PRIVATE ARMY

by

LIEUTENANT-COLONEL

VLADIMIR PENIAKOFF

D.S.O., M.C.

'POPSKI'

JONATHAN CAPE
THIRTY BEDFORD SQUARE
LONDON

frontis: THE AUTHOR]

FIRST PUBLISHED FEBRUARY 1950
SECOND IMPRESSION 1950

Dewey Classification

940.5481

PRINTED IN GREAT BRITAIN IN THE CITY OF OXFORD
AT THE ALDEN PRESS
ILLUSTRATIONS PRINTED IN COLLOGRAVURE BY HARRISON & SONS, LTD.
LONDON AND HIGH WYCOMBE
BOUND BY A. W. BAIN & CO. LTD., LONDON

CONTENTS

CONTENTS

PART THREE

JAKE EASONSMITH

PART FOUR

POPSKI'S PRIVATE ARMY

PART FIVE

ITALIAN PARTISANS

CONTENTS

ILLUSTRATIONS

MAPS

INTRODUCTION

THIS is the story of what happened to me in my middle age between the beginning of the year 1940 and the end of 1945. Up to the times I am writing about I had found little contentment, and I believe that my contemporaries had the same sterile experience; but during these five years every moment was consciously happy. My excuse for asking strangers to read a book mainly about myself is that they may be interested in the record of events that led me and a few friends to considerable happiness.

My tale is of war and hard work and enterprises, sometimes stirring but more often ludicrous; of sudden reversals of fortune; of people in high places who were not ruled by convention and others who were; of lowly men of foreign nations whose devotion to our cause exceeded our own; of bloodshed and violence, but more of cunning and deceit and high spirits and the pleasant cudgelling of brains and then again more hard work; above all of friendship.

Only to the fools amongst the men of my generation will the realization come as a surprise that we liked war.

Of my first forty-five years there is little to be said that is relevant to this story. I was born in Belgium to Russian parents of an intellectual type now extinct: they showed an old-fashioned turn of mind in having me taught English as my first language and later by refusing to send me to school, which they considered inadequate. For years I had never less than three tutors who pumped knowledge into a precocious brain; as well as music, riding and fencing masters.

From this rarefied atmosphere I passed in 1914 to a Cambridge college, a precious intellectual prig, with high scientific ambitions, and conscientious objections to war. I left at the end of my fourth term to enlist as a private in the French Army. I was in a hurry and couldn't face the months of training I would have had to go through had I applied for a commission in the British Army. The French were obliging: eleven days later I reported to my battery, a fully-fledged gunner. I was too young to be much affected by military life: as I remember, I enjoyed it mildly and acquired a knowledge of the French way of life and a distaste for the French people which increased considerably in later years. It all ended with twelve months in hospitals and convalescent camps, and I was invalided out of the army shortly after the 1918 armistice.

I had gone practical and, turning my back on a donnish career, I trained as an engineer. I worked hard at a succession of jobs in which I didn't believe much and in 1924 I settled in Egypt where I devoted many years to the manufacture of sugar. In the meantime I married and had two children, read, travelled, made a few friends, flew a plane and motored in the desert in an indestructible 'Model A' Ford, rudely nicknamed 'The Pisspot', of which more later.

PART ONE
ALONE

CHAPTER I

DEFEAT OF THE LEVANT

AFTER I had settled in Egypt I kept few ties with Belgium, a small, dull country, I thought, with which I was bored. Furthermore I had belonged in that country to a clique of highbrows with whom it had been fashionable (and, funnily, still is, as I have recently discovered) to deride the Belgians for being a loutish and inferior breed. I have changed my mind now about that country, but for years I seldom visited Belgium and neglected most of the friends I had.

Living in Egypt I was automatically incorporated in the local European communities, all more or less easternized in spite of their British, French, German, Italian or Greek origin. This half-million of non-Egyptians are elaborately stratified. Going by outward appearances I suppose my label should have been as follows: 'Belgian engineer. First generation in Egypt. Mixes more with the British than with his own Belgian community, yet practises no kind of sport. Does not play bridge. At home also in the French and Italian colonies. Does not cultivate the Egyptian Pashas and is not a member of the Mohamed Ali Club. Unlikely to reach eminence in the local business world.'

In fact the Levantine atmosphere that pervades the European communities in Egypt made me uneasy and slightly scared of its debilitating influence: as the years went by I anxiously watched myself, expecting to find the symptoms of rot — the mixing of languages and the gesticulating hands.

Local Europeans, Levantines and Westernized Egyptians lead a dreary life. Endeavour is limited to fierce, unimaginative money-making and the more unrewarding forms of vanity. The thrills of love are provided by a season ticket at the brothel and mechanical affairs with the dry, metallic, coldly lecherous wives of your friends. No hobbies. Games are played, to be sure, out of snobbishness, copying the English. Adventure is provided by daily sessions of bridge, rummy or poker, and gambling on the cotton exchange. Books are valued in a way: a wealthy Armenian cigarette maker caused an upheaval when he provided his new flat in Gezirah with a *library*. I was invited to inspect impressive bookshelves: the bindings were gay and suspiciously new: in their thousands, they covered the walls from floor to ceiling. One panel was green, another blue, another antique calf. On inspection I discovered five sets of the complete works of Victor Hugo, three of Balzac, seven of Paul Bourget, four of René Bazin. The antique calf were fakes, not books at all but boxes cunningly fitted with backs cut off old books. Anyhow the owner, who speaks fluently (and simultaneously) eight languages, is illiterate.

This way of life is so boring that I never could understand why it is valued at all: indeed the death of friends and relatives is suffered with the regulation amount of tears and hysterics but otherwise with perfect equanimity. But when it comes to personal danger: what agonies of fear, and orgies of self-pity! Cowardice is boasted of and praised as a virtue — the main, the fundamental virtue, the one that keeps going these poor cardboard lives. The wise man is the one who experiences most fears, for thus he can protect himself against more dangers. In fact these shams, who spend their lives copying people they don't understand, have only one feeling that is genuine: fear. They are terrified of physical pain, of disease, of losing money, of losing face, of accidents, of discomfort, of hard work and all; they are constantly scared and they like it; revel in it. And why shouldn't they, the poor wretches? The fear of death is the only real motive they have for going on living.

I am by nature cautious; running deliberately into danger goes against the grain. But if I can enjoy taking risks and don't mind physical hardship I believe I owe it to the puppets amongst whom I lived for sixteen years. It seemed natural to strive after a way of life opposed to theirs.

Levantines are only a nasty scum covering the great mass of fellaheen, the peasants on whom they prey. I liked the latter, simple folks with their roots deep in the soil — so deep indeed that they could hardly be thought to emerge at all from their Nile mud. I worked with them, understood them and spoke their language: in return I received friendliness and devotion. In a land of sham, pretentiousness and half-baked aspirations they were genuine: kindly, human, ignorant, hard working and unaffected. But I wouldn't try to live as one of them, the poor, starved, cringing, cowardly wretches.

I had more respect for the scanty Badawin who, in small numbers, still roam the deserts of Egypt. Weak offspring of the masters of the world, they retain a smouldering memory of the Arab conquest and they still maintain a nearly dissolved link with their parent tribes in Arabia. Poor and all but extinct, roving nomads like their forefathers, they are still acknowledged as masters by their fellaheen neighbours, who fear them without reason, for there is no strength in them.

It grieved me to find a noble race so fallen and I attempted to build them up into authentic Arab characters, an effort of constructive imagination which owed much to Doughty's *Arabia Deserta*.

From 1925 to 1928 I worked in the sugar mill at Nag Hamadi north of Luxor, in Upper Egypt. For eight months in the year, between the sugar seasons, my duties were light and gave me abundant leisure for Palgrave, Burton, Doughty, Lawrence and Gertrude Bell, writers on Arabian travel; slowly and at second hand I fell under the spell of the Arabs.[1] My mind gradually set on Arabian discovery, and travel in Arabia became my ultimate aim. At that time neither Philby, nor Bertram Thomas, nor Ingram had yet made their great journeys in southern Arabia, nor had Ibn Sa'ud been taken over then by the oil interest; thus big rewards could still be picked up by the explorer in Arabia.

With these plans in mind I discovered Haj Khalil and I undertook to train him in the traditions of his forefathers. He was only a petty sheikh of twenty Badawin tents, owner of a few acres of sugar cane on the edge of the desert, and a small-scale labour contractor for the sugar

[1] I use this name, as it is used in the Muslim world, to denote people living under a tribal organization who derive (sometimes fancifully) from the original tribes of Arabia at the time of the Prophet. Egyptians are emphatically not Arabs, though Arabic speaking and of the faith. Badawin and Arab are practically synonymous in Arabia, Syria, Palestine and Egypt, but not Cyrenaica where the name Badawin is not used.

mill, but he had in him noble stirrings and the seed of greatness. Now settled in comfortable middle age, he had in his youth ridden to and fro to the Sudan driving camels for sale to Egypt, and had considerable desert lore. He and his brother Mifla, an uncouth camel boy, were my guides as we rode our camels in the desert near Nag Hamadi on short trips of four or five days. I learnt then the rudiments of life in the desert: landmarks, how to read tracks, where water can be found, pastures, the care of camels and the courtesies of the nomads. Khalil is the only Arab I have met who could explain and teach desert lore. On one of our early trips he made me dump my topee — a very uncomfortable headgear when riding a camel — behind a rock in a wadi. A few days later, coming down the same wadi on our way back he called out: 'Where is your large hat?' and laughed when I had to admit I had no idea. He said the wadi would next take a bend to the north-east, then sweep round to north-west — then three small bushes in a row — a rock shaped like a coffee cup — a gravel ridge about as high as the palm of my hand — a cave — a boulder like a camel's head, and behind the boulder: my topee. Thus was I trained to memorize landmarks.

In return for his tuition I taught him the ancestry of his tribe, the Rasheidis, who they were related to in the Hejaz and how they were an offshoot of the Qoreish, the tribe of the Prophet. He was not entirely ignorant of these matters, having been on the pilgrimage and a guest of his brethren in the Hejaz, but until I came, he had not thought much of it, being more concerned to push himself as a business man with the French who ran our sugar mill than to revive the traditions of his decayed Badawin. Insidiously I diverted his mind to things other than an ambition to cut a fine figure as a wealthy village omdah and put his mind to other things. I told him of the deeds of Sherif Hussein's Arab army in the late war under Lawrence and the great battles they fought as allies of the English King. Haj Khalil was a true Badu, with a feeling for romantic situations and with political ambitions; he was fired with the pride of his race, but as there were no opportunities for him to shine in battle he had to be content to set about and make himself the leader of the scattered Badawin who pastured their meagre flocks in the mountains between the Nile and the Red Sea.

In this, with my backing, he succeeded very well, and when we entertained our guests, the ragged, bearded visitors from the desert judged him a true sheikh of the Arabs in his golden head-band and white robes and with his generous hospitality of the coffee cups. For my own role in the pageant they couldn't find a place in their tradition; the legend of the great English travellers to Arabia had not reached them from across the Red Sea; but they were not embarrassed, as, in spite of their destitution, they had enough pride left to take for granted the flattering attentions of a foreigner and an infidel.

The situation was farcical because Haj Khalil, as an Arab sheikh in the grand tradition, was phoney — his desert subjects were no more than gipsies, and what was I, as an explorer, but a week-end tripper? But nobody took things too seriously: the Arabs were flattered, gained in self-respect and, no doubt, were able to turn to practical advantage in their dealings with the fellaheen their enhanced prestige and their greater cohesion. For my part, I was learning to handle the nomad Arabs safely, at home, so to speak, and in such a manner that mistakes were of no consequence. I could look forward to setting out on my Arabian journeys, when the time came, with some confidence and without being too green.

Although I knew I would some day break my ties, for the time being I refrained from doing so, not being ready yet. So I went about my jobs, first in a sugar mill, then in a sugar refinery (which stands one step higher in the industrial hierarchy), and for several years I pursued the ordinary activities of industry and, on my yearly leave, the polite pleasures of European travel.

CHAPTER II

PLAY WITH THE DESERT

IN 1930 I transferred to the Sugar Refinery at Hawamdiah, outside Cairo. A refinery, unlike a sugar mill, works not just four months, but the whole year round: my leisure was now limited to week-ends and occasional holidays, and consequently I had little time to spare for Arabs and desert. Also I had exhausted the possibilities of make-believe in this connection.

I took up flying and on many Sunday mornings I sat in the Almaza flying club waiting for the Egyptian instructor to turn up: for some mysterious reason he was always late but I quite often got my twenty minutes' tuition. I eventually qualified for an 'A' licence after sixteen hours in the air and one hundred and twenty hours in the club house. Later I occasionally flew to Alexandria, Port Said or Miniah, but without much real pleasure because flying is a dull business. There is an exhilaration in the first solo flights and in the few stunts which the beginner is taught to do; cross-country flying on the other hand is very much like driving a tram, especially in Egypt where the weather is always clear and map reading presents no problems.

In the early 'thirties I heard about a Major Bagnold[1] and his friends who were making motor journeys in the desert. They had reached the Gilf el Kebir and Oweinat, where Egypt, Sudan and Cyrenaica meet, 680 miles from Cairo and over 300 miles from Kharga oasis, the nearest supply point. They had penetrated the Egyptian Sand Sea and altogether they had covered thousands of miles in the Western Desert in Ford cars. They navigated with sun compasses, used theodolites and wireless sets to fix their position by the stars, and they drove over rocks and sand dunes which had been considered impassable to motor vehicles.

Here was something new in desert travel, and I experimented on my own to find out how far and how safely I could go with a single car.

[1] Later Colonel (now Brigadier) and O.C., L.R.D.G.

I had a Ford two-seater that I converted into a box-body truck fitted with balloon tyres: this was the Pisspot I have mentioned before and it had travelled over 120,000 miles when it came to a sticky end at Mersa Matruh in the second year of the war.

With a circular protractor, a disk of ivory from the Muski in Cairo, a knitting needle and an aluminium frame, I got the Refinery workshop to construct a sun compass. The first model, mounted on gimbals with an oil damper to cut down oscillations proved over-elaborate. However I found I could dispense with gimbals altogether and the instrument I finally used looked home made but it was easy to set and it kept me on my course with sufficient accuracy.

When navigating with a sun compass the azimuth of the sun must be known for every hour of the day, and at any particular time of the year. The appropriate tables being out of print, on the day before going on a trip I had to clamp the sun compass on a bench in the garden and make a note, every half-hour, of the position of the needle's shadow. It was a long and tedious process but, working thus from the bottom, I found I eventually acquired the simple art of navigation so thoroughly that I ran no risk of making a mistake even if I happened to be tired or flustered. This was important because, travelling alone in the desert with no one to check my navigation, an elementary mistake in the setting of the compass might easily have led to disaster.

I didn't attempt to build a theodolite.[1] I went to the other extreme and bought in Switzerland a Wilde theodolite, so elaborate and so expensive that the transaction broke me and I had to curtail my rock-climbing holiday and slink back to Egypt. Though I soon found out that a common surveyor's theodolite would have served me just as well, the pleasure of handling this lovely instrument made up for the climbs I had not been able to make in the Dolomites.

To receive the time signals I used a stop watch and a small, dry-cell, commercial wireless set, an unreliable contraption on which, *sometimes*, I managed to hear the time pips from Helwan observatory.

[1] On land to fix a position astronomically, the angle of a star above the horizon is measured by means of a theodolite (at sea and in the air a sextant is used). The time of the star observation must also be known, and for this purpose a wireless time signal has to be received.

Thus equipped, and provided with the Nautical Almanack and The Royal Geographical Society's *Hints To Travellers*, I spent many nights struggling with a star chart. At first Vega, Betelgeuse, Aldebaran, Castor and Pollux were seldom where I thought they should be, but in due course they lost their fickleness and kindly turned up in the region of the sky where they were expected. 29° 52′ 10″ North and 31° 14′ 20″ East was the position of my house in Hawamdiah. At first I was happy if the stars put it within twenty miles and not in mid-Atlantic or in the Gobi Desert: then I became more proficient and got my astrofix within three miles, which was good enough.

For my training in dead-reckoning navigation I plotted on the map a course of a hundred miles or so, beginning and ending at features well identified on the map, and then I navigated my truck with sun compass and speedometer as closely as possible along this course. The distance between my objective and the spot at which I actually ended was the measure of the accuracy of my navigation. I once ended up fifty feet to the west of my objective, the doorway of St. Sergius Monastery in Wadi Natrun, but that was a fluke: the going had been excellent, I had been specially careful and I had taken nearly two days to cover 120 miles. This coincidence, however, revealed to me how surprisingly accurate careful dead-reckoning navigation can be. Before that lucky hit I had felt that though I had watched very carefully for hours the shadow of a knitting needle on an ivory plate there was no reason at all why, at the end of a long day's drive in a featureless desert, I should from the top of the next rise lift a pyramid on the horizon. After that success, however, I gained confidence, and though I might be as much as ten miles out at the end of a difficult run I never thought I was lost.

For a solitary traveller, as I generally was, driving and navigating at the same time is a trying job. Every time the course is altered an entry should be made in the log book and the truck must be stopped while it is done; in broken country or in a winding wadi this may happen every few minutes and the going becomes extremely slow and tedious. In soft sand, where it would be fatal to stop, long stretches of the course may have to be memorized. When the going is very rough, in rocks or amongst boulders, the driver has to concentrate on watching the ground a few yards ahead of his front wheels and never gets a chance of looking at the compass or the speedometer, nor even at any of the larger landmarks which might enable him to keep a rough track of his course. As a result I had a certain difficulty in estimating the course over the sections where accurate readings had not been possible, and I sometimes had to walk back on my tracks for several miles with a hand compass, till I picked up a landmark.

Soft sand was my greatest problem. I became skilful at spotting and avoiding bad patches and at skimming over treacherous surfaces when no detour could be made. When I did get bogged down I had to unload completely, dig and lay planks under the jacked-up rear wheels. Progress was at the rate of a few feet at a time and it once took me a whole day to cover three hundred yards. Then the load had to be ferried across and stowed on board. Instead of planks I experimented (without any success) with rope ladders, canvas mats and strips of coconut matting under the wheels. It was Major Bagnold who invented the steel channels which finally solved the problem and came into general use during the war.

Our war-time journeys took me over ground that I couldn't have dreamt of attempting alone: but there was then plenty of man-power available to push and dig, and also in due course we acquired vehicles with a four-wheel drive. I sometimes regretted perversely that the fine art of desert driving was no longer required.

However, I was not thinking of war then, but still of exploration in Arabia and though, for financial reasons, I expected I would be limited to one vehicle, I never intended to undertake any serious travelling without a companion or two. My aim on these solitary trips was to train myself under exacting conditions and make sure that on my journeys of discovery I wouldn't encounter difficulties that I hadn't already solved during my training.

An advantage of these lonely trips was that I couldn't afford to be slack in my preparations. I had made up my mind that on no account would I rely on search parties to rescue me if I got lost or ran out of petrol or broke down. To make quite certain that such a disgrace wouldn't happen to me I never let anybody know to what area of the desert I intended going. I carried an impressive number of spare parts for the truck and I made sure, at home, that I could fix them single-handed. I endeavoured to provide for the most unlikely accidents, and as a result I overloaded my poor Pisspot to such an extent that I nearly broke its back. Practically the only spare I didn't carry was a cylinder block.

More through persistent good luck than skill, I had so far always succeeded in bringing my truck home, but I could not of course eliminate completely the possibility of a breakdown or of getting hope-lessly bogged, and as the range of my trips increased and took me a hundred and fifty miles out, or more, I got worried about the means of walking back in case I had to abandon my truck. I had no doubts about my ability to find my way back to the Nile Valley, the simplest of problems, but I had to drink and eat on the way and I didn't fancy a fifty-pound rucksack. A young schoolmaster friend called Jeffrey Bunn found the answer. His fancy was to walk in the desert, and for his water, kit and food, he built himself a hand cart mounted on motor-cycle wheels which he once pushed all the way from Ma'adi, near Cairo, to Sokhna, on the Red Sea coast, taking a week over the trip and living in comfort. I had a similar 'pram' made of aluminium tubing; it could be dismantled and stored in the back of my truck, and with a sufficient reserve of water and food I felt justified in taking my lonely trips further into the Western Desert than I had ever done before.

By the spring of 1939 I had long ago achieved my purpose: desert travelling had for me ceased to be an adventure. My navigation was sufficiently reliable to give me at all times the feeling that I knew roughly where I was; I didn't worry about mechanical breakdowns and I could with an easy mind, enjoy the freedom of my loneliness and play at filling up the map. Even in the sections of the desert which I reached, the Egyptian Survey maps had many more blanks than features; I liked to fill in dunes, rocks and wadis. I was very happy and free on my lonely trips and glad to be away from Cairo.

I grew more ambitious and wished to make for the furthest limits which had been reached at that time by the elaborate expeditions of Bagnold, and I started planning a trip to Oweinat, a mountain peak that springs up to six thousand feet out of a flat desert 700 miles to the south-west of Cairo. A journey of this length required a chain of dumps of petrol, water, food and spares, with smaller dumps in between for an eventual walking trip. My plan was to take with me a companion, but one car only, and I settled down to work out routes, distances and supplies. It soon appeared that with only one small truck to play with and not much free time, the preparations would take several months. With the small load my truck could carry I would have to cover four or five thousand miles on journeys from my base in Kharga Oasis, to establish my dumps. It couldn't be done on week-end trips. Every year I took two months' holiday from sugar refining which I spent in Europe, travelling: I decided to stay in Egypt this year and carry on with the dumps.

Then one day in May 1939 I told a friend in the Embassy about my plans. 'Oweinat,' he said, 'has now an Italian Air Force landing ground. I don't think you will be allowed to go there.' 'Who is to stop me?' I said. 'Wouldn't you like me to tell you all about the place when I come back?' 'Not interested,' he replied. 'It is just a landing ground. But we don't want a frontier incident. Our Italian friends are being a little difficult, and we can't have them starting any funny business just now.'

I thought he was a pompous diplomatic fool, talking as if he was H.M. Government; and I told him so, annoyed at his assumption that he could make me put off my plans.

When I had cooled off I thought it over: up to that time I had persuaded myself that Hitler didn't mean business, I had laughed at warmongers, and, having some direct knowledge of conditions in Germany and in Italy, I had explained many times that these countries were in no condition to go to war.

Now, I was shaken, and looking back on my memories of the previous year in Germany and in Austria, where I had been just before the Anschluss, the notion grew on me that I had been utterly mistaken and that war was indeed coming. And when I considered the French people, as I knew them all too well, demoralized, scared, torn by mean hatreds, given over to the enemy, I decided that weak as I thought the German Army really was, it wouldn't have any difficulty in disposing of the French Army. And what other force was there in Europe that could scare them into keeping the peace?

I recognized my desert wanderings as the glorified week-end trips which indeed they were; and I put Oweinat out of my mind, as I thought, for ever. But three and a half years later, from the top of the Gilf el Kebir, I fancied I caught a glimpse of the mountain floating in a shimmering mirage on the southern horizon, as I made my way to Kufra.

I had other plans now and a fortnight later I was on my way to London. If England was going to war, I was going to be in it.

CHAPTER III

OVERTAKEN

SINCE I had left Cambridge in 1915 to join the French Army I had been in England only for short spells — yet I regarded England as my country and loved it with a somewhat ridiculous fervour: as a boy, having loved an incredibly enchanting mistress and broken away, will go on loving her memory all his life. And even today, this battered land has some of the secret delights and casts the same spells that carried away the heart of a youth of seventeen, thirty-three years ago.

London in June 1939 was in an uncomfortable, panicky mood that frightened me and made me sick with anxiety. Let Frenchmen, Italians and Levantines go into a flap; but England showing signs of hysteria was really alarming. As a defence and to keep my own sanity I took up the attitude that the alarm was caused by Nazi propaganda and that we had only to ignore it all and the Germans would climb down. I laughed at the talk of war and strangely enough I converted many to my views: the fact that I came from abroad gave weight to my opinions. In a time of panic the outsider is easily credited with great wisdom, and the very attention given to my views made me more and more uneasy and convinced that trouble was coming. There was nothing more for me to do in England; apart from helping to dig those pathetic trenches in Hyde Park my services were not required and with a heavy heart I went over to France to see what was happening there.

National prejudices may be often caused by ignorance: not so with the dislike I had of the French, for it resulted from much intimacy. (Unwisely, I had persisted for too many years in living and working with them, in France and in Egypt.)

Meanness, pretentious vulgarity, devastating selfishness, parochialism, bogus culture, surliness and conceit are undoubtedly part of a Frenchman's make-up, but I don't think I would have minded much —

for I acknowledged many redeeming features — if I had not been completely put off by such small things as the tone of their voices, their manners and the smell of their houses. Personal distaste was at the root of the poor opinion I held of these people, for it is natural to find fault with those you dislike; for all my bias, I wouldn't have dreamt of imputing to them self-abasement and servility. Objectionable people, perhaps, with many unpleasant habits, but — at heart — proud and brave.

And now, in the late spring of 1939, it seemed that they were no longer either proud or brave.

Those who held advanced political views were unhappy: they foresaw, either a war in which France would be defeated or, if war could be avoided by more appeasement, a complete subservience to Nazi ideals. In either case everything they held good in life would be lost. The others, in their various ways, held remarkably similar views: France was weak, broken and tired, no more a first-class power, in fact not a power at all. She could not fight, would not fight and was bound to be defeated if, by some incredible folly, she did go to war. So why talk big and threaten and attempt the impossible? Wisdom was to strike no attitudes, make the best of a bad job and come to an accommodation with the Germans. And wasn't there much to admire in the new Nazi way of life? It had made the Germans prosperous, orderly, happy and united. The French were exactly the opposite. It stood to reason that if she went the Nazi way, in a modified, humanized, Frenchified form, France would reap the same advantages. The time had come to discard obsolete antagonisms and to spot your enemy where he really was: not the German across the border but the politically-minded, irresponsible working class in your own country.

I don't often argue with Frenchmen; so I declared myself convinced by my friends' logic, wished them good luck in their wisdom, and departed for Germany with the feeling in my mind that, in the coming struggle, France might well be on the side of the enemy.

Outside Germany, in those days, Hitler's lying and bullying made life unbearable but, inside the Reich, the ugly rumblings were nearly inaudible; and the mind was free to enjoy the funny sight of the Nazis at home. It was all very gay and entertaining: the paunchy, dark little men Heil-Hitlering right and left, the ill-fitting comical uniforms, the parades and the banners, and, in the forests and the mountains, the hiking parties of sunburnt boys and girls. Coming from France was like leaving a gathering of old maids to join a children's party, riotous and slightly hysterical. I didn't know then that the party leaders were corrupt and self-seeking; ugly rumours of the concentration camps had reached me indeed, but as ever since 1914 I had learnt to discount atrocity stories I put these aside for future investigation and decided, provisionally, that all was well and that the Germans had acquired a regime that suited them. Suited them so well in fact that it was impossible to discover what was really going on below the gay surface. I had no intimate friends in the country who would open their hearts to me: indeed I had for a long time been concerned at my failure to become really friendly with any German. They were courteous, considerate and hospitable, but every attempt at finding what they really thought of the plans of their leader led to a blank wall.

I became uncomfortable during the last days of my stay in Germany, guessing more and more at a stupid conspiracy behind the pleasant façade, and annoyed at being treated like a spoilt child who is humoured when he asks questions but must on no account be allowed to meddle with the affairs of his elders. Also, I didn't believe that the war, if it came, would be as kind to the Germans as they thought, and I felt sorry for the poor blighters, so gay and confident and so pleased with themselves.

On my way back to Egypt and the routine of sugar refining I stopped in Milan. I was quite at home in Italy, where I liked the people and always had the pleasant delusion that I would find out what was going on behind the scenes. Friends who liked me and, in their flattering way, looked up to me and made much of me, contributed to the pleasantness of my stay.

In Milan there was a group of friends, headed by Giancarlo Dosi Delfini, who met occasionally at his town flat, where I was always certain of picking up information. Marchese Dosi is a man of monstrous girth and fantastic ugliness, partly natural indeed, but much increased by a face wound received in the first war. He has the devastating, cynical sense of humour which is a particular creation of the northern Italians, and an earthy common sense expressed in a diction of unbounded vigour. Never a member of the Fascist Party, he had nevertheless risen to be the head of one of the largest industrial concerns in Italy. On business he travelled much in central Europe, Germany and Sweden, and being a man of great intellectual powers and wide inquisitiveness he managed to be always informed of all the cross-currents of European politics. His friends, who shared up to a point his political independence, were men of intellectual achievements, and between them, being lawyers, scientists, bankers and in the upper ranks of the civil service, covered most of the activities of the state.

All successful, they kept their distrust of the Fascist regime within very private bounds — in the intimacy of Dosi's flat, however, they could let themselves go and I was treated to a devastating tale of inefficiency, graft and corruption amongst the men who controlled Italy. Dosi and his friends were convinced that Germany would be going to war before the year was over, that Italy would follow sooner or later and that it would all end in disaster. Working on their pooled information they concluded that one year was the longest time that the economy of their country could be expected to stand up to the strain of a major war. After that period, would come the plunge and they were looking forward gloomily to this disaster which was the only means, they thought, of getting rid of Mussolini and his followers.

Men of character all, upright and brave, with a sense of responsibility to their country, they were satisfied that there was nothing they could do to save it from its infamous masters but to let country and tyrants slide together into the abyss, trusting that the tyrants would be broken and the country would eventually recover. They were not of the breed of conspirators, who in Italy are not generally drawn from the ranks of the old families; they took their world as it was, did their best by it and considered attempts to upset the established order unbecoming for gentlemen.

Mass hysteria which had been so conspicuous in Germany had, I found, completely died out in Italy. The Fascist regime being seventeen years old had outlived its early enthusiasms; based no longer on the generous support of an active minority nor on popular applause, but on the self-interest of successful job hunters, it lived on bribery and intimidation. Military parades and party rallies drew little public and what cheers there were came from the paid gangs.

It came as a shock, therefore, to find a young friend of mine in Rome suddenly converted to emotional Fascism. I had known him for fourteen years as a cynical derider of all enthusiasms, level-headed exponent of the virtues of detachment and common sense: he had witnessed recently a specially good military march past and as a result he raved now (rather shamefacedly) about the glorious destinies of Mussolini's Empire. I laughed — he apologized for his outburst, but added: 'You can't understand, you haven't seen those wonderful troops!' I had no doubt that the units on that parade had been well turned out and perfectly drilled but, if Dosi and his friends were to be believed, they were also the only ones in the whole Italian armed forces to be adequately equipped and trained. I was very desirous to check up on this, but though nothing is more difficult than to SEE an army, particularly in peace time, I thought that the recently reinforced garrison of Rhodes in the Dodecanese might be a good sample of Italian fighting forces, and, the island being small and the garrison reported to number over eighty thousand, it seemed reasonable to expect that soldiers would be pretty conspicuous in so restricted a place.

It was as I expected: the place was swarming with Italian soldiery. They were a ragged lot, in tattered uniforms, mostly barefooted or shod with canvas sandals of local make, and hungry looking. To my civilian mind the question of footwear was conclusive: the Italian Army couldn't have much fight in it.

CHAPTER IV

LEFT OUT

I ARRIVED back in Egypt at the beginning of July 1939. Not curiosity had set me on my trip, but really a guilty conscience. I had felt for a long time that my generation which had, in its youth, survived the first war, bore a large share of responsibility for the peace of the world: my own generation particularly and neither the elder statesmen nor the youngsters who had come of age after 1918. To be sure I had taken this responsibility very lightly: I had followed with amusement the spread of Fascism in Italy, then, with more concern, the rise to power of the National Socialists in Germany, but I had remained half-wittedly convinced that no nation would be foolish enough to go to war. I wanted to remain undisturbed by rumours and to carry on with the day's work, as any other course of action might lead to a state of panic and play the game of a foolish minority of warmongers.

Such had been my state of mind before I left for Europe. The knowledge I brought back that war was inevitably coming convicted me, in my own eyes, of unforgivable complacency. I didn't entertain the idea that anything I personally could have done might have altered the course of events, but that was no comfort in not having put up a fight.

I might have done as my sister (killed in a motor crash a few months previously) had done: she had devoted herself altogether to work for the League of Nations and had taken to Spain, at the time of the Civil War, a field hospital, raised and maintained by the Belgian Socialist Party. I had thought her then a dear funny crank and full of delusions; but it appeared to me now that she had followed the wiser course while I had misspent my abilities manufacturing sugar and cultivating sterile hobbies. I felt very guilty and for several weeks after my return I turned things over in my mind, seeking for a way: then Hitler invaded Poland and dispelled my doubts.

Now that war had broken out the rights and wrongs of the quarrel didn't matter any longer: the simple fact was that, to my knowledge, England was in danger of falling under the control of the Germans and my simple duty was to assist those who strove to prevent such a misfortune. To the best of my ability, I had to take a share in fighting the war.

An intolerably vivid picture in my mind of smooth German bullies laying down the law in England and the English-speaking countries over the world was then at the root of my determination to fight and remained so, right through the war. I didn't hate the Germans, nor did I believe then that they were particularly evil or wicked — even if I had, it would hardly have been a motive to fight, for hatred is a silly, troubled emotion, the child of fear and weakness, which is in its proper place in the nursery only. During the fighting I never appealed to feelings of hatred and although I know that my men sometimes fleetingly experienced it, it was not in the heat of battle, but in other circumstances, as will appear later in this story.

Simple as my duty was I foresaw many practical difficulties in carrying it out. Just as keen as myself, there were in the world thousands of eager busybodies, all asking to be allowed to help. His Majesty's Government, caught unready in a major war, had no doubt trouble enough in employing to good advantage the manpower already at their disposal without bothering about taking on untrained volunteers. I was sure that if I just went and offered my services I would be told to run away and be a good boy — and quite rightly too.

Goodwill and the bare wish to serve were obviously not enough; my only chances of getting where I wanted were either to apply for a job that I could do as well or better than anybody, or to undertake duties unpleasant enough to repel most other volunteers. With this in mind, and terribly hampered by my ignorance of the requirements of modern warfare, I attempted to assess my position, and this is the picture I drew:

My nationality was Belgian: in Great Britain I was counted an alien, a friendly alien probably but nevertheless a *neutral*, for Belgium had not yet become involved in the war. My national status was going to be a great disability.

I was forty-two years of age, five foot ten and nearly fifteen stone. The French Army had invalided me out in 1919 with an eighty per cent disability, and though my physical condition was not really as bad as this figure implied, I was rather short of breath and my legs required some care if I was to walk any great distance. Blood pressure was a little too high also and on that account I had failed to pass the latest medical examination for the renewal of my pilot's licence. On the whole it seemed that my physical state was going to be a liability.

And now the assets: A good deal of technical and administrative experience — a few languages — some knowledge of most European countries and of the Middle East — I could fly a light single-engined plane, sail a small boat, drive a truck in the desert — and I could navigate all three.

With these meagre accomplishments I had to find means of making myself useful either to the army, the air force, the navy or some form of war industry.

For the army, my one year's service as a gunner twenty-four years ago seemed hardly to count as a qualification: I had really no military experience worth talking about and I didn't care for marching. Linguistic and geographical knowledge would lead only to dreary office jobs in Intelligence or the Censorship, which I was not prepared to undertake. I was strongly prejudiced against the more active forms of spying as depicted in thrillers — my only source of information on the matter — and though I have done much intelligence work since those days I still feel that spies are pretty despicable. It is a fine point of ethics and I have been very near the borderline, but in my own estimation I have never sunk to the status of an 'agent'. Of staff work I had no knowledge whatever. The Engineers might offer an opening. On the whole I didn't fancy myself as a soldier: I was shy about my waist line and I strongly suspected I would be laughed at if I offered my services to the army. With a reservation about the Engineers, I decided against it.

CHAPTER V

AN ELDERLY SUBALTERN

WHEN I went to the Refinery at seven in the morning on
May 10th, 1940, I collected rumours of a German invasion of
Holland and Belgium. These were confirmed at lunch-
time by the *Egyptian Gazette* and I thought at once that probably by
now Deswarte had already been killed. Ten years younger than myself,
he was the only friend I had kept in Belgium and I loved him dearly.
When he had visited me in Egypt eight months previously, he had told
me that, being a lieutenant in the infantry reserve, he would on general
mobilization command an anti-tank platoon. His role was to take on
the spearhead of the enemy armour and his orders were to fight to the
last man and the last round of his anti-tank rifles. I hadn't reckoned
with the possibility that the German armour's spearhead and Lieutenant
Deswarte might not find themselves on the same road on that first
morning of the war, which is exactly what happened and he survives to
this day after many adventurous escapes.

My second thought was that my personal status had altered: I was
now an *allied* alien and the War Office should be informed of the fact
without delay.

Of my native country, I thought it was only getting what it deserved
for clinging so obstinately to a disastrous neutrality — a misguided
policy which had put it in the position of having to stand up, unsup-
ported, to the German Army. That this policy belonged rather to M.
Spaak than to the Belgian people at large was a consideration that didn't
occur to me at the time: I wasn't in the mood for such niceties.

After lunch I took my car — not the Pisspot but a newly-bought
white Mercury saloon — and drove from Hawamdiah to Headquarters
British Troops in Egypt in the Semiramis Hotel on the Nile embankment. Decorous military bustle had brought new life to the faded
Edwardian splendours of the most ambitious of Egyptian hotels and it

seemed a joke having to obtain a permit before entering the familiar hall. On the fifth floor, in a bedroom emptied of its furniture and with the wash basin decently camouflaged, sat Major Emery who for years had been my neighbour at Sakkara where he dug for antiquities with remarkable success.

Like the few Egyptologists who have achieved greatness Emery had had no academic training in this bogus science, but had started life as a marine engineer. To an uncanny gift for discovering tombs under the sand in places where the pundits had decided nothing would be found he added a lively genius in interpreting the results of his excavations; the nebulous ancient Egyptians came to life under his hands. I had watched him open unrifled tombs and sort out the contents with the meticulous care of a detective. Intuitive imagination helped by a prodigious memory gave him the clue to the life which had ended five thousand years ago in the body whose desiccated mummy lay before our eyes: the strange implements of stone and copper lying round the sarcophagus he identified as weapons, tools and kitchen utensils, the familiar objects of everyday life. In a very early tomb he found flat, long, copper objects with serrated edges, which puzzled everyone. While someone prated of hieratic rods, Emery cleaned and polished one of the objects, considered it, handled it, and going over to a shed behind his house took up a wooden plank. While I held it he proceeded to cut it across with the hieratic rod: he had discovered a very ancient saw, the father and mother of all saws. He had, since the beginning of the war, left the Department of Antiquities of the Egyptian Government to be commissioned in 'Intelligence' and apply his human gifts to interpreting the living enemy instead of the ancient dead.

Versatile, he had dropped his civilian bluntness and acquired the detached manner of the staff officer. He was my guide and my sponsor in the unknown world of military hierarchy. I put my case to him and he conceded that being — since that morning — a citizen of an allied country I stood a good chance of being allowed to join His Majesty's Forces. He rang up several mysterious powers and the truncated half of their conversations, which I overheard with a beating heart, led me to believe that I would report the next morning to Kasr el Nil Barracks for a medical examination. Not so fast in fact did the military machine function but nevertheless a course of action was laid out for me: I was to put in an application for permission to enlist in the British Army which would be forwarded to the War Office. When authority had been received from London, I would have to satisfy a medical officer and I would then be commissioned as a second lieutenant in the General List. A commission was so exactly what I didn't fancy that, like a tactless idiot, I blurted out that I wanted honest service in the ranks and not silly games as a gentleman: I had no military experience and it would take years to train me into an officer! Emery, who had even less military knowledge than me, being too young to have served in the first war, gave a start, as well he might, and reverting to civilian directness said: 'What about me? — I am a major eight months after joining the army. Don't be a fool. I resent being called a silly gentleman, but coming from you I suppose I don't really mind, but if you talk in that vein to our friends here they will think you are trying to be snooty or that you have a bee in your bonnet: in both cases they will consider you a very undesirable recruit for the army. At your age the army can only offer you a job as an officer and *in an office* and you will be lucky if you get it.' I appreciated his wisdom and determined to hold my peace for the time being.

I had to keep the Sugar Company in the dark about my plans lest they would forestall me, claim my services and pull strings to keep me out of the army. They were running short on staff with several Frenchmen called up and soon the Italians to be interned; I had to watch my step very carefully for the next few months for, having given away all my available money, I was now dependent on my salary to keep myself and my family from month to month.

Reverses that summer followed their melancholy sequence: Belgium fell, France followed, even faster than I expected; we evacuated Dunkirk; Italy joined Germany in the war and our forces in the Middle East were now faced with an enemy.

I didn't doubt that we could deal with the Italians locally but the general situation looked black: short of putting my faith in a miracle I couldn't see how England could now escape being defeated. Our soldiers in Egypt had remained serenely unruffled to be sure, but their optimism seemed to proceed more from lack of imagination than from any special knowledge and I prepared my mind for the final struggle. Personally I was still out of the battle: I wanted to smuggle myself somehow on board the *Revenge* before she went into her last fight. So I pestered shamelessly and blindly everyone I could get access to: the commander-in-chief, the brigadier A. & Q., the military secretary, the staff captains 'A', Major Jenkins in particular, the deputy security officer, whom I had known as a civilian, and I wrote clumsy letters to the War Office. They all bore with me with a courteous equanimity which was more than I deserved.

On October 2nd, 1940, Jenkins rang up to say that a reply had been received from the War Office and would I report the next day to the medical officer in Kasr el Nil Barracks?

The medical officer was young, kind and, I suppose, romantic. I laid my cards on the table with false candour: at my age, I said, and with my special qualifications, my ambition was to be posted to Intelligence: an office job to be sure, but in which I hoped to be able to make myself useful. I knew my limitations and that there was not the remotest possibility of anyone thinking of employing me in a fighting capacity where slight physical disabilities, if I had any, would put me at a disadvantage. Middle-aged men, however, have their vanities: mine was to be passed as fit — in the highest medical category. It couldn't do anybody any harm, so perhaps he could see his way to put me down as A.1. He smiled and agreed that an office job was indeed my obvious destination: he gave me a cursory look over and filled the forms as I had suggested.

On October 6th, I was commissioned, got myself a uniform and bravely put up one pip. On the seventh I applied for a posting to the Libyan Arab Force. On the ninth I was ordered to report for an interview to Colonel Bromilow, O.C. 102 Military Mission, which was really the Libyan Arab Force. I lied no more than was necessary but I succeeded in giving the impression that I would be a useful recruit to the Force. I spoke deprecatingly of my service in the first German War and I believe he assumed I had been a gunner officer of some distinction in the French Army, which still carried a reputation for efficiency and purposefulness. I mentioned of course that I spoke Arabic fluently, which indeed I did, but not the Libyan dialect, and that I had for years handled thousands of Egyptian fellaheen, which also was true and about as good as running a rabbit farm as an introduction to commanding Libyan Arabs. An account of my dealings with the Badawin and of my journeys in the Egyptian deserts and in Transjordan clinched the matter. Colonel Bromilow was no fool: he had seen much service in Iraq and he understood the Iraqi tribesmen well enough; though he knew little of the Libyans (but not less than anybody else in Egypt at that time) he realized perfectly that they were not fellaheen; but he was desperately short of British officers for the Libyan Arab Force and he had to take what he was offered. As it turned out he didn't strike a bad bargain when he took me on: I remained fifteen months with the Force and I had a share in licking it into shape.

CHAPTER VI

GATE KEEPER

TENS of thousands of Libyan Arabs, refugees from Cyrenaica and survivors of General Graziani's planned massacres, had fled to Egypt between 1926 and 1931, when their nineteen years' long war against the Italian conqueror was brought to an end by the capture of Kufra Oasis.

Destitute, and nearly without cattle, they had settled on the fringe of the Western Desert from Burg el 'Arab near Alexandria to the Fayum and even as far south as Beni Suef. They were semi-nomadic and very miserable; some of them had completely forsaken the traditional life of the desert and had joined the cosmopolitan riff-raff that make a shady living around Alexandria harbour, but allegiance to their spiritual leader Sayed Idris el Senussi, himself an honoured refugee, and common memories (amongst the older men) of life on their own pastures, held them together and gave them a precarious unity. They are tribal Arabs from Cyrenaica, of the Senussi sect of Islam: puritan Mohammedans to whom alcohol is abhorrent, few of them smoke and none ever uses a swear word nor indeed the mildest abuse. Practised in the foul Egyptian obscenities I had great difficulty in controlling my language in my early dealings with the mealy-mouthed desert warriors. Once, exasperated beyond endurance by a pig-headed recruit but exercising restraint I called him nothing worse than an ass. This mildest of insults had surprising effects. Marching up from the ranks the lean tribesman handed me his rifle: 'If I am a donkey,' he said, 'I am not fit to be a soldier,' after which he sulked for three days in his tent and was finally appeased only by a public apology and my solemnly given and courteously disbelieved assurance that, with us British, the donkey was held in high consideration, second only to the lion.

I use indifferently to denote the tribal Arabs from Cyrenaica, the names Senussi Arabs, Libyan Arabs, Jebel Arabs; though it may seem confusing it is only a small fraction of the number of names I could use if I were to follow the various local customs.

I believe it was Colonel Bromilow who first thought of raising a force amongst these refugees. When I joined it the Libyan Arab Force had been in existence for three months and numbered about three thousand Arab volunteers: warlike enthusiasm had combined with the attractions of regular food and pay in inducing a good response to the call for recruits.

What was to be done with these Arabs was a matter about which contradictory views prevailed. Colonel Bromilow, an experienced cavalry officer of the old school and a man of enthusiastic imagination, wanted to train them into irregular guerrilla groups which, under British officers, would skirmish on the flanks of our regular forces in the desert and penetrate into enemy territory on reconnaissance tasks. It was on the understanding that such would be our role that ten of the officers, including myself, had joined the Force. We all left it when it became apparent that it would never be more than a semi-military formation; and we all found hazardous jobs that kept us pleasantly busy till the end of the war. Two of these officers, Bob Yunnie and Jean Caneri, joined forces with me at a later date and they will appear frequently in this story.

Middle East Headquarters, mistrusting the fighting capacities of their Libyan battalions, wanted to employ them on guard duties in Egypt, relieving British troops for the battles in the desert.

O.E.T.A. (Occupied Enemy Territory Administration) considered them from the political aspect and required their services as a police force to keep order in Cyrenaica during our repeated periods of occupation.

Colonel Bromilow was in a good way to achieving his aim but, devoted as he was to the Force he had himself initiated, he was a regular officer and had his career to consider. All too soon he had a chance of promotion and left us to take command of the Iraqi Army. The commanding officers who succeeded him had no experience of Arab troops nor any interest in them: the appointment was just a stepping-stone leading to something more lucrative and more congenial, and thus the

Occupied Enemy Territory Administration had its way and the Libyan Arab Force ended up as a gendarmerie.

I knew nothing of these influences when I reported to the Senussi Camp at Kilo 9 on the Alexandria Road near Mena on October 10th, 1940, but congratulated myself on having outwitted the friends who had plotted to tie me to a desk in Headquarters. A guerrilla force of Arab tribesmen was the opening I had hoped for and I set to work to make the most of it.

I had had a strained interview with an Egyptian director of the Sugar Company, who had said: 'When I want to throw out a berberine servant I am expected to give him a week's notice. Reckoning on the ratio of salaries, you should have given us at least a year's notice. Your present behaviour is scandalous; you will hear more from me.' In fact I heard nothing for months, till suggestions were made to the Company which eventually brought their attitude in line with Western practice.

Bryan Emery had briefed me in the fundamentals of military etiquette: saluting; addressing superior officers; what to do with my hat on entering an office; when to stand a drink in the mess, and other points of that nature. It was done in five minutes, but so comprehensively that it saved me from awkwardness for the whole of my military career. This was all the training I received before reporting for duty.

The Libyan Arab Force was somewhat untidy. It was nominally organized in battalions and companies like a regular infantry unit, but beyond their names we knew little of the functions of these formations. The battalion to which I was posted as a company commander counted two regulars: the commanding officer would turn up for a day, give us hearty and gallant words, and then disappear for a week; the adjutant, a subaltern, had to all practical purposes assumed command of the battalion and issued daily orders which all tended to increase his personal comfort. Every morning we company commanders had to find plausible reasons for declining to build a motor road leading to the adjutant's tent or stalls for the adjutant's polo ponies; then, with the help of instructors from the Egyptian Army, we drilled our men right through the day. After we had retired to our tents the recruits, with undiminished enthusiasm, got together and drilled one another so that our sleep was punctuated by echoes of the words of command (in Arabic) of the footdrill.

Our commanding officer became more elusive — the adjutant attempted more strenuously to run the battalion for his own benefit: prepared as I was, in my ignorance, to take everything in the army for granted, I couldn't help feeling that our situation must be unusual. I took leave one afternoon to go down to Cairo and interview Bryan Emery on the duties, powers and privileges of a battalion commander and his adjutant. He was a little hazy about these matters, having never served in a unit, but he called for expert opinion and I returned to camp well briefed and provided with a copy of *King's Regulations*. This red volume is fascinating to read and well repays study: in the light of my new knowledge I laid my plans and waited for my opportunity. It came a few days later when the crazy Arab driver of one of our three-ton trucks, crammed full of men, lost control of his vehicle and overturned it, spilling its human load over the road. We had seen the accident happen from the top of the hill where our mess was perched, and I drove down with the adjutant to give help. Most of the men were shaken but unhurt and were picking themselves up dazedly as we arrived. The driver, with a flattened head, looked dead, three other men were lying in blood, and an elderly Libyan soldier, with a white beard, though he showed no signs of injury, lay groaning and made no efforts to get up. Our adjutant was a young coward and a bully; the sight, even the thought, of physical violence, always put him in a state of hysterical excitement. He kicked the old man in the stomach, urged him in foul words not to play the fool but to get up and lend a hand, then kicked him again, viciously. The old man, though his eyes were open, seemed to me unconscious and suffering from concussion. As it turned out he had a fractured skull. I told the adjutant to pull himself together and stop worrying a dying man. He spluttered, but calmed down and submitted when I ordered him back to his tent and told him he was under arrest. I was senior to him, having been promoted to captain a few days previously, and he realized it even better than I did.

Having disposed of the casualties and cleared up the mess I returned to camp where, with the help of my precious *King's Regulations*, I did my best to write a report on the incident in military language. It stated that the adjutant had been put under close arrest on a charge of assaulting a private after he had become a casualty while on duty and I forwarded the report by dispatch rider to the Officer Commanding the Libyan Arab Force, 'my own commanding officer being absent and out of contact'. I felt very doubtful about the correctness of my expressions but I hoped I would kill or, so to speak, at least grievously injure two birds with one stone.

The next morning a senior officer from our Headquarters in Cairo came up to the camp. His first questions naturally concerned the whereabouts of the battalion commander, whose duty it would normally have been to deal with the matter. I had, reluctantly, to admit that I hadn't seen him for several days. The adjutant couldn't help either as all the information he had was that the colonel might be staying in a flat in Alexandria.

During the following days the military machine worked according to its own rules, and, as far as I was concerned, entirely behind the scenes. The presumptuous adjutant disappeared for ever, though, in the light of my later knowledge, I must assume that he escaped court martial on this occasion as my evidence was never called for. The colonel turned up a few days later and called a conference of the officers in the battalion to tell us that he had been offered another appointment and that much to his regret he would have no further occasion to avail himself of our collaboration. He thanked us all very heartily and we had a riotous farewell party in the mess. He then also disappeared for ever.

Up to this time I had been merely acting an unrehearsed part in a farcical pantomime of which no one knew the plot. With the arrival of our new commander I became more of a soldier. Lieut.-Col. Paley, of the Rifle Brigade, turned the battalion from a purposeless rabble into a military formation: what was even more important to me, he set about teaching me my new profession. He and I were acquainted from before the war and we had frequently met during the last few months when he was head of the Intelligence Department at Headquarters in which Bryan Emery was his second in command. I could help him in his new appointment with my knowledge of Arabic and an ability to handle Senussi recruits, and so he found it worth his trouble to instruct me in the rudiments of the military profession.

In spite of indifferent health, he worked, it seemed, day and night; defying the Egyptian climate he chose the hottest time of the summer days for his office hours, for the men were then resting in their tents, and he could deal in peace with his administrative problems. In the beginning, however, he didn't bother much about the office: we made daily inspections of the men's latrines, cookhouses and sleeping quarters — clean latrines became for me the very essence of military efficiency, to the point that even now my first words on taking over a new command would be: 'Let us have a look at your latrines.'

We attended the sick parades, we tasted the men's food and their tea and listened to their complaints. When we had done with their physical well-being, we organized their leaves and arranged for admission to the cinema at the neighbouring Indian Army camp. Then our rounds took us back to have another look at the latrines.

In the meanwhile the pool of three hundred British rifles, which was all that Middle East Command had been able to allot to the whole of the four battalions in the Libyan Arab Force, had been withdrawn and replaced by an unlimited supply of captured Italian rifles. These weapons were anything up to sixty years old — the more recent ones dated back to the 1914 War — and were in a shocking condition, but each man was eventually equipped with a rifle that would (in a way) fire, and ammunition was plentiful, if unreliable. Until 1912 the Arab tribes of Cyrenaica had been independent under the nominal suzerainty of the Turks. Then the Italians had invaded Tripolitania, and, having conquered it without any appreciable resistance, they attempted to settle also in neighbouring Cyrenaica. The Senussis, however, would have nothing of the foreign invader, and although they had to relinquish the coastal towns, Benghazi, Derna and Tobruq, they prevented the Italians by force of arms from occupying the interior of the country. Isolated from the outer world, they fought their guerrilla battles with

45

weapons and ammunition captured from the enemy. Under the leadership of Omar Mukhtar the struggle continued with varying fortunes until 1929 when, General Graziani having massacred more than half the population, and Omar Mukhtar having been captured and hanged, the Arabs at last submitted to the foreign conqueror.

Thus all our older men were familiar with Italian weapons. But contrary to our expectation, their marksmanship turned out to be pathetically inaccurate: a romantic delusion had to be discarded and much time spent on the firing range before we could hope that a few at least of our bullets would reach the vicinity of their target. We also obtained captured Italian light machine guns: these weapons of a new design of extreme ingenuity, light, pleasant to handle and of a good appearance, had only one fault: they wouldn't fire. I tested many: under the best of conditions, when spotlessly clean and oiled precisely to the right degree, they couldn't be relied upon to fire more than a burst or two: so in our battalion we discarded them.

When I first joined the army I had pictured a fighting force as a body of brave men who engaged the enemy with fortitude and endeavoured to destroy him with a variety of weapons and an unlimited supply of ammunition. The duties of the leader were limited to maintaining the morale of his men and outdoing the enemy in cunning and endurance. What happened to these men in the intervals between the battles and how they came to be in the neighbourhood of the enemy at all, were matters which I didn't consider as relevant. Under Paley's guidance the picture altered to something as follows: a few men, always too few, endeavouring to bring to bear on the enemy inadequate, fragile and irreplaceable weapons, provided with too little ammunition. These men, who eased their bowels every day, had to be fed, clothed and kept in good health and spirits for months before the opportunity came to lead them into battle; they had to be moved over vast distances with their kit and their equipment, which they kept losing and wearing out. The men themselves, through various agencies, kept trickling away from the unit and reinforcements had to be brought in and trained in a continuous stream.

Colonel Paley's contempt for battle training worried me considerably. Very much later in the war I realized his wisdom: it is impossible to teach men how to fight without taking them into battle.

I learnt also from Paley to express myself in army language, and he showed me a few ways of inducing staff officers to act against their better judgment, and how far it is safe to break the letter of the law. There is an art in disobeying orders and no commander who has not mastered it can hope to win a battle.

On June 10th, 1940, Italy declared war on the Allies. On September 14th, General Graziani moved forward from the Egyptian border at Sollum, and though he met with no resistance from our troops, he had exhausted himself when he reached Sidi Barrani, sixty miles away, and there he stopped.

On December 16th, 1940, General Wavell attacked Sidi Barrani, took it, completely defeated the Italian Army, captured some two hundred thousand prisoners and pushed forward four hundred miles to a position south of Benghazi.

On March 31st, 1941, General Rommel, in command of the German Afrika Korps and of an Italian army, struck south of Benghazi, and rolled back our forces as far as the Egyptian border. However, seventy-five miles in the enemy rear we held Tobruq, which was invested for eight months.

On November 18th, 1941, General Cunningham attacked at Sollum, relieved Tobruq and pushed forward as far as El Agheila beyond Benghazi.

Having sat in Mena camp, gatekeeper to the desert, for over a year I caught the see-saw on its second upward swing and arrived in Tobruq a few days after its relief, overland with the combined transport of two battalions of the Libyan Arab Force.

CHAPTER VII

MUDDLE

I WAS in a vile mood because three weeks earlier I had been transferred from the battalion, in which I had worked so hard under
Paley for nearly a year, to take temporary command of another
battalion which had been unfortunate in its commanders: it had at
first been under a nice country gentleman, courteous and obliging, who
liked riding, but also liked the bottle. His drinking bouts lasted four or
five uninterrupted days and nights and occurred once a month. Happening to have to preside at a court martial during one of these bouts,
he came to grief and found himself very suddenly awaiting shipment
for home in a transit camp near Suez.

His successor was a man of culture who could write pungent
English, but he stuttered so fantastically as to be, for all practical purposes, dumb. We timed him one morning at breakfast in the mess
when over four minutes passed before he could say: 'I wasn't talking to
you.' Another of his weaknesses was to tell his Syrian girl-friend about
his plans and I often heard the movements of his battalion discussed by
Cairo social gossips long before the orders were out. The poor man
was torpedoed and drowned on his way back from Tobruq: his death
was a loss to the crude humours of our mess but undoubtedly a gain to
the army. He was the man I replaced, pending the appointment of a
new battalion commander.

Under these two commanders the battalion had not made much
progress: the subordinate officers, with the exception of the adjutant,
were mostly rejects from other battalions, half-wits, who had no
idea of what they were supposed to do. The men were untrained
except in foot and arms drill and couldn't even fire their weapons.

Such was the command I had been given at the moment when my
own men were at last going into action. I raved but there was nothing
useful I could do about it: the battalion was under orders to sail to

Tobruq and somebody (apparently I) had to command it. I was promised a relief as soon as available; by now I knew that such promises, in the army, mean nothing at all.

Taking into action an amorphous crowd of Senussi Arabs and bewildered British officers was an unpleasant prospect. I had been given a free hand and I made a generous use of my powers. Within a week I had sacked the four company commanders and half the non-commissioned officers and had started weeding out and regrouping the men.

My battalion became a very unhappy unit. The officers, with the exception of the few whom I had promoted, wore long faces; by day and by night I made their life a misery. And I encouraged all demands for transfer from the battalion. Behind my back, as I well knew, a steady flow of recrimination reached, by devious routes, our Head-quarters in Cairo. I hoped to alarm them by the drastic nature of my reforms and thus speed up the appointment of a proper battalion commander: what I wanted was to return to Paley's battalion as a company commander.

My scheming was not successful: a battalion commander was indeed appointed, a very pleasant officer who had had a normal career in the Indian Army and lately in the Sudan Defence Force; accustomed to orderly, well run and correctly administered units, he was so much taken aback when I revealed to him the nature of his new command that he refused to let me go, confirmed all my measures and kept me as his second in command.

As I have said, I went overland to Tobruq with the transport and stores. The battalion was to follow by sea on December 18th, and when their ship was overdue by several hours I found the Port authorities in Tobruq very sad. They wouldn't say anything at first but finally admitted that something had gone wrong with the shipment of Christmas turkeys. This was not a code name: the Polish ship that carried our battalion had also in its refrigerated hold sixty tons of turkeys. She struck a mine and had her bows blown open. She didn't sink for several hours, the whole battalion was taken on board the escorting vessels but the troops' Christmas dinner went to the bottom. In my heart I could have wished it had been the other way round.

I need not have worried about the behaviour of my Senussi battalion in action: we were allotted only guard and police duties. Under command to Area we had our Headquarters at Derna and our furthest detachment was at Barce. We were 'Base' troops and not very good ones. I gave up striving and passed the time touring Cyrenaica and cultivating the sheikhs of the inland Arab tribes. The battalion I shamelessly left to its muddle.

On January 18th, 1942, reports were received in Derna of an unexpected German armoured force moving on to El Agheila. I was much struck by the fact that a large number of enemy tanks could have been landed and grouped in Tripoli without any information reaching our Intelligence Service — a gap in our defences which I thought I might one day fill.

Weak and stretched, with some of its best units diverted to Greece, the Eighth Army had been caught on the wrong foot and could not hold the German attack which came on January 21st: a general withdrawal was ordered and Area at Derna went into a mild flap. I am a little vague about what happened during the next few days because the colonel was away at Army H.Q. most of the time and I had the job of pulling in our detachments and of concentrating the battalion at El Qubba. Then the colonel turned up with the news that he had managed to have us considered as combatant troops and put under command of the 4th Indian Division covering the withdrawal of the Eighth Army. I congratulated and thanked him — with a wry smile he expressed the hope that we shouldn't disgrace ourselves. I couldn't give him much encouragement.

The day was all of a bustle with the Indians arriving and troops passing through El Qubba and next morning at first light we moved towards Derna with some of the Indian troops and took up a position on the edge of the escarpment in broken country. I reconnoitred, allotted localities to each of our companies and took the company commanders over the ground. I then returned to Battalion Headquarters off the main road, where the bustle had now died down and that deathlike calm reigned which falls over the whole of nature between our further outposts and the still unreported enemy: the birds themselves had become silent.

At midday, having given time to the companies to establish themselves, I went round their positions. One of the company commanders, following the contour of a hill, had placed all his men in such a position that the only objective they could fire at was our own battalion transport, well down the road to the rear. I asked him from what direction he expected the enemy to come. He didn't know: had the enemy arrived yet? Against all rules of discipline I called to one of the Arabs: 'Where is the enemy?' Silent and glum the man jerked his thumb over his shoulder. I noticed a gun position neatly dug in with four men serving one of our captured Italian machine guns. Surprised, I asked: 'Will it fire?' The answer was 'No.' — 'Do the men know it?' — 'I expect they do, but it will give them confidence to have an automatic weapon. I must do something to keep up their morale.' I expect the best encouragement *I* could have given to the company's morale would have been to kick their commander down the hillside. I overcame the temptation and contented myself with making him collect the offending weapon and take it himself down to his trucks. A man of twenty-eight years of age, educated at one of the old public schools, he had passed out with good marks from the Middle East Tactical School's Senior Commander course. He was to play on us one more prank that day and then his active military career came to an end.

The fates were kind to us: the enemy never turned up that day.

At dusk we moved out of our positions and made down the escarpment road into Derna town, the colonel leading and myself bringing up the rear. The rendezvous was Tmimi, a low escarpment in the desert, thirty miles east of Derna and one-third of the way to Tobruq. On the escarpment at Tmimi the pursuing enemy was to be held during the next day.

There was still much traffic of lorries in Derna when we arrived after dark, and our vehicles, trying to find the easiest way through the town, got split up into small groups.

The traffic emerging from the town all converged on to a narrow very steep road that climbs the escarpment in a succession of sharp hair-pin bends. It was packed tight with vehicles, grinding up a few yards then stopping for long intervals. We got even more split up, with not only Indian trucks between us but also those of several other units which had been delayed in Derna to this last hour of evacuation. There was no panic in this apparently disorderly retreat but only a quiet, good-humoured determination of each driver to get along to his appointed rendezvous, and an undercurrent of confidence that the confusion would sort itself out in the end, as indeed it did.

Our adjutant riding a motor-cycle managed at intervals to move up and down the traffic and to keep contact with some twenty of our trucks strung out over a couple of miles of the road. He came to me with the news that one of our last trucks loaded with ammunition, had broken down on a bend and was holding up the traffic. I walked down to find that the clutch had gone and an attempt was being made to take the vehicle in tow. Overloaded with loot, it was far too heavy to be dragged up the steep incline, and, thinking of the hundreds of trucks held up behind it, I made up my mind to tip it over the brink. With much pulling and shoving, helped by men from the neighbouring trucks, we backed it against the stone parapet which we then pro-ceeded to breach with picks. The truck plunged down the ravine in a vertical drop, then went bouncing down rocks and boulders, the ammunition exploding in lovely fireworks, till it finally came to rest far down, a blazing wreck. Nobody paid much attention but our men gave a ghostly cheer and the whole column started once more on its upward grind. I learnt later that a notorious spy, of the Derna Arabs, whom we had captured earlier that day as he was trying to cross over to the enemy lines, had been left 'asleep' in that lorry as it went over the side.

We sorted ourselves out when we reached the plateau on the top of the escarpment and proceeded towards Tmimi along a less congested road. I watched the speedometer carefully for fear of overshooting: the night was very dark and Tmimi is just a fold in the stony rolling desert, not much of a landmark, even by daylight. I stopped at a faint flicker of light by the roadside and I had the luck to come across a friend, a sapper officer, who knew that our rendezvous was exactly two and a half miles ahead, over the top of the next rise. There I found our colonel on the road with some officers of the Indian Division, flicking torches at the oncoming vehicles and dispatching them to their leaguers. The colonel led my party in: we had now collected the whole of Headquarters and the companies save one, commanded by the officer who believed in boosting the morale of his men by giving them unserviceable weapons, which was still abroad. I made my way back to the road and waited. By four in the morning the Indian officers checked their lists and turned in. Dawn came but no Libyans; none of our troops by this hour were intended to be between Tmimi and the enemy; our company had either been captured or it had slipped by unobserved in the dark and pushed on beyond the meeting place. In that case they couldn't have gone much further before realizing they had overshot the mark, and must have bedded down a few miles down the road; I expected them back very soon after light. They did not turn up at all because their commander had taken them all the way to Tobruq: he had travelled ninety miles instead of thirty without noticing, so he told us, that anything had gone wrong and, having got that far he didn't see any point in trying to join up again: 'As we were withdrawing anyway, I was sure you would all turn up in Tobruq in the end.' I don't really believe *now* that he had intended to avoid the battle, but in his poor muddled brain he must have forgotten that he had been given a rendezvous at all, and he had driven on and on till the sight of familiar Tobruq made him pull up.

There was a haze over the plain at Tmimi as the sun came up: curtains of dust over moving vehicles, and, rising high above them, black mushrooms of smoke. Many dumps and the big landing ground at Tmimi, being incompletely evacuated, had to be destroyed at this last hour. A number of troops were getting on the move, also the big R.A.F. trailers; in the opposite direction field guns were coming up in support of the Indian Division. The going was fair all over the plain: so no one kept to the road and vehicles moved in every direction. Nothing could be seen but hazy forms looming out of the dust and fading out again, but, in the still morning air, crystal clear sounds cut across the distant hum and buzz and supplied the images that the eye couldn't see. A vast, cheerful purposefulness filled the plain.

By midday the expectant front-line hush fell once more; our friends had left us to protect them against an interfering enemy. From the sea to the distant hills, an escarpment runs here, at right angles to the coast and the road. On the upper plain were the dispersed Indian vehicles, our own and the divisional artillery. On the downward slope of the escarpment, dug in with their weapons, were the men, overlooking an empty plain that rose slowly to hills on the horizon with the road winding its way to the sky line.

We placed one of our remaining Libyan companies to defend a narrow front in very soft sand dunes; I joined then Captain Stewart who commanded a company of the 1/1 Punjabis and I refreshed my soul with the sight of his experienced troops preparing for action. The air was clear now over the lower plain in the afternoon sun; standing on the edge of the escarpment I could see the Indians below me on the forward slope, and as far as the hills on the sky line four or five miles away, out of which the enemy was expected to debouch.

As neither the Germans nor ourselves had any aircraft over Tmimi that day, the engagement took an old-fashioned turn with reconnaissance on both sides done from the ground: sitting on top of the escarpment in God-like knowingness I could not only see with my own eyes the movements of the battle, but also guess what went on in the minds of the commanders on either side, for they had no knowledge which was denied to me. On this only occasion I found it possible to follow the development of a battle from a seat in the very first line: usually to the fighter all, except a narrow sector, is confusion and uncertainty and a general view can be perceived only in the peace of Headquarters far in the rear, where maps and messages tell the tale at second hand. Strangely this directness gave, in my mind, to the battle of Tmimi an appearance of deep unreality.

About two o'clock the sound of five bursts of machine-gun fire drifted over from the plain. Three of our own armoured cars appeared from a fold in the distant hills and made a leisurely way back to our lines. Watching the strip of road where it dipped away out of view over the sky line I had a glimpse of a German armoured car returning to their lines. Contact had been made between the opposite armoured patrols, a few shots exchanged, and both sides were reporting back. The last of our cars stopped at the foot of the escarpment where the crew got out to do something with mines on the road; then it joined the others on the road on my right and passed out of sight behind me. For half an hour nothing happened, then some German vehicles moved over the sky line and went into a fold of the ground. Ten minutes later, more followed. For another half-hour nothing. Then a solitary shell whined high overhead and sent up a small puff of dust and grey smoke far behind me. For many minutes quiet — then slowly, three thuds from our field guns. The battle was on, but except for the leisurely noise nothing was happening. The Indians behind their rocks were sitting back and chatting cheerfully in their thin sweet voices, flashing white teeth.

German vehicles moved cautiously towards us, spreading over the lower plain, in and out of sight as they dipped into wadis and out again. Puffs of dust sprang up around them, but made no difference to their deliberate movements. At a quarter to four whines of a different kind sounded overhead with slowly increasing frequency and dispersed bursts began to dot our upper plain amongst the vehicles and also the slopes where the men lay. A sharp, dry crack issued from each burst: the Germans had now brought mortars within range of our positions. From down below they couldn't see what they were firing at and were contented to pepper the upper plain. As our mortars had a shorter range than the German ones there was still nothing for the Indian infantry to do and they went on chatting. Our field guns intensified their fire, searching out the enemy.

I turned round to see a cloud of dust obliterate my car, the antiquated Pisspot, which marked the position of our Battalion Headquarters five hundred yards behind me, and I wandered back to investigate. The shelling was not heavy enough to be uncomfortable: indeed I found it exhilarating and I dodged the bursts with a pleasurable excitement, under fire at last for the first time in this war.

The Pisspot had received a few splinters but no vital damage and none of our officers and men lying around it in shallow slit trenches had been hurt. Our colonel, who with the rest of our people was under fire for the first time in his life, asked: 'What kind of shelling would you call this?' — 'Light and desultory,' I replied, upon which he got up and looked round with interest. The others winced and ducked in their trenches at every sound, so I sat down on my heels and took pains to demonstrate to them the relationship between the flashes and bursts they saw and the noises they heard. Sound travels quite slowly, the speed of projectiles through the air can be more than twice as great, but the transmission of visual images is practically instantaneous: as a result of these differing speeds the perception of the elements of a battle is thrown out of the proper sequence. Thus if a gun fires at you and its shell falls short, the events perceived may be in this order:

1 — Seen: flash at gun muzzle at departure.
2 — Seen: burst of exploding shell as it hits the ground.
3 — Heard: report of exploding shell.
4 — Heard: whine of shell through the air.
5 — Heard: report of gun at departure.

When a gun is firing overhead the sequence may, according to your position and the shape of the trajectory, change to: 1-3-2-4-5 or 1-5-3-2-4. With weapons on both sides firing projectiles of varying velocities with high or flat trajectories, the picture becomes somewhat confused. All cases have one comforting feature: the long whine, that most unnerving of noises, is always emitted by a shell which has long gone past you and is in fact no menace at all.

Their minds now busy trying to sort out the origin and the meaning of what they saw and heard, they perked up considerably and were soon quite jolly. A very young subaltern, however, crouched at the bottom of a slit trench, miserable, white in the face and shaken. I got him out, held him under the arm and walked him up and down, hoping to get him to come and take an interest in the battle from the edge of the escarpment, but he couldn't be prevailed upon and grew slightly hysterical. I had to take him back to his burrow where he promptly went to earth and whimpered: 'We are doing no good here, let us go away. Why don't we go away?' I was not going to let him spoil my pleasure and I couldn't leave him to make a fool of himself, so, to save his face, I scribbled some message and ordered him to take it to Division Headquarters well back and out of range of mortar fire. I pointed out the truck he had to make for in the distance, told him to walk there quietly and picking up my revolver from the seat of the Pisspot I added, 'If I see you run I shall have to shoot you,' which, if he only knew, was a perfectly futile threat as I am incapable of hitting a man at ten paces with a revolver. He went off with a slow, stilted gait and I didn't see him again till next morning.

I drove the colonel slowly in the Pisspot amongst the flying splinters and stones to the positions of our company in the dunes. We found the men where I had put them under good cover and after some searching discovered also the company commander. Nothing much was coming their way and they were fairly happy but a little worried because from where they were they couldn't see how the battle was going and they thought their officers had left them. I told them not to worry and to keep a good look out, but obviously the going was so abominable in front of their positions that there was no question of an attempt being made by the enemy in that quarter. The colonel stayed with the company to return later on foot and I drove back to the Punjabis, leaving the Pisspot at our Headquarters. On the way I stopped to have a can of beer with the cheerful British crew of a field gun and marvelled at finding artillery right up in the front line: their role was to stop at point-blank range any tanks that might attempt to climb up the road on to the escarpment. I told them that no tanks had been sighted yet and I wandered off, pursued by their friendly banter.

The mortaring was heavier now but still quite enjoyable: dispersed it had no nasty concentrations that feel that the enemy has seen you and is after you personally. Stewart thought that with an hour only to go before sundown the enemy would attack at any moment, and surely enough, five minutes later, clumsy half-track troop-carriers appeared in numbers on the lower plain and disgorged their men eight hundred yards from the foot of the escarpment. The Indians stopped chattering and opened up with short, well-spaced bursts, and German bullets came spattering and drew sparks from the rocks around us.

For some reason I like machine-gun fire less than shell fire, but I was so enthralled by the way the Indians worked that I couldn't help enjoying myself. Stewart suggested I might now go home and, taking the hint, I walked out of sight behind some rocks to save him the bother of having a 'tourist' on his hands while he was engaged with his company. He and his men, quite unperturbed, went about their business with accuracy and a great economy of movement, and cheerful grins lightened up their now dusty faces. A few men fell and were quietly carried away. A call for ammunition came up and I joined the party that went for the ammunition truck, for idleness was weighing heavy on me. A shell landing on it sent it up in thick clouds of black smoke. Picking our way amongst the bursts we made for another, drove it to the escarpment edge and manhandled the boxes down to the gun positions. I hope Stewart never heard of my share in the work (if he did, he very tactfully refrained from mentioning it) for it was a silly way to behave and quite unnecessary, as the situation called for no urgency.

I could see the Germans — by now they seemed to be quite numerous — moving forward methodically from cover to cover, a section at a time, over the rough lower plain, carrying their weapons towards the foot of the escarpment. There were plenty of pieces of metal and chipped stones flying about on both sides and each man took good care not to expose himself unnecessarily, but no passion — anger or fear — went into the conflict. The familiar risks of battle were accepted unquestioningly: the elaborate, strenuous work of attack and defence was done carefully — a well-known routine that caused no excitement.

At a quarter to six the German fire seemed to thin out and I could see small groups of their men dashing back to cover. Very few of them had reached the foot of the escarpment and there was no reason why they should press the attack now with the sun just down and darkness coming very shortly.

I decided I had played about enough, and expecting the order to withdraw our company I made my way back to the Pisspot and washed my face. The Germans had slackened their machine-gun fire as they pulled out but they gave us an extra pasting with mortars: I suddenly found myself lying flat on my face, blown over but unhurt. When the bits stopped showering down I counted twelve paces to the whitish smudge which showed where the shell had hit the ground and was delighted to find it had landed so near, as if my luck in avoiding the flying pieces was something to my credit. The Pisspot disappeared once more in a cloud, but she was not to perish yet for a long time: a tyre had been ripped open by a splinter but I had a spare (in those days of penury!) and I drove away in her, eventually.

The order came to stand by to move out at eight. I drove to the sand dunes: the company had anticipated orders, and was lying dispersed by the roadside. I said nothing and marched them back to their trucks. Fate had again been kind to us and had sent no enemy against our positions.

The German fire stopped when darkness fell. The Indian streams of tracer thinned out with precision and only now and then broke the unnatural silence. An unconquerable weariness sent me to sleep as we drove away.

CHAPTER VIII

MOUNTAIN AIR

THE day after the battle of Tmimi was spent at Akroma a few miles west of Tobruq. During the night we had gone through the troops which were to stop the enemy on the new line at Gazala; our fighting was over. We drew rations, dug latrines, got lost repeatedly in a sandstorm, and slept whenever we could. I called several times at Corps Headquarters in the Turkish fort on the hill and made a friend of the intelligence officer.

The next day found us in Tobruq waiting for orders. There we found again our lost company, and the battalion was complete once more; not that I cared, because I had made up my mind to leave, and when a few days later the battalion was ordered back to Egypt and it became obvious that it would never more be employed as a fighting unit, I found my colonel helpful. He was a fighting man who, soon after his return to Egypt, got himself a more congenial appointment and left the Libyan Arab Force — he must have been pretty well worked up, for he granted me leave to attach myself to any unit in the forward area that would take me, gave me a letter for Corps Headquarters and lent me a Ford pick-up with a driver. My own driver, over eager, had taken the Pisspot back to Egypt.

My intelligence friend at Corps Headquarters had no job for me and I went in search of the King's Dragoon Guards, a mechanized cavalry regiment with which our Libyan battalion had operated for three days before being attached to the Fourth Indian Division.

Lieut.-Col. McCorquodale commanded the regiment and he had, half jokingly, offered to give me a job if ever I left the Libyan Arab Force. The latest location of the regiment known to Headquarters was at Gazala; so off to Gazala I drove, in a cheerful mood, free and happy to be, not latrine-gazing in Egypt, but once more bustling in a forward area. So very bustling that night that when I reached Gazala about midnight there was nobody to stop me on the road and I drove light-heartedly into no-man's-land. Gazala, Akroma, Tmimi are just names on the map for there isn't a single built-up town or village between Tobruq and Derna. There are wells of those names somewhere in a hollow, but there is no conspicuous landmark on the road. Although the night was dark and still, I sensed a hush, and becoming suspicious, I drove on gingerly till I perceived the shapes of armoured vehicles asleep by the roadside. I stopped the car, the engine ticking over, in a patch of deeper shadow, and walked on to find that, as I feared, the sign on the vehicles was a black and white German cross. So back to my car, unperceived by the slumbering enemy, and dead slow in reverse half a mile up the road till I thought I could safely turn round without raising an alarm. Back in our lines I found sleeping South African armoured cars. The trooper I woke up, after much prodding through the open side-door, knew nothing of any English armoured cars; he took me to his troop commander, and then on to Squadron Headquarters where a sleepy captain poured me out half a mugful of brandy and got busy on the wireless to his Regimental Headquarters. Thither, by request, I was conducted, and after more brandy, a sergeant was discovered who thought he had seen some of the K.D.G. vehicles I was looking for south-west of Akroma the day before. On this slender information, having thanked my South African friends, I drove back on my tracks and dawn had broken when I found once more the hill and the fort of Akroma. I nosed around without success till about mid-day, when I was stopped by a driver who wanted to know if he was on the track to El Adem. I put him right and asked the oft-repeated inquiry: luck was with me this time for he had that morning left the K.D.G.s moving into a leaguer seven miles to the south-west. Two hours later I found them and drove up to the commander's armoured car.

Colonel McCorquodale couldn't take me on the establishment of his regiment but attached me to 'A' Squadron for intelligence duties and liaison with the Arabs. As I had no desire to remain with the regiment for ever this arrangement suited me well.

After the ambiguous, fumbling half-heartedness of the officers in my late battalion, coming to work with men who made fighting their business was like escaping from smelly hovels to the air of the mountains. It is not incongruous to praise them for taking their duties to heart, for in those days there were many who didn't. I soon discovered other virtues attached to this armoured-car regiment: we had a job and there was no need to go begging for employment, officers and men knew what they were doing, were interested in their work and liked it. As they had no leisure to think about much else they kept cheerful and in good spirits.

I spent an afternoon learning the mechanics of my new trade: talking on the wireless, driving the cumbersome Daimler armoured cars and handling the B.S.A. gun; then for the next few days I went out with routine patrols along the newly-formed line stretching to the south from Gazala on the coast to Bir Hakim. Nothing much happened: though we frequently saw the enemy I don't remember having been really engaged. I learnt, however, something of the tactics of fighting in vehicles, and this knowledge stood me in good stead in later days when I handled armed jeeps. That our jeeps carried no armour made no difference as the plating on the armoured cars wouldn't stop even a rifle bullet.

All too soon the regiment was ordered back to Cairo for a rest and refit, my attachment came to an end and I found myself once more in Mena Camp, recaptured by the Libyan Arab Force, second in command to Paley's battalion. This happened towards the beginning of March 1942.

Paley and his battalion had had an adventurous time during the withdrawal. Stationed near Ajedabia, beyond Benghazi, at the time of the German attack, he had deliberately let himself be overrun and had operated for some time in the enemy rear. Then, finding a battalion too cumbrous a unit for guerrilla operations, he had marched it back to our lines, two hundred and thirty miles through enemy territory. He had followed a route on the confines of the desert in the southern foothills of the Jebel Akhdar, where the enemy hadn't had time yet to establish more than a few weak posts; his six hundred-odd men had been fed by the local Arabs and when he reached Tobruq after thirty-four days he hadn't lost, I believe, more than thirty men.

Captain Yunnie, a lean Scotsman from Aberdeen, to whom I had given first training when, newly commissioned, he had joined the Libyan Arab Force, had taken over my company in Paley's battalion. A pure civilian — he had been an insurance agent for some years before he had enlisted in the ranks at the age of thirty at the beginning of the war — he proved himself during the difficult withdrawal and acquired a taste for independent action and hazardous enterprises. More will be said about him in this story.

On the march they had been much helped by one of their Arab officers, Sa'ad 'Ali Rahuma, who had negotiated with the local tribes for the provision of food, had always been informed of the dispositions of the enemy and had been largely responsible for picking the route. Sa'ad 'Ali was a discovery of mine: an old scoundrel he undoubtedly was, cantankerous, vain and untruthful, but I had supported him against everyone in the early days, and I was glad to find that my high opinion of his capacities had been vindicated on this march. Colonel Paley recommended him for a Military Cross, which he got, the only officer, British or Arab, to be decorated for service with the Libyan Arab Force.

Paley was now about to be appointed second-in-command to the Iraqi Army, under Colonel Bromilow. Before leaving he arranged that I should be put in command of a new detachment called the 'Libyan Arab Force Commando', and from that moment I never looked back.

CHAPTER IX

MY OWN PLANS

AFTER my return from Cyrenaica and my brief service with the K.D.G.s I knew what I wanted to do: it was to build up a network of intelligence covering the Jebel Akhdar from Derna to Benghazi (now held by the enemy) — to take control of the friendly Arab tribes in that area and, as a minor object, to destroy enemy petrol dumps. I wanted to blow up dumps only when it would seriously embarrass the enemy at a critical moment and on a large scale; I was completely opposed to undertaking minor acts of violence such as raids and ambushes on isolated trucks or individual soldiers. I considered such small operations to be of no military usefulness whatsoever, and their only possible result would be reprisals on our friends the Arabs and the upsetting of my intelligence organization.

The Arabs as a source of information had not been untapped. The 'Long Range Desert Group' (L.R.D.G.) ran regular motor patrols in the desert to the south of the Jebel Akhdar: they occasionally left a couple of Arabs at some spot and picked them up again on their return trip three weeks later with such information as they had been able to collect from local gossip. Several British officers also had made trips of some duration in the Jebel: the most remarkable of these was John Haselden, a cotton broker from Miniah in Upper Egypt. Son of an English father and a Greek mother, born and bred in Egypt, of all Englishmen I have met he came the nearest to being able to pass himself off as an Arab.

Intelligence obtained by such haphazard methods was necessarily fragmentary and frequently out of date, as it appeared unfortunately in the commando raid on General Rommel in which Major Geoffrey Keyes, v.c., was killed on November 17th, 1941. Not only was Rommel away in Rome on that day, but the house in Beda Littoria which Keyes attacked was never used as a residence by the German commander-in-chief, who lived at that period in a cave in Wadi Kuf outside the town.

My aim was to collect intelligence — continuously — over the whole of Axis-occupied Cyrenaica and to be myself on the spot to appreciate the implications and the credibility of the information brought in — to check on news of importance and, if necessary, go and see with my own eyes — to direct and co-ordinate the work of my informants, and to pursue and develop promising clues. I wanted to present Eighth Army Headquarters, not with disconnected pieces of information, but with a co-ordinated picture of the enemy position in Cyrenaica kept up to date day by day.

At that time the German-Italian front line was at Gazala, west of Tobruq. Their supplies came by road from the ports of Benghazi and Tripoli, respectively three hundred and eight hundred miles in the rear. Their supply dumps and reinforcement camps were placed in the area extending from Benghazi to Derna, the fertile mountainous heart of Cyrenaica which I call, by an extension of the local usage, the Jebel Akhdar — the Green Mountain. Keeping watch on the Jebel Akhdar I would be able to inform Eighth Army of the supply position of the enemy, and of their movements of troops and of armour.

To achieve my plan I wanted to establish myself permanently in enemy territory and take with me only a small number of Arab soldiers as a personal bodyguard and to handle stores and run errands. Some of these men would be trained in demolitions to form a small striking force for eventual operations against petrol dumps. For my communications I required two wireless sets and British signallers to work them. The bulk of the intelligence work would be done by local Arab civilians. To the intelligence officers at Eighth Army I gave a hint of what I proposed to do and asked them to keep an eye on my reports; to get the support of the Libyan Arab Force I concealed my hand and spoke only of demolitions. The indifferent success achieved by the Libyan troops that had gone out to Cyrenaica had already caused the disbandment of one of the five battalions, and further retrenchments were likely. The officer commanding the Force hoped that small spectacular stunts by his newly-formed 'Commando' might, if properly advertised, help to avert the axe and thus preserve some substance to his command. Middle East Headquarters, whose sanction was requested for the scheme, were equally favourable for the reason that at a stage in the war when major reverses were following one another in a depressing succession, any positive achievement, even very small, was welcome to maintain morale. The spirits of staff officers need more watching over even than those of the rank and file, for they know too much: I am sure my friends at Middle East Headquarters expected me to provide them with tiny but picturesque successes that would, for a while, take their minds off our big failures in the desert and in Greece. Thus 'Libyan Arab Force Commando' was formed to provide me with the men I wanted for my own schemes.

In fact I was provided with more men than I thought I could employ, but I kept my own counsel and selected, from the whole Force, twenty-two Arab other ranks, one British sergeant to look after them and one Arab officer, all volunteers. Thus, though I was over-staffed, I made a small call on the slender resources of British personnel in the Middle East, an argument to which Headquarters were very sensitive.

The Arab officer I had asked to accompany me was Lieut. Sa'ad 'Ali Rahuma and he had accepted eagerly: he liked me and he liked even more the prospect of becoming a man of importance amongst his own people.

Everybody helping, my preparations proceeded happily. The whole party received training in demolition work: loud bangs went off day and night in the neighbourhood of Mena Camp, and many a forty-gallon drum of petrol went up in flames. Sa'ad 'Ali revealed a sur-prisingly accurate knowledge of detonators, primers and fuses, which, added to the fact that he admitted having spent much time in Palestine, led me to suspect that, after he had fled penniless from Cyrenaica following on the Italian pacification in 1931, he had made a living by hiring his services to the Palestinian Arab terrorists. Which was indeed what he had done, as he told me on a later occasion, and a very good living he had made of it, on French gold.

By the end of March 1942 my little party was ready. Minute as it was, my new command was independent and it was for me the ful-filment of eighteen months of training and waiting. I valued it above its intrinsic importance as a promise for the future: I felt confident that with such a start I should, with good management, be able to keep myself on active operations, without a break, till the end of the war, which I put at ten years hence.

The possibility that I should survive that long seemed remote, and as, while I remained a soldier, I had no use for a private life, before leaving Egypt I set about arranging my affairs on the assumption that I would never come back to be a civilian.

My two young daughters had been evacuated to South Africa the preceding summer and were at school in Durban. I made for their maintenance elaborate financial arrangements which took into account the possibility of an enemy occupation of the Middle East, and then dismissed them from my mind for the next few years. My wife, with whom I had been on terms of friendly disagreement for a long time, was living in Cairo doing a job of a very secret nature at Middle East Headquarters. We arranged to divorce and got through the proceedings quite easily, through the friendly offices of the Belgian Minister in Egypt. She married again some time afterwards.

I sold my car, gave away my civilian clothes, sent to the Red Cross such of my books as I thought might suit hospital patients, and piled up the remainder with pictures, letters and the rest of my belongings into two rooms at Hawamdiah.

Ties all severed, family responsibilities shaken off and forgotten, and material belongings reduced to the contents of a bed-roll, an army pack and two haversacks, and of course the still undefeated Pisspot, I set out cheerfully to fight the war on my own.

The Pisspot ended its career in Mersa Matruh, where it was handed over to workshops for a minor repair while I proceeded to Jaghbub with my men. When I returned a few days later to collect it, a friendly young officer said: 'I have done you a good turn. That car of yours was not desert-worthy — it was not even road-worthy, and anyway it was a civilian type. I have returned it to Base as being "beyond local repair". Here is your chit: you can get a new car from El Fayed.' I thanked him kindly for his good intentions, but the chit of course was of no use to me, as the poor old Pisspot was my private property and not an army vehicle at all. Thus it ended ingloriously, on a scrap heap in Egypt.

PART TWO

THE SENUSSIS

CHAPTER I

WADI BUMA

IMPROVISATION and dash are foreign to my nature, unknown risks make me uncomfortable: I am never so happy as when I can spend my time making cautious preparations. Slow and unhurried, I have of course many times deliberately let golden opportunities slip by, unused, because I didn't feel ready for them; but, on the other hand, every one of my enterprises has had some measure of success, and my losses have, always, been low and easy to make good.

A set plan, worked out to minute details is not what I mean by preparedness: on the contrary, there is no more formidable obstacle to success. What I like to do is to go myself beforehand over the country and get the feel of the plains, the mountains and the valleys; the sand, the rocks and the mud; at the same time, I listen to the local gossip: find out who commands the enemy and what are his pastimes — who my friends are and how far they are prepared to help me and what are the presents that will please. Then, when I come back later with my men to carry out my evil schemes, I can let the plan take care of itself. If I have got a picture in my mind of the general conditions and a clear view of what I want to achieve, if I know roughly what there is over the next hill and the one after, I needn't worry: a workable plan of action will present itself to my mind when required — with no painful striving.

This will explain why, having brought my party as far as Jaghbub Oasis, I left it there to proceed on a preliminary trip to the Jebel with only Sa'ad 'Ali Rahuma, one Arab private called Hamed, and a stock of cigarettes, tea, sugar and white calico to be used as goodwill gifts and currency.

In those days anyone who had business in enemy-occupied Cyrenaica booked a passage on the Long Range Desert Group 'Bus Service' to the enemy's back door. The Jebel Akhdar, the 'Green Mountain ranges', run parallel with the Mediterranean coast, one hundred and seventy miles from Derna to Benghazi. They rise abruptly from the sea in precipitous rocky cliffs, to reach a maximum altitude of nearly three thousand feet, then drop in a succession of ranges of decreasing height to the great inland desert plain, fifty miles south of the coast. The northern slopes which receive a fair rainfall (I have even seen a thin covering of snow at Beda Littoria on a January morning) are covered in evergreen oaks where the forest has not been cut down for the Italian agricultural settlements. Going south the trees grow stunted and scarce, to be replaced by scrub and finally by scanty desert bushes along the dry wadi beds. Further south again the gravelly sands and rocks are barren, with only a few clumps of bushes here and there, flowering and sweet smelling during the short spring and dry the rest of the year. This inner desert, completely uninhabited, stretches over eight hundred miles of hills and rolling plains to the high peaks of the Tibesti mountains, where a few primitive tribesmen pasture their flocks — then another eight hundred barren miles to Lake Chad in French Equatorial Africa. Isolated in the waste, five hundred miles from the coast, the tiny Kufra Oasis lies in a depression where, having flowed underground one thousand miles from the equatorial rain belt, sweet water wells up and irrigates palm groves and gardens of millet.

Debased town Arabs live in stone houses in the coastal towns, Benghazi and Derna, and inland at El Merj, which the Italians call Barce, in its rich, red, cup-shaped plain. The remainder of the Jebel and the foothills to the south are the home of the true nomads, who pitch their tents from well to well as they follow their grazing flocks. Except along the trade routes to the oasis of Jalo and Kufra, they never wander into the southern spaces where their cattle would find neither pastures nor water.

These truly desert wastes were used for their travels by the Long Range Desert Group. I have avoided tiresome initials so far but this unit will appear often in my story and it will be called L.R.D.G. Its full designation Long Range Desert Group appears now for the last time.

The L.R.D.G., having solved many problems of desert travel and navigation, ran their motor patrols from Egypt to Tripoli, twelve hundred miles, with a soul-satisfying regularity. Except through enemy action they had never lost a truck nor missed a rendezvous. A free, cheerful, tireless, efficient body of bearded men, they were the most pleasant companions I have ever had. I graded their squadrons, drawn from various parts of the Empire, on a scale of human excellence, which ranged from the New Zealanders high on top through the Rhodesians and the British Yeomanry down to the squadron drawn from the Guards Regiments. The New Zealanders, farmers in civil life, took easily to a roaming life in the desert. They had from the first a resourceful, happy assurance and set a standard which the others tried to follow.

Colonel Bagnold, a shy, scholarly man, had founded the L.R.D.G. in the very early days of the war, with the help of Prendergast, Shaw and Clayton, who had been with him on his travels of exploration before the war. He had invented a sun compass and adapted astronomical methods which made navigation easy and accurate; his trucks, altered and improved, could, with the help of steel channels (another of his inventions), drive over all the obstacles found in the desert. A condenser devised by him did away with water consumption by the truck engines and increased considerably the range of the vehicles.

His next brilliant achievement was getting the pick of the army for his unit, and such was the power of his leadership that he even contrived to fire Guardsmen with an enthusiasm which overrode their customary ill-natured squabbles. L.R.D.G. patrols of five thirty-hundredweight trucks, carrying five men each, drove out regularly from Egypt through the southern desert, their undisputed domain, and after a journey of a thousand miles, like raiders from the sea, reached undetected the coastal area held by the enemy. They ranged from Tripoli to Lake Chad on a variety of missions, mainly of reconnaissance and survey. The regularity of their journeys was occasionally upset by the enemy, but such was the excellence of the men and of the equipment that geographical obstacles and mechanical breakdowns never interfered with their schedule. Each patrol carried a wireless set and remained in daily contact with Headquarters.

On the evening of April 25th, 1942, five days out of Siwa with Captain Hunter's patrol, I sighted the Jebel, a brown smudge on the northern horizon. The next morning we topped a low rise and trundled down into a plain covered in flowers and dotted with acacia bushes, the lower reaches of Wadi el Ghelta, near Haqfet Jiljaf. Sheep, goats and a few camels grazed the sweet-smelling brush, the first life we had seen since we left Siwa, three hundred and eighty miles away. We pulled up under cover of a steep wadi bank, a few hundred yards from a village of tents, and I sent Sa'ad 'Ali to talk to the Arabs.

An hour later he returned with half a dozen of them and we squatted on the sand in the shade of some acacia bushes. Sa'ad took me aside to advise me not to waste much time or treasure on our guests as they were men of no importance. Sa'ad 'Ali's appearance was ludicrous. He had the build of a jockey, wore an ill-fitting, soiled and crumpled British Officer's tunic (with a dirty purple and white ribbon of the Military Cross) and slacks, his wizened, dark face under a cap-comforter, with brown monkey eyes vivacious, sharp and clever and a humorous smile that broke up his face in hundreds of creases and wrinkles. His wit was sharp; after he had scored a point he would break into a disarming silent laugh, mouth open like a child. His mannerisms were many and catching: and I still use a grimace to express playfully indignant surprise which I acquired from him.

Our guests, simple shepherds of an obscure sub-tribe, would in more prosperous times have worn coloured braided waistcoats and full-bottomed Turkish pantaloons, yellow elastic-sided boots and a white cloth turban wound over a brown felt skull-cap. As it was, after two years of war and blockade, their apparel was mostly of ragged cast-off garments from the three armies which had marched up and down their country. Their dignity was only saved by the jerd, a rectangular piece of woollen material fourteen feet long and four feet across, which every Arab of Cyrenaica wraps nobly round his body, toga fashion. Sa'ad 'Ali once said: 'The Italians showed us in a film the glory of the Romans. *We*, obviously, not *they*, are the true descendants of the ancient Romans for we still dress as they did.' And he was quite right, for the jerd *is* a toga.

army camps, and most of the forest had been cleared in such a way that we could venture there only with extreme caution. But to the south of the southern road the country, being wild and poorly provided with tracks, was seldom visited by the enemy. Again between the northern road and the coast, where the escarpment plunged down to the sea, the warlike Dursa tribe kept their country fairly free of Italian or German troops. Ninety-five miles to the west were our own lines extending from Gazala to Bir Hakim. We had, however, a friend much closer than that: Wadi Shegran had been used for a long time by the L.R.D.G. as a back door to the enemy positions. John Haselden had been picked up here the preceding November after the unsuccessful attempt on General Rommel's life at Beda Littoria, and three weeks before my own arrival Major Chapman had been left here with two British wireless operators to investigate the possibilities of a commando raid on the traffic of the northern tarmac road. According to an arrangement made on the wireless, he had posted an Arab to contact us in Wadi Shegran. This man, whom we found driving a small flock of sheep and goats, told us that Major Chapman had established himself in a canyon-like wadi less than an hour's walk away, and undertook to go and fetch him. Chapman, long and lanky, had been a schoolmaster in Cairo until he joined the army, leaving in Egypt a wife and three small children about whom he worried ceaselessly. With a studious, academic mind and a hypochondriacal disposition, he suffered nonsense from nobody, and applied himself with no delusions of glamour to the tasks he had set himself. However matter of fact his behaviour might be, he could not be satisfied with a humdrum military career. Discontented with the Libyan Arab Force, he had left it early to take an appointment with a cavalry force raised in Syria amongst the Druse hillmen, which he had left again as soon as the Syrian campaign had ended, to undertake his present assignment with no trace of enthusiasm but with a dogged determination. By nature a debunker, he applied rigid tests of common sense to the foolhardy undertakings he had engaged himself in.

He arrived in the dark of the night and was rather disgruntled: the Shegran-Slonta line of approach had been overworked, the Italians had heard rumours and were very nervous. In particular a man called Selim, of the Barasi tribe, who had been our main contact in this area, was strongly suspected by the Italian commander at Slonta of helping the British and had been interrogated by him several times. Selim himself turned up the next night and confirmed the bad news. He had been questioned once more by the Italians on his pro-British activities that very day and he was taking a very dangerous step in visiting us. I immediately saw that it was unfair to compromise him any further and I decided to break new ground.

Sa'ad 'Ali approved: he distrusted the Barasi anyway. Full of prejudice, his words were: 'The Barasi are all informers, let us go to the Obeidat' — the largest and most powerful of all Jebel tribes whose territory extends from Lamluda to beyond Tobruq in the east. At very first light Sa'ad set out on foot by himself to find transport, leaving me with Hamed and the stores amongst the boulders of the Shegran. Chevalier, who had come out to help with the projected commando raid, stuck to his original plan and went into hiding in Chapman's canyon waiting for an opportunity to be guided north to the road.

In the evening Sa'ad returned with three decrepit, ragged Arabs leading a horse, two camels and a donkey. Avarice alone had induced them to hire out their broken-down animals, and they studiously ignored the fact that I was a British officer. Sa'ad wouldn't remain where we were one moment longer: he hustled and bustled, our small stores were loaded on the unwilling animals and off we went in the night. I rode the horse, with a back-breaking Arab saddle, Sa'ad 'Ali perched himself on the donkey on top of an enormous bundle — the rest of the party walked.

Past Sidi Musa our cross-country journey took us, a grey sheikh's tomb, then under the cliffs of Ras Juliaz where we entered the forest, climbing all the time. Dawn found us near Qasr er Remteiat, a ruined Roman — or perhaps Greek — castle on a hilltop which gives its name to the district. Here Sa'ad 'Ali called a halt in a clearing of the forest, a wide meadow dotted with bushes and cut deeply by dry watercourses lined with trees. I appreciated the cunning choice of the camping site: the water courses were deep enough to give us good cover and shade, and anyone approaching us from the woods would be in full view across the clearing. We paid off our guides and their beasts, and they slunk off and were gone in a moment in the early twilight. We kept the horse, however, having found it vigorous in spite of its sorry appearance. A few pounds of tea and two lengths of calico were the price paid for our mount, cheap enough indeed, but it had the Italian Army brand and was a dangerous possession for a poor Arab.

We sipped our tea; Sa'ad 'Ali scratched himself and said: 'I haven't had a wash since we left Siwa, I am itchy all over. Now is the time for a bath.' With a grubby towel and a cake of soap from his haversack, he disappeared over the bank, to come back after an hour shaven and shiny. Hamed followed then to perform the same function. I thought that so much cleanliness was against the rules of the game and I felt there was something vaguely heroic about an eight days' growth of beard, but Sa'ad wouldn't have it and insisted that Hamed on his return should take me to the well for a wash.

Starting on each side of the broad top of a hill were two low dry-course stone walls: they ran down the slope at a converging angle to meet after a few hundred yards over the mouth of a cistern hewn out of the rock and lined with masonry. When the torrential winter showers fall the walls act as the sides of a funnel to collect and guide the rushing waters down the hillside into the cistern. Thousands of these cisterns are dotted over the Jebel, nearly all of Roman build and some of them as large as the inside of a fair-sized house. They are the only water supply in the whole of the mountains for there are no true wells, nor, with the exception of the Wadi Derna, any permanent running streams, and the inhabitants are entirely dependent on them to water their cattle and for their own drink. Yet the labour-hating Arabs have let their Roman cisterns fall into disrepair, save a very few.

When I started undressing Hamed left me, with a can and a length of rope, at the square opening to the cistern, and went and squatted with his back to me at a little distance, for these Arabs are modest and would not be seen in their nakedness. In time I nearly reached to the Arab standard of cleanliness but, in common with all my British companions, I never could quite rid myself of the fancy that these frequent washings took something away of the romance of our boyish adventures.

As I had put myself entirely in Sa'ad 'Ali's hands there wasn't much I could say when, returning to camp, I found him not furthering warlike designs but preparing to bake bread. Though not at all religious — I seldom saw him pray except in company and then very perfunctorily — Sa'ad had all the good Senussi's distaste for tinned food — infidel food — and would consume it only in the most extreme emergency. Hence his resolve to bake bread. He scraped a hollow in the ground, lined it with flat stones and lit a blazing bonfire over it of dead tree branches. On a flat rock he mixed his flour, water and salt, kneaded the dough, slapped it and banged it, white to the elbows and grinning like a cheerful devil. When the fire had burnt itself out to embers he scraped the stones clean, put flat round cakes of dough on the hot stones, and covered them again with embers. He then seemed to lose interest, walked away, busied himself with other things and finally lay down under a tree and dozed off. Suddenly he jumped up, called to Hamed: 'The bread is ready!' and they both scraped off the embers hurriedly lest the critical moment be passed and the bread burnt. The loaves, about a foot across and two inches in thickness, were pulled out and set to cool. The outer crust, black and charred, had to be scraped off: the bread itself, though unleavened, was firm, crisp and delicious. We made a meal of it with cheese and tea and then we composed ourselves to sleep.

At sunset Sa'ad 'Ali sent Hamed to bring in the hobbled horse from its grazing. He intended our man to seek out Metwallah bu Jibrin, who he thought might be with his people at one of the wells near Remteiat, and ask him to come and visit us. Hamed was instructed carefully where to go, who to see and what to say, and definitely ordered to be back within thirty-six hours. Having repeated his instructions, he rode off in the gathering darkness.

We spent the next day, Sa'ad and I, sleeping and talking. The following morning Hamed had not returned, nor did he appear during the day, so we slept and talked again. The only living creature apart from ourselves was an owl that we saw flitting from tree to tree. The Jebel, with its green trees and abundant undergrowth, is strikingly empty of wild life. The reason is that there is no open water for the creatures to drink from. This owl, however, managed to make a living and in the general quiet we heard its dismal cries at intervals by day and by night. Buma is the local name for an owl, and Sa'ad, who was getting impatient at Hamed's delay, addressed the bird: 'Oh Buma, as you see we are still here in Wadi Buma near Qasr (castle) Buma, drinking from Bir (well) Buma. We have come out to fight the armies of the enemy and all we have found is a Buma. In our old days, the major and I, if we can still talk like men and do not hoot like you, Buma, we shall sit drinking tea and recall our brave deeds at the Battle of the Buma.' The bird gave a few hoots and Sa'ad took up: 'Oh Buma, don't mock poor old Sa'ad. He trusted Hamed, the fool who broke the glasses, with his last horse, he trusted him and now he has got lost, and the horse has broken a leg. When we go back to Egypt, if ever we do, our friends will ask: "How many Christians have you slain, oh warriors?" and we shall answer: "Of the Christians we killed not one, but we sat and listened to a Buma." '

I guessed what was on Sa'ad's mind. He wanted to go himself and fetch Metwallah bu Jibrin or some other trusty friend but he feared that if he left me alone I might think he had deserted me. On the other hand we couldn't both go together on account of our stores, which it would have been inconvenient to abandon, but mainly because the first approach is a matter in which great care must be taken to compromise nobody, and I was too obviously a British officer and my Arabic was too poor to risk a meeting with the wrong person. So I said to Sa'ad: 'Don't abuse the Buma, she is good company and I will be very happy with her.' He pulled a comical face at me but all he said was: 'We shall see tomorrow morning.'

The next morning, the third since our arrival in Wadi Buma, Hamed had not returned. Sa'ad packed a small haversack and departed. His advice to me was to lie low — if any Arab discovered me I was to say that my camel had strayed and my guide, my 'khabir', had gone after it. Of my destination I had better say nothing except that I was travelling north. If after two days Sa'ad wasn't back, I was to make my way back south-west to the Shegran as best I could.

I was left alone with the Buma and I sat down under the bank to read Philip Guedalla's *Life of Wellington*. Next morning I was still under the bank, alone in a silent landscape and utterly happy. I had done everything that had to be done, nothing remained but to wait for my plans to mature and during the interval I was free, without worry and at peace with myself. Such periods of waiting were the only rests I took during the war: they offered so complete a relaxation that I never felt the strain of action.

Towards evening I saw movement under the trees at the far corner of the clearing and a moment later peace was shattered as a waving rider came galloping across the meadow and pulled up in front of me with a hint of a flourish. Sa'ad 'Ali leapt down, greeted me briefly and inquired after the Buma.

'I have brought Metwallah bu Jibrin. He is in the woods with his friends. In the saddle, Major, in the saddle, we are moving on.' Sa'ad was a hustler, strangely for an Arab; he made me climb on to his mare to make a dignified appearance before his friends, but the short Arab stirrups, adjusted to Sa'ad's diminutive legs, dangled just below my knees and rather spoiled the nobleness of my bearing. However Metwallah, standing under the trees with two of his friends, gave me a grave welcome when I hoisted myself out of the saddle, and after the formal introduction and compliments, he asked me to accept his hospitality for that night.

In the background stood the horses and three of Metwallah's camels with their attendants These Sa'ad took with him to load our stores and on his return he wouldn't let us tarry over our courtesies but, still in his hustling mood, he said: 'Tonight we shall talk. Now we want to get away from the Buma,' and turning to me he gave a low derisive owlish hoot.

CHAPTER II

COUNTRY LIFE

NIGHT had fallen when we dismounted amongst dim trees and rocks. Dogs were barking in the distance. Metwallah pushed on to his tent to make sure that the coast was clear, found all safe and came back to lead us in. I stooped low on entering as the roof reached to four feet from the ground and I found myself in the reception half of Metwallah's home — on one side a flimsy canvas partition cut off the domestic half where women and children live; on the three other sides the low outer curtains were rolled up to let in the breeze. Wooden sofas covered with carpets and a few hard pillows were all the furniture, and on them we squatted down, our legs folded under us, in the light of two oil lamps of the old-fashioned type with glass chimneys. A wooden bowl, the size of a large wash basin, filled with sour milk, was handed round and we drank deeply in turns, holding up the heavy bowl with both hands. Sour milk, from goats and ewes mixed, called 'leben' locally, was to be my standard food as long as I stayed with the Arabs, and I thrived on it; it is not considered as a real meal by the Arabs but more as a refreshment offered to the thirsty and hungry traveller the moment he arrives. An hour later, in preparation for the dinner, a boy came round with a metal hand basin bearing a cake of soap on its raised middle. He poured water over our soaped hands from a long-spouted pitcher and then handed us a towel. We all squatted on the ground round a low table which was then brought in and on which was placed a bowl of steaming ''esh'. This is a meal of barley flour flakes, boiled in water and soaked in melted butter. On festive occasions it is sometimes sprinkled with sugar. We turned up the sleeve on our right arm, said: 'In the name of God the merciful, the compassionate' — by way of Grace — and dipped into the bowl in silence. As soon as we had had our fill, it was removed to be finished off by the minor guests and attendants, squatting outside the

tent, and in came a boiled kid on a brass tray. Metwallah, our host, tore
the joint to pieces with his hands, handed me the choice shoulder piece
on a flat loaf of hobs, bread similar to that baked by Sa'ad 'Ali in the
Wadi Buma, by way of plate; the others helped themselves (the host
always last — and he eats hurriedly after he has made sure that the guests
are well looked after) and we all fell to, still in silence. Melted butter
had been poured over the kid's meat, making it a rather messy dish, and
it required more skill that I then possessed to eat it, without staining my
clothes, off a limp loaf held in my left hand, and sitting on the ground.
Noticing my awkwardness, my host spread a hand-towel over my
knees and regretted he could not provide a Roman (meaning European)
board and proper cutlery, but, he added laughing, 'Now that you have
come to live with the Arabs you will have to learn to eat as we do.' To
which I agreed and indeed I soon became skilful at eating in the natural
way, with the fingers. When I had finished Metwallah offered me a
piece of meat torn off the bone he was holding, which I accepted, but
when I refused a further helping no more food was pressed on me, for
such is the etiquette amongst the Senussis. Not so in Egypt, where
good manners require the guest to be stuffed beyond his will.

As soon as we had finished, Metwallah called for his servants: the
tray with the reduced carcass was removed and soap and water went
round once more. We washed our hands and lips, rubbed our teeth
with a soapy forefinger, rinsed our mouths and then lay back on the
pillows. Glasses of water were handed round and a little later tea was
brought in. Hardly a word had been spoken during the meal but now
the gates were opened and talk flowed.

Metwallah's position was unique amongst the Senussi Arabs who
helped the British during the enemy occupation of their country: cattle
owner and tradesman, he led, in peace time, a dual life: in his town
house in Derna, he was a wealthy trader with connections overseas,
in Europe and in Egypt — in the Jebel with his flocks, a traditional
nomad Arab. Though very wealthy, he was not a sheikh and had no
political ambitions. What the nature of his participation had been in
the long struggle against the Italian invader from 1912 to 1929, I have
not been able to find out with certainty. I don't think he fought in

person: I have always thought of him as a banker with a great devotion to the cause, helping to finance the poor Senussi Army — at no loss to himself. In the present crisis he had taken a definite stand on our side and, remaining always carefully in the background, he preferred cautious help. What I wanted from him on that first night were his views on the leading men of his Obeidi tribe, the cynical opinions of a man through whom passed the main threads of intrigue, but who, determined to remain behind the scenes, took no sides in tribal rivalries.

Through the night we gossiped: from sheikh to sheikh, and to meaner men too, our talk followed a zigzag course. Who was a reliable friend and who was half-hearted, who was vainglorious, who ambitious, who mercenary? To these Arabs, a closed community, gossip and intrigue are the very breath of life: Metwallah and Sa'ad 'Ali threw themselves into the game with passion; and all I did was to put a question now and then and listen. Sa'ad of course had been out of the country for many years and his interests tended to concentrate on events of the old Italian wars. About two in the morning they were hard at it, recalling battles long gone by and I let myself go to sleep on my bench. Later in the night Sa'ad shook me awake, offered tea, and, much refreshed, I brought my friends down from the ecstasies of reminiscence to concrete plans for the morrow: they had talked themselves out and were ready for action.

While listening to the gossip I had decided that my best course would be to visit personally as many as possible of the leading men. My presence in the Jebel, thus openly advertised, would give them confidence in the ultimate success of British arms. I would explain my plans, ask for their co-operation and make them feel that we were all working together on an important scheme, simple, clear and perfectly understood. Of course I ran the risk of being betrayed to the enemy, but I banked on confidence breeding confidence: I thought that, though a man might easily be tempted to give away a British officer by whom he has been stealthily summoned to an anxious midnight interview in the woods, he would hesitate to betray a guest who had walked openly up to his tent and had accepted his hospitality as a due. Dispensing favours not begging for them, boldness, not timidity, was, I hoped, the way to acquire prestige and authority. Anyhow, I had much at stake and I could not afford to worry overmuch about risks.

We made a list of the men I would see and worked out a route. With nomads, ever on the move from well to well, visiting is a problem, but Metwallah, wise and encyclopaedic, knew or guessed where everyone was likely to be found. When dawn broke we went out and walked some distance into the woods: I didn't want yet to be seen in the village of tents by a chance visitor. We needed mounts for our trip and Metwallah arranged for a choice to be offered for sale. No good mares were available; we finally picked on two stallions, the best, we thought, of a very sorry lot. Though horsemen all, the Senussi Arabs were very careless of their animals: perhaps the difficulty of feeding them on barley, which, in war time, was badly needed for human consumption, was the reason, or the fact that the Italians had taken away the best long ago, but I did not see a single horse in good condition. We bargained at leisure and when finally a price was agreed on — so many glasses of tea leaves, so many of sugar and so many cubits of cloth — we had the job to count out our strange money. Sa'ad kept a very small glass for this purpose but piled it conscientiously as high as it would hold. A cubit is the length from the finger tips to the elbow: with a man of Sa'ad's diminutive stature it is a very short measure indeed but, to my surprise, we never had a complaint on that account. The horses paid for, we hid the bulk of our supplies, which we did not intend to carry with us on our tour, in a dry water cistern. An Arab shepherd was made responsible for the treasure which was all measured out before being stored; a boulder was pushed over the mouth of the cistern and the shepherd undertook to pasture his flock of sheep and goats in the neighbourhood and keep an eye on possible looters. Nothing was missing on our return. As Hamed was still abroad, Metwallah provided us with two retainers on horseback.

Hamed returned to me weeks later, footsore, with a long and sad story. He had failed, being indeed a timid fool, to find Metwallah and had gone instead to visit his mother in a distant pasture. Rumour having reached him at last of our whereabouts he had left our horse with his mother and walked back to us. When he was brought to me, crestfallen and apologetic, I sent him back, tired as he was, to recover the horse and he finally returned just in time to be evacuated to Egypt. Such was his inglorious share in our campaign.

Towards evening we set out, myself, Sa'ad 'Ali Rahuma and the two boys lent by Metwallah, on the first lap of our visiting tour. We were very careful, in those early days, to travel only in the darkness so as not to be seen by casual travellers who might spread rumours. Later, when my presence in the country was known, officially so to speak, to thousands and my status as a friend of the Obeidi sheikhs well established, I took to daylight travelling without running into much trouble. We rode across country and as the enemy always kept to the very few tracks, the risk was small of meeting him unawares.

I can't remember exactly how long my tour lasted because I got no regular sleep but only a few hours here and there, by day or by night, and after a while the distinction between one day and the next became slightly blurred. I rode usually most of the night, timing my arrival at my new host's for the very early morning. Stopping at some distance from his village of tents I would send in Sa'ad and one of Metwallah's men to announce my visit. While they were away I wrapped myself up in a jerd and slept for an hour or so. Then I would go over to my host's tent, exchange civilities, drink sour milk and talk while the meal was being prepared. Generally some of my host's friends came and shared our dinner. This, by the way, was invariably similar to the one we had on the first night with Metwallah. Sour milk, boiled 'esh with melted butter, followed by boiled kid and barley bread. There was no other food in the Jebel in those days, and from year end to year end the daily fare was identical, with the exception, of course, that meat was only served on festive occasions and then only if there was time enough to kill a kid, clean it and cook it. I found this food satisfying and never tired of it, though after some months I developed a craving for fresh vegetables and fruit. But I kept extremely fit and so did the Arabs, amongst whom I found practically no disease.

During the afternoon there was more talk in the tent, with intervals of sleep, and after dark we rode away once more. On the fifth or the sixth day of this tour of country houses, having visited several minor characters, I made for Kaf Herwa to meet Sheikh 'Ali bu Hamed el Obeidi. I had got to like him four months previously in Derna when I had judged him to be the most powerful man amongst the Obeidat. A tall lean man of fifty, with flowing gestures and a soft voice with tender tones covering passionate fires; a subtle brain, a sharp wit, a natural assumption of authority, a knowledge of the Western world, master of intrigue and of the devious route, he led in fact the Obeidi tribe whose nominal head was 'Abdel Qader bu Bridan, an old sheikh of over eighty years of age. Before the war (our war), having made his peace with the Italian conqueror, he lived in some splendour, with a house in Derna and another in Alexandria in Egypt where he spent several months each year.

Since the beginning of the present war, although his son was openly with the British in Egypt, a young officer in the Libyan Arab Force, he had, with dextrous duplicity, kept on good terms with the Italians, having led them to believe that his influence alone prevented a general armed rising, not only of the Obeidat but also of the other Jebel tribes. The Italians were very ignorant and with the memory of nineteen years of humiliating rough handling at the hands of the Senussis they easily fell a prey to the Arab bogy. With their German masters keeping in their hands the control of military operations but relying on their despised ally to keep the peace along the lines of communication, the Italians were very nervous: their policy towards their uneasy Arab subjects was a mixture of appeasement and bullying.

'Ali bu Hamed played on their fears and succeeded in maintaining a precarious balance: his advantage was that, with his spies in every place, he was in fact all the time at the heart of the enemy's councils, whereas the Italians, ill-informed and lazy, were double-crossed even by their miserable paid informers. 'Ali bu Hamed had fought the Italians all his life and he hated them; he had no particular love of the British but he wanted us to liberate his country – after the liberation, when it came, he wanted to be in a position of influence with the new masters and he foresaw that their goodwill might help him to succeed 'Abdel Qader bu Bridan as Sheikh of the Obeidat, when the old man died. For the Germans he had no particular feeling, though, like many of the Arabs, he gave them the esteem which is due from warrior to warrior. The common saying was: 'The Italians are dogs, the Germans are men.'

'Ali bu Hamed had to be careful not to give any hold to Italian suspicions: he lived at that time with his family and retainers, not in tents, but in caves called Kaf Herwa in a wadi, wild, to be sure, and difficult of access, but not more than three miles from Acqua Viva, an Italian military post on the main road. I offered to meet him safely, far from his home, but he sent word that, for this first interview he wanted me to be his guest and he would send for me at Qaret Um Alfein the following night. The message added that, as he could talk the Egyptian dialect, there would be no need for a third person to interpret while we talked. This, I knew, was no reflection on my knowledge of Libyan Arabic, poor enough at that time in truth, but a hint that he had no wish to have Sa'ad 'Ali Rahuma as a partner to our discussions, for he disliked and despised my lieutenant whom he considered a mountebank — a brave soldier indeed but too much given to boasting — and of too obscure a tribe to be allowed to patronize an Obeidi sheikh.

At midnight 'Ali bu Hamed's messenger arrived at my host's tent, draped in a black jerd and mounted on a black horse. Off we rode into the dark windy night like a couple of ghosts. After an hour's blind riding over broken and rocky country we stopped in a craggy defile where my guide made me dismount, threw his dark jerd over me, asked me to wait and vanished into the night. Later a tall shadow came noiselessly out of the darkness, a hand pressed mine and I heard the well-remembered low melodious voice greet me with anxious solicitude His arm affectionately pressing mine, 'Ali bu Hamed guided me up the wadi, helped me up a slope, through an unseen crack in the cliff, and lifting a curtain he led me out of the black night into a vast, bright cavern, lit by four dazzling pressure lamps, and all hung with carpets. Carpets underfoot, carpets on the walls and in the centre two sprung sofas piled with soft pillows. 'Ali turned to me, disentangled me from my jerd, and putting his hands on my shoulders smiled at me with joy. The stage management was superb and my amazement unfeigned. 'Ali laughed, cut short the usual formal greetings, helped me take off my shoes, made me comfortable on the pillows and clapped his hands. A servant appeared from an inner recess of the cave carrying teapot and glasses. The meal — sour milk, 'esh, boiled kid — followed immediately; we washed, drank more tea and time being short, we talked. I said: 'Sheikh 'Ali, my friend, the British Government and your Amir, Sayed Idris el Senussi, knowing the friendship that is between you and me, have sent me to you so that, with your assistance, I may guide, advise and help your people and all the faithful Senussis in the Jebel Akhdar, in their struggle against the common enemy. My Government wants also to be informed of the enemy's intentions, dispositions and strength. Not rumours of a thousand tanks in El Abiar which turn out to be nothing more than a water lorry and two motor cycles in Lamluda — we want facts. To get them we want spies in enemy headquarters, in the airfields, in the dumps and the stores. We want eyes watching every road and every harbour, day and night.

'Lastly,' I said, 'the British Government may at a future date request me to bring in raiding parties to blow up dumps. This will only happen when our armies will be marching forward and the work will be done in such a way that no Arabs can possibly be implicated.' I said no more on this subject but reverted quickly to my first point: 'As to advising the Arabs on their best course of action,' I said, 'I have noticed during the last few days that some of our friends are hot-headed and want arms to fight the enemy. I must tell you that such action is precisely what we don't want. Pinpricks against the Italians will not help our army, they will bring disastrous reprisals against the Arabs, which we will not be able to prevent, and my Government will lose its eyes and its ears. We don't want direct action yet, later perhaps — not now.' 'Ali bu Hamed said: ' 'Abdel Qader bu Bridan is very old but his blood is still hot. He wants to fight. He believes the war is nearly won and that if we don't move now we will miss our chance — then the English will think we did nothing to help. He has many friends.' I saw his difficulty and I told him I intended calling a conference of all the Obeidi sheikhs under 'Abdel Qader and I would find means of damping their ardour without shaking their faith in the British victory. 'You and I can persuade them,' I said. 'But nobody need know that we have made our plans together beforehand.' 'Ali bu Hamed nodded dreamily: 'It is better that way. Now what information will you want about the enemy?' I told him — in great detail — and he undertook to expand his network of spies to meet my requirements. His main source of information were Italian-speaking Arabs employed as servants in headquarters and messes. The Italian officers spoke quite freely in their presence and left documents lying on desks, never suspecting that their ragged servants understood and even read their language. At night the servants met friends in the street or under the tents of neighbouring shepherds — words were exchanged and later a rider disappeared into the night with a well-memorized message.

'Ali bu Hamed promised to arrange for messages to be transmitted to my headquarters when it would be established. 'They won't come from me,' — I nodded acquiescence — 'Sheikh 'Abdel Jelil bu Tayeb will see to it.' 'He is a man of honour,' I said. 'You and I need not meet again in private. It is better so.' There was no need to dissemble with 'Ali bu Hamed: we understood one another perfectly. He gave me the names of the men he wanted to be invited to my conference of sheikhs and we parted with few words, the night being nearly spent.

I reached Qaret Um Alfein before dawn, roused Sa'ad 'Ali Rahuma and set out to call on 'Abdel Aziz bu Yunes whose tents were pitched five miles away in a dreary steep wadi of black shingle near Bir el Dei. I had picked on this vain and very stupid young man, thick-set with a broad black moustache, because he was a nephew to old Sheikh 'Abdel Qader bu Bridan. He entertained the foolish hope of succeeding his uncle as Sheikh of the Obeidat, instead of which he came to an untimely end a few months later for his betrayal of me to General Piatti, the Italian Governor of Cyrenaica. But when Sa'ad 'Ali walked into his tent that morning and announced my visit, he was delighted and relieved because he had feared I might call on 'Ali bu Hamed, the rival claimant to the succession, and not on him. We were given a princely reception Sa'ad 'Ali, cheered, I suppose, at having avoided a snubbing interview with his old enemy, was in an uproarious mood. He cracked jokes with our many fellow guests at the dinner party and called to the old lady (our host's mother) behind the canvas partition, claiming that he had been a suitor of hers thirty years ago. The old crone even came crouching from under the curtain and shyly shook hands with me: she took heart under the playful banter and with a mischievous twinkle in her old eyes protested that she had never as much as looked at that wizened little monkey. She then retired to her side of the partition and we started talking business. She, and the other women of the household, could of course hear every word that was spoken but neither then, nor in any tent nor on any occasion did a secret leak out through women's gossip.

The business of the day of course was the sheikhs' conference and it pleased everyone. Here at last was official recognition of the Arab cause: not dark midnight confabulations between an unknown British agent and an obscure shepherd, underhand meetings behind bushes that led seemingly to nothing, but a full dress gathering of all the stars in the Senussi world called by a British officer in uniform, specially sent for the purpose by his Government, and the Senussi spiritual leader, Sayed Idris el Senussi. Kaf el Qsur was chosen as a suitably central and sufficiently concealed spot for the meeting and the date fixed at twelve days hence to give time for the most distant sheikhs to arrive.

Sheikh 'Abdel Qader bu Bridan's only surviving son (the others had all been killed in the Italian wars), a delicate youth of seventeen, was with us that day, staying with our host, his cousin. He was dispatched to summon his father from Mekhili, fifty miles to the south. Such was the enthusiasm that the boy did not wait for the end of our council: he learned his message word for word, mounted his mare and departed. An Arab does not prepare for a journey: he wraps his jerd around him and is gone. Food and water will be got from Arab tents on the way.

By midnight all the messengers had left to deliver the invitations — in my name and that of 'Abdel Qader bu Bridan. Overcome with weariness from much talking I curled up on the wooden couch and slept till dawn. At daybreak Sa'ad 'Ali rode away, bound for Metwallah's tent at Er Rteim. They were to be responsible for the commissariat: we reckoned that between our guests and their retainers, eighty men at least would have to be fed for three days at Kaf el Qsur and I relied on Metwallah to provide food and servants in a style suitable to an historic occasion. Meanwhile with 'Abdel Aziz and two of his men, I went down to have a look at the enemy traffic on the road, two miles away. It was not the tarmac but a very good motorable track, which we called the 'Martuba by-pass': I suspected that it took most of the traffic going westwards to the enemy main forces at Gazala, avoiding the tiresome descent from the escarpment to Derna and up again to El Ftayah, and I planned to establish a permanent watch on the track. On this occasion 'Abdel Aziz showed sense and took me to a spot from which a good long stretch of the road was visible in both directions. Cover was not too good but sufficient for my purposes. We left our mounts behind a sheikh's tomb called Sidi Shaher Ruha and proceeded over a broken plain rather sparsely grown with scrub till I stopped and made myself comfortable under a bush forty yards from the track. Three men on foot are not very conspicuous and anyway army drivers never take their eyes off the road, so the chances of being noticed were slender and the lack of shade made it unlikely that a convoy would stop here for the midday rest.

It was a busy day on the track that morning: a steady stream of vehicles went by in both directions and from where I sat I could see the faces of the soldiers as they drove by. There is something deeply satisfying in watching the enemy war machine from the wrong side of the fence and this, my first opportunity, gave me much pleasure. A snooper's enjoyment, no doubt, but marred by no guilty conscience; with, indeed, a sense of virtuous achievement and a happy knowledge of having outwitted the enemy. I had never seen so many German soldiers in all my life as I did that morning; watching them I thought: 'Smug-faced fools, you think the enemy is ninety miles away! If you only knew! He is a stone's-throw away, sitting under a bloody bush and writing down in his book every bloody vehicle of yours.' I had ruled several pages of a notebook in columns with headings: Mark III tanks, Mark II tanks — five-ton trucks with troops — ditto with supplies — staff cars, motor cycles and so on. The right-hand page for westwards traffic, left-hand for eastwards traffic. The density of traffic was about two hundred vehicles an hour, which kept me pretty busy and I filled up the pages, with considerable satisfaction.

By noon traffic became scarcer and I had periods during which no vehicles were in sight. Then the periods lengthened and by two o'clock the road seemed permanently deserted. The sun was overhead, the heat was considerable, I felt drowsy. A lonely truck roared in the distance, appeared round the bend, loaded with German troops, was entered in my book and passed on. I lay back and stretched my legs: my two companions were asleep, their head cloths drawn over their eyes. Then I realized something was wrong: I had not heard the last truck grind up the next rise after it had passed us. I lifted my head and I saw it halted on the track, five hundred yards away. Through my glasses, in the shimmering heat, I saw the men out of the truck, gathered in a bunch. 'Brewing up,' I thought. I touched my companions on the shoulder, they woke up without a start and turned their eyes as I pointed. I lay back and 'Abdel Aziz kept watch. Ten minutes later he touched me: I turned on to my stomach and looked through the glasses at two mirage-distorted figures: they came nearer and resolved themselves into two German soldiers. The glasses lowered, I judged the distance to be still quite safe and I said to 'Abdel Aziz and his companion: 'Go back to the sheikh's tomb — I shall meet you there later,' and I cocked my tommy gun. 'Abdel Aziz got up and walked away — he was just an Arab in the landscape, no one would notice him. His companion grunted: 'I am staying,' and we both crawled behind our bush and kept our heads down. The two Germans, a private and a feldwebel, had a rifle and a pistol between them. They were now quite near and seemed to be making for our bush: as they had not unslung their weapons it was likely that they were not suspicious, but still they were making straight for us. Very carefully I shouldered my tommy gun. Between us and the two Germans was a rather conspicuous small tree, about twenty yards away from our bush. I slid the catch to 'single shot', brought the foresight to bear on the feldwebel and decided to fire when he reached the tree. If I succeeded in bringing both men down with no more than three or four shots, I hoped that the others, at the truck, would not notice and I would have time to withdraw unperceived in spite of my (as I thought) conspicuous uniform. The feldwebel advanced with a glassy stare. I drew breath, aimed at the pit of his stomach and started squeezing the trigger. As he reached the tree, however, he stopped, turned away from me, and his companion did the same. I released the trigger hoping that I would not, after all, have to kill these two men that I didn't know. They undid their belts, slid down their slacks and squatted in the shade of the tree. I let my weapon rest on a stone and looked at my companion: he was quite unmoved but he turned his head towards me and his face cracked into a tiny smile.

For a quarter of an hour these two squatted chatting at the top of their voices, then they hurried back to their truck and drove away. My Arab said: 'You might have killed the two Christians.' 'Yes, but there are many Germans besides them. May God let them live till the end of the war.' The Senussis used the word *Nasrani* (Nazarene) so commonly for *enemy* that they forgot that the original meaning of the word, which is of course *Christian*, would apply equally to myself and to most of the British Army.

I told my companion: 'You should have gone with 'Abdel Aziz.' 'Oh no,' he laughed, 'I am your khabir. If you die, I die.' Strictly speaking, not he but his master 'Abdel Aziz was my khabir, but I thought better not to argue and simply said: 'God bless you', and let the matter drop. A khabir is the guide, the sponsor, to whom a stranger is entrusted and as long as he hasn't brought his charge back to safety it is understood that the khabir is responsible in every way for his comfort and his life. The relationship is easily and casually entered into. Once undertaken, the duties are binding unto death. But death is of small moment to a good Senussi compared to a breach of good form; the return of a khabir having lost his charge would be very shocking indeed.

I resumed my watch of the road till an hour later when 'Abdel Aziz and his second henchman, who had been left at the tomb, appeared in the distance with plates of food carried in handkerchiefs. We left the newcomer to keep an eye on the traffic and retired to the shade of a watercourse for our meal.

A few more vehicles passed till sunset, and then, just before dark, I made the snooper's scoop: fifteen German Mark III tanks going up to the line, with their attendant vehicles. German tanks in those days

95

were the bogy of our Headquarters (with very good reason) and the main object of a road watch was to detect and report any tanks coming up. Two hours after dark, having confirmed that, as I thought, the enemy didn't travel by night, we all returned to 'Abdel Aziz's tent. I was well pleased with the day's work: the Martuba by-pass was, as I had guessed, used extensively by the enemy and it would be easy to set a watch on it. Moreover I had, with my own eyes, seen German tanks and made a note of their markings, and with childish eagerness I wanted to pass the information back to Army Headquarters without delay. The only means I had of getting in touch with Headquarters was Chapman's wireless set in the canyon near Wadi Shegran, and Sa'ad 'Ali was the only man who could direct a messenger to it. So back to Er Rteim I rode, leaving about midnight and arriving shortly after dawn. I found Metwallah and Sa'ad 'Ali already (or was it *still*) up and told them what I wanted. They discussed the matter and decided that Mohammed bul Qassem was the man to take my very important message down to the wireless — if he could be induced to go — and the man was sent for. He was a grizzled warrior of a surly disposition, dark-featured and scowling. Sa'ad told him that a message of the utmost urgency had to be carried — Mohammed said he wouldn't go — Metwallah insisted — Mohammed didn't know the wadi with the radio — I asked him as a personal favour: he said he would take orders from nobody. I said, never mind, I would go myself. Mohammed bul Qassem asked: 'Where is the message?' I gave it to him and we all got up. Sa'ad took Mohammed apart and standing with his head to one side, tense and absorbed, gave him directions in a whispered sing-song chant. He told him the landmarks of the thirty mile route: a bush, then a hill, a bush again, a ridge, a rise, a wadi, a hummock . . . then at last a kharruba tree, over a rocky ridge and down into the canyon. Mohammed bul Qassem listened with averted head and vacant eyes. When Sa'ad 'Ali stopped talking he grunted and walked away. At three o'clock the next morning, as I lay asleep in Metwallah's tent, he shook me by the arm, and handed me a message form: Chapman's acknowledgment. He had walked, over unfamiliar mountains, sixty miles in seventeen hours.

I left Sa'ad 'Ali and Metwallah busy counting sheep and collecting pots for our party and I went and stayed near Qasr Wertij with Sheikh 'Abdel Jelil bu Tayeb. He was the kinsman whom Sheikh 'Ali bu Hamed had mentioned to me in his Arabian-Night cave, who was to work out the details of my intelligence service. Here was the perfect follower of a great man: middle-aged, level-minded, efficient, hard-working and kindly. He had received his orders and had carried them out diligently. His relationship to me was strangely paternal: he considered it his duty to guide me. With unusual insight he realized that, in spite of deceptive appearances, I was really a stranger to the Arab world — his world — and he undertook to coach me.

We settled the practical side of my business: where I would place my wireless sets, who would be my regular messengers and how much they should be paid. He gave much attention to the kind of information I considered useful and to the means of getting it.

For the road watch he produced an elderly man called Jibrin with three grown sons, whose tent at that time was pitched near Sidret Haraij, only two miles off the Martuba by-pass. I spent a day with him watching the traffic to show him how I wanted the work done and to make sure he could identify the different types of vehicles. When I left I arranged that he would start work as soon as I came back with the wireless set. His sons would take turns as daily runners to my headquarters. Later, trained by Chapman, he became head of an important firm of 'road-watchers'.

The next few days before the sheikhs' conference at Kaf el Qsur were spent in leisurely talks with Sheikh 'Abdel Jelil bu Tayeb.

CHAPTER III

OBEIDI CONFERENCE

FROM the well-wooded mountain tops we rode southwards, winding down Wadi Qsur. At the Kaf, the landscape is desert suburb: clumps of trees and a little grass along the wadi banks; the bed is of boulders and gravel for, dry now in May, in winter it runs a full spate of torrential yellow water and carries torn-up trees whose black skeletons line the banks like the remains of a forest fire. The hills on both sides are crumbling and barren, shapeless and desolate. At a sharp bend of the wadi, however, a high yellow cliff is exposed in which are many caves, walled in by the 'Romans' for some purpose of their own. The Arabs don't build, and wherever hewn stones are found together they say the Romans put them up. Eleven hundred years ago the armies of Islam took this province from the decaying Roman Empire, but so uneventful has been the pasturing of flocks ever since that to the inhabitants it seems that living memories nearly take them back to the greatness of Rome.

The caves that give their name to the spot, empty now, were used to store grain in more prosperous times, and the higher ones, which had not been fouled by cattle, were clean and free of ticks. I found myself a home high up the cliff side: it was reached by a pleasant climb up a crack in the rock and had two windows overlooking the northern mountains.

Sa'ad 'Ali and Metwallah, with the food and the servants, had already settled in the wadi when I arrived, and so had some of our guests. The others came riding in during the next day. Sheikh 'Ali bu Hamed arrived early and retired to a cave. I had posted watchers on a hilltop, some distance down Wadi Qsur and when, towards sunset, they reported the approach of Sheikh 'Abdel Qader bu Bridan I rode out to greet him. A robust, thick-set man of over eighty with a white moustache and pointed beard, the hoodless burnous he wore under his ample white jerd made him look far too bulky for his small prancing mare, whose trappings and black and scarlet tassels hung to the ground. He boomed out in a deep gruff voice and we shook hands repeatedly without dismounting. Riding to camp together we exchanged the customary formal greetings. There is no more meaning put by the Arabs in these words than by us when we say and reply: 'How do you do?' — 'How do you do?' — and a little later, perhaps 'Well, how are you?' — 'Thanks. And how are you?' — and later again over a drink 'All the best!' 'Your very good health' — 'God bless.' As befits a leisurely and dignified mode of life, the Arab greetings are more in number than ours and are exchanged a great many times, usually in a toneless clipped voice, and replied to alike, with a slight inclination of the head and a lifting of the hand towards the heart. It was, however, a recognized peculiarity of the well-bred amongst the Obeidat that they put in their greetings those soft lingering tones of tender concern which 'Ali bu Hamed used to the point of affectation. Not so 'Abdel Qader bu Bridan whose affectations lay, in the opposite direction, towards blunt manliness and a rough humour.

Later in the evening we squatted down to a meal, about sixty of us; some of the sheikhs being still on their way, the formal proceedings did not start till the next morning.

During the night the remainder of our guests rode in with their attendants and spread themselves up and down the wadi, horses and camels hobbled and put to graze; fires were lit and tea boiled. I left Sa'ad 'Ali to entertain our friends and retired to my Roman home up the cliff for a reasonable night's rest: the morrow was to be a day of many words and I would need a fresh mind and clear wits.

At sunrise 'Abdel Qader bu Bridan led the prayers, tea was handed round and then I called the sheikhs into the shade of an overhanging rock at the foot of the cliff. They squatted down in a many-rowed circle and I faced them with 'Abdel Qader bu Bridan on my right, and 'Ali bu Hamed on my left; Sa'ad 'Ali, behind me, was ready, when necessary, to interpret abstruse turns of speech and to tell me the names of the speakers, many of whom were of course unknown to me. I stood up and said, picking my words:

'In the name of God the merciful, the compassionate! Sheikh 'Abdel Qader bu Bridan, Sheikh 'Ali bu Hamed, Sheikhs of the Obeidi clans and families, Arabs of the Jebel Akhdar, faithful Senussis, brothers! It grieves me that on this solemn day I should be unable to address you in the proper way and with adequate words. My tongue is black for I am not a scholar but a soldier, a man, not of knowledge, but of war, who comes to you from his foreign land, ignorant of your language but yet a brother to you, a brother in arms, to fight with you the war against our common enemy, the oppressor of your land, the murderer of your kinsmen, the robber of your flocks, the enemy of the faithful.'

I stopped to take breath, while 'Abdel Qader nodding in polite approval repeated in his rumbling bass: 'The murderer of your kinsmen, the robber of your flocks, the enemy of the faithful!' and a murmur went round the assembled listeners. I looked round to Sa'ad 'Ali, who winked and whispered: 'Excellent, carry on. Don't mention your black tongue any more, it is a word of Egypt.' I went on:

'Your spiritual leader, your Amir, the venerable Sheikh Sayed Idris el Senussi, God bless him, has offered his help and that of his people to my king, who is the King of England. At the present moment the Arab battalions of exiles are fighting side by side with their English brethren, and also with the faithful from India, with the men from Australia, New Zealand and South Africa, in fact' — I added lamely — 'with soldiers from the whole world.

'The black and white standard of Sayed Idris, the crescent and star of the Senussi, flies alongside the flag of the King of England. But this is not enough: the British Government knows that they have no more faithful friends, no allies more eager to join in the battle than you, the Senussi Arabs of the Jebel, than you assembled here today, the Arabs of the Obeidi tribe, oppressed, invaded, massacred but undaunted, expelled from the pastures of your fathers by vile Sicilian settlers, poor, hungry, but still and evermore, men and fighters — my Government know you and they want your help.'

'Abdel Qader bu Bridan rumbled the chorus: 'Oppressed, invaded, massacred but undaunted, expelled from the pastures of your fathers by vile Sicilians,' and an appreciative murmur came once more from the assembly. I had by now completely run out of big words and the remainder of my speech had to be said in vernacular — in the vilest pidgin.

'My Government want your help and they want to help you. Because of this wish, I am here with you and I am going to stay with you. I command the Allied forces in the Jebel. I want your sheikhs, I want all of you to tell me what you need and if it is possible, it will be provided. I want you to know that you can come to me when you are in trouble. I want you all to help such of my people as I will bring here — to guide and to shelter them. Above all I want you to bring to me all the information you can get about the enemy. I want you to be the eyes and the ears of the British Army.'

Rather exhausted and very pleased with my eloquence I was going to sit down when I caught an anxious look from 'Ali bu Hamed, and I remembered that the essential had not yet been said. So I started once more:

'We are strong and confident of success but God alone knows the hour of victory. In the meanwhile we need every man who can fire a rifle and you also will be called upon. You are all warriors — many of you have considerably more experience of war than I have — so it is not for me to remind you that in war you must strike at the right moment. If you strike at the wrong moment, neither you nor your brothers survive to regret the mistake — and the enemy rejoices. What I don't tell you, you can guess; what I will tell you now, is that today is not the right moment for you to strike. I also tell you that the moment will come, and I shall be there to give you your orders and provide you with weapons to fight your enemy.'

I stopped and stood, as if uncertain and debating with myself the advisability of saying more. Then, tossing my head, and addressing 'Abdel Qader bu Bridan, in a lowered voice:

'I shall tell you something that will make you understand why I want you to wait. We are preparing a surprise for the enemy, a surprise that is coming from over the sea and out of the sky. Over the sea — out of the sky. Do you understand?'

'Abdel Qader stared out of rather protuberant eyes and said uncertainly: 'I understand.' I turned to 'Ali bu Hamed who said softly and clearly: 'I understand perfectly, Excellency the Major: birds, eagles.'

I turned to Sa'ad 'Ali as if to ask him also if he understood but what I said in a very low voice was: 'The old man opposite, with the grey beard and the camel stick — is he important?' — 'Yes, Major,' said Sa'ad 'Ali quite loud, 'I know what you mean,' and he whispered the name 'Tayeb bu Jibrin.'

I walked across to the old sheikh: 'Do *you* understand Tayeb?' He nodded gravely. I went round the circle of my listeners saying: 'You have understood, 'Abdel Jelil bu Tayeb? And you, Metwallah? And you, 'Abdel Aziz? And you? And you?' The chorus came all round: 'We understand.'

Back in my place I resumed:

'When the surprise is ready, your hour will be very near. You have heard Sheikh 'Ali bu Hamed. Eagles, he said. Our eagles will want nests to lay their eggs in. You, all of you, are going to find nests for our eagles' eggs. That is going to be your work now. And the nests will be surprised!'

A subdued decorous chuckle came from the ranks.

'With you be the peace and the mercy of God and his blessings,' I said suddenly and sat down.

Sheikh 'Abdel Qader bu Bridan now started talking. The ceremonial opening to his oration was altogether beyond me: I only caught a word now and then in the sonorous flow of his eloquence. Illiterate as befitted a gentleman of his generation, he was an artist in words and expressed himself in classical Arabic. The seventh-century dialect of the Qoreish, which the Prophet's immediate successors used in the compilation of the Qoran, is used all over the Arabic-speaking world from Oman to Morocco for ceremonial speeches and also — in theory — for all written literature, even newspapers. It differs from the various vernaculars as much as classical Latin from French, Spanish or Italian, and I had little knowledge of it. I waited to hear my name mentioned and acknowledged the unintelligible compliment with polite bows, then I let my mind wander, relying on Sa'ad 'Ali to recall me when necessary. I looked at the crowd around me: nearly every petty sheikh from Tobruq in the east to Lamluda in the west and as far south as Mekhili had left his tents and was now squatting in the Wadi Qsur listening to seditious speeches. Out of sight over the mountains, but only seven or eight miles away, German convoys followed each other over the dusty track to Martuba and the east: it seemed hardly possible that the enemy should be unaware of my games and miss an opportunity of putting an end to British subversive activities. The Italians had held the coast of Cyrenaica for over twenty-five years – since 1929 they controlled the whole of the interior; they had large settlements dotted over the fertile parts of the Jebel, in Giovanni Berta, Luigi di Savoia, Beda Littoria, Maddalena, D'Annunzio and Barce, luxury hotels in Derna and Cirene. They should know what was going on in this, virtually, their own country. Surely at any moment now, armoured cars would appear over the hills and wipe out our gathering. But nothing happened – a tribute to the loyalty and the craftiness of the Senussi Arabs and the complacency of their Italian masters.

The old sheikh had lapsed into colloquial and was saying: 'In the days of *our* war when the call came to raid the enemy you remember how it was: only those of us who had less than *three* rounds of ammunition were excused from the fight. And where did the rounds come from, and the weapons themselves? captured from the enemy. Cut off from the outer world, alone, penniless, we fought for twenty years. Now, we can have English help, a wealthy nation in the world – not three rounds a head but perhaps a hundred. Shall we sit back and watch our English friends from over the sea chase *our* enemy from *our* country? The major has asked us what he can do to help us: we want weapons and ammunition – nothing else.'

Thus 'Abdel Qader bu Bridan ended his speech in the first round of the argument. The call to arms was taken up by one speaker after another and grave murmurs of appreciation from the audience rewarded the eloquent. The day wore on. I grew restless, and when a camel boy, a mere lad of seventeen, got up in the back row and started on a fiery but halting speech, I said to 'Abdel Qader: 'Are we not wasting time?' – 'Let him have his say,' replied the old man. 'He is a freeman and entitled to speak. He is young and drivels but he will learn.'

The solemn old men of the tribe nodded approval and the youth was allowed to bring his maiden speech to a repetitive and lame conclusion.

In the early afternoon, 'Ali bu Hamed stood up with dramatic suddenness and spoke for the opposition:

'The Dursa, our brothers the Dursa, are fighting the Italians now.' The Dursa, a warlike Senussi tribe, live on a strip of land between the northern road and the sea coast from Appollonia to Tolmeta. From the rich uplands where the Italians had settled, they had been evicted, but the precipitous wooded gorges where the escarpment plunges three thousand feet down to the narrow coastal plain were theirs — strongholds and hide-outs from which they had recently been raiding Maddalena, a large Italian settlement. Little more really than the pilfering expeditions of men made desperate by starvation, their operations were cunningly described by 'Ali bu Hamed as a military campaign.

'The Dursa,' he went on, 'are hard pressed. Planes have been brought against them and Italian troops, Alpini, are being gathered now to attack them in their wadis. The Dursa must be helped — their need is greater than ours, they have first call for help. Brethren, we must ask the major to bring arms and ammunition and we shall get them over to the Dursa. I say: overlook our own straits and help the Dursa or they will be wiped out.'

The crafty fox carried the assembly. Speeches were made in support of immediate assistance to the Dursa and the risk of a premature rising of the Obeidat seemed averted. I was well pleased and in the final speech for that day I undertook to bring into the Jebel on my next trip weapons and ammunition for the Dursa. Later, I said, we would build up dumps of arms for the Obeidat. There was no immediate hurry and I would see that they were issued in time. Other forms of material help remained to be discussed: I suggested we might deal with the matter on the morrow and we adjourned for dinner.

One problem, however, suffered no delay: while the meal was being brought in I went into a private conference with 'Ali bu Hamed and arranged with him that he would send immediately messengers to the four main Dursa sheikhs to ask them to meet me six days later at Sidi Ahmet bu Rweiq.

The dinner was very happy, we were pleased with the day's work. 'Abdel Qader and 'Ali bu Hamed, the rivals, both felt they had scored off the other, the tribe was united, everyone rejoiced in the planning of great deeds and we all knew we had scored off the Italians.

After the final pacification in 1929 when half the Arab population of Cyrenaica had been massacred by General Graziani, the Italians had tried conciliation. 'Abdel Qader had been made a Knight, a Cavaliere, of some Order and was given a large jewelled star worn on a broad blue ribbon. Then, at the beginning of the war, he had been summoned before the Military Governor, General Piatti, he told us, and warned that unless Arab aid to escaping British prisoners of war ceased, his Order would be taken away from him. He removed the star and ribbon, put them in his pocket and asked: 'Am I no more a Knight?' — 'Certainly not,' said Piatti, furious. — 'But I am still 'Abdel Qader bu Bridan, am I?'

The old man roared with laughter as he told the story, hugging himself, showed me the Star and repeated: 'Am I still 'Abdel Qader bu Bridan?' He then called on 'Ali bu As to give us his poem on Graziani. This was a ballad of many stanzas, each line in a stanza ending in the same rhyme; the delivery slow and clear, impressive and very strongly stressed. The last line or two of each stanza were taken up as a chorus by 'Abdel Qader and others. The ballad told of Graziani's cruelties, of the rebel sheikhs he had contrived to be thrown alive out of a plane over their own tents, of the mass deportation of all the Jebel Arabs, their families and their cattle to Mersa Brega, of his treacheries and his bullying. It then went on in a triumphant mood to tell of his utter defeat at the hands of the English and ended scurrilously with an imagined interview between Graziani and Mussolini.

Several other poets came forward with their compositions referring to incidents in the history of the tribe, some of them going back to pre-Italian days of inter-tribal warfare and celebrating the defeat of the Barasi at Lamluda. But the bulk of the poems were about the struggle against the Italians, which had been the background of these people for two generations.

Sheikh 'Ali bu As, a grizzled old warrior with only one eye, a noted poet in the tribe, had meanwhile retired within himself and I could see him by the firelight, muttering and beating the measure with his hand. When he started to declaim, all talk stopped, for he was admired. He told of the events of these very days, of the stirring summons reaching the Arabs in their lonely pastures, of the mounted travellers converging by day and by night on to Wadi Qsur, of the English major and his outlandish speech, of the words of the great sheikhs, of the stammering camel boy, of the dinner and the feast and the reciting of poetry. He drew great laughter with a description of Piatti, insolent and fooled, writing to Mussolini that all was well in the Jebel. He concluded with a prophetic description of the final rout and massacre of the enemy and the glory of the English Army, the Amir Sayed Idris, the Arabs in general and the Obeidat in particular.

One after another my guests fell asleep. Sheikh 'Abdel Qader bu Bridan wrapped himself head and all in a black jerd and lay himself down by the fire. 'Ali bu Hamed retired to a cave and I climbed up to my eyrie by the flickering light of the dying fires.

The next morning early we went into committees to discuss practical arrangements. I knew what was expected and said I would bring tea, sugar, flour and cloth, as much as our trucks would carry above the arms and ammunition. I then took each of the sheikhs in private and asked them what gift would be most acceptable to them.

At midday I addressed once more the whole assembly. I told them that my Government had solemnly undertaken never to let their country come again under Italian rule after the victorious conclusion of the war. They took my word for it and expressed decorous gratefulness. There was another claim that they wanted me to settle: the Sicilians (the Italian settlers) must be prevented from coming back to their farms after the war. I had discussed the matter in private and had tried to avoid raising the question, but as 'Abdel Qader bu Bridan was determined to bring up the matter in public if I didn't, I said:

'As for the "Sicilians", when our armies occupy the Jebel Akhdar, those of them who have been left behind by the Italian Army will be deported to Tripoli. My Government will take over the farms and dispose of them to the best of the common interest.'

My audience was pleased enough by my assurance that the hated Sicilians would no more be seen; they would also have liked a promise that the Arabs would be allowed to pasture their flocks over the land which had been put under plough — but they didn't press me for it.

I proceeded to thank them, wish them good luck and concluded with a promise of stirring deeds.

'Abdel Qader handed me two written addresses, one for the British commander-in-chief, the other for Sayed Idris. The wording had been discussed interminably and finally put down in pencil by Sheikh 'Abdel Jelil on leaves torn out from my pocket book.

Dark, lean and mysterious, 'Ali bu Hamed slipped away in a hurry lest the Italian command grew suspicious of his long absence, but 'Abdel Qader departed at leisure for his southern pastures.

I rode away to Er Rteim with Sa'ad 'Ali and Metwallah. With much entertaining our stocks had run low, we were completely out of cigarettes and Sa'ad 'Ali's temper suffered accordingly. He became so irritable that we had to stop chaffing him and he rode in sullen silence. Towards evening we stopped at a well to water the horses, in spite of his abusive protests, for he wanted desperately to get back to our cache and his store of tobacco. So distracted was he, that when we started again he mounted from the right-hand side and found himself in the saddle facing the tail of his horse. We burst out laughing, he glowered at us and nearly lost his temper: then only he realized his predicament and joined us in mirth.

I took a strong line with the Dursa sheikhs when they turned up on the appointed day. I told them their action was ill-timed and badly conceived and could only cause embarrassment. In the future they should take care to undertake no such operations without my order. The poor creatures were rather harassed, having been through anxious times, on top of which had come a dangerous ride through the Italian settlements to meet me, and they were like children who have got out of hand, landed themselves in trouble and welcome the comforting scolding of their elders. I told them I would give them what help I could in the way of weapons, but it would take time, and advised them in the meanwhile to break off operations straight away, retire to their mountain fastnesses where the Italians had no troops to pursue them, and start negotiation with the enemy, who, I assured them, would be glad to give them good terms. I was counting (and rightly) on the Italian fear of the Germans and their desire not to appear unable to control their own Arabs. Any of their tribesmen whom the Italians might insist on having handed over, I told them to send to Abiar bu Sfaia in the south of the Obeidi country, where I would eventually arrange to have them picked up by an L.R.D.G. patrol and removed to Egypt. I also undertook to arrange with the Obeidat to give them asylum. I was glad to be able to send them back home, comforted, and I made my own way to Er Rteim, Metwallah's tents and my temporary headquarters.

During the four more days I had before catching the return L.R.D.G. patrol at Wadi Shegran I went to look for a suitable back door entry to the Jebel in the south where I could come in from the desert on my next trip and I also made arrangements for the transport and the storage of the immense amount of supplies I intended to bring in.

I was faced with a problem that was rather worrying: how was I to induce the staff in Cairo to supply me without delay with all the stuff I had promised? I decided that the fancy branch of Middle East Headquarters under whose direct command I came were too bewildered to take any notice of my requests and I resolved instead to put my faith in Eighth Army. I was quite certain that they would appreciate my policy of 'arming the Arabs so that they shouldn't fight'. My first job was to make them sweet, and to this end that very same night I sent Mohammed bul Qassem on a second trip to the wireless set in the canyon, with two memoranda: one for 'Intelligence' Eighth Army with a summary of the military information I had picked up during my trip, including some pretty good bombing targets, the other for the Western Desert Liaison Officer, with the political gossip. I hoped thus to find Army Headquarters already well disposed when I arrived in the flesh. It was a gamble because if I came back to the Jebel without being able to show the Arabs tangible proofs of my self-assumed greatness, I might as well stay at home.

On our way south we nearly ran into an adventure. To save time, and grown careless, Sa'ad 'Ali Rahuma and myself on horseback and one of Metwallah's Arabs riding a camel, had chosen to ride along the motor track leading to Mekhili, in daylight. Sa'ad 'Ali, his uniform covered by a jerd, would not have been too conspicuous if he had not had a tommy gun slung across his shoulders; I was wearing as usual a very dirty khaki drill shirt and slacks, with a pistol in a holster on my army belt, and a broad-brimmed New Zealand hat. We heard a car coming up behind us and had just time to move off the track when it came in sight with two Italian officers and a driver. They drove past slowly, looked at us, laughed — at our grotesque appearance I presume — and, unobservant fools, passed on. We avoided motorable tracks after that encounter.

I visited several dry wells and caves suitable to store my treasures if ever I brought them in, and I renewed my acquaintance with an old friend of Sa'ad 'Ali's, who had been up at the sheikhs' conference. This kindly old man called Musa had large flocks pasturing at that time north of the Baltet ez Zala'q; he promised to provide me with camels to carry my stores on my return trip.

We rode on, and, one day ahead of schedule, I scrambled down into the canyon to meet Chapman and Chevalier and get the news from the outer world.

Both these officers were very unwilling to return to Egypt the next day with the L.R.D.G. patrol as they had so far achieved nothing and felt frustrated. I invited them to stay on in the Jebel and operate with me: they accepted and I undertook to square things with Headquarters. It was arranged that during my absence they would move up with the wireless set and their two operators to the Obeidi country with Sa'ad 'Ali Rahuma and organize the road watch.

Olivey and his patrol turned up the next day punctually, having completed a task further west, and I drove off with them, on our way back to Siwa. When I entered the private world which they carried with them like a ship at sea, the character I had acquired while I lived with the Arabs dropped off, and I reverted to my usual self.

CHAPTER IV

WAYS OF LIFE

I HAD never tried to impersonate an Arab and I couldn't have done it if I had wanted to, for I am a desperately incompetent actor. Awkward in fancy dress, incapable of imitating a foreign accent, unable to assume a character, self-conscious in front of a camera, I can only be myself. Thus the ease with which I adapted myself to Arab ways was due to no histrionic gift nor was I accepted by the Senussis because they mistook me for one of their own. To them I remained always a stranger — a very friendly one — and I never tried to make them forget that I belonged neither to their race nor to their religion. Yet, as soon as I was amongst them, slipping without conscious effort into a new personality, I adopted their manners and their prejudices. I liked them and admired them so well that I had no difficulty in sharing their outlook: although I never really behaved like an Arab, in a way I thought and felt like one. I find a deep satisfaction in such a change of character, which I have experienced also with other people: Italian partisans and Russian soldiers during the war, and others again after it.

Although in our mutual understanding we forgot easily our differences, they were so great that it would seem that there should be an unscalable barrier between a Senussi Arab and an urbanized Westerner. The Senussis, through the accident of their history and the barrenness of their land, were, at the time I was living with them, a small isolated group whose mode of life had remained little changed since the Arab conquest, eleven hundred years previously; an anachronistic, self-contained community, nearly completely cut off, not only from the Western but even from the Muslim world. Their pilgrimage was seldom to Mecca but commonly to the oasis of Jaghbub where lies the tomb of Sayed Mohammed bu 'Ali el Senussi, founder of the Senussi sect and grandfather to the present spiritual leader, Sayed Idris el Senussi.

Until 1912 they had been under the sleepy suzerainty of the Turks who bothered little about their internal arrangements, but offered no encouragement to foreign visitors. Then came the Italians who, after defeating the Turks, became the nominal masters of the land. But they occupied effectively only the coastal towns: the dogged resistance of the tribes prevented them from spreading inland. During this long drawn out conflict the Arabs had little access even to their own towns and were cut off from Egypt. Thus they came to remain in a sense true Arabs, while the rest of the Muslim lands from Egypt to Morocco were being Westernized.

In the days before the Italian conquest they had grown barley and even wheat: but the arable lands in the fertile plain round the town of Barce and on the uplands near Beda Littoria had been taken away from them and Italians (mostly Sicilians) settled in their stead. When I knew them they did indeed cultivate a few acres here and there in the wadis running southwards, miserable crops of stunted barley, sown after the winter rains, but their economy was pastoral. Their flocks were of sheep and goats and a few camels, and their food mainly of milk and butter. The increase of their flocks they sold in the coastal towns Benghazi and Derna (and, before the war, in Sollum for export to Egypt), where they bought flour, tea, sugar, clothes and the few implements required for their austere households. Of industries they had none, with the exception of the weaving of the roofs of their tents, which was done by the women on very primitive looms, of yarn spun by the men from the wool of their animals. The low walls of the tents were made of sacking and not of their own weaving.

Outside the coastal towns there was not a single Arab house made of stone but they all lived in villages of tents, ten to fifty tents to a village. Their only furniture were the low wooden benches on which they slept and a few small chests, nor could they own anything more cumbersome, for all their possessions had to be loaded on camels each time they moved camp, which happened not when the grazing was exhausted but when the cisterns from which they drank and watered their animals came to be empty.

The men looked after their flocks and traded their animals, but otherwise worked not at all: not because they were lazy but because work, an occupation fit only for slaves, was despised and considered a degradation; in the activity which befitted a free tribesman, in war, they exerted themselves ceaselessly and took infinite pains. Untaught and illiterate, their lives were ruled by a rigid code of behaviour: to preserve it they were at all times prepared to lay down their lives.

Bred to despise trade, abhor violence and revere laboriousness and the activities of the mind, I could, it seemed, have no link with these ignorant warriors: yet the pure austerity of their behaviour fired me with an enthusiasm which overrode our differences. Thus it was that I shed the sophistication of my Western ways and shared joyfully the clean pattern of their simple lives.

Travelling with the L.R.D.G. our lives also followed a well-planned pattern: familiar duties left us delightful leisure. On the march, the patrol commander's truck went first, picking the route; then the navigator, then the wireless; the other trucks followed — the fitter came last: his job was to help whoever fell out with mechanical trouble. In the open desert, where there was little risk of detection, we avoided the hazards of travelling in the dark, and journeyed from sunrise to sunset, stopping for an hour or two in the middle of the day for lunch and to allow the wireless operators to get in touch with Headquarters. In single file, a quarter of a mile or so apart, was our usual formation, but we spread out considerably right and left in the areas where we thought enemy planes might be roving. When a plane was reported we stopped in our tracks to lay our wakes of cloudy dust which made us conspicuous from the air.

Before starting in the early morning we ate our breakfast of tea, porridge, bacon, biscuit and jam. Each man's water bottle was filled for the day and we drove off. Later in the day, when the patrol leader put out a coloured flag, the trucks pulled up and we went to collect our lunch of biscuit, cheese, tinned fish and pickles. Then until the signallers, having completed their job, took down their aerial, we sat on the ground in the shade of our truck and read books, for the heat of the day did not induce talk. At dusk the trucks came to rest close together and we all went with our mugs for our daily ration of rum and lime powder. On a fire of dry desert bushes dinner of bully beef stew and spices was cooked, to be followed by a slice and a half of tinned peach or apricot, and tea. Round the fire we talked and joked till, night drawing on, one after the other we went up to our truck and laid ourselves to sleep on the ground. The signallers went on hammering at their keys long after everyone else was asleep.

Five men composed the crew of a truck and five or six trucks made a patrol.

On our third day out a message came at midday from Headquarters in Siwa. Deciphered it said that a party of commandos, attached to L.R.D.G. for desert experience and training, were at that time laying a petrol dump in Wadi Mra'a, sixty miles to the rear of the German front line, eighty miles south of the coast and five hours' drive from our position. They had no wireless and, as weapons, only small arms. So far we had considered this wadi as our own preserve, but now our air force had reported enemy activity in the very area where the defenceless commandos were laying their dump. We were instructed to go and get them out. Olivey, our commander, took two trucks with him, sent the remainder of his patrol on to Siwa under the sergeant, and set a course for Wadi Mra'a. Towards sunset amongst low gravel hills I had a glimpse on the skyline of a truck moving southwards. A moment later it disappeared, but I had taken a bearing and we immediately gave cautious chase, setting a course south-west to intercept it. On the next rise we caught sight of it again, then lost it, then came again upon it, close enough to study it through our glasses. It seemed to be a British water tanker — a bowser — but it might well be used by the enemy, for, at that time, after our alternate advances and withdrawals, so many vehicles had been captured by both sides that the make of a truck was no indication of its temporary ownership. It was travelling alone, however, and the pursuit was not likely to lead us into a trap: we pressed on and finally overtook the vehicle, which did not stop until one of our trucks actually crossed its path and signalled it to rest. It carried a lonely British driver, a little dazed and tired, but smiling; having pulled up he sat behind his wheel and spoke only in reply to our questions. He told his story clearly enough, and

H

gave no sign of excitement, neither then nor later, after he had been refreshed, although he had good cause to be upset. He had been lost for three days when we came upon him, without food and with only a little water that he had drained out of the radiator of his truck. He had little more than a gallon of petrol left, and had it not been for the chance look I had given in his direction at the moment of his fleeting appearance over the horizon he and his truck would have come to a final rest a few miles further south.

A very dumb driver of a unit attached to Seventh Armoured Division, at Bir Hakim, he had been detailed to take his truck into workshops for a minor repair. The work completed he had asked the way back to his leaguer. Somebody told him to follow the direction in which pointed a truck standing in its tracks, for six miles, and he would find himself at home. He then went into a tent to get his papers signed: when he came out somebody, he said, must have turned the indicator truck round, for he had travelled not six but over eighty miles and never found his unit. Up and down he had driven, following one after another of the tracks with which the desert was criss-crossed; he had come across a signpost pointing to Jaghbub (where the Fourth Indian Division was), but he hadn't liked the look of it — it seemed German he thought — and had driven off in the opposite direction. I asked him why, having realized he was lost, he had not driven due east which would have brought him back inevitably to our lines, but all he could say in reply was a puzzled query: 'What is east?' I tried to explain about the sun rising and setting, but he dismissed these technicalities with a patient smile, as being altogether beyond him. He said: 'I knew that following the tracks I would get somewhere — I was bound to meet someone.' A very brave man and quite unperturbed, he could not be made to realize how near he had been to a senseless death. We marvelled at the army employing men so utterly ignorant.

At dusk we made our way down into Wadi Mra'a, a deep crack that threads its serpentine way for many miles through the surrounding desert, and found the commando camp in some bushes under the high, steep western bank. The commandos were put to reload the petrol tins they had already dumped and it was decided to move out the next morning at first light. During the night we heard, in the still desert air, a clatter of trucks moving on the other side of the hill and we caught the reflection of headlights in the sky. The R.A.F. had been right in their report and it appeared that the Germans, like ourselves, thought the Wadi Mra'a a good hiding place for a dump.

The uncouth commando drivers, all brawn and empty heads, were instructed how to keep formation, and we left for home a little before sunrise, Olivey leading with his two trucks, the eight unarmed commando three-tonners following, and myself in the recovered water waggon (to which I had transferred for comfort) bringing up the rear. We had gone about a mile and were still on the flat, sandy wadi bottom when over the western ridge appeared one German eight-wheeled armoured car and, a moment later, another.

These formidable vehicles had every advantage over our convoy: speed, agility (the monsters could drive indifferently forward or in reverse), a defensive armour which our heaviest gun could not penetrate and any of the shells they could send over, landing near our petrol-laden lorries, would send them up in flames. We were helpless and trapped.

At that moment the sun came over the eastern horizon and shining in the German's eyes made them stop on the ridge while they tried to make out what we were. I saw a man come out of one of the armoured cars and stare with his glasses in our direction. Olivey made a quick decision: he ordered his trucks to about turn, spread out in arrow-head formation and follow him towards the enemy. Off we went, bumping along as fast as we could and eleven golden plumes of dust rose behind us up into the morning sky and over the rising sun. We might have been anything – possibly tanks. I watched the foot of the ridge come nearer, wondering if the Germans would wait till we reached it. If they did our bluff would be called and further deception impossible. I watched, and suddenly there was only one eight-wheeler on the skyline – a moment later the other monster backed out of sight and we had won the day. The German armoured cars must have rushed back to their convoy and got it under way, for we never saw them again – and visiting the place a few weeks later an L.R.D.G. patrol found the remains of a German petrol dump, hastily abandoned.

Olivey wheeled right and had some trouble in checking the enthusiastic commandos who would have topped the rise. We made a peaceful passage back to Siwa, and three days later I sat in Lieutenant-Colonel Prendergast's office on the top of a hill, while he rang up Eighth Army Headquarters to arrange my visit to them. Prendergast had been a member of Bagnold's early expeditions in the desert before the war and he had now succeeded him in command of L.R.D.G. I overheard him mentioning on the phone somebody called Popski and when he had done he turned to me, and, somewhat embarrassed, he said, 'As you heard we call you Popski. Nobody can understand Peniakoff on the phone. Do you mind?' I assured him I was delighted with my nickname and remembered that my namesake was the comical hairy little bolshy in — was it the *Daily Mirror?* — comic strip. Whether I liked it or not, Popski I had become and Popski I have remained to this day.

Army Headquarters at Qambut, east of Tobruq, was a number of heavily camouflaged tents and caravans widely dispersed in a dusty plain. Nobody knew where anybody was, and having left my car at the military police tent I wandered around till I hit the 'Operations' caravan.

With my head full of my own schemes I hadn't lately had much time to consider the general situation: it was a shock to realize that no one at Army Headquarters had confidence in our ability to resist a German attack. The prevailing view was that when Rommel chose to advance there was nothing to stop him reaching Egypt. In a sense the morale of our forces was low: there was little confidence in our own strength and no faith whatever in our High Command. And yet everyone was cheerful. Eighth Army staff in particular, already at that early period and before Montgomery's reforms, were shining models of friendliness and helpfulness. They trusted me and assumed that my requests were reasonable and justified. Much to my relief (for I had been anxious about their response to my demands), they granted everything I asked for and took steps to provide me with the odd assortment of supplies I wanted to take back with me to the Jebel.

I was pressed to return urgently to the theatre of my operations and to prepare myself to spread 'alarm and despondency' (an expression that was just then coming into fashion) as soon as I would be given the sign. Destruction of petrol had the highest priority, which suited me well enough. For my political schemes with the Arabs I received a free hand, and I was given a tactfully non-committal written reply to the sheikhs' address. I had a session with 'Intelligence', told them what I had found out, then I was asked questions that the German quartermaster general alone could have answered. However, I undertook to do my best and left Headquarters with the pleasant delusion that the fate of Eighth Army was in my keeping.

I drove back to Siwa the same night, non-stop, and ransacked the suq for my warlike stores. What couldn't be purchased locally was flown to me from Cairo. Some items on my bill of lading were as follows:

Calico, white	yards	1600
,, red	yards	900
Pots, tea	dozen	6
Nails, horseshoe	lb.	20
Sweets, boiled	cwt.	1
Leather, shoe	sq. feet	200
Scarves, head	dozen	2
Girdles, embroidered	pieces	12
,, gold thread	pieces	4
Slippers, coloured	pairs	12
Thread, cotton reels	gross	12
Caps, skull (with tassel)	dozen	2
Chocolate	lb.	40
Bloomers, red (ladies')	pairs	6

Apart from a month's army rations for my party of twelve, the L.R.D.G. quartermaster supplied me with (amongst other items):

Tea	lb.	600
Sugar	cwt.	6
Flour	cwt.	24
Cigarettes, tins	dozen	50

Strangely the British Army in the Middle East was unable to provide me with a saddle and I finally purchased a looted Italian one in the Jebel from an Arab.

L.R.D.G. supplied me also with the weapons which I meant to show to the Arabs as a token of our intention to make them fight when the the time came. (That in my opinion the time would *never* come was no business of theirs and only Sheikh 'Ali bu Hamed knew the secret of my duplicity.) These arms came from a store of obsolete weapons discarded by the L.R.D.G.: Boyes anti-tank rifles, two-inch mortars, captured heavy Italian machine guns and others: an impresssive array well suited to my purpose. I also got a .45 Colt automatic for Sheikh 'Abdel Qader bu Bridan, and a small pocket pistol inlaid with mother of pearl for Sheikh 'Ali bu Hamed.

My own weapons, ammunition and explosives made up the load. I took twelve Arab privates with me from the twenty-two I had left behind at Jaghbub — the remainder I transferred to Siwa with their British sergeant, to be looked after by the L.R.D.G., till such time as I might require their services. I also took with me a new British recruit, a very young subaltern whom I had known as a schoolboy in Cairo. A nice red-headed lad, eager, level-headed beyond his age, he had just completed his course at the Officers Cadet Training Unit; he had taken a special course in explosives, he could talk Arabic, and he had not been spoiled by service with a base unit. I hoped to train him in my ways and get some help from him. His name was Shorten.

CHAPTER V

SPREAD OF ALARM

THE patrol that took us out was commanded by David Lloyd Owen, then a captain. In 1944 he came to command the L.R.D.G.

The rendezvous with Musa had been fixed Arab fashion, rather vaguely, 'North of the Baltet ez Zala'q'. A balat (or baltet) is a shallow lake in the plains south of the mountains; it fills up with muddy rainwater, pouring down the wadis during the winter, then dries up: by August it is a dry mud pan with a hard surface perfectly level and without a ripple, over which our trucks could race in any direction. In May, as we were then, the Baltet ez Zala'q, twenty-fives miles south of the foothills, was still a sheet of water roughly fives miles square and a few feet deep. The Arabs bring their flocks south from the mountains at this season, water them from the lakes and let them crop the desert bushes, a more wholesome food, they say, than the more abundant mountain vegetation.

With cumbrous stores weighing nearly seven tons I was anxious to reach my rendezvous early in the day; thus I hoped to have time to inquire of Musa's whereabouts and reach his tents before dark. It turned out differently. We reached the southern shores of the balat in the early morning: the rippling water was tempting. We all bathed, then had a late breakfast. We lingered so long that, when we were ready to move on, the time was nearly on for the midday wireless transmission, and we delayed our departure to allow the signallers to exchange messages with Headquarters in Siwa. Rounding the lake on the western shore we came across recent car tracks and a camp site. Our Arabs got to work, tested the moisture of the remains of food attached to opened tins, found the sand under the dead embers of the camp fire still lukewarm, analysed footprints and car tracks, and after a leisurely whispered consultation, decided unanimously that an

Italian patrol of five light trucks carrying not less than twenty-one men had stopped for a meal in this spot about noon on the previous day, and had driven off in the direction of Mekhili. The knowledge that the enemy was patrolling this remote and usually deserted area increased my determination not to be dumped before I had reached a spot where I could get transport; it had the opposite effect on Lloyd Owen who wanted to get rid of me and my heavy junk as early as possible and be free to regain, undetected by the enemy, the open desert further south where he had to relieve another L.R.D.G. patrol. Their work at that time was to lie off the Triq el 'Abd, and watch enemy traffic using the short cut from Benghazi to the east.

The going along the lake shore was in soft sand and very slow. We tried the high slopes on our left and found them covered in sharp-edged boulders which slowed us down even more and ripped open two tyres. Furthermore they were barren and uninhabited. Most of the afternoon had gone before we came across our first Arab and he had no knowledge of Musa, who didn't belong to his tribe. We made once more for the low ground near the lake in the hope of meeting someone who could help me. We got bogged — tempers grew short — I had to use charm to avoid being dumped amongst the migrating water fowl who seemed to be the only inhabitants of the lake shore. We pushed on, however, and just before sunset I caught up with an Obeidi Arab who undertook to guide us to Musa's tent. Unfortunately my guide believed that where a man could walk, an overloaded truck could follow: in the growing darkness we found ourselves engaged in a confusion of large boulders over which our lorries lurched and rolled. Then one of the trucks blew a tyre and Lloyd Owen's patience snapped. He came over to me with an awful scowl on his usually humorous countenance and declared his conviction that my guide had no idea where he was leading us to. I had to agree with him and I gave up the struggle. Orders were given to unload and ten minutes later the retreating trucks rolled out of sight in the dusk. Cases of tea and rolls of calico lay in confusion amongst a wilderness of rocks. My only link with my friends in the Jebel was a very old and very shaken Arab with a grey pointed beard, who seemed completely lost and bewildered.

In fact he was only sick as a result of the first motor ride in his life.

My twelve Arabs were undismayed. They might feel lost in a town but never in the desert. We drank tea and cooked a meal; then two of my men set out with the guide to fetch Musa. Shorten was enjoying his first taste of adventure: he would, I am sure, have been disappointed if everything had gone without a hitch. I felt, as I often do, unhappy in the dark — a remnant of childish terrors — but I comforted myself with the thought that no Italian trucks could possibly reach us over the rough ground we had just covered with the L.R.D.G.

At ten minutes past three that morning I was awakened to greet Musa, who had just been brought in. Tea was made and we exchanged gossip. After my departure from the Jebel, ten days ago, he had been visited by Sa'ad 'Ali Rahuma and they had picked on a natural cave in a small wadi running into Wadi Gherna, forty miles away, as the best hiding place for our stores. Sa'ad 'Ali had then left him to visit sheikhs round Barce further west, Chapman and Chevalier and the wireless operators were established in a wadi at Er Rteim, in the neighbourhood of Metwallah's tents.

Musa said he had camels ready to carry our loads but when, at dawn, he saw the amount of junk we had brought he was troubled and he feared he would not be able to lift everything in one journey. He then walked back to his tents and returned later with twenty-eight camels of various ages and sizes, having collected every animal capable of carrying a load. Two of the camels had riding saddles for myself and Shorten, three or four had pack saddles — the remainder were bare and the loads had to be tied on to their backs with ropes. A host of youths and children had driven the camels in with shrill cries; in great apparent confusion we started loading up. The first stage was to ferry everything across to Musa's tents. When this was done I sorted out what I would take with me and two of my men were left behind to look after the flour, tea and sugar which I had to leave in Musa's keeping. At five o'clock that afternoon we set out on a forty mile trip to Wadi Gherna with twenty-six camels (two of the original lot had proved unmanageable) and twenty-one men. The waning moon rose about midnight and lit our ghostly plodding. Camels and Arabs, vociferous at the loading, are dead silent on the march and though the untrained animals gave trouble and the brittle, home-made ropes that held up the loads kept breaking, not a sound was heard. Senussi Arabs don't get flustered when they are in their natural surroundings; bolting camels were recaptured quickly and efficiently, shedded loads tied up again, and not a word uttered louder than a whisper. At dawn we were in the foothills, winding up the rocky Wadi Gherna. At nine o'clock, hidden in boulders and trees, an opening showed in the cliff that towered on the right bank. In we went, in single file, up a steep and deep tributary of the main wadi. The unwieldy beasts climbed with unexpected agility over the tumbled rocks. At ten our guide called a halt, the first since we had left the day before, the camels were unloaded, hobbled and left to graze, and while tea was being boiled everyone joined in carrying the stores into a deep natural cave high up the side of the ravine.

At that moment a three-engined German plane came over the mountain top and flew exactly overhead, so slowly, it seemed to me, that I thought it had stopped in mid-air to look at us. We all froze in our tracks till it finally dragged away, then we sprang to camouflage the more conspicuous weapons with branches. The plane came over a second time a few minutes later, even lower and slower than at first. It must have decided that we were just another lot of Arabs because nothing more happened. We kept stores in that cave for over a month without ever being bothered.

When all our gear had been stowed away in the darkness of the cave I had a meal and slept for an hour. I then left Shorten in charge of the party (with instructions to do nothing without the advice of my Arab sergeant), sent Musa's camels back home and rode away towards Er Rteim. Walking alongside my camel was my guide, an elderly, white-bearded Arab. He had a concave profile, like the man in the moon in my book of nursery rhymes, and was quite witless.

My mount was tired and hungry and kept lowering its long neck to snatch at tufts of scrub as we went, pulling the rough camel-hair head-rope painfully through my fingers. We had to climb over two thousand feet on rough ground — our pace became progressively slower: we took twelve hours to cover twenty-five miles: when we arrived at Metwallah's tent the sun had risen a long time ago.

I had slept for seven hours only out of the last eighty and had been twenty-nine hours in the saddle. I was pleasantly weary but by no means exhausted. With Metwallah was Sa'ad 'Ali, who had just arrived back from his visits of prestige to the sheikhs in the west. While we ate they gave me the gossip of the Jebel and we then rode down to my new headquarters in a discreet and well-wooded wadi, about an hour's ride away.

I found the two wireless operators in good spirits, though their life was hard: they spoke no Arabic and knew nothing of what was going on around them; at a later date they got to be irritated by one another to the point that, to avoid quarrelling, they had to put up their quarters under separate trees a quarter of a mile apart. Chapman and Chevalier were away establishing the road watch on the Martuba by-pass: they turned up the next morning.

On that day, the fourth since my return to the Jebel, we got ourselves organized. I left Chapman, with Chevalier to help him, in charge of the road watch, the wireless station and the intelligence service generally. One of them would always be present at our headquarters to interrogate the Arab informants as they came in, check on their information, and make out the messages to Army. In this matter we set ourselves a high standard of accuracy and we refused to give in to the temptation of transmitting information which we couldn't vouch for. Even so, we soon found we had to compromise and we graded our reports as follow:

Plain, unqualified, statements were about facts we vouched for personally.

'*Confirmed report*' meant that several independent informants had brought in first-hand information that tallied.

'*Reliable report*' referred to information brought in by one only of our trusted and proved Arab informants. It had to be first-hand and we submitted the man to a long and searching interrogation to find out what exactly he had seen or heard.

Rumours, even widespread rumours, we absolutely refused to mention in our messages, though of course we had to take them into account for future investigations, for they were generally founded on fact — often a very small fact. I missed thus what might have been the greatest scoop of all: the presence of Mussolini himself, incognito in the Jebel, as I shall relate in due course.

We soon had a number of regular informants working full time for us: we trained them in our ways and sent them out on special investigations. The curse of our trade was the amateur sleuth who brought in elaborate and detailed information of which not a word was true. We got caught in that way on an occasion when we had left young Shorten in charge of Headquarters for twenty-four hours. I found him beaming the next morning when he handed me the message file:

'GERMAN TANKS,' it read, 'FIFTY-TWO MARK III, FORTY-SEVEN MARK II STOP LORRIES SIXTY-THREE STOP MOTOR-CYCLES TWO STOP LEAGUERED JUNE IST NORTH OF SLONTA ROAD STOP MAP REFERENCE BENGHAZI O.532 376 STOP STAYING SEVERAL DAYS STOP BOMBING TARGET A I STOP INFORM R.A.F.' This fairy tale had been brought in the night before by a notorious busybody, a very plausible liar by whom poor Shorten had been taken in. I signalled:

'MY MESSAGE SEVEN OF TWO REFER STOP TAKE NO ACTION STOP INFORMATION INACCURATE TRANSMITTED BY MISTAKE STOP PLEASE APOLOGIZE R.A.F. STOP WHAT ARE THEY DOING ANYWAY?' The last words referred to the fact that none of the bombing targets I had given so far had received attention. The fact was that our very small air force was hard pressed at that time bombing Benghazi and Tripoli daily, trying to stop the flow of supplies coming at these ports and thus delay the impending German offensive: it had no machines available for casual targets.

I told Shorten unkindly that he was a gullible fool and disconcerted him by refusing to check up on his sensational scoop. 'There might be twenty tanks,' he said. 'Perhaps no more than ten — but even then . . .' But *I* thought there were none at all.

I had now a small dump down at Musa's tents north of Baltet ez Zala'q sixty-five miles away — another in the cave of Wadi Gherna twenty miles away — another at Headquarters. I wanted to keep some food and ammunition at the two first places as a reserve in case of disaster, with men to guard them, but the bulk of the supplies were to come up to Headquarters at Er Rteim with the main party of men. The weapons would be displayed there for the fiery Obeidi sheikhs to see, and to judge me a man of my word. Some of the arms, however, would have to be carried over to the Dursa, who, to be sure, had followed my instructions and made a truce with the Italians, but were still in a state of smouldering rebellion.

I made Sa'ad 'Ali my quartermaster and put him in charge of these complicated movements. He also had the job of delivering the gifts I had brought for my friends.

The next problem was of remounts. Of the three horses I had purchased originally, one was still away with Hamed, one had been ridden to death by Sa'ad 'Ali, leaving us with only one poor creature. I bought eight camels and four horses, which would make us in a sense self-supporting in the way of transport. In an emergency I could now move my little force and its essential supplies without calling for help. For my own use I got myself a white mare with the brand of the Italian Army. Christened Birdybird, she was no flyer but did me good service till the end of my stay in the Jebel. She had brittle hooves and kept on casting shoes but she was reasonably fast and had much more stamina than most horses in the Jebel. The problem of finding enough barley to keep the horses in good trim was a permanent worry and I often thought I had better discard horses altogether and rely only on camels: they were slow but they fed themselves. All these purchases were paid for in what was then the normal currency in the Jebel: tea.

I had now completed my domestic arrangements: I next turned my mind to finding the means of spreading 'alarm and despondency' as had been suggested by Eighth Army. I couldn't help feeling that the size of my force was too small to be able to cause any serious material damage to the enemy war machine and I treated the matter somewhat as a joke. However, it would be fun to have a crack at the enemy and to let off loud bangs in earnest. It would also help us to overcome the boredom resulting from the monotonous routine of intelligence work. Both Chevalier and Shorten had asked to be allowed to take a hand in any fun that may be going — more serious-minded, Chapman turned down our boyish enthusiasms and declared his intention of carrying on with the work while we played our pranks.

Already on the first day of my arrival I had sent word to all my Arab helpers asking them to find me large (if possible unguarded) petrol dumps, and the same instructions were given to every informant as he came in to my camp with his piece of news. I dispatched such of my own men as I could spare to various parts of the Jebel on a similar quest. To prevent heart-searchings, which the prospect of reprisals might cause, I let everybody believe that the petrol dumps when found, would be bombed from the air. As soon as I could free myself of administrative duties I went and called on 'Abdel Jelil bu Tayeb, my spiritual adviser, and impressed on him the urgency of my quest. He thought he knew a man who would be able to help me and promised to send him along as soon as he could be found.

Two days later, at my headquarters, a short, lean, rather ragged Arab was brought up to me. He dispensed with any but the barest civilities and in a low and singularly deliberate voice he said that his name was Mohammed el Obeidi, that he had been sent by Sheikh 'Abdel Jelil bu Tayeb, that he knew of an Italian petrol dump in the neighbour-hood of a place called El Qubba (or as the Italians call it: Giovanni Berta), that his tent was not far from the dump and he knew the area well. Having said that much he stood silent, waiting.

His countenance was pensive, he seemed to be following an intricate pattern of inner thought. A grave, sombre man, of few words, when he was pleased, which was seldom, no more than a ghost of a smile lighted his features. An old soldier, he had spent a lifetime fighting the Italians, he knew equally the virtues of long patience and of swift action. I liked him from the first moment.

126

The interrogation followed its course:

'You know the dump?'

'Yes.'

'You have seen it yourself?'

'I have been in it.'

'How do you know it is petrol?'

'I have seen the black drums.'

'How many drums are there?'

'I don't know.'

'Are there a thousand?'

He made a mental calculation: 'More.'

'Are there two thousand?'

'I don't know.'

'When was the dump made?'

'In winter, soon after the Italians came back after the British troops left.'

'Has it been used since?'

'No.'

'Where is the dump?'

'Near the houses of El Qubba to the east. South of the road.'

'How far from the houses?'

'I don't know. Near.'

'Can you see the houses from the dump?'

'You can see the fort.'

'Is there a guard?'

'No. There is a wire fence on posts.'

'Are there any troops in the neighbourhood?'

'There is the camp of tents north of the road. In the village there are the workshops where the Italians repair the trucks, and the stores where they issue the rations. At night the trucks that travel on the road go into the car park.' (El Qubba at that time was a staging post on the main German line of communication.)

'Can the dump be seen from the air?'

'I don't know.'

'Are the petrol drums covered?'

'No. But there are trees and the whole place is overgrown with thistles.'

'Can you take me to the dump?'

'I can take you inside the wire at night. There is no difficulty.'

'Even if I am in uniform?'

'Even in uniform.'

I liked Mohammed el Obeidi more and more. His information was accurate and to the point. I was sure he was not romancing. And if there were really more than a thousand forty-gallon drums of petrol in that dump and I succeeded in blowing it up at the right moment, there might be a small amount of 'alarm and despondency' in the enemy camp after all.

I told Chapman that I would be leaving for El Qubba the next afternoon, taking Chevalier with me, and one of my Arabs, and asked him to get a demolition party of three Arabs under Shorten to stand by till I sent instructions. Shorten was down at the dump in the Wadi Gherna but due back two days later.

That night a message came on the wireless for me. It said: 'SPREAD ALARM AND DESPONDENCY.' So the time had come, I thought, Eighth Army was taking the offensive. The date was, I think, May 18th, 1942. On the 19th in the late afternoon, with Chevalier, Mohammed el Obeidi and one of my Arabs, I rode off from Er Rteim. The trip was timed to take us across the Martuba by-pass about two in the morning and to reach Sidi bu Halfaya before daylight. When we got there Mohammed el Obeidi took us to a huge, dry Roman water cistern hewn out of the rock on the top of a spur. The horses were put to graze and we made ourselves comfortable and drank tea in the three-roomed cistern which was to be our home for the next week.

At dawn I made my way cautiously to the western edge of the spur. A few yards from the opening of our cistern a vertical cliff fell three hundred feet to the wadi below. On my left, half a mile away on the opposite side of the wadi, I could see an Italian ammunition dump with trucks loading and, further to the left, a stretch of the Martuba by-pass on which the daily convoys were beginning to raise dust. To the right a wide panorama opened with, on the skyline six miles away,

the ambitious Italian monument that stands up on the hills beyond El
Qubba. We took turns during the day, Chevalier and I, alternately to
sleep and to watch through our glasses the Italian ammunition dump.

This dump might provide a useful alternative target, if the petrol
dump at El Qubba could not, for some reason, be attempted, and I
asked Chevalier to reconnoitre it at close quarters in the dark hours of
the next night, taking with him our Libyan soldier, while I went to El
Qubba with Mohammed el Obeidi.

I started immediately after dark — too early really — for we were
much vexed with the barking of dogs and were compelled to make
repeated detours to avoid Arab tents where the inhabitants were not
yet asleep. I didn't care to be seen by anybody so close to an important
enemy centre. Yet it could hardly be avoided and when a rider appeared coming directly towards us we had to stop and greet him, for
any other course would have made us suspect. While Mohammed el
Obeidi, quite changed from his ordinary taciturn demeanour, engaged
the rider (an Arab returning to his tents after a day spent at El Qubba) in
voluble talk, I grunted a few non-committal noises and drifted along
out of sight in the dark. I heard Mohammed el Obeidi explain away my
churlish behaviour by saying that I was a rich merchant from Jalo
Oasis travelling to Derna and very cross and hungry because Mohammed,
my guide, had blundered and lost his way. I thought the story would
not have taken in a mouse but the other man tactfully accepted it and
commiserated with Mohammed el Obeidi on the troubles of a guide.
He offered to take us both to his tent and give us a meal but my guide
managed to disentangle himself politely and rejoined me, chuckling
grimly. It must be realized that not I but *Mohammed el Obeidi* was the
man who risked his life in this adventure: if the worst happened I would
become an honourable prisoner-of-war, but my friend had a good
chance of ending his life strung up by an iron hook through the jaw.
For such was the kindly Italian method of dealing with disaffected Arabs.

A little later we alighted at the tent of Mohammed el Obeidi's brother,
where we left our horses and ten minutes' walk took us to the dump.

Enclosed with a rustic three-wire fence it covered about ten acres of
scrubby ground, dotted with trees and overgrown with tall dry thistles.

I 129

The petrol was laid in lots of twenty-five to thirty drums lying close together on the ground. The lots were irregularly dispersed in the undergrowth but were not too difficult to discern, even on this moonless night. For two hours I walked up and down within the wire, counting the lots and making mental notes of landmarks. I found ninety-six lots: at an average of twenty-seven drums to the lot that dump held over one hundred thousand gallons of petrol. It seemed good — I wondered what snag there might be; with one or two exceptions all the drums I had lifted were heavy and apparently full. With a tool I had brought with me I unscrewed a few stoppers and verified that the contents were indeed petrol. Mohammed el Obeidi had served me well.

On one side the dump abutted on to a track leading to the main road, about five hundred yards away. Crossing the wire on my way out I saw a glow coming from the lights of El Qubba, but the little town itself was hidden by a low rise.

We arrived back in the cistern at Sidi bu Halfaya before daylight. Chevalier and his Libyan soldier were in: they had been unable to find the ammunition dump in the dark, and had returned having achieved nothing. I was annoyed because it was an easy task — the distance was no more than half a mile. Chevalier couldn't be blamed as he had no experience, but the Libyan, I knew, could have had no difficulty in reaching the dump and reconnoitring the approaches. He had had the whole day to map out a route of which every yard was visible from the top of our cliff. I said nothing but marked down our soldier as being a fool and faint of heart and resolved never to employ him any more on a job of this kind. His failure didn't matter much to me anyhow because, having decided to attempt the destruction of the petrol dump at El Qubba, I concentrated exclusively on this project.

I wrote a message to Chapman asking him to send up the demolition party with the explosives and gadgets required. I told him the size and the layout of the petrol dump and the manner in which I intended laying the charges. He would then have no difficulty in sending up the right stuff. We understood one another perfectly in these matters.

I had to wait till dark before dispatching the Libyan soldier with the messsage. I then told him that, in spite of the fact that he had been unable to find the ammunition dump half a mile away, I knew he was quite capable of riding in the dark sixteen miles to Er Rteim. If he got there safely before dawn, delivered the message and guided back to us the men that Chapman would eventually entrust to his care, no more would be said about the matter of his unsuccessful reconnaissance. He gathered my meaning, nodded (with relief I thought) and went off. I hoped I had made the best possible use of a very imperfect instrument.

From that moment till the arrival of the demolition party there was absolutely nothing for me to do and I fell into a delightful inactivity. I slept sixteen hours a day, ate and the remainder of the time I lay in the sun and watched the kite hawks wheel in the sky. Chevalier fretted and was bored and wanted to play paper games. I knew he was worrying, for he was cursed with a premonitory imagination; my duty was to soothe him and take his mind off the coming ordeal, but I couldn't do it, I was too lazy. I was out of the world of strife and wouldn't be recalled. If I failed him then I hope he has forgiven me.

On the second day of waiting Mohammed el Obeidi brought me back to our schemes. He came to me where I lay on a rock and asked permission to speak.

'When you asked to be taken to see the petrol,' he said, 'I thought you had in mind, after making sure of the target, to send on your radio a message to your airplanes, and they would come to bomb the dump. I realize now that such is not the case. You have seen the dump, you have sent a letter with that simpleton to your friend the tall major, but yet you are still waiting here. I assume then that you intend blowing up the dump yourself and that you are waiting for your men to come up and help you to do it. I must tell you, Major, that I don't like it, because, if it is done in that way, the Italians will think that the *Arabs* set fire to the petrol and there will be reprisals. My family, my friends, all have their tents around El Qubba. They may have to pay the penalty: some of them will be hanged, the others will be deported — their cattle will be taken from them, and they will starve. They are my people, Major: I don't like it.' He said these words in his deliberate way and paused as if listening to an inner voice. I knew only too well that the success of my scheme was in his hands. If his intention was to betray me and I couldn't talk him out of it, it seemed I would have to kill him. I had a pistol down in the cistern, but I liked the man. In a few minutes I would have to make up my mind.

Mohammed resumed:

'Why don't you trust me, Major? Why don't you open your mind to me? Tell me your plan. You are in command, you know best. If the airplanes can't do the destruction *you* know why and *you* know what has to be done. This is war and not the time to think of families. If you know that the petrol has to be burnt and that it can't be done in any other way than by walking in and setting it on fire — so be it. I don't like it but I am a soldier, Major. What has to be, has to be. You must tell me your plan; I can help you.' He waited. I had to decide at once one way or the other, there was no middle course. I believed he was sincere. If he turned out to be a liar, I would be proved unable to judge men, unfit to command, unsuited for the tasks I had chosen for myself, bound anyhow to fail sooner or later. I was on test, not he. I made up my mind and I told him what arrangements I had made.

'When will your men arrive?' he asked.

'Late tomorrow night or the night after.'

'Mounted?'

'Yes.'

'How many will you be altogether?'

'Eleven.'

'How many men on the job?'

'Nine.'

'After you have been in the dump and laid your gadgets, how long will it be before the fire starts?'

'Three hours.'

He nodded, wrapped his jerd round him and walked away towards El Qubba. I had twenty-four hours — till his return the next evening — to wonder if I had been a fool.

He came up briskly, sat down and spoke as follows:

'There is hurry. Soldiers have begun yesterday to load petrol from the dump. I hope your men arrive tonight. When they arrive they will be tired: they will rest here in the cistern till the next evening. Then, starting at ten, the nine of you and myself, we shall walk, carrying the explosives, to a dry cistern near my brother's tent at El Qubba, where we shall arrive before light. In the cistern there will be food and water. No one, under any excuse, will leave it during daylight—not even to relieve nature. On the slope outside there will be a little boy with his sheep and goats. If he sees anything alarming, such as armed soldiers making for the cistern, he will whistle in this way to warn you.

'At sunset more food will be brought. At eight-thirty you will be ready to go over to the dump, carrying only what is indispensable: explosives, one weapon I should say for every three men, and a few rounds of ammunition. The remainder of your kit will remain in the cistern. I will take you to the dump where you will arrive at nine. I will leave you there and you will do what you have to do. Not later than ten forty-five you will make your own way back to the cistern, where I shall be waiting for you. You will collect your kit and we shall walk away to Kaf el Kefra.

'In the meantime your two surplus men will drive the mounts, carrying your rations and any kit left behind, to Kaf el Kefra where we shall find them when we arrive. There is water in a pool under some rocks and we can rest at the Kaf until the evening. We shall then ride back in the dark to Er Rteim.'

I said: 'It is good. We shall do as you say. I am grateful to you.' Mohammed el Obeidi grunted and went down into the cistern to boil himself some tea. He was my master in the art of war, and since that day every plan I have made has had his perfect 'operation order' as a model.

I couldn't find Kaf el Kefra on my map and the landmarks leading to it mentioned by Mohammed el Obeidi were all unknown to me: I had to be contented with the knowledge that it was 'not far to the west of El Qubba and south of the main road'.

I wanted to leave the enemy with the impression that the petrol dump had been raided by a motorized party and not by local Arabs.

I remembered being told that after the unfortunate raid on Rommel's headquarters the parties waiting on the coast to be picked up by submarine had been lost because someone had carelessly dropped a map marked with the rendezvous. I wanted to do deliberately what had then been the result of an incredible folly, and I spent the next hours in marking a small-scale map with an imagined route, leading in to El Qubba from the west and leaving it towards the east, then curving down to the south in the direction of the open desert. The route I marked in yellow pencil, the halting points in green; a red circle surrounded the approximate position of the petrol dump, with a brown question mark. When I had drawn fasces in black for the Italian troops in El Qubba and a purple swastika for the Germans in Derna I thought that my map looked pretty convincing. I scribbled a few sums in the margins (petrol consumption for five vehicles doing eight miles to the gallon and such-like calculations), then an address, Mademoiselle Laura Vanetti, 9 Rue Morpurgo, Alexandria. Next I folded the map backwards and forwards several times till the creases looked worn, then I spread it out and crumpled it up and spread it out again, laid it on a flat rock and wiped my shoes on it, smeared it with fat from a tin of bully beef, burnt two cigarette holes in the right-hand edge and carefully tore it half down the middle. I then folded it up and put it in my pocket, ready for use.

Shorten with the demolition party arrived that night in high spirits. They rested, then they passed the time preparing the explosives. We used a device christened the 'daisy chain', made from gun-cotton primers threaded on a five-foot length of prima-cord, an instantaneous fuse that looks like a thick blind-cord. Gun-cotton primers, the explosive on which we relied to set the petrol on fire, are in the shape of a truncated cone, the size of a large pipe bowl and have a longitudinal hole through their centres. Five primers went to each daisy chain, spaced out and held in place by knots in the cord. At one end of the cord a detonator was fixed with adhesive tape: into the detonator we crimped a time-igniter, an automatic device that was meant to set off the detonator at a fixed time after the safety-pin had been withdrawn. On this occasion we used three-hour igniters. For our own safety daisy chains and detonators were carried separately and assembled at the last moment only, after the chains had been laid under the petrol drums.

We adhered strictly to Mohammed el Obeidi's schedule. About one in the morning, after three hours' stumbling walk, we arrived in the outskirts of El Qubba. Late as it was the little settlement still showed a few lights; a screeching wireless played Italian jazz in the army brothel on the hill, where I had once been billeted at a time when the place was ours. An electric welding plant in the workshops threw fitful flashes of cold, violet light. After our fearful march in the dark the mean lights and the thin noise coming from the well-known piddling Italian settlement of less than sixty houses were magnified by contrast and filled the landscape. I fell into a dream-like fancy: the trees showing against the glow were a city park; beyond it were wide streets full of lights. Trams clanked, cars slid by, well-dressed people walked the pavements and sat in crowded cafés, where bands played soft music. Over the cinema neon lights flickered. I didn't click back into reality till long after we had slipped into our cave-like cistern.

The food provided by Mohammed el Obeidi's brother was good and plentiful. Our bellies well filled we all slept late into the next day. Our little watchman outside had no occasion to whistle. I was told later that two Italian soldiers had crossed the foot of our slope, but the child seeing them unarmed and their purpose but an idle wandering had wisely refrained from giving the alarm. The last hours of waiting wore heavily on my two British companions: Chevalier was gloomy and irritable; Shorten, excited, talkative and restless, laid down the law about the fine points of the art of demolition, and I had to interfere tactfully to prevent a quarrel. The Arabs, fortunately, were self-possessed and chatted drowsily together.

At seven-thirty that evening a small boy slipped in, carrying on his head a tray with a hot meal. At eight-thirty we hung our daisy chains round our necks, put the detonators and time-igniters in our pockets, and walked over to the petrol dump. We crossed the wire, and collected round a small, white rock, where I gave my instructions: I had divided my force into three parties of one British officer and two Arabs each. To each party I allotted a sector of the dump which I described to them as well as I could by the landmarks — trees, rocks and bushes — that I had noted on my previous visit. Starting from where we stood they were to work their diverging ways into the dump, laying one daisy chain under each of the cluster of drums they could find in the dark. Each party had twenty daisy chains and they were to lay as many of them as they could, bearing in mind that we were all to collect again at the white rock at ten-fifteen. On no account were they to be late at the rendezvous for, I said, I wouldn't wait one minute beyond the appointed time. Unused daisy chains were to be brought back. I repeated my discourse in Arabic, asked each man if he had perfectly understood where he was to go, what he had to do and where and at what time was the rendezvous. Our watches had been synchronized beforehand and off we went. There was no moon but the sky was clear and, though the stars gave us enough light to work by, the darkness was sufficiently thick to make us feel safely invisible. Across the dump, in the distance, shone the headlights of three Italian trucks which were being loaded with petrol drums. I welcomed this activity for, I thought with pleasure, the enemy would find his dump gone up in flames at the precise time when he had planned to use it. It seemed unlikely that he would be able to replace this large amount of petrol so quickly that the course of the battle would not be affected.

We worked methodically and unhurriedly. My two Arabs lifted a drum and I laid a daisy chain underneath — then, while I fitted detonator and igniter (which has to be done with some care), one of them kept watch by me; the other walked ahead and prospected for the next lot of drums. In this way, and helped of course by my previous knowledge of the topography of the dump, we wasted no time.

It was too easy — I felt like a sneak, trespassing in the dark and, what is more, plotting to damage somebody's property. Wasn't I taking unfair advantage of the good-natured confidence of the owners of the dump who hadn't even thought it necessary to put a guard on it? Soon, however, the pleasure induced by our smooth team-work dispelled my initial distaste: for I was no more a cowardly burglar but an honest workman doing efficiently a good job of work.

From lot to lot our broken way took us closer to the Italian lorries.

Their lights were a comfort to me, they dispelled the anxiety I often feel in the dark, and anyway, by day or by night, the sight of the enemy is always exhilarating. Soon I could hear the men talking in Italian, as they handled the heavy drums. With many blasphemous repetitions, they cursed the officer who had caused them to be detailed for this unwelcome night work. We worked up as close to them as I thought reasonable, then made our way back. We were well ahead of time and we disposed of our three remaining daisy chains on lots we had skipped on our way up.

At eight minutes to ten with twenty-three minutes to go, we squatted near the white rock. Two minutes later Chevalier and his two men loomed out of the darkness and joined us. They had used all but two of their daisy chains. We waited in self-satisfied peace. At ten past ten I posted one of the Arabs two hundred yards ahead in Shorten's sector to guide him in, in case he had trouble in finding the white rock. At twenty-five past the Arab returned, having neither seen nor heard anybody. I waited till a quarter to eleven: Shorten's party was then half an hour overdue. They must have come to grief in some unexplained silent manner, for they couldn't have lost their way: I took the decision (awful to me) to abandon them and withdraw the remainder of my men. We walked away in single file, and had gone perhaps thirty paces when the man behind me touched my arm and dropped to the ground. I did the same, and looking back towards the rock I discerned shadowy shapes moving. Our last man got up and made carefully back towards them. A moment later he brought up Shorten and his two men. I whispered weakly: 'You are late.' I was so shaken with relief that for a few seconds I couldn't think. He started talking and brought me back to my senses. 'We shall talk presently,' I said. 'Follow Chevalier.'

Back in the cistern, while the others gathered their kit, I had him up: he stood to attention, the silly idiot, with a foolish grin of satisfaction on his pink face and started his report.

'Sir. I laid sixteen daisy chains in sixteen different lots of petrol drums . . .' I cut him short.

'Why were you half an hour late?'

'Was I, Sir? I didn't think I was that late. Surely?'

'Why were you late?'

'Well, Sir, after we had laid our sixteen daisy chains I noticed that the primers were immobilized by a single knot on the cord. Now, Sir, on the demolition course, we were advised to tie a double knot to make sure of the explosive wave propagating itself from the cord to the primer. So I went back to all the lots and tied a second knot in the sixteen daisy chains. Ahmed and Sayed have been most helpful, Sir.'

'Christ Almighty,' I whispered, 'of all the f—— fools in the army, the f—— dregs is what I get. What do you think we are doing here? Running a bloody demolition course? I'll propagate an explosive wave up your f—— arse. You are sacked. Dismiss.'

I felt better — Shorten grinned in the light of my torch — he appreciated my language and was too pleased with himself even to feel guilty. I looked round:

'All set? Out we go,' and, Mohammed el Obeidi leading, out we went.

Time was running short. The first charges had been laid shortly after nine, two hours ago. If the delayed igniters worked properly the dump would start blowing up in an hour — or less — illuminating the countryside. We had to get away before this happened and the alarm was given — and I had still a job to do. I had arranged with Mohammed el Obeidi that he would take us along the side of the dump on to the main road. When we reached it I got everybody across, took the marked map out of my pocket and fixed it in a bush by the roadside, hoping it would look as if it had blown out of the back of a truck. The six remaining daisy chains and a few igniters I laid neatly in the ditch, together with a packet of cigarettes and a field dressing, as if they had been forgotten and left behind in a hasty departure. I then rejoined the rest of my party across the road. We skirted tents — a reinforcement camp that held up to two thousand troops — dispersed on the north side of the road. There were dim lights in some of the tents but we saw nobody about. When we had cleared the last tents I called to Mohammed el Obeidi to slacken the pace a little. With the camp and the road between us and the dump I thought we were safe for the time being:

it was unlikely, if the alarm were given, that the enemy would search for us at first in his own territory: he would rather assume that we had escaped to the south, towards the desert; or to the east, towards our own lines — not to the north-west where there was no cover and every village held troops and Italian settlers. We had, however, to get out of this area before dawn and we were taken by Mohammed el Obeidi in a wide curve to avoid El Qubba, then across the road once more and on to the mysterious Kaf el Kefra.

We had hardly dipped into a gully beyond the camp when a dull boom came from the dump, a dark red flame rose in the sky and fell again, leaving a glow behind it. Chevalier, who was walking with me, turned round without stopping and muttered softly: 'Oh Lord!' With a timid disposition he was a man of courage and persistently involved himself in improbable adventures. Pig-headedly he fought his natural inclination to take things easy: hardly out of one breath-taking scrape and still panting, he searched for some new way of getting himself scared. He was generally successful in his enterprises and, surprisingly, survived the war to return to cotton-broking in Alexandria.

We stumbled on in the dark led by Mohammed el Obeidi at the swift, tireless Arab pace. The glow in the dump behind us had died out. I was worried about it: that first explosion had been premature and had probably been caused by one only of our charges, but I thought it would have been sufficient to keep the fire going till the others went off.

We walked on. By one o'clock nothing had happened though all the charges should already have gone up if the time-igniters had functioned properly. With a sinking heart I felt the despair of failure overcome me. Weary and dispirited I walked on, suddenly so tired that, had I been alone, I would have lain down to sleep. Time dragged on: in my mind I kept going over the sequence of charge-laying: primers, fuses, detonators, igniters. How could they *all* have failed? We had laid fifty-four daisy chains and one only had exploded — without much effect apparently. I decided to keep up hoping till one-thirty. The half-hour came and nothing happened. Cursing the makers of our gadgets I admitted failure. As nothing could be done about it my spirits immediately began to revive and I started working out in my mind a plan to blow up a bridge on the railway line between Benghazi and Barce. I looked at my watch; my despair had lasted half an hour.

At five minutes to two the skyline behind us exploded. A broad curtain of yellow flames lifted to the sky and stayed there, lighting the bare landscape around us. Rumbling thunderous explosions followed one another throwing up more flames. Drums of petrol, projected upwards, burst in mid-air, blazing globes of fire that floated slowly down. A moment later a rolling wall of heavy, billowing smoke, lit to a fierce red by the fires burning on the ground, had taken possession of half the horizon and reached to the sky. It seemed incredible that the petty manipulations we had done so quietly in the dark could result in such a glorious catastrophe. It was more than we expected; our reward was ten times what had been promised, such a munificence made us wonder; we felt slightly awed and very powerful.

For a whole hour the blaze increased in intensity. Our men kept falling out to gaze back at the wonder and then caught up again at a trot. The glare of the burning dump lit our way and made the going easier. Then, as we increased our distance and intervening hills threw longer shadows, I found myself once more stumbling in the dark and hard put to it to keep up with our indefatigable guide. On we walked. Overcome with exhaustion, I renounced my self-respect and asked Mohammed el Obeidi how far we were now from Kaf el Kefra. 'Not far,' he replied laconically and we plodded on.

The first light of dawn came. The fire behind us shone with un-diminished fierceness. We plodded on. The sun rose: we were in a barren wilderness of sandy hills and scrub. My head swam with fatigue; to keep awake I tried working out a sum: *The Germans have two hundred tanks — they do five miles to the gallon — in battle they run fifty miles a day. How many days' supply are one hundred thousand gallons of petrol?* I kept losing the threads of my argument and starting again from the begin-ning — then I got a surprising answer: *sixty-two days*. This was too good, it couldn't be correct. Patiently I began again. This time the answer came: *a third of a day, eight hours*. As a period as short as that was rather disappointing back I went to my premises. Mohammed el

Obeidi came up to me and said: 'Kaf el Kefra is now near.' We were all well tired out by now but we went on under the warmer sun. I worked once more on my problem and got as an answer: *twelve days*. It seemed satisfactory and I lost interest. We walked ... Our guide said: 'Beyond that hill is Kaf el Kefra.' I laughed out aloud because of a joke of ours: 'When you start on a trip the guide says the objective is *far* — after four hours' walk he says it is *not far* — four hours later he says it is *near* — four hours' walk again and he says it is *beyond that hill* — then you walk another four hours before getting there.' With dragging feet and an aching body I tramped along for another eternity, then I looked up again: the sun was hardly higher in the sky, which was surprising. Someone said in Arabic: 'There comes Musa riding a camel.' And indeed I saw a rider approaching across the yellow plain—one of our men, mounted on one of our camels. We had arrived. Musa slid off his camel and shook my hand with fervour — he patted me on the shoulder and pointed to the eastern horizon where a solid black cloud of smoke stretched from north to south.

We scrambled down into a semi-circle of low cliffs below the level of the plateau, dotted with caves: Kaf el Kefra. It was only half-past seven.

Musa and Yunes, the two men who had brought our kit and the animals from Sidi bu Halfaya, boiled tea for us and cooked breakfast. Squatting in the soft sand, quite revived, I looked at Mohammed el Obeidi; to my amazement his usual dark composure had gone: he was grinning and chuckling to himself.

'What is it, Mohammed?'

'Those Italian soldiers who were working last night in the dump. They are now under close arrest. The charge is "Smoking while handling petrol and thus causing grievous damage to Mussolini's property,"' and, for the only time in my experience, he burst out laughing. We all laughed, we shook with uncontrolled mirth, we rolled in the sand, sobered down and then spluttered out again. We thought his remark infinitely funny, it summed up beautifully for us the events of the last week.

I took guard duty for the first hour, before turning in to sleep. I climbed up to the plateau and looked down: our men were all invisible, asleep in the caves — the camp fire had been carefully covered with sand, the empty food tins buried. Our camels and horses were out of sight, grazing up and down the wadi. It was well. On the horizon the black wall of smoke billowed lazily.

The Arabs around El Qubba, including Mohammed el Obeidi's brother and his family, were all rounded up by the Italians and closely interrogated. They were released after a few days. Eventually a copy of the official Italian report on the incident came into my hands. It attributed the fire to the action of a *British motorized Commando*. I couldn't say whether this was the result of my attempts at deception or should be attributed to the desire of the local Italian commander to put the blame on a mysterious raiding party entirely beyond his control. After all he *might* have put a guard on the dump!

Tactfully no mention was made in the report of the amount of petrol destroyed but I was amused to learn that a dump of small arms ammunition which, entirely unknown to me, lay on the far side of the petrol dump, had been caught in the conflagration and had also blown up. Apparently the thistles and the dry undergrowth had spread the fire and even several of the tents in the camp on the far side of the road had been burnt.

A few days after our return to Er Rteim one of our amateur spies came in bursting with important news: British planes had bombed El Qubba and completely destroyed an immense petrol dump!

CHAPTER VI

SETTLEMENT IN THE JEBEL

As it was followed by no reprisals against the Arabs, our success at El Qubba established our prestige right through the Jebel. I received congratulations even from the cautious 'Ali bu Hamed. Sheikhs from distant tribes, whom I had never seen before, came to visit me and proffered their services. This enabled me to extend our network of intelligence as far as Benghazi, where many supplies were landed, about which I was very glad to have regular information.

A drawback to our popularity was that sheikhs now came to me with their problems, asked me to settle their differences about water-points and tried to make me take a hand in tribal politics. I did my best but I had neither the time nor the staff to carry out properly the duties of Governor of Cyrenaica.

Chapman in the meanwhile had got his road watch functioning with an astonishing degree of efficiency. Every night, for nearly five months he wirelessed to Eighth Army a detailed account of the enemy movements on the main line of communication during the preceding twenty-four hours. His show was run as a business. He had watchers on the road, relays of runners, supervisors, everyone paid a monthly salary, with premiums for regularity and fines in case of inaccuracy or slackness. Every few days he would go and watch the road himself from morning till night and check the result against the report of his Arab watchers further up the road. In this way he kept them on their mettle and made sure that they wouldn't concoct their lists of vehicles in their tents, far from the tiresomeness of road watching. He succeeded in firing his helpers with enthusiasm for this tedious work and gave them a love of accuracy which is very foreign to the Jebel Arab's nature.

Chapman gave me a black report on Sa'ad 'Ali Rahuma's activities as a quartermaster; an investigation revealed the disastrous extent of his lavishness. I relieved him of his administrative duties and sent him to reconnoitre the railway line running from Benghazi to El Abiar and Barce. As I was particularly ill-fitted to be my own quartermaster I sent an urgent request to Middle East to send out Grandguillot, a Frenchman from Alexandria, now a captain in the British service, of whose administrative abilities I had good reason to have a high opinion. I knew that he was looking for a job and would be willing to quartermaster for us.

In the meanwhile, putting aside more congenial tasks, I set out to visit our dumps. I was climbing out of our deep wadi at Er Rteim when I saw, coming towards me, an Arab leading a horse on which two men were riding. I soon recognized the man, an Arab called Sayed el Barasi whom I had employed casually to collect information, a good man and of a pleasant disposition; but the riders puzzled me. They were unshaven and in tatters, yet there was something indefinable about them that put me in mind of the R.A.F. Sayed el Barasi told me he had brought those to me, would I see what they were? I had a sudden notion that they might be Italians, disguised, sent out to spy on me and addressed them abruptly in what I thought might be their language. They looked up languidly and replied in halting but unmistakable cockney. They were, as it turned out, two of a crew of eight who had baled out of a bomber near Benghazi six weeks earlier. They had wandered a long while in the inhospitable desert south of the Jebel, had been picked up by friendly Arabs in a state of considerable exhaustion and passed on from tent to tent till they had fallen into the hands of Sayed el Barasi, who, being familiar with our camp, had brought them in to me for inspection. When they realized that they were talking to a British officer, their countenances lit up a little, but, thinking that I was only a fellow sufferer (in slightly better condition than themselves) and being tired and bewildered, they disbelieved my account of my position, or they assumed that my mind was wandering. It was only when I brought them to my camp and poured them each half a mugful of whisky that they realized, with an expression of angelic delight on their poor tired faces, that they were indeed saved and had found someone who could look after them. I handed them to our wireless operators, recommending that they should be fed very sparingly, wrapped in blankets and left to sleep. That night their names went out on the air to the R.A.F. — and their families.

Sayed el Barasi, in the meanwhile, having talked to some of our men, came up to me and, after I had thanked him and given him a reward, asked if I would employ him as one of my regular staff. I replied that, as he well knew, I was always willing to give him work but as he had his family and flocks to look after and couldn't give me all his time, I couldn't take him on my staff. 'Never mind my family and my flocks,' he said, 'I want to work for you permanently. Will you take me? I have also got a horse.' I agreed to this and told him he would be attested and enrolled as a private in the Libyan Arab Force. He would then receive the same treatment as the men I had brought with me from Egypt. I was puzzled, however, and inquired from my men about his motives. I learned then that his journeys on my account having become known to men of his tribe — the Barasa — amongst whom was an informer in Italian pay (I remembered Sa'ad 'Ali Rahuma's dictum: 'The Barasa are all traitors'), he had been betrayed and, in his absence, a party of Italian police had raided his village, burnt his tent, killed his cattle and taken his wife away as a hostage. His children were looked after by relatives — having lost everything he had come to me for employment. A lesser man might have flaunted his sacrifices and the losses he had suffered; not so this simple Senussi who only asked *as a favour*, to be allowed to join us in fighting the Italians. He didn't think it seemly for a man and a warrior to try and make capital out of his losses or to importune a friend with the tale of his misfortunes.

I sent Sayed el Barasi to investigate the prisoner-of-war cages near Benghazi. I thought I might find it possible to organize escapes and bring some of our prisoners back to Egypt. His instructions were to find the location of the camps, how many they held, of what troops (British or Indian) and to find out about the guards, the wire and the state of the defences generally. A tall order, but he rode away contented enough (I had bought his horse off him but let him ride it).

The plan had been suggested by the arrival in my camp of three escaped prisoners, brought in independently by Arabs a few days after the two air force lads. They had escaped from a camp — somewhere south of Benghazi, they thought, but couldn't say where it was — and had had the good sense to keep to the southern foothills of the Jebel where they met many Arabs who fed them and sped them on. In this way they reached me quite rapidly and in good condition, though they had walked about one hundred and forty miles. It seemed to me that with a little organization in the prison camps and amongst the Arabs on the way it would be possible to keep a steady trickle — or even a flow — of escaping prisoners making their way back in comfort to our lines.

I signalled the L.R.D.G. asking them to divert a patrol to collect the five men I had now in my camp. Their reply came the next night: R1 Patrol (New Zealand) would call three days later at Haqfet Jiljaf in the southern foothills, arriving about sixteen hundred hours at the usual rendezvous. So we put our five escapees on camels and sent them down with an escort of our soldiers. They reached the rendezvous in an easy two days' ride, were picked up as arranged and arrived in Egypt in due course.

Poor Shorten went with them: sacked. He was a lovable lad and extremely brave but as yet too young and irresponsible for my jobs. I couldn't employ him with Arabs who were much better at the game than he was. I gave him a glowing testimonial and he joined the S.A.S. Regiment shortly after his return to Egypt. Later I was sad to learn that he had got killed when his jeep overturned during the chase that followed the battle of El Alamein.

I was getting a little worried about the number of visitors who came daily to our camp at Er Rteim. We were getting *too* well known and inevitably sooner or later the wrong kind of person would be calling on us. I moved my headquarters to a wadi near Khawlan, closer to the Martuba by-pass where Chapman had his road watch and was thus a more suitable location for the wireless set. There was water nearby, and there were friendly tents in the neighbourhood from which we could get milk and occasionally a kid or a lamb. I left two men at Er Rteim, to screen the visitors and send on to our new camp only those they could vouch for. The wireless operators welcomed the change in the very dull routine of their lives.

My investigation into the state of our stores had resulted in a long list of requirements sent out on the air to L.R.D.G. In reply a few days later I got a signal which said:

'R2 PATROL WILL CALL BIR BELATER JUNE 4TH TWENTY-ONE HUNDRED HOURS CARRYING SUPPLIES AS REQUESTED STOP GRANDGUILLOT AND TWO ARABS WITH SUPPLIES TRAVELLING WITH R2 STOP MIDDLE EAST REQUEST YOU GIVE HIM EVERY ASSISTANCE MESSAGE ENDS.'

Grandguillot was the officer I had just asked for — to be my quarter-master. Such expedition in complying with my demand was astounding; I felt I had never given Middle East Headquarters their due. The last sentence in the message puzzled me — wouldn't I naturally give every assistance to an officer joining me at my request? — but I dismissed the matter lightly as being beyond my comprehension.

Chapman, Chevalier and myself rode down in great spirits to Bir Belater to meet Grandguillot. Dick Croucher and his patrol of New Zealanders rolled in on time and we had a party. New Zealanders are pleasant and Croucher, unaffected and humorous, was an old friend of mine: for an hour we discarded the Arab way of life and the intricacies of tribal politics, we forgot the road watch and our plans to damage enemy property: we chatted and laughed and drank beer and rum-and-lime. Then they departed again, leaving us to load our camels with the treasures they had brought.

Grandguillot, a French international tennis player from Alexandria, liked to play the part of a stage Frenchman. He shouted and got excited and, though he didn't actually kiss us, he made me feel that he might do so at any moment. He had two Libyan Arab soldiers with him and a large number of mysterious, heavy, sausage-shaped bags. On our leisurely ride back to camp I gave him an outline of our position and our activities and told him what I expected him to do.

'I would love to help you,' he said, 'but I shall have my own work to see to.'

'What is your work?'

'I can't tell you.'

'How come,' I said, 'don't you know?'

'I do — in a way,' he replied, somewhat embarrassed. 'I am not allowed to tell you.'

'Why?'

'It is secret and I have been specially instructed not to tell you.'

'Haven't you been sent here at my request?'

'Did you ask for me? I was never told.'

The situation was ludicrous and we both laughed. I pointed out that if I didn't know what his job was, I couldn't help him, and without my active support he would not be able to achieve much in the eastern part of the Jebel which, in a sense, I controlled: he might *perhaps* succeed in doing *a little* — but, whatever he did, I would be informed of it automatically day by day, and his awful secret would be out of the bag. So hadn't he better be sensible and tell me *now* what it was about? I might be able to help him.

Grandguillot was no fool, and he understood well the position we were in in the Jebel; he was also a well-trained soldier and the orders of his commanding officer were to be obeyed — up to a point. He meditated a moment then leant from the saddle and said in French:

'Ce sont des cons' — referring to our masters in Cairo — 'mon vieux Popski, mais nous allons être plus malins qu'eux.' Then he told me that a new organization had come out from England to the Middle East, with the object of helping our prisoners-of-war to escape from enemy cages and to make their way back to our lines. He had joined this organization and had been sent to the Jebel with orders to establish a chain of food depots along the routes which the escaping P.O.W.s might take and to induce or bribe the local Arabs to guide them from depot to depot till they could be collected at a suitable spot and picked up by the L.R.D.G. The mystery bags, he said, contained special, scientifically prepared rations, and he had with him forty thousand lire to bribe the Arabs.

I said the scheme seemed sound enough, and could be made to work, — with some alterations to suit existing conditions. In fact I had had a similar plan in mind for some time and would be glad to help him.

'What is beyond me,' said Grandguillot, 'is why the colonel

wouldn't let me talk to you about it. Security is security to be sure. But *somebody* must know what I am doing.'

'How old is your colonel?'

'He is a lieutenant-colonel really and quite young — perhaps twenty-eight, or less.'

'A regular officer?'

'I believe so.'

'I don't think it was for the sake of security,' I said, 'that he ordered you to be discreet. There may be another motive behind his odd behaviour. A month ago, I imagine, your colonel was a mere captain. He had friends, he knew how to pull strings, perhaps he was lucky; anyhow he managed to get himself appointed to a good staff job that carried promotion. Good jobs and promotion mean a lot to a regular officer and I fancy he does not want to lose either. He wants to make good. On this new business of his, he has sent you behind the enemy lines where he knows I have been operating for some time. Popski, he thinks, knows all the ropes. If he finds out what Grandguillot has been sent out to do, he will help to be sure, will get some prisoners out and then *claim all the credit for himself*. He has the ear of Eighth Army and will get away with it. Now if Popski liberates *all* the prisoners, sooner or later somebody will want to know why the organization specially set up for that purpose gets none. Perhaps the show will be disbanded, perhaps its commanding officer will be replaced by a man of more experience — maybe Popski himself, who is only a major, will fancy the appointment.

'Should this happen,' I concluded my lecture, 'your present boss would lose his rank and may have to revert to regimental employment. Which God forbid!'

Grandguillot said I had imagination and should write psychological novels. His own considered opinion was less involved: his colonel was a *sinistre imbécile* who hadn't realized that the only possible way of keeping me out of the picture was to do nothing, nothing at all. And where would *that* get him?

We came to a friendly agreement: we would work together the schemes to recover escaping prisoners and Grandguillot would get the credit for as many as we brought back. In return he would take over my administration and share our fortunes. I was well pleased with the arrangement: hard-working, methodical and efficient, he was an asset to my party and furthermore he was a pleasant companion, full of fun and of unexpected knowledge. As to the escaping prisoners, as long as the poor blighters were brought out safely, I didn't care to whose account they were chalked up.

CHAPTER VII

VINDICATION OF SA'AD 'ALI

W H E N I received the message inciting me to spread alarm and despondency, I assumed that Eighth Army was about to take the offensive: ever since, we had been watching the behaviour of the enemy for signs of how the battle was developing. Army received our information but gave us none in return, the B.B.C. news was deliberately out of date: we had to rely on our guesses.

Enemy road traffic increased considerably, the shallow port of Derna was put to use by coastal craft and sailing boats, and every day large flights of German transport planes landed their cargoes at El Ftaiah, on the escarpment above Derna. At night the eastern sky was aglow with fires and flares — which I took to be caused by the R.A.F. bombing enemy landing grounds and dumps. There could be no doubt that the battle had started but we looked in vain for signs of an impending German withdrawal. On the contrary: stores and troops were going up and none coming down, we even spotted a convoy carrying bridging equipment for which no use could be imagined before the German Army reached the canals of Egypt. The gossip reaching us from Italian officers' messes spoke of the varying fortunes of a developing German offensive. Grandguillot, though fresh from Siwa, knew only that a big battle was on and that it was thought it was going well for us. In fact Rommel had forestalled our offensive by attacking us on May 27th, 1942, with armoured forces south of Bir Hakim and with infantry (mostly Italian) at Gazala. For three weeks the battle was fierce but fairly static with alternations of successes and reverses. For us in the Jebel it was a period of intense activity and we undertook several demolition operations with some success. We were confident that a British victory was near, the Italians, on the whole, shared our views, and the Arabs, in the presence of such an unanimity, couldn't help but feel that the battle had already been won. As a consequence, conditions were easy for us and, although we had never been so active, we took few precautions to remain concealed.

Then the nightly illuminations which had heartened us receded, decreased and finally ceased altogether; the road traffic fell back to normal and the big dumps around El Qubba were found empty, completely transferred forward. Sheikh 'Abdel Jelil bu Tayeb rode in one morning to tell me he had heard a rumour that Tobruq had fallen, and during the day and the following night more and more reports came in confirming, with an increasing accuracy of detail, that this had indeed happened, on June 20th, with the capture of over twenty thousand of our men.

Some fool invented a spurious 'ancient prophecy' to the effect that 'whoever holds Tobruq holds Cyrenaica'. The Arabs went repeating it, scaring each other: in twenty-four hours a full-sized flap had developed. 'The Italians had won the war, they would remain in Cyrenaica for ever. Reprisals against the Arabs would soon start.' Everyone suspected his neighbour of being a basas — an informer — and I was asked when I would remove my compromising headquarters to a more remote area. I thought it was a sensible suggestion but I didn't think it wise to increase the panic by running away in a hurry; also I had been caught on the wrong foot: several of my men were away on distant jobs, some of the camels were grazing at some distance, and our camel gear, ropes and containers were in a shocking state of disrepair. I prepared to move to a more discreet and less populated area (my present headquarters were only five miles from the main road), planning to leave in three days' time. Very early on the morning of the second day Metwallah arrived with the information that an Italian party led by a basas (unnamed) would leave Lamluda at dawn to come and round us up. He advised me to move out at once. I knew only too well that if we were discovered by an Italian patrol, even if it failed to capture us, all the Arabs in the neighbourhood — and included in this number were all our most faithful friends — would be made to pay the penalty for harbouring us; I had no choice but to decamp. Dawn found us on the move, our stores precariously tied on to our camels with pieces of decayed rope, the men themselves heavily loaded. Thanks to Sa'ad

'Ali Rahuma's hustling, we had managed to lift everything we had, but frayed ropes kept snapping and loads falling off; we hadn't been going for two hours before we had to stop and slink into a shallow gully where we thought we would not be too conspicuous. I heard some riders coming, and peeping through the bushes over the bank of the gully I recognized Metwallah and three of his friends galloping along. He pulled up when he saw me, said hurriedly he was going to Derna to get the news and show himself to the authorities, and galloped away. Having to hide behind hedges was humiliating enough — the realization that my friends and supporters were running away from me put me in a fine state of dejection. In complete misery I sat down in the gully, at a loss what to do next. My companions sat in gloomy silence, waiting for a lead, but I had been caught in the flap and couldn't find a word to cheer them. I was beaten.

Sa'ad 'Ali Rahuma came and squatted next to me, very quiet, very self-possessed. He said: 'The heavy weapons we have got and their ammunition were meant only to impress the sheikhs. They will not be needed till better news comes. Our explosives too are heavy and can be spared for a few days. Perhaps, Major, you will think fit to dump them here. If we do that we shall be able to carry the remainder of our stores: the wireless sets and small arms and the food. I believe there is a disused well near here, where we could hide our equipment. Let us ride over and look for it, you and I, and see if is fit for our purposes.'

I agreed languidly. Sa'ad 'Ali sprang on to his horse and made it scramble noisily over the bank of the gully. 'A fig for the basasin,' he said and waved his hand, the middle finger crooked, a rude gesture he must have learnt in Egypt. Interpreted it means: 'My finger up his backside.' We rode in silence till he reined in on the edge of a smooth meadow and cast a glance at me as I slumped sadly in the saddle. 'I shall race you to that tree,' he said. 'One, two, three — go!' Off we clattered, he on his scraggy bay and I on Birdybird, my white mare. (For once she had four shoes on!) At the tree he was leading by two lengths. 'Not fair,' he said. 'You are twice as heavy as I am. I shall give you now a start.' Back we galloped: he won again, easily, 'Wait,'

I said, 'I shall beat you yet,' and I unbuckled and threw down on the grass my heavy belt with the pistol in its holster and the ammunition pouch. 'Three lengths start I'll take and goodbye to you.' I won the third lap by a head. We walked our panting horses back to where I had dropped my belt, Sa'ad 'Ali chattering away: 'When I was a young man we had horses, real horses. We prided ourselves in our horseman-ship. I was a good rider: I could have galloped round this meadow with a silver dollar poised on the toe cap of my boot and never dropped it. I wonder, Major, have you got a silver dollar?' I hadn't, but I found a flat stone which I balanced on his foot. He cantered away carefully but the stone soon fell off. 'What can you expect with a horse like mine?' he grumbled. 'Now you try, with your comely "Berdberd".' I lost the stone even quicker than he had and came back laughing. Sa'ad 'Ali Rahuma's face crinkled up in an impudent grin:

'I believe the major is happier now.'

'A thousand thanks to you. Now where is that cistern?'

We found its concealed entrance amongst tumbled rocks near the top of a hill. I complimented Sa'ad 'Ali on remembering the existence of this well after all those years. 'There are over ten thousand disused cisterns in the Jebel and I know them all,' he boasted.

This particular one was well suited to receive our dump: dark, dry and deep, its bottom could be reached only with a rope or a ladder, enough to keep the casual pilferer away. We rode back to the gully where my party was still crouching moodily. Sa'ad 'Ali was in his most hustling mood: he dispatched a party to the cistern with a first instal-ment, and leaving one man to keep an eye on animals and stores, he led us all to a bank overgrown with the long stalks of alfalfa grass.

'Now boys, to it. Cut the grass. The long stalks are the best. Come on boys. Have you been idle so long, you pampered soldiers, that you have forgotten how to make ropes?' He set to with an incredible energy till he got every one of us cutting frantically. He sat himself by the mounting pile and with quick, deft movements rolled and twisted the coarse stalks into strands and then into ropes. Whatever this re-markable man set his hand to — kneading dough, shoeing a horse or rope-making — he did with the economy of gestures and the quick aptness of action of a practised professional. In this respect he was unique amongst his people who despise manual labour and, when compelled by necessity to put their hands to some work, are found to be all thumbs. Three of our older men joined Sa'ad 'Ali at his labours and emulated his deftness, clumsily.

His hands engaged, Sa'ad 'Ali Rahuma kept up a stream of bantering abuse and would allow his helpers not a moment of relaxation. I rode over to the well. The work there completed, I returned to find yards of coarse rope stretched on the ground. The men were tired and happy, and when an Arab we knew came slinking in to warn us with awe that he had just seen a basas hot on our trail he was greeted with general laughter. Sa'ad 'Ali had restored our morale.

By mid-afternoon one hundred and seventeen yards of rope had been made and we started loading up. Sheikh 'Abdel Jelil bu Tayeb, whom I had sent for, arrived, urbane and cool. I discussed the situation with him and decided to move camp that same night to Bir Semander in Wadi Ramla twenty miles to the south-east.

With our loads well secured and our minds at ease we covered the stage during the night. In the early morning we settled under acacia trees on the banks of the dry wadi. I shared a tree with Grandguillot; Chapman and Chevalier took another two hundred yards away; the remainder of our men spread themselves further downstream. That evening our wireless opened up and we put our usual intelligence report on the air. We didn't mention our changed fortunes to Eighth Army: they had, we thought, enough worries of their own, and we felt quite capable of looking after ourselves.

Every other night a party went to Bir Semander to draw water. Relays of runners kept up communications with the road watch. The flap died down very rapidly in the Jebel and our informants found once more their way to our new camp. There was, however, no disguising the fact that we had less and less to do. As the battle moved eastwards and reached the Egyptian border two hundred miles away the Jebel became a backwater, a military void. My immediate problem was to keep up the faith of my Arab friends in the ultimate victory of our side. In their eyes I was the British Government; so long as they saw me amongst them, plotting my schemes with their help, they wouldn't take much notice of the confusing rumours that filtered through from 'Radio Derna', and they would believe that, as I told them, the with-drawal of the British Army was a cunning trap laid to catch Rommel with an extended line of communication and deal him a crushing blow on our own ground. I should have been much surprised had I been told then that my mendacious prophecy was to come true.

To show the Arabs that I was still active — and also in the hope of being able to arrange mass escapes — I sent reconnaissance parties to several points from Tobruq to Benghazi to find out in what manner the twenty-thousand-odd prisoners captured at Tobruq were disposed of.

In our changed circumstances, however, I had no more use for a large party and I decided to send back to Egypt the bulk of my men with Grandguillot and Chevalier. Chapman thought he would like to stay on with me; we decided to come to a final decision on the matter when we had received fresh news from the outer world. I sent a message to L.R.D.G. asking them to pick up a large party and fixing a rendezvous at some distance from our present camp. They promised to send a patrol about the middle of July.

My party was growing daily. The Italians, believing they were once more the masters of Cyrenaica, had started reprisals against the Arabs they suspected of having helped the British, and as a consequence refugees came trickling in to our camp hoping we would evacuate them to Egypt. Then one morning a little South African was brought in. He had escaped from a prison camp near Benghazi ninety-two days previously and for over two and a half months he had wandered by himself in the inhospitable southern desert where in the dry season no Arabs go. He had lived on a little water he found now and then in the radiators of abandoned vehicles and scraps of food left in opened tins, making his way slowly eastwards through the endless desert. At times his mind had wandered and he had been unconscious for several days. Yet such was the greatness of heart of this little clerk who had spent his life in an office in Johannesburg that, after he had been only a day with us he asked to be allowed to remain in the desert and help us with our work, rather than being evacuated to Egypt by the next convoy.

I granted him his wish for a while till I had to give in to pressure from South African Headquarters who insisted in sending him home to the Union. His name is unfortunately lost to me but I hope he, or some of his friends, may read this book and I may thus get in touch with him once more: men of such staunchness are uncommon.

It was Dick Croucher who turned up with his New Zealand patrol. He told a strange tale: Eighth Army, weakened but by no means crushed, was standing up to the Germans, still in Cyrenaica but falling back steadily on to the Egyptian border. Headquarters in Cairo, on the other hand, had fallen into a flap and were preparing to remove themselves elsewhere — Palestine or the Sudan, he thought. The diplomats also were packing and he had seen bonfires of burning archives in the Embassy gardens. Civilians, European and Levantines, were scrambling away to the Congo, South Africa, India and Australia — wherever they could find a plane or a ship to take them. Amongst the troops in Egypt, he said, all was confusion: everyone was running around, either pestering harassed staff officers or issuing impossible orders to bewildered underlings.

At first I had listened with amusement to Dick Croucher's humorous account of what he had seen in Cairo a few days ago but when he came to say that his orders were to withdraw the whole of my party (including myself) and to take us to Cairo, to the very centre of this unsavoury mess, a wave of panic came over me. I didn't mind fighting a losing battle against the enemy (I had learnt to take military reverses without fuss) but I was terrified at the prospect of having to fight our own General Staff as a jobless officer in a panic-stricken rabble far in the rear. Rather than submit to this indignity I would remain in the desert, carry on with such jobs as I could find to do behind the enemy lines and take the risk of being left stranded in Cyrenaica till the end of the war if things went wrong with Eighth Army and Egypt fell to the enemy. I hate panic and mass hysteria so much that the possibility of becoming, perhaps for years, a fugitive in enemy land seemed a better lot than becoming involved in the confusion Dick Croucher described so well. I didn't then fear capture much because I was confident that if I was surprised and taken I would escape again soon. Later I lost some of my cocksureness and I came to dread the prospect of spending years behind barbed wire: of all the hazards of war, captivity is the one against which I am the least well armed.

I found many arguments to reinforce my determination not to go back to Cairo: I couldn't let down my Arab friends — I had still the possibility of collecting information which might be useful to Eighth Army, and my scheme to liberate some of our prisoners-of-war was taking shape. My real motive of course was that behind the enemy lines I was free and my own master.

Chapman also was disposed to stay on, though he didn't tell me what his motives were. He just said that he didn't feel like going to Cairo. Worried as he was about his family in Cairo, this decision required great courage. Though we lived for months in the closest intimacy of purpose we never revealed our inner thoughts to one another: a confidential talk would have embarrassed us both. Chapman asked our two British wireless operators if they would volunteer to stay with us and they agreed readily to do so, without apparently giving much thought to the matter. Neither did I, for I had used up all my cunning in handling the Arabs and I tended to take for granted the co-operation of our British soldiers. I was embarrassed when I had to deal with the very few problems they presented and I let Chapman tackle them, which he did very skilfully. I had yet to learn the handling of British troops.

In a wireless message to L.R.D.G. Headquarters I explained my scheme for the liberation of prisoners-of-war and asked them to send a patrol in a month's time to collect such of our men as I would have been able to get out of the cage. The next morning their reply arrived: they agreed to my request but made it quite clear that the general position was so uncertain that no one could tell for sure if in a month's time there would be any patrols at all operating in the Jebel. I thanked them and said I would take the risk.

CHAPTER VIII

ESCAPE FROM PANIC IN CAIRO

DICK CROUCHER drove away in the early afternoon, taking with him Chevalier and Grandguillot, the escaped prisoners, Sa'ad 'Ali Rahuma, the Libyan soldiers (save two) and the Arab refugees — about thirty men all told. His parting words, unexpectedly emotional, were: 'Goodbye Popski. I shall never see you again.' Chapman, myself, two wireless operators and two Libyan soldiers remained, with one month's supplies. All over the sandy wadi, and particularly where dry desert bushes had been crushed down, the trucks had left unmistakable track marks which I was puzzled how to obliterate. The problem was solved by driving a flock of sheep and goats up and down the wadi: by sunset the tiny hooves had churned up the soft surface so completely that no trace remained of the passage of our vehicles. We dumped some weapons, left behind by men, under rocks, against an emergency, and we walked back in the dark to our camp in Wadi Saratel.

We decided, Chapman and I, to share out the work in the following way: I would liberate prisoners and he would organize hide-outs in case the Germans occupied Egypt and the L.R.D.G. failed to relieve us at the end of August. We thought that in the wooded crags and the cliffs on the northern coast, where the inland plateau drops three thousand feet to the sea, we would be able to hide indefinitely if the local Arabs gave us food: these Arabs were the Dursa, to whom I had given a scolding at the time of their rebellion. Accordingly Chapman left for 'Dursaland' the very next night, with his Libyan, who knew the country well. They were both riding camels. The return trip would be about one hundred and fifty miles.

I stayed alone with the wireless operators and my Libyan in the Wadi Saratel, waiting for my emissaries to come back from various places on the coast where I supposed prisoners might be collected. Till they arrived I had absolutely nothing to do, and for some days my physical activity was limited to the pulling of my rug round the tree under which I camped, following the shade as it moved from west to east. I had only one book left: *The Canterbury Tales*, and it didn't matter at all that I had read it several times. At first I had guessed my way through; at each reading I understood a little more: thus the book was ever new.

Rumours were brought to me that Mussolini himself was in Qubba. I disbelieved them. Then a man I trusted well enough came with a tale of having seen him disguised as a sergeant in the market at Qubba, not once but on several occasions. He had seen Mussolini before the war at public functions and swore he recognized him. The story seemed too circumstantial and the fact so incredible that I decided to take no action till I had confirmation. I didn't even mention the rumour in my daily message to Army, for I didn't want to lower my standard of accuracy, and moreover, I was not much interested. Unprovided with vehicles I had no means of kidnapping the fat blusterer, and I drew the line at assassination. Eventually I got confirmation of his presence in Cyrenaica: as the matter might have had some political significance I informed Eighth Army after all.

Then I heard that the Germans had two large transit camps in Derna where our prisoners, captured at Tobruq, were kept for a few days on their way to Benghazi. Here was my chance: with a thousand or more prisoners coming in, and going out again, every week, the nominal rolls could not be kept very tidily, nor would the guard be very strict. It might be easy for prisoners to escape from the camps; and they might have a chance to get clear before the hue and cry started. So I set off immediately, to examine the camps and make arrangements for escapes.

As I didn't know the country round Derna well enough to travel alone by night I rode up to the tent of a Sheikh Mukhtar, ten miles up Wadi Saratel, and asked him for a guide — a khabir. He promised to do his best at once and sure enough I had hardly got back to my tree when a decrepit old Arab rode up on a very tall camel. 'I am Omar bu Qasem,' he said. 'We are going to Derna together to see 'Ali el Barasi. Have you got a mount or will you ride my camel?'

'I shall ride my mare,' I replied. 'Let us go.' I folded my jerd, picked up a haversack, called to my Libyan soldier to saddle Birdybird, told him I was going to Derna for a week leaving him in charge of the wireless operators, mounted and rode away with Omar.

Darkness fell as we scrambled out of the wadi. Omar struck a course over a slightly rolling, stony plain and we rode in silence. The night was very dark, the sky was overcast as one of the rare summer storms was brewing. Birdybird kept stumbling and our progress was slow. I looked at my compass now and then: Omar kept us on a steady course, slightly north of north-west. How he did it I don't know, for no stars were visible nor could I notice any landmarks on the ground except a few low bushes and patches of soft sand now and then in shallow dips of the hard gravel plain. Even by daylight the landscape would have appeared featureless. We had ridden three hours when he pulled up and asked me if I could see the white superstructure of a well somewhere ahead of us.

I peered very carefully through the woolly darkness and saw nothing. 'Can you see it?' I asked. Omar said in a querulous voice: 'How could I? My right eye is quite blind and the left one is not much better. You can't expect me to see a thing; this is a dark night.' My heart sank: like a fool I had entrusted myself to a blind guide on a black night, and I was lost. Derna, forty miles away, suddenly appeared unattainable. Quietly Omar said, 'We ride on.' He pulled up again after ten minutes: 'Please dismount and put your head near the ground. I think you will now see the well against the skyline.' I did so and sure enough a small rectangular shape showed up, dark against the faintly lighter sky: the well, about one hundred yards ahead of us.

Omar gave no sign of relief, for he had never had the faintest anxiety. 'This is Bir bu Hataja. We won't go any nearer because it is much in use and our tracks in the soft sand might be seen tomorrow morning. All the Arabs know the tracks of your mare. We go on to Bir Qash-qash which is on stony ground, to water the animals.' Our track now lay up a narrowing rocky wadi with sides rising steeply it seemed to at least a hundred feet: there was no doubt about the way and an hour later we climbed up on to the plateau at the head of the wadi where stood the well. Omar took from his saddle bag a coil of rope and an empty petrol can and we watered Birdybird and also the camel. While we were drawing water I tried to get Omar to explain how he found his way: I had no more success with him than with other Arabs on many previous occasions. As usual I got the puzzling reply: 'I know the way.' It was a perpetual disappointment to me that though I had been walking and riding backwards and forwards over the Jebel for months I had still got no nearer to acquiring a sense of direction in any way comparable to that of the dumbest Arab. At night without a compass, even over familiar ground, I inevitably strayed from the direct route when there were no conspicuous landmarks: any Arab child could have given me lessons. In fact it is quite common to meet a toddler of eight or ten all by himself two or three days' walk from anywhere, gravely following the tracks of a stray camel. There is of course no magic and no sixth sense in their ability in finding their way: landmarks, so minute as to escape our notice altogether, remain fixed in their memory; not only visual landmarks but also the feel of the ground underfoot. Moreover they have in their mind a picture of the general structure of the country: on a featureless plain, they can distinguish watersheds and slopes. Dry, sandy watercourses faintly marked with poor bushes seem to us distributed haphazardly; the Arab recognizes them as part of the general drainage system, flowing ultimately to one of the big wadis: Ramla, or El Fej, or Belater. In a similar way, walking in a side street in London, though I have never seen it before, I may know that following its general direction I shall ultimately arrive in Oxford Street. The desert Arab is hopelessly lost in a town.

We rode away from Bir Qashqash and had been going some time when we heard dogs barking faintly. Omar asked me if I had any food with me. 'Only a tin of bully,' I said, 'which I would like to keep for an emergency. And anyhow it is Christian food and not suitable for you.' He asked me to stay where I was and made off in the direction of the dogs, returning after a while with four loaves of bread and a small lump of cheese. 'There were seven tents,' he said. 'An old woman in one of them called to me when she heard me coming. I lifted the flap and told her I was a traveller and hungry: she gave me the food. It should last us till we get to Derna.' It was then about three in the morning.

Shortly after dawn we stopped in sight of the German Road (the Martuba by-pass) somewhere west of Kharmusa, intending to cross it during the afternoon lull in the traffic, and in the meanwhile we made ourselves comfortable in the shade of an acacia tree and ate our meal.

About eleven o'clock we saw a lonely camel rider crossing our tree-dotted wadi a hundred yards away. As he had seen us I sent Omar to call him to our hospitality. He turned out to be an Arab of an obscure western tribe of low reputation, which accounted, I supposed, for his extraordinary bad manners; indeed, against all courtesy, he kept asking questions: who we were and where we intended going and what was our business. Omar went and lit a fire in a hollow some distance away, taking teapot and glasses with him; he called to me after a while; I walked over, leaving our guest. 'This Arab may well be a spy. We must shake him off somehow or he will follow us to Derna.' 'Go and talk to him,' I said. 'I shall make the tea. Be careful you don't touch his glass for there will be *special* tea in it.'

Left alone I slipped five tablets of morphia into one of the glasses. I had been told that seven tablets were a fatal dose, so I hoped that five would induce a nice long sleep but leave no unexplained corpse behind. I contrived that our guest should take the doctored glass — I had made the tea particularly strong and sweet so as to cover the taste of morphia — and I went on listening for over an hour to the idiotic stream of questions of our bumpkin friend. At last he grew drowsy and finally fell asleep. We made him comfortable in the shade of a bush, covered him up with his jerd and when the traffic on the road died down we rode over. It had been pleasant to hear once more the rumbling trucks on the road and to catch a glimpse of the enemy through the trees where the road crossed the wadi: it stilled a secret feeling of futility which I had been suppressing, not quite successfully, ever since our withdrawal to Bir Semander.

Two hours before dawn we arrived, Omar and I, at the edge of El Ftaiah plateau on the escarpment above Derna and we dipped into one of the precipitous gullies that run nearly vertically down to the coastal plain, six hundred feet lower down. We climbed down as far as our mounts could go and stopped in a hollow amongst rocks and boulders, thick with trees and bushes, grass and even moss, for a small trickle of water seeped out of the rocks, ran a few yards across the hollow and fell out of sight in a sheer drop, a tiny waterfall. Omar unloaded the camel and advised me to take some rest while he went to make contact with 'Ali el Barasi and some other of our friends in Derna. He would be back, he said, about midday, and rode away on Birdybird. I lay back in my bower, glad to sleep, having been up for two days and two nights.

The sun was just up when I woke in my enchanted retreat. After months in the desert where all water is in cisterns or in stagnant pools, there is a magic in running water, even if it is no more than would come from a dripping tap. I fancied glades and mossy banks, dragonflies and fish rising. I washed and made myself tea and lay back again, very happy, waiting lazily for Omar to return. Then I remembered the camel. Omar had said that he would leave it unhobbled as it wouldn't stray: if I wanted it all I had to do was to whistle. The brute, however, had strayed and never answered. After a while I got vaguely worried and strolled to the head of the gully. No camel. I ventured on to the plateau, whistling at intervals. It was silly, losing a camel and going about at dawn, whistling for it: I wanted to get back in the hollow and watch my little stream, and the bushes growing out of the rocks. In the desert nothing grows on rocks, the vegetation is all in the hollows and the dry watercourses. I rounded a hill and came across an Arab with a flock of goats and sheep. I realized at once that I would have some difficulty in explaining my presence but he had already seen me and anyhow I wanted to get my camel back, hobble it tight and lie once more on the damp moss. I walked up to the Arab, a young man of no particular brightness, dressed in an assortment of cast-off army clothes, and asked him if he had seen my camel. 'It has strayed, and I am looking for it,' I added rather self-consciously and, I am sorry to say, with a suppressed giggle. It was a well-worn joke with us in the Jebel that we kept meeting improbable people in unlikely places and all they had to say to account for themselves was: 'I am looking for my camel.' How likely would it seem to this Arab shepherd that a strange, middle-aged European officer, in uniform, should indeed be looking for his camel on the outskirts of Derna town in the early hours of the morning? What business had I got with a camel at all? The situation was preposterous and I laughed outright, ruining my very slender chance of having my story believed. The Arab, however, was an Obeidi and well-mannered: he answered my greetings politely and regretted that he had seen no stray camel at all that morning. Which was a lie, as it appeared later; the camel at that very time was sitting, tightly hobbled down, outside his tent half a mile away.

'Come along,' I said, 'and have some tea.' He followed me, leaving his flock at the head of the gully. He drank tea, looking curiously at my few possessions, obviously trying to draw conclusions as to my identity. Finally he brought himself to ask: 'You are not Arab?' 'Of course not, I am English.' 'In that case where is your khabir?' I explained that my khabir had gone to collect some of my Arab friends and would be back at any moment. He laughed: 'You are not English, you are German.' This was an unexpected development and I launched into long explanations, trying to convince him that I was indeed English: I spoke to him of the sheikhs of his tribe, I showed him an Egyptian pound note, a portrait of Sayed Idris, English cigarettes. He wanted to know who my friends were in Derna, but that of course I wouldn't tell him. After all *he* might be in German pay. He let me talk and talk and finally gave his verdict: 'You are a German posturing as an Englishman and trying to catch out the Arabs. You want to find out who is helping the British. I am going now to report to the German post on the road that I have found an English officer.' 'Stop, wait a moment, you will be sorry to have done such a thing. Do you want to be called a basas by all the Obeidat? I am really English you know.' He was shaken, thought a moment, then said: 'No Englishman would be such a fool as to come here without a khabir. I am off to the military post.' 'Sit down,' I told him very gently. 'You will understand that I can't let you go and give me away to my enemies. You will stay with me until my friends arrive. If you try to go I shall have to shoot,' and I showed him my weapon. 'That is fair,' he said. 'You are quite right — you can't let me go,' and he sat down once more, much relieved in his mind to have dispensed with the need of making a decision. We chatted amicably for quite a long while, till he got worried about his flock. 'Look,' he said, 'I can't lose my sheep because I have had the privilege of meeting you. Would you mind coming with me to gather them? We can then keep them near this gully of yours and we shall not miss your friends when they arrive.' I thought the arrangement was fair and for the second time that morning I found myself walking up and down the plateau whistling. We got the wretched little beasts together and spent another hour very pleasantly talking of the marvels of the great cities. Then there was a scramble and a rush and Omar bu Qasem arrived with 'Ali el Barasi and two more friends from Derna, all mounted. I gravely introduced my prisoner (who knew 'Ali well enough), and we all sat down to our greetings. I told Omar I was very sorry, I had lost his camel. 'Not at all, don't worry,' he replied. 'The camel has been found. It is being looked after by this man's people.' There was something farcical in the air at El Ftaiah that morning — as there was to be right through my stay in Derna — and we all laughed and chattered.

From where we sat on the plateau the main Derna-Tobruq road was just in sight in the east, and I had a good view all round. I drew my companions' attention to a group approaching us from the south: 'That's our breakfast,' they said. And so it was, carried on the head in metal dishes by members of the household of my former prisoner whose tents were just out of sight in a dip of the ground. A most colossal breakfast and a very merry one. I was the only one to keep a look-out and later I reported two figures coming over from the road. Through my glasses I could see they were armed but my companions would not be alarmed and went on eating the boiled kid, till two Italian soldiers appeared quite close and making straight for our breakfast party. I was whisked away back into my gully while a screen of Arabs advanced towards the soldiers and masked my undignified retreat. The dishes had come down with me and I was in no danger of starving. Ten minutes later Omar appeared grinning: 'False alarm; they were soldiers from the road post, who wanted to buy eggs and had lost their way to the tents. They are out of the way now — come back and finish breakfast.'

'Ali, my new friend, was a wealthy Arab of the Barasi tribe who had settled as a merchant in Derna: he was very eager to help me. When I had explained my intention of arranging escapes he was full of suggestions and tried to give me a very detailed description of the two camps in which the prisoners were kept, but though I knew the town well enough he couldn't make me visualize the topography to my satisfaction. I wanted to present the prisoners who might be willing to escape with a detailed plan: where to cross the wire and a route to follow after getting out, and I couldn't do this without seeing the ground myself. We decided then that I would spend the next day in the Turkish fort on the escarpment overlooking the town and observe the P.O.W. camps through my glasses. In that way, he thought, I would be able not only to see the lie of the land, but to observe the disposition of the camp guards and their movements. 'From the fort,' said 'Ali, 'you can see Derna as on the palm of your hand.'

'Ali was devoted to our common cause: he was also, I soon noticed, very ambitious, and his enthusiasm for my plan derived largely from the hope that the operation, if successful, would put him in the limelight and allow him to steal a march on the Obeidi sheikhs who were already well known to the British authorities. He, on the other hand, through lack of opportunity, had remained so far in the background. He wanted official recognition and I gave it him in the shape of a document I wrote out appointing him '*Chief Controller of British Agents in Derna, Wadi Derna and El Ftaiah*', with the '*honorary rank of captain and a monthly salary of fifteen hundred lire payable in advance on the sixth of each month*'. As a token that I was entitled to make such appointments I paid him six months' salary in advance.

When I had finished with him I moved to a high knoll and spent the rest of the day watching the German landing ground which was in full view below me on the far side of the road. I saw forty-two transport planes take off empty for Crete all in one flight at 10.00 hours and return loaded with petrol and troops at 16.00 hours. It was apparently a daily routine: a rash one as it appeared a few days later when a squadron of our Beaufighters shot down in the sea thirty-eight of these planes on their return trip. One of the last messages transmitted from my wireless before it broke down had given the R.A.F. the tip. I tried to account for one of these planes myself, with what success I don't know. After dark that same day, I walked over with my former prisoner to the landing ground, which was poorly guarded, and deposited in the tail of one of the Junkers all the explosives I had with me, four pounds of gelignite with a twelve-hour delay igniter, in the hope that it would go off and split the fuselage while the plane was in the air on its outward trip the next morning. No more than a nasty practical joke (for the loss of one plane would not worry the Luftwaffe), yet it might annoy the Wehrmacht who would feel compelled to employ more troops to guard the airfields at night. My guide, who had the job of waking the guard at the entrance to the airfield every morning when he brought them milk for their breakfast, was delighted at the prospect of meeting his clients with the private knowledge that *he* had put a tiny seed of destruction in one of their formidable machines.

Back from the airfield I slept till moonrise, about two in the morning, when 'Ali el Barasi came to take me to the fort where he wanted to arrive before dawn. A long steep scramble over rocks and screes took us down nearly to sea level where we turned left into the canyon of Wadi Derna. A footpath wound its narrow way up the wadi between low garden walls, orange and pomegranate groves, and vineyards passing many mud-built houses, all asleep at this hour except for the furious barking of dogs which reverberated and thundered from the high cliffs. A swift stream of sweet rippling water runs down the wadi, widening into pools, or enclosed within secret banks, spanned by wooden bridges, clear and bubbling. On each side, sometimes two hundred yards apart, sometimes leaving only room for the bounding stream and the path here cut out of the rock, rise the vertical rocky walls of the wadi. Brightly red and yellow, they stretch upwards for six hundred feet, crags and pinnacles and great slabs of stone. According to the winding of the watercourse pink moonlight now reached the bottom of the cleft, now left us in darkness and lighted only the upper floors of a fantastic architecture. There wasn't a sigh of wind: the moist air was thick with smells of flowers and trees; the heat oppressive. My companions walked fast, apprehensive less somebody be woken up by the dogs and question our wanderings: the settled Arabs were by no means as united against the Italians as the tribal nomads inland; my friends called them contemptuously Derna Arabs — Arabs without a tribe — and suspected every one of them.

We walked thus an hour, I think, then started climbing out of the wadi, up a tributary gully. In a moment I was out of my dream world, back amongst the familiar dry boulders and dusty screes of the desert scenery. I reached the fort panting and far behind my companions.

The town and harbour can indeed be seen from the old Turkish fort but not by any means as on the palm of the hand. As the distance to the furthest prisoner-of-war camp was over two miles I realized at once that I should have to look at it from much closer if my visit was to be of any practical use. I asked 'Ali to find some means of taking me to the outskirts of the town two hours before sunset: I would then find my own way to the camps. He grumbled and argued: the streets, he said, would be full of troops in the late afternoon. That was precisely what I counted on: the Germans would take me for an Italian, the Italians for a German, and I would pass unnoticed in the crowd. He agreed that if I *had* to walk the streets the crowded hour was probably the best, but couldn't he go in my stead? I declined his offer: giving up the argument, he called to his three friends and discussed the matter with them at great length in low whispers while I kept my glasses on the white town lying on the plain below me. For eight hours I kept my watch and saw much of interest: coasters unloading in the small harbour, convoys of lorries running into the barracks inside the Benghazi Gate where we had had a supply point at the time when Derna was ours (it was obviously used for the same purpose by the Germans), tents stretched along the coast west of the town: rest and reinforcement camps, I guessed, some Italian, some German. Intricate calculations, mainly guesswork, led me to the figure of twelve to fifteen thousand as the number of troops in and around Derna. About one o'clock, in the growing heat of the day, the bustle slowed down everywhere. At two, not a soul was astir. I got into the shade of a wall and curled up to sleep.

At four o'clock 'Ali woke me up. I mounted a donkey that had been driven up to the fort while I slept, wrapped myself head, face and all in my jerd, leaving only my bared feet showing, and rode away hunched up and head rolling, supported on each side by an Arab: a patient taken to the doctor *in extremis*, a dying man about whom — we hoped — nobody would bother. I was led down to the town and into the courtyard of a friendly house of ill repute where I cast off my jerd, pulled on my shoes, and, taking the plunge, strolled out, trying to behave like a soldier coming out of a brothel, frightfully self-conscious, very scared and remembering my feelings when, as a small child as yet unable to swim, I was made to jump into a deep pool.

Round the first bend in the narrow alley the sight of a police feldwebel walking towards me sent me into a wild panic: the district might have been put out of bounds and my being in it, instead of a safeguard, as it was intended, might be the occasion to be taken directly to a police post. My discomposure must have been apparent, but attributed to another cause than fear, for the German as he passed gave me a dirty grin and cracked an obscene joke *in broken Italian* about games unsuitable for my age. His unkind remark revived my courage; if the *German* feldwebel had judged me to be *Italian* my deception was working as I expected and all was well. When I reached the end of the alley my knees were still wobbly, but my mind was at rest, and I launched myself quickly into the main street. It was full of soldiers, Afrika Korps, Luftwaffe, Italians, all dressed in drill like myself — uniforms originally of many shades of khaki but now bleached and discoloured to a nondescript sandy yellow, amongst which my own dirty British shirt and slacks did not particularly stand out. There were hundreds of soldiers strolling in that street, every one of them an enemy: not one bothered to notice that my dress was different and alone of its kind.

I started along the houses, ready to bolt up a side lane, then realized that the more comfortable I felt the less I would be noticed: if only I could manage to forget altogether the singularity of my position it wouldn't matter even if I wore red and green and feathers in my hat, nobody would think of questioning my right to be in Derna on August 6th, 1942.

This knowledge gave me the assurance to go and jostle my way at a good pace down the middle of the street, bumping occasionally into one of my enemies. But I hardly looked at them now: I was turning over in my mind the problems of escape for my prisoner friends, and I hurried towards the first camp I wanted to examine. I had a job to do — and over four miles to walk before dark: I wasn't going to let anyone delay me. I even came to have a feeling of fellowship towards these other lads, soldiers like myself, with duties not dissimilar to mine; in a confused way I felt that we were all on the same job. I worked up to a state of bliss, awareness of my unusual position nearly dismissed from my conscious mind; not completely though, for I had to be on the look-out for officers and be ready with an Italian salute for a German officer and vice versa.

Apart from the officers I looked no one in the eye, for nothing discourages overtures, friendly or hostile, better than a vague abstracted stare: one doesn't go up to a stranger walking purposefully who, by the look on his face, is absorbed in his thoughts and is only just aware of his surroundings.

I walked out of town through the Benghazi Gate: a few hundred yards further on in the open plain on my left and just off the road stood my camp: tents closely packed within a perimeter of barbed wire, with elevated wooden platforms at intervals, on which stood the guard. Poles carrying electric lamps showed that the camp would be lit up at night in the usual way: they were far apart and I judged that they would leave useful areas of semi-darkness. I made for the far side of the camp, skirting the wire at a distance of fifty yards, looking curiously at the prisoners and making no pretence of being there for any other purpose: I just kept walking, neither hurrying nor loitering and observing the ground as I went. One-third of the way along this side, which faced inland away from the road towards the escarpment, a narrow dry runnel about three feet deep ran at right angles into the camp; the untidy wire barrier had not been stretched quite to the bottom, and I decided it would be fairly easy for a man to crawl unseen along the runnel, under the wire and away. The nearest watch tower was a hundred yards away and the only light in the neighbourhood seemed to be a small searchlight on the tower. Inland, away from the camp, I made a note of landmarks which might help a man to find his way in the dark towards the mouth of the nearest wadi running down from the escarpment, twelve hundred yards to the south.

I had just jumped over the runnel when in the very still evening air I heard a faint commotion in the camp. I looked round, expecting a challenge from the guard or a burst of fire: but I saw only that some South African prisoners — I could tell them by the red tabs on their shoulder straps — were crowding up to the wire and I imagined they were discussing my appearance. I took a few more steps, stopped, lit a cigarette, to give any inquisitive member of the guard a token of the ease of my conscience, then walked away at an angle, increasing slowly the distance between me and the camp. No one, however, took any more interest in me, and having completed the circuit I approached the road once more near the end of the camp furthest from the town.

With the information I had collected alternative plans of escape were taking shape in my mind; I liked the way things had turned out: the guard was not too fierce, the wire haphazard and the deserted plain would offer a fairly safe get-away towards the escarpment. With several hundred prisoners in the cage the chances were that a few adventurous spirits would be found amongst them to attempt an escape.

I had now to make for the other camp, a mile and a half away at the opposite end of the town: as I got on the road and began to retrace my steps towards the Benghazi Gate a longing overcame me to scrap this part of my programme and to fade away quietly towards the friendly safety of the escarpment wadis. I suddenly was desperately weary and repelled by the prospect of a long walk through the town and back, along that terrible, crowded street. Hadn't I achieved enough for my purpose? The conditions of escape from the other camp, which was in the buildings of the old hospital beyond the Tobruq road, would be rather unfavourable and the get-away difficult, as it would have to be through the town. Wasn't I foolish, having had luck with my first attempt, to run the risk of being caught on my way to a second and much less promising one, and thus ruin the whole undertaking? It was indeed unfair to the men detained in the hospital not to try and give them also a chance of escaping, but I was the only judge of what could be done: they were unlucky in being in the wrong place, a fate they shared with thousands of other prisoners in distant places I couldn't get at.

I dragged my feet along the road as I turned these matters in my mind, fighting my weariness of heart, and with my interest in the whole scheme completely dead. I finally decided to cancel my visit to the hospital. I can see now that my decision was wise: one under-taking was quite enough, I couldn't really get a larger number of escapes from two camps than from one, and the risk of being caught while trying to improve unnecessarily on a very sound scheme was certainly not worth taking.

About three-quarters of the distance along the road from the camp to the city gate I had noticed a small track turning to the right off the road and leading to a clump of tall bushes. This track I now made for, intending to make my way from the bushes to the escarpment, and I stepped along the road, much fresher for having made up my mind.

A few yards before reaching my turning-off point I looked up and saw, just beyond the Benghazi Gate, a group of twenty to thirty Italian soldiers come out of the quartermaster's stores and walk away towards the town. The unwelcome sight of so many enemies made me realize in a flash that my decision, however sensible, had been inspired by fear: if I didn't face the dangers of the crowd now I knew I would never stand up to any danger in the future. Running away today was as good as running away once and for all. So I walked on, past the track, past the Gate, into the town and trod my way once more amongst the crowd, gingerly and with a quaking heart, convinced of the utter futility of my quest but determined to see it through.

I thought a shock would help me to recover my nerve and a moment later, peering fearfully up a side alley, I saw an Italian youth running towards me. He had a fatuous grin on his thick lips, a misshapen nose and flapping ears, a perfect booby. As he was about to reach the main street I took a step into the alley so that he crashed into me with some violence. I was braced and escaped being knocked over, but the lad was winded and startled: I held him up by the shoulder and shook him soundly, hissing out angry meaningless German noises: 'Strum strum heidelpferd — strum knöbelstein — strumbelneck — strum strum strangverneckerst niegerloos.' (I was back in the nursery, talking German 'Pingo' with my sisters.) The lad gasped and gaped; when I let him go he ran back up the alley and out of sight. Two pleasant-faced German N.C.O.s grinned at me from the other side of the street; I gave them a little wave of the hand and plunged away in the crowd.

The rest of the trip was quite pleasant. I made up a story for myself: 'All the men about me were prisoners, my prisoners — I was their camp commander and I pretended not to see them so that the poor wretches shouldn't have to salute all the time.' Thus grave and detached I wandered at last up to the hospital building. It stood on a low cliff overlooking the sea, the compound was full of tents nearly to the cliff edge. I walked up and down the beach, apparently wrapped in contemplation of a very picturesque sunset, but casting an eye now and then at the red rocks above me. I soon found what I was looking for: in three different places easy chimneys led down to the beach: the wire on top was perfunctory. The camp must have been designed in a hurry and it had obviously been assumed that the cliff was unscalable.

The sun dipped into the sea behind Ras bu 'Aza. I waited a little longer, then, in the gathering dusk, I made my way once more along Derna's main street, a happy man. I had done what I had set out to do and I was now quietly going home, looking back on the day's work. The tremulous plunge I had taken three hours earlier really belonged to my distant youth, when my apprenticeship had been served, and I had now become a master of my craft. My former fears appeared to me pathetically immature; in fact I saw now that I had nothing to fear at all: for, supposing I was recognized and apprehended, I would only be taken to one of *my* camps (for my captors would assume I was just an escaped prisoner) and all I would have then to do would be to apply to myself one of my own escape plans and get away the next night.

Thus I built up a newly-found courage. The apprehension of personal danger can easily be mastered once the lesson has been learnt that nothing worse than death can be expected — and the prospect of death, though it can be a bother, is not particularly terrifying to most

174

of us. Thus the stage is reached where danger loses its awesome horror, and it becomes easy to overcome the urge to run away. Each time a man has *not run away* he becomes less liable to be afraid in the future: he can now enter a bout of fear and come out again without surrender; fear is no worse than a fit of the colic — damned unpleasant while it lasts but the easier to withstand the less fuss is made. But if a man run away but once he may never recover his nerve.

Some men of course are too stupid and unimaginative even to experience fear at all — many such heroes find their way into the army — and there are also others, who enjoy wallowing in terror: for them there is no remedy but to send them home.

There is another fear, the fear of failure, which to me is a much more formidable enemy. Insidious, it takes the shape of an irrational conviction that if I were to fail in one enterprise I could never be successful again in any other: that is why I have to take infinite trouble in the preparation of each of my undertakings, and why, once engaged and things going wrong, I can hardly bring myself to listen to reason and pull out in time.

This day in Derna however had been a success all round, and I made for home with a light heart. Passing German Headquarters I caught sight of 'Ali, who, it seemed, had been shadowing me most of the time; after I had given him a discreet sign of recognition he walked on ahead and led me into a dark, narrow lane; a moment later an urgent whisper called me under an obscure archway. 'Ali with his friends were there with the old donkey: I mounted, a jerd was thrown over me and without more ado we rode away. My fate, for the time being, was out of my hands, and as I jogged along I composed in my mind the instructions I wanted to write for the prisoners in the cages.

On top of the escarpment I was taken to the tent of one of 'Ali's friends, where I found all a bustle for my reception. Two smiling girls, whose firm, high breasts showed through their wide sleeves when they lifted an arm, hurried with friendly laughter in and out of the tent, with rugs and cushions, soap and water, and then a long drink of leben. We were all happy and talkative, slightly excited and happy to be together: I have never had a friendlier, merrier homecoming. To be sure, having slept no more than six hours in the last four days, I was a little drowsy, but it didn't matter: I enjoyed the party and the pleasant prospect of a long night was ahead of me. The solicitude of my friends went to my heart: they had had an anxious time watching my movements from afar, and now, happy with relief, they wanted to show, with their homely celebration, how glad they were of my safe return. With the exception of Omar, who was an Obeidi, all the others were of the Barasi tribe: none of them had I met before our meeting at El Ftaiah, the day before. These Barasi gave more freedom to their womenfolk than any Arabs I have known, which may account for their lively cheerfulness, remarkable even amongst the sociable Senussis. The Egyptians, on the other hand, who live entirely apart from their women, are very glum and would not deign to lower themselves by laughter.

I fell asleep on my bench, expecting to sleep late next morning, but I was woken up two hours before dawn to be taken away as some suspicious characters had been seen lurking about. The two daughters of my host came to shake hands, an unusual courtesy amongst the Arabs with whom leave-taking is the occasion of only the shortest, shame-faced compliments. One hour's walk took us to another tent in a hollow of the escarpment plateau, and here I was left alone to sleep out the remainder of the night. When I woke I found 'Ali waiting for me with paper and envelopes which I had asked him to buy in Derna, and I set about writing out five copies of instructions for each of the two camps. I wrote to the prisoners that they had friends outside the camps who were ready to help any of them who attempted to escape; I suggested places, means and times for crossing the wire and indicated a route to follow when clear of the camp. I added a rough sketch of the camps and a hand-drawn map of Derna and the area inland as far as the escarpment to each copy of the instruction. My plan was that the escapers should get out of the camps early on a dark night (the easiest part of the undertaking) and find their own way to the escarpment, trying to make for one of the wild gullies that I indicated on the map. There they would be met by my Arab helpers, into whose hands they were to put themselves entirely. The Arabs would collect them in suitable spots, feed them, and eventually bring them to my camp, somewhere in the neighbourhood. I ended with a recommendation to wear the strongest footwear they could lay their hands on. I had seen too many escapers attempting a three hundred mile walk in dilapidated gym shoes. As a token of bona fides I enclosed in each envelope one Springbok (South African) cigarette.

I couldn't give them more details as the documents could easily fall into the wrong hands, and I wanted to compromise my Arabs as little as possible. While I gave the escapers the impression that my camp was quite near (they all assumed eventually that it was just on top of the escarpment) I told 'Ali that I would be found in the lower reaches of one of the wadis: Saratel, Ramla, El Fej or Belwetat, roughly in an area extending from Amur el Jill to Zumlet en Nawamis, some forty-five miles from Derna. To deliver my messages to the prisoners I counted on the fact that the Italians in charge authorized a few local Arab boys to enter the camps with eggs they sold to the prisoners. 'Ali had a few friends amongst the petty tribesmen and undertook to bring them up for my inspection and to receive my instructions. As writing the instructions and drawing sketches and maps would take me a whole day, before setting to work I settled with 'Ali and his friends the other major points of our scheme: numbers which would be needed for the screen of men waiting for the escapers at the foot of the escarpment and the provision of food. He then left me to my labours.

When I had finished I took a clean sheet of paper, sharpened my pencil and wrote out the following document:

To: Generale Piatti, Commando Superiore, Barce.
From: O.C. British Advanced Headquarters in Cyrenaica, Libya.

It has been brought to the notice of this H.Q. that a certain number of Senussi Arabs resident within the area of my command have been apprehended by your orders and put to death without trial. The only crime of these men is that, following the dictates of humanity, they have given, at various times, asylum to unarmed members of H.M. Forces who have escaped from prisoner-of-war camps. The execution without trial of the above-mentioned Senussi Arabs no less than the

M   177

cowardly and barbarous method employed in carrying it out are in direct contravention of international law and the usages of war as recognized by civilized nations. This H.Q. has forwarded to H.M. Government the names of the Senussi Arabs thus tortured to death by your orders, together with the particulars, dates and places of their execution. H.M. Government will take every step in their power, as well during the present hostilities as after the conclusion of the war, to bring to judgment any person responsible for the commission of such crimes. In the meanwhile, so as to ensure that such acts of barbarity shall not recur, I have ordered my commanders in the field to take measures of retaliation in the eventuality of any new executions of Senussi Arabs coming to their knowledge. These measures of retaliation will consist in the shooting of one officer of the Royal Italian Army for every Senussi Arab executed. These Italian officers will be selected amongst the members of your staff. The shooting of the a/m Italian officers will be carried out by members of H.M. Forces operating in Cyrenaica.

POPSKI, Major
O.C. B. Ad. H.Q. C.

August 7th, 1942.

Appendix (A) — Nominal roll of Senussi Arabs executed from January 21st, 1942, to August 1st, 1942 inclusive.

Appendix (A) included the names of several of my local helpers who had fallen into Italian hands when the fall of Tobruq and our retreat to the Egyptian border had given heart to the Italian bullies who administered Cyrenaica. The method they employed to put to death Arabs suspected of giving help to the British was to hang them by a steel hook inserted in the jaw and leave them to die of shock.

This letter was eventually slipped into the mail box at German H.Q. by an Arab sweeper. I received no acknowledgment from General Piatti but, coincidence or otherwise, until I left Cyrenaica I heard of no more executions.

My hosts for the day were an unusual couple: I sat down to dinner with the man *and his wife* (the only time such a thing happened to me in all my experience of Arabs), and I discovered that even Arab husbands are liable to be henpecked when my host spilled melted butter on a straw mat covering the tent floor and his wife raised a hullabaloo. He was made to rush out for a pot of boiling water and lift and sponge the mat before we resumed our meal.

I moved that night to a cave in a wooded hillside overlooking the sea and I worked there the whole of next day with 'Ali. Two egg merchants were produced (one for each camp) and briefed. I advised them to give my messages to N.C.O.s rather than to privates and to make sure that the recipients were quick-witted. The lads (they were no more than twelve years old and pretty sharp) eventually acquitted themselves of their task with great success.

I then interviewed the men whose job would be to intercept the fugitives on their way to the hills. They were to be careful not to alarm the prisoners by springing suddenly on them in the dark, but shadow them for a while, then send *one* man alone to make contact. I gave them each a document stating that they were in my employ and I left money with 'Ali to reward them according to their deserts.

I moved again that evening, to one of 'Ali's stone houses in the upper reaches of Wadi Derna, above the waterfall, where we ate a farewell dinner for about twenty guests. There was an alarm when a neighbour (of dubious allegiance) came to inquire what the fun was about, and I was bundled indecorously behind a sofa. But the unwelcome guest stayed only a short while and we resumed our mirth. It was remarkable how merry we all were, surrounded by enemies and with the threat over my hosts' heads of finding themselves the next morning hanging from the gallows with a steel hook through the jaw. I of course ran a considerably lighter risk.

I was relieved to depart about eleven o'clock that night, for I felt my presence amongst them added unnecessary danger to the already precarious position of my hosts, and there was nothing more I could do to further my plans. In fact, not only did they take the larger share of risks, but they did all the work, and the credit for our final success, such as it was, should go to them. Birdybird and the camel, which I hadn't seen for four days, materialized at 'Ali's back door; we took our leave, Omar and I, and rode off in the night. We crossed the Martuba bypass before dawn, pushed on right through the following day, and arrived on the site where I had left my camp in Wadi Saratel in the early afternoon.

The camp was gone. In case somebody was laying in wait for us we rode straight on, without stopping, pretending we had no local interest whatever, then took a wide circuit out of the wadi, found the neighbourhood deserted, rode back to the spot where the camp had been and dismounted to investigate. Everything had been tidied up — not a match stick had been left lying. Omar was puzzled by the tracks of two camels that he couldn't account for but I decided they were those of Chapman's mount and his Libyan's.

Omar wanted to follow the tracks which moved westwards; I knew however that if Chapman had been in charge of the move we should find the tracks doubling and redoubling on themselves in a knotted intricacy (for he was very cunning); so, to save time, I decided to call on Mukhtar as he would know where my party had moved to. Mukhtar, however, had also moved house and we had to ride nearly up to Bir Belater before we found an Arab who could tell us that Chapman had come back from Dursaland two days before with a party of refugees and had thought it wise to move camp to Wadi el Fej somewhere north of Amur el Fej. We set out immediately on the fifteen mile ride, watered our animals at Bir Semander in Wadi Ramla, lay down and slept till dawn in Wadi el Fej, picked up Chapman's tracks, and rode into his camp half an hour later.

I slept most of the next three days. On the evening of the fifth day after my return from Derna an Obeidi, whose tents were a few miles away, walked up to me and, after greetings, said: 'They have arrived.' I called for Chapman and we rode over together to find fifteen or twenty men lying in the sand round a fire: the first batch of escaped prisoners. They were so exhausted that we couldn't find one who would take an interest in us, which rather hurt my feelings! Their indefatigable Arab guides had made them walk forty-five miles with only one break of an hour. They had never been trained to such feats of endurance, for the last six weeks they had sat inactive and underfed in prisoner-of-war camps, and furthermore, when they had started, they had been given to understand that their destination was 'Quite near'. Their guides, on the other hand, quite fit and wonderfully pleased with themselves, were looking forward to a fat reward (which they got).

We gave our new friends leben and tea — they were too tired to eat — and we left them where they were, to sleep it out till morning, when, footsore and stiff, they hobbled over to our camp.

Our new recruits were mostly South Africans with a few men from England. When they recovered, after two or three days, they forgave us what they had considered a deplorable practical joke. They turned out to be a cheerful lot, extremely resourceful and quite capable of looking after themselves. One of them, a Londoner, had not come from the cage at all. He had been wounded in the knee during our withdrawal six months previously: unable to keep up with his companions he had been picked up by an Arab, who had taken him to his house in Wadi Derna. His wound had been tended with dressings bought by his host, and had finally got well. As soon as he could be moved he had been carried to another house, then to a cave, then to another house and so on, never staying more than three or four days in the same spot. On the food provided by his hosts, far in excess of their own meagre rations, he had grown fat, and they had provided him every single day with a ration of seven cigarettes bought from Italian and German soldiers. Knowing the scarcity of cigarettes in the Jebel at that time, this last touch seemed to me to belong to a fairy tale: but the lad, who was of a methodical disposition, had kept a diary in which he had entered day by day every item received from his kind hosts (with some idea at the back of his mind of repaying them some day), and sure enough the entry 'Cigarettes, 7' appeared regularly.

We had now the responsibility of a growing family. The first lot of escaped prisoners was followed by others, Chapman had brought some Dursa refugees with him from his trip, and other Arabs came in, all of whom had to be fed and looked after till they could be evacuated to Egypt. Feeding was our greatest problem: having collected all my dumps I still had a sufficiency of flour but everything else was running very short: our meals were frugal and had to be very carefully planned. I bought a few kids and sheep from my neighbours (who were very short themselves) and I sent to Derna for fruit, fresh vegetables and German and Italian Army cigarettes. We never went really hungry but I had to give so much thought to food, with my party growing every day, that months later I still woke up in the night turning over supply problems in my mind.

I was running out of money also. I sold all our animals with the exception of Birdybird and two camels, then I issued I.O.U.s. When I was finally relieved I owed over half a million lire — mostly for salaries and my debts were all settled in one fantastic orgy of paying out.

Chapman and I had early made a wise arrangement: we lived separately — he under his tree, I under mine, two or three hundred yards away. Thus we never got irritated with one another. Every two or three days his Libyan soldier would come over and say ceremoniously: 'Will the major please come and dine with the major tonight at seven?' and I returned the compliment. At these meals we produced little tit-bits carefully saved: half a bar of chocolate, a small tin of dressed crab, half a dozen fresh grapes from Derna. Once we crowned a standard meal of bread and bully with two small raw onions, a treat indeed.

The various groups in our party were all camped separately: we had the South African camp, the wireless operators', the Dursa, the Barasi, the Obeidat, all dotted along the wadi. We lived peacefully.

The last of our charging sets for the wireless batteries broke down. We heard the B.B.C. news one night announcing the fall of Mersa Matruh, then no more. The last message we had received was from Cairo: it was so garbled that after three days working on the cipher all we could bring out was one sentence: 'God bless you' — which didn't sound too optimistic. (We discovered later, back in Egypt, that this message was only a reply, composed by some emotional idiot, to our news of the arrival of the first batch of escaped P.O.W.s.)

We were now quite cut off, and we decided with Chapman that the time had come to make arrangements for the future. Assuming Egypt to have fallen, we had two possibilities: either to go in hiding, perhaps for years, in the country of the Dursa — not promising, as Chapman had discovered on his last trip — or to make our way to Kufra, an oasis four hundred and twenty miles to the south from where we could reach the Sudan, which we hoped would still be in British hands. We resolved to attempt the trip if L.R.D.G. failed to relieve us at the appointed time. The journey, avoiding the regular caravan route which started from Jalo, now in Italian hands, would involve a stage of twelve days camel riding without water. I got in touch with old Musa, my friend of Baltet ez Zala'q, who undertook to start training camels for this long waterless trip. In two months' time they would be ready, but he thought we should postpone our departure till the coolness of the winter.

Two of the South Africans, mechanically minded, undertook to improvise a charging set and get our wireless to function once more. The petrol engine part of one set was still in good order; it was the dynamo which was irretrievably burnt out. Someone of us knew of a broken-down Italian motor-cycle lying abandoned somewhere on the Kharmusa-Mekhili track. We sent a party out to find it: after four days they returned with a small dynamo off the motor cycle, apparently in working order. The South Africans now built a wooden frame and contrived somehow to clamp on to it the petrol engine from our charging set and the Italian dynamo. The two had now to be connected by a belt cut out of leather straps which had also been collected from abandoned Italian equipment. One morning at last I heard the chug-chug of the engine and I walked over to where the South Africans were laughing over this success. The dynamo was running, and, what is more, giving the required voltage: it had been a gamble, for we had no idea at what speed it was meant to run. There was, however, a snag: the dynamo, built to be belt driven, was fitted with a pulley but the engine wasn't, and the belt had to be run off the coupling: to keep the belt on it had to be held between two guiding rods, and the friction wore the soft leather across in little more than five minutes. Our engineers were not to be beaten: they cut dozens of belts ready for use and fitted on a new one as the old one wore out. It remained, however, a slow process because each new belt had to be sewn on: they considered themselves very successful when the dynamo ran fifteen minutes in the hour. They stuck to it day and night and on the third day our exhausted batteries began to revive, but we dared not switch on the wireless yet. At this stage our engineers' labours were interrupted.

CHAPTER IX

HIDE AND SEEK

SHEIKH 'ALI BU HAMED came riding down our wadi, stopped his mare opposite the tree under which I was sitting, alighted and put his arms round me. I hadn't seen him since the sheikhs' conference at Kaf el Qsur — a lifetime ago it seemed. In view of his cautiousness, he was the last man I expected to visit me (by daylight too) at a time when all hope of a prompt liberation of Cyrenaica had vanished.

He came directly to the point: ' 'Abdel Aziz bu Yunes, Sheikh 'Abdel Qader bu Bridan's nephew, whom you have long since ceased to employ (and for very sound reasons, as I well know) has been mortally vexed by the withdrawal of your confidence. In his anger the fool decided some time back to turn basas — informer; he wrote to General Piatti, then went to see him insistently several times with the information that British officers with a wireless set were operating in the Jebel. Piatti laughed at him and dismissed him with hard words. The general was well informed of what was going on within his command: the English were *all* back in Egypt — in fact they would very shortly be pushed out of Egypt — and he did not approve of petty sheikhs wasting his time with cock-and-bull stories. These sheikhs had better mind their own business. So 'Abdel Aziz went home with more anger than ever in his heart.

'Then, ten days ago, I don't know why, Piatti sent for 'Abdel Aziz and asked him if he knew where the British officers were. "Yes," said 'Abdel Aziz, "in the Wadi Ramla."

'General Piatti,' said 'Ali bu Hamed, 'then called for me and for Sheikh 'Abdel Jelil bu Tayeb, my kinsman, and other sheikhs of the Obeidat, and told us that this 'Abdel Aziz bu Yunes knew of English officers in Wadi Ramla. We all swore that there was not a single British officer at large in the whole of the Jebel. In the past one or two may have come in and run out again, when the English lines were at Gazala, but, long since, we hadn't even heard rumours of any such things happening. Piatti said it was our business to know, not to peddle rumours, and he was determined to clear up the matter once and for all. So he is sending a motor patrol to comb your district, looking for you. Myself and 'Abdel Jelil and 'Abdel Aziz will be travelling with it, and we all leave from Mekhili tomorrow noon. If you are found, 'Abdel Jelil and I both hang — if not, something unpleasant might happen to 'Abdel Aziz.'

'God bless you,' I said. 'Let it be 'Abdel Aziz. Where shall we move to now?'

We decided on the next hide-out. 'Ali bu Hamed promised to send me a runner every night with the news of the Italian patrol, and took his leave. We loaded our few belongings, obliterated our tracks and walked away. We had a watch of two Arabs stationed at Zumlet en Nawamis a conspicuous hillock which was our rendezvous with L.R.D.G. We sent them word to tell the L.R.D.G. patrol, if they turned up, to keep clear till the alarm had blown over.

During the next five days we played at hide and seek with the Italian patrol. Every night, as arranged, a runner arrived and told us what route was intended for the morrow, and we shifted accordingly. The dice were loaded in our favour to be sure, but it was still a sporting event: the Italians drove in trucks, whereas the fifty-odd of us walked, leaving a conspicuous trail, restricted in our roaming by the need to keep within a night's ride of one of the only four live wells available, as we couldn't carry more than one day's supply of water. The Italians, assuming in their innocence that we would be hiding in one of the main wadis where bushes and caves could give us a certain amount of cover, stuck to these watercourses; but we took to the open high plateau between the wadis. A gently undulating surface of stones and gravel, sparsely dotted with scrub, provided no hiding places and our camps were visible for miles. As the plateau was quite accessible to motor traffic, the Italians could have driven out of the wadis, if they had chosen: in which case they would have stood a good chance of making a catch. Through a combination of good management on the part of our Arab friends, who acted in fact as guides to the motor patrol, and of the ineptitude of the Italians, we succeeded in eluding their inquisitiveness, though on the third day they drove so near to us that we heard the roar of their engines down in the wadi. On the fifth night Sheikh 'Ali bu Hamed signalled that Wadi Ramla had been declared clear of enemy by the Italians, who were now moving further west, and he advised me to move into it. We found a deeply encased bushy stretch of the wadi, where we made ourselves comfortable in the shade, rested our poor feet, and got the South African engineers to resume their work on the wireless batteries.

The Italian patrol went home. 'Abdel Aziz bu Yunes tried to take refuge with them, but General Piatti ordered him back to his tents, and 'Ali bu Hamed saw to it that the order was carried out. A month later he was found with his throat cut, a suitable death for a 'basas'.

On the third morning of our repose, as the sergeant was reporting that he was about to test the wireless set with the revived battery, one of our Arabs who had been keeping a look-out from the top of a hill came in with the news that he had heard a noise as of vehicles in a south-easterly direction; a little later another man reported having just seen unidentified trucks winding up our wadi, about two miles off. I sent word all along the line to get under cover and walked over to Chapman's bower, where he lived inside a particularly thick and high bush. I found him shaving and told him the news. He looked at the unaccustomed tommy gun in my hands and said, completely unmoved:

'Is there anything we can do?'

I thought of the fifty unarmed men in our care. 'Nothing at all.'

'Right,' said Chapman. 'I go on shaving,' and smiled through the lather.

I laid down my weapon and seated myself at the entrance to Chapman's bower. Our men had all taken cover and hardly breathed: but enough fresh litter lay about to open the eyes even of the most town-bred Italian. I could hear now approaching trucks grinding in low gear through heavy sand. When, through the branches, I saw the first one come slowly round the bend in the wadi — suddenly quite close — I got up and stepped forward to stop it: if there was to be a surrender, let it be decorous and orderly, with no winkling out of reluctant bodies and no shooting. As the truck drew nearer I recognized it: a thirty-hundred-weight Chevrolet carrying five bearded men, familiar, grinning L.R.D.G. faces. It pulled up and Hunter jumped down; I shook his hand, pretending I had known all the time who was coming. Chapman came out of his bower when he had finished shaving.

Hunter and his seven trucks were two days early: alarmed by our silence on the wireless he had thought we might be in trouble and had hastened to the rendezvous at Zumlet en Nawamis, where he had found our two Arabs who guided him to our camp.

The news Hunter brought was good: the enemy had been stopped, exhausted, at El Alamein, our flap had died out and an offensive spirit had spread amongst our troops since the arrival of a new commander of Eighth Army. Many plans were afoot, of which he knew only that the L.R.D.G. would be involved, and that somebody had said that, if he was still alive and free, Popski would be required for one of the operations.

Cheered by the prospect I dismissed from my mind any inclination to let Hunter go back to Egypt without me, and gladly renounced the throne of the Jebel. My Senussi subjects were not, I think, sorry to see me go, and looked forward to a pause in the constant anxiety which our safety had lately been to them. I assured them that their country would be liberated, and that I would be back before the winter; strangely enough, they believed me and, stranger still, it turned out as I said.

Before I went however I wanted to tie up loose ends and leave everything in good order. We called in those of our creditors that could be reached in time, appointed representatives for the others and, with funds brought by Hunter, paid out all our debts. Birdybird, my white mare, I sent to 'Ali bu Hamed, my dearest friend amongst the Senussis, to whose secret and powerful support I really owed what success I had had.

An old Dursa sheikh, Chapman's protégé, being a scholar, was appointed head clerk and chief accountant. We worked with him for thirty-six hours, at the accounts first, then writing testimonials and instructions. I left a little food, and fixed another rendezvous in case more prisoners were got out of the cages.

On the second evening we all piled on to Hunter's trucks and drove off towards Siwa. On the way, however, we were instructed to go to Kufra instead, as Siwa was being evacuated by our troops; so we called at Hatiet el Etla, a patch of scrub and bushes north-west of Jaghbub, where the L.R.D.G. had a secret dump. We filled up with petrol and food and drove off across the sand sea on the four hundred mile trip to Kufra.

I remember little of that trip: I had been for over five months continuously behind the enemy lines, and my mind was affected by 'Jebel fever'. The problems and the responsibilities of the last months kept buzzing round in my head — nothing else in the world mattered to me. I spent an impatient day in Kufra, then boarded a plane for the six hundred and seventy mile flight to Cairo. I landed at Almaza in the evening, got a taxi and reported directly to Headquarters Middle East, leaving my kit at the gate. I was hurt to find that everyone had gone home at eight o'clock without waiting for me, and the duty officer, though courteous and kind, didn't think my business urgent enough to justify ringing up his brigadier at the Turf Club. Indeed he urged me to go home and have a bath and a drink and a good night's rest, and come back the next morning. I gave in, feeling confusedly that by my weakness I was compromising the whole issue of the war.

PART THREE

JAKE EASONSMITH

CHAPTER I

DRAKE AND MORGAN

THE next day I received a lesson in humility. The fancy headquarters who were supposed to be responsible for me had been
completely renewed since I had visited them six months
previously. Furthermore, during the flap, they had moved to Palestine, then back to Cairo, mislaying their records in the process. As a
result, when I called, nobody knew me, nobody had even heard of me,
nor was anybody interested in me in the least. I thought they resented
my existence altogether. However, I was asked to report again in a
day or two, while a search was made in a great pile of files lying in the
cellar. When I came back a smug major told me with venomous satisfaction that the question was now quite clear: my unit, the Libyan
Commando, had been disbanded months ago, and consequently he
was in no manner responsible for me any longer. Who was then? He
didn't know. I launched forth in my best style of invective, referred to
shifty little sissies sitting on their backsides in dim Cairo offices, put
in doubt his ancestry, his integrity, his sobriety and his sanity, threatened
him with the Army Council, Mr. Churchill and the King, and finally,
more reasonably, with his commanding officer. His colonel in the
meanwhile had come into the room attracted by the noise, a good-look-
ing man with a meaningless face and exquisite manners, who seemed
to be amused by my invectives and the dismay of the unpleasant
major. He took me to walk up and down a little garden at the back
of the house:

'I wouldn't worry Micky,' he said. 'You won't get anything out of
him. Nor out of me either. Administration is not our strong suit.
Have you seen your King lately?'

'I beg your pardon?'

'I was at school with him, you know. A fine fellow, wouldn't have
thought he was Belgian. Not too bright — his brother Charles has all

the brains — but a good horseman. Archie thinks there is a certain physical likeness between him and me. I wouldn't say so, would you?'

'Certainly not.' I replied. Then, trying to bring him to the point, I asked: 'What branch of Middle East H.Q. do you come under?'

'It's a bit obscure, I'm afraid. There has been a certain amount of reorganization lately. He always goes to stay with my mother, if only for a day, whenever he comes over to England. Well, it has been nice to meet you. The best of luck to you.'

An orphan, unacknowledged and unwanted, I left the dynasto-maniac and wandered about Middle East Headquarters in search of a sponsor. I finally drifted into a newly-formed branch which, I was told, co-ordinated all military activities behind the enemy lines. Shan Hackett, a very young colonel, was in command, a witty, active, short cavalryman, who had heard of me and greeted me as a friend. I was too stupidly embittered to respond to his bantering: instead I poured out my grievances:

'Five months on operations . . . back to Cairo to find my unit disbanded, myself without a posting and my pay stopped for the last four months.'

Shan Hackett moved his short legs, sat back in his chair and burst out laughing.

'Now Popski, for your private reasons you fade out into the desert. You go and fight a private war with your private army for your private convenience, taking orders from no one, and when you choose to come back you expect H.M. Government to pay you for your fun!' My surly self-righteousness dissolved, the last fumes of Jebel fever blew away, and I was ready once more to behave sensibly.

Shan Hackett was a man after my own heart; he set things going with a touch of light fantasy and treated nobody too seriously: an attitude which, in my heavy-footed earnestness, I ever vainly tried to achieve. He suggested I should take part in one of the raids that were being planned at the moment. Then on my return he thought I should raise a force of my own to operate on the lines developed by me in a report I had sent back from the Jebel some time ago. I was surprised that he should have read it.

I was introduced to a turmoil of planning activity. In that late August of 1942 Rommel was expected to attack Eighth Army at El Alamein; the operations I was getting involved in aimed at interfering with his line of communication from Benghazi to Tobruq and upset his supplies at the time of the battle. My sense of propriety was shocked at the light-hearted manner in which the problems were tackled: ten per cent planning, ninety per cent wishful thinking. I had become rather a prig in military matters and I fancied myself as an expert; moreover I was a passionate champion of the L.R.D.G. and I would not consider any other unit had a right at all to operate in the desert — our desert.

The rooms occupied by M O 4 in Middle East H.Q. were not lacking in boyish enthusiasm: very young men developed mad schemes to make an end of Rommel and the Afrika Korps; with a few hundred men, armed, it seemed to me, with little more than pea-shooters, they were going to capture the whole of Cyrenaica from Benghazi to Tobruq and leave the enemy troops on the El Alamein line without a base in their rear — to die of fright, I presume. John Haselden, who was my age and should have known better, showed a more youthful spirit than anyone. His scheme was to drive into Tobruq with eighty men (mainly commandos) pretending to be British prisoners-of-war, carrying tommy guns hidden under their great coats. Their three trucks would be driven by German Jews in German uniforms, pretending to be German soldiers escorting the prisoners, who would have no difficulty in getting past unsuspicious road guards. They were to proceed at dusk to the port area and capture the coastal batteries. At dawn the next morning the Royal Navy was to land troops from two destroyers and several M.T.B.s, seize and hold the port, liberate four thousand of our prisoners. What was to happen later was obscure.

Haselden wanted me to join this party: discussing the plan with him I discovered that he relied for ammunition and supplies on what he would find in Tobruq.

'Don't be a fool,' he said, 'there will be no difficulty. Tobruq is full of everything.'

I decided to keep away from Haselden's party and told him I would rather go to Derna, as I knew the country so much better. The projected raid on Derna, which was to be an L.R.D.G. responsibility, was dropped and I got myself transferred to the Barce raid, also with my friends. I shall tell more of it in a moment. Other raids planned for the same night of September 13th, 1942, were: L.R.D.G. on Benina airdrome, the Sudan Defence Force on Jalo, and Stirling with the S.A.S. (Special Air Service) on Benghazi, another ambitious scheme. Benghazi was to be surprised with about two hundred men, then sixteen thousand prisoners were to be let out of the cage, armed from enemy dumps, and the town and port held for a week, till a landing party brought over from Malta by the navy had taken over. I objected that to my certain knowledge there were no P.O.W. cages in Benghazi — all the camps were far to the south. All right then, they would be brought up from the south!

With the exception of the Barce raid all these schemes failed: Haselden's party ran into Tobruq and were all killed with the exception of two men, the navy lost two destroyers and several M.T.B.s, Stirling never entered Benghazi and retired with losses, Benina was not reached at all. And yet I can't say what success they might have had, if *surprise*, the one condition on which they all depended, had been achieved. The night of September 13th, 1942, might well have been a nightmare to the enemy if, out of the blue, his line of communication had been attacked by mysterious forces in five different places spread over two hundred and fifty miles. German and Italian Headquarters would have been flooded with conflicting messages, reporting a party of parachutists on Benina landing ground and an armoured division in Barce, and a certain amount of confusion might have resulted. As it was, unfortunately for us, our bright young men were far too excited to hold their tongues: when they were turned out of Middle East H.Q. in the evening they gathered in the bars and night clubs of Cairo to discuss again their childish plans: their friends joined in with suggestions picked from boyish books that they had pored over in earnest only a few years before, Drake and Sir Walter Raleigh, Morgan and the Buccaneers were outbidden, new stratagems poured out in a stream of inventiveness, while circles of admiring Levantines formed round the excited youths, and the barmen's ears visibly stretched while they mixed their drinks in feigned aloofness. Later at night lovely dark Syrian heads on crumpled pillows listened carefully to their blond bedfellows: military plans mingled with the raw pleadings of inexperienced passion. Early next morning the telephones in Gezirah and Qasr el Dubara buzzed with shrill Levantine voices exchanging notes in French, Italian and Greek, mixed with English military expressions and names of units. The Cairenes loved to impress their friends with a knowledge of our future operations, and wasted no time in spreading around any scrap of information they had managed to collect: amongst them, indistinguishable, just another bridge-playing Levantine, was the Italian agent, sitting pretty with an easy job indeed. No romantic disguises for him, no purloining of secret documents, no treacherous accomplices to be kept in order, no risks at all in fact, no expenses and no trouble: he just stayed at home and answered the telephone. A host of enthusiastic voluntary helpers, unwitting and unbidden, provided him with solid material for daily reports, which, enciphered, went on the air from a discreet wireless set in a villa off the Pyramid's Road.

How efficiently gossip and bedtime revelations could be translated into military intelligence was revealed to me a year later: at midnight on September 9th, 1943, having landed in Italy earlier in the evening, I called on the commander of an Italian division in Francavilla, half way between Taranto and Brindisi. While the general was being got out of bed I chatted over a bottle of whisky with one of his staff captains, a clever lad, who had held an 'Intelligence' appointment on the General Staff in Cyrenaica. He quoted from memory our order of battle for the five raids of September 13th, and said he had got all the information complete and sorted out as early as September 3rd or 4th, ten days before the attack. The only information he had not received concerned routes and timings of the parties moving up: this was an L.R.D.G. responsibility and they were trained to keep their own counsel.

CHAPTER II

BUFFALO BILL

WE started from the Fayum on our way to Barce with no knowledge of how thorough the indiscretions had been; although I had been much alarmed by the chatter and the confusion in Cairo, I hoped that our present party, being purely L.R.D.G., would have been spared the worst of publicity. My austere conception of warfare did not harmonize with fantastic planning; considering myself a professional soldier — on what grounds I don't know, for I had not yet fired a shot in earnest — I despised the amateur efforts of the young men who were shortly to pay heavily for their ill-informed enthusiasm. I was glad to be away from it all, on the move once more, after little over a week in Egypt. It didn't occur to me that I might have been in need of a longer rest after five months behind the enemy lines.

The expedition I was now on was really a holiday to me: my responsibilities were limited to providing local information when we arrived near Barce, and I was under the command of an officer whom I admired and loved. Jake Easonsmith, a wine merchant of Bristol, at the time I am writing about was a major commanding a squadron of L.R.D.G. Simple and upright, he had a directness that gave confidence to troubled minds. His deliberate speech, warmed by a slow smile, reflected an inner sureness, a perfect balance, and a mature considera-tion of life and death; it had, as no other man's, the power to put me at peace with the world and myself. If he ever had doubts, he never showed any: with him all was secure. Unflustered, undaunted, he raised our lives above strife into a limpid world of spiritual values where our duties were clear and pleasant. Under him we all did our best and worried not about the success; he led us without using any of the tricks of leadership, for it was a privilege to do his bidding, a means of joining him in a superior adventure as if he had some hidden knowledge which made worldly success of little moment, but gave immense value to our striving. What mattered was to follow him in his rectitude. He talked but little and never gossiped: his life was his own, and when he wasn't at work he followed his inner thoughts. I served him with a devotion which I have given to no other man.

We left the Fayum on September 2nd, 1943, with twenty-two vehicles in three patrols, New Zealand, Rhodesian and one of Guardsmen, bound for the Egyptian Sand Sea, a route of extreme difficulty which had been selected because no one in his senses would have expected us to take it.

We struck the sands at Ain Dalla, and for the next three hundred miles we coaxed our trucks and our jeeps across the loveliness of the great sand dunes. The long successive ranges of tangled sand hills, five hundred feet high or more from trough to crest, had bold, sharp curves and deep shadows on the soft slopes. Valleys of sand, sometimes three miles wide, ran roughly north and south between the ranges, completely lifeless but for, every two or three days, a rounded bush of vivid green, its fleshy leaves swollen with sap, fresh, shiny and alone. The wind-fashioned landscape recalled the beauty of mountain snows: the shapes were alike, and, as off an Alpine peak, blown plumes streamed from the tops of the dunes, but not a stone broke the purity of the sand, whereas in the mountains rocks stick up incongruous through the clean lines of swept snow. The upper ridges of the dunes were white with yellow depths – not the blue-white of snow; the lower slopes and the valley bottoms had colour: from butter yellow to pale purple, rippled or infinitely smooth, they stood out boldly in the morning, then dimmed to a common grey under the midday sun. From the higher dunes a wide tangle of ranges showed, razor-edged ridges, crescent-shaped circuses, nearly vertical slopes, drawn with acute precision. In Nature there is nothing tidier than blown sand.

Our route lay at right-angles to the successive ranges: up and down we drove our trucks, with much labour. The flat bottoms of the valleys were treacherous: sailing across a table-smooth plain I would feel my wheels go sluggish, and see the featureless sand drifting past me slow down and stop. Looking round I would find the other vehicles, dispersed right and left, also bogged. Alone in the distance Jake's little jeep crawled on. He had finer perceptions than most of us and could spot bad patches of sand where we could discern no difference. On the flat each truck would extricate itself by the unaided efforts of its own crew. With steel channels six feet long laid under the wheels, one man driving with care, the others pushing, a few yards at a time, the vehicle reached a firmer surface. Driving up the slopes and over the ridges called for infinitely more skill, and at times all the men available from the three patrols had to help in getting one vehicle at a time over a tricky stretch. Lines of steel channels were laid to make a kind of rail road: further ahead men waited with channels ready to be thrown under the wheels as soon as they were seen to start a spin in the sand. The art of channel throwing was difficult: the few who had mastered it were in constant demand.

Much depended on the selection of the route: on approaching a new range Jake Easonsmith drove ahead in his jeep and tried here and there till he found a route to the ridge. Hard slopes are generally steep, and moderate ones soft and boggy: it was a question of striking a happy mean. Moreover sand slopes moderate enough to be climbed by a loaded truck generally fall off nearly vertically on the far side of the ridge. Our method was to rush the slope and deliberately bog the truck on the top. A team waiting on the ridge would then manhandle it gently on to the downward slope: if you bogged too early you couldn't be pulled over, if too late you took a flying leap of forty or fifty feet. It was slow work and strenuous, but in no way heart-breaking because we knew the difficulties and did not expect quick progress. Nobody grumbled on a day when we covered only eight miles: we were I think well pleased with our skill in getting all our vehicles as far as we had over a very difficult range of dunes.

I was crossing the sands for the second time only, and I suspect that allowance was made by my companions for my comparative inexperience, and also for my age: I was nicknamed on the trip 'The Old Major' (as opposed to Easonsmith, 'The Young Major'). I think I was made to do less than my share of digging and shoving and carrying channels. I certainly was not exhausted at the end of the day and had enough vitality left to enjoy the pure splendour of this land.

The officer commanding the Guards patrol had not fallen under the spell of Easonsmith. One morning, as we were halted at the foot of a high dune, with the New Zealanders ahead under Nick Wilder breaking the trail, he said to me in a peevish mood:

'All this waiting doesn't make sense. Jake thinks he is the only man who knows the sands. I shall find my own route.'

Off he drove in his jeep, leading his patrol. Retribution came terribly quickly: half an hour later Very lights came over a dune two or three miles along the valley, signals of distress. He had rushed up an unreconnoitred slope and reaching the razor-back top with speed to spare had dashed down the opposite slope, his overturned jeep rolling over him and his gunner. The officer suffered from a squeezed skull, the gunner had a spinal lesion and was paralysed from the waist downwards. He died many months later in hospital. The officer recovered without much damage; his face longer and narrower than ever. Jake said nothing and waited for the medical officer we were carrying on this trip to attend to the casualties and make his report. He then made arrangements by wireless for the two men to be evacuated by air from Big Cairn.

Big Cairn, six feet high, was built by a very early L.R.D.G. patrol on the west side of the Egyptian Sand Sea in a featureless plain. It was a regular landmark for L.R.D.G. patrols, and on this occasion a dump of petrol, water and rations had been laid for our use, from Kufra. From Kufra also, two hundred and fifty miles to the south-west, came a plane for our casualties. The first time it missed Big Cairn, but made it the second day, and we proceeded on our way with only a few hours to spare if we wanted to be outside Barce on September 13th.

On the twelfth, having had no further delays, we were driving westwards along the southern foothills of the Jebel Akhdar somewhere south of Marawa, when we came across fresh tank tracks. I assured Jake Easonsmith that there had certainly been no enemy tanks in this area the last time my men visited it about a month earlier. Nor was there, in the normal course of things, any reason why the enemy should bring tanks into this backwater, five hundred and fifty miles from the front line. I said:

'The barman at the Cosmopolitan has been hearing news.'

Jake gave me a quizzical smile and said nothing. It seemed that we had wasted our trouble in taking the arduous route through the Sand Sea. The enemy had other sources of information.

The next morning, September 13th, Jake called a halt in a sparsely wooded wadi five miles from Benia and fifteen miles south-east of Barce. The Rhodesian patrol had left us the day before to join up with Stirling's party further west. They were to raid Benina airdrome. Our remaining fifteen vehicles were dispersed in the wadi and camouflaged.

Our original plan had been to arrive two days earlier: two Libyan Arabs whom I had brought with me were to walk into Barce, make contact with their fellow tribesmen, get the information about the enemy, and return to our camp before we went in to attack on the night of the thirteenth. Owing to the accident in the Sand Sea we had arrived much too late to carry out this programme. Our discovery of the presence of tanks made it now even more necessary than we had foreseen to get information of what was going on in Barce: Jake decided to drive my two Arabs as near Barce as he could reasonably go by daylight, drop them and come back to our camp. I instructed the Arabs to collect hurriedly what information they could and to meet me again at Sidi Selim, a sheikh's tomb about six miles from Barce, that afternoon at five o'clock. I gave them money — perhaps too much. The short time available hardly left them time to achieve anything useful; it was the best we could do.

I stayed in our leaguer and put out scouts with instructions to stop any Arabs seen wandering in our neighbourhood and bring them to me, with the double object of getting information and of preventing the news of our arrival from leaking out and reaching the Italians. By the early afternoon I had collected a dozen Arabs, who put up with their temporary confinement with good grace. One of them had been in Barce the day before and confirmed the recent arrival of a few tanks; he also had a rumour of twenty thousand troops collected in the big rest camp at El Abiar thirty miles to the west.

During the morning the two patrols had been lazily busy cleaning the guns and tidying the loads, then the men had gone to sleep in

200

[facing: JAKE EASONSMITH

the shade of their trucks. At three o'clock Easonsmith collected everybody under a tree and gave his orders.

The enemy, mainly Italians, had a landing ground on the outskirts of the small town of Barce, fifteen-odd miles away. On this landing ground they had aircraft. Headquarters were in the main street, in a hotel. The garrison, such as it was, lived in barracks outside the town on the road leading to El Abiar. There was a possibility of the enemy's disposing of several light tanks. They also had light A.A. defences.

We had two L.R.D.G. patrols. A British raiding force was on the outskirts of Benghazi, seventy miles to the south-west. The main British forces were at El Alamein, five hundred and fifty miles to the east.

His intention was to destroy the enemy aircraft on the landing ground at Barce on the coming night, and simultaneously to create a diversion by attacking the enemy headquarters and the garrison.

To this effect Popski would drive in a jeep to Sidi Selim, leaving at four o'clock. He would wait there for his Arabs to arrive. When they came he would sort out their information and have it ready for the main party when it arrived.

After a meal at six-fifteen, as night fell, the two patrols led by Easonsmith would drive off to Sidi Selim, arriving at seven. T patrol wireless truck would remain there and make contact on the air with Stirling's S.A.S. force outside Benghazi. Our medical officer, Dick Lawson, was to remain with that truck and wait for any casualties that we might bring back from Barce later during the night.

At nine the whole raiding party would leave Sidi Selim for Barce. On reaching the outskirts the New Zealand patrol would make for the landing ground, the Guards for the barracks, Popski with one Guards' truck would hold the road leading out of the town.

Rendezvous were fixed for stragglers.

When Jake had done, with maps and air-photos and a postcard I described the town and the buildings which I knew well. I hoped it would thus be easier for the parties to find their way in the dark. Barce has two Italian-built streets forming a T, with a square and the railway station where the two strokes meet. Off these two streets are a maze of alleys with small Arab stone and mud-brick hovels. We should come in along the left-hand top stroke of the T. Italian Headquarters were half way down the vertical stroke, the landing ground at the bottom of it. The right-hand top stroke led to the barracks.

At four o'clock, with the sun still high, I went off in my jeep with a driver. A quarter of a mile down our wadi we hit the Benia track and turned right: the country was hilly and wooded and the track followed a sinuous course. Rounding a corner, my driver said:

'Let them have it, Major.' Taken by surprise (for that was the kind of soldier I was then) I fumbled with the twin Vickers machine guns as I watched a motor-cycle come towards us ridden by two Italian officers. Before I was ready to fire they were passing us, and, instead of killing them, I waved and smiled and shouted a cheerful 'Ciao'. They replied and their cycle gave a wide lurch as they both turned their heads to look at their unrecognized friend. Then they passed out of sight round the bend. I had of course played the right move, but I thought I must pull myself together and be quicker on the trigger: the days of snooping and hiding in ditches were over. With two L.R.D.G. patrols at my back I felt I ought to open fire on a German armoured division — if I met one. I looked at my driver; he didn't seem to mind.

Further down the track, at Sidi Rawi, I saw on the right-hand side a rough shelter which looked like a road post; it was not manned, or the men were asleep inside. Just off the road I saw long low huts and I stopped a moment to watch; horses were being led to water by what I took to be Tripolitanian soldiers: it was all very sleepy and peaceful. I pushed on along the track through a shallow rocky gorge and arrived at Sidi Selim, a white sheikh's tomb just off the track. We parked the jeep and camouflaged it, then looked for my Arabs: I gave three times the hoot of the Buma, then again and again, but they had not yet arrived. Well concealed, we waited.

At dusk just after six o'clock, a plane flew low, coming from Barce and following the track. I wondered if it would catch our patrols on the move, but they hadn't started yet. They waited till complete darkness, which would be about forty minutes after sunset, about a quarter to seven. At half-past seven I heard a few shots in the distance. Then silence. We cut the telephone wires that ran on poles along the track to prevent the alarm being given in Barce, then, after waiting twenty minutes, we drove back along the track in the dark. I was nearing the last bend in the gorge before reaching the post at Sidi Rawi, when a hullaballoo broke out: tracer went flying over the hill and a rattle of several machine guns. We pulled the jeep off the road and up the bank as best we could to avoid misunderstandings when our trucks arrived: when I saw them coming round the bend, I signalled with a torch and was hailed by Jake. All was well and we went on together to Sidi Selim. At the post which I had found deserted Jake had been challenged by a Tripolitanian sentry called Hamed, whom he had promptly disarmed and captured. An Italian officer had turned up and been killed, then Jake had chased out the occupants of the huts and destroyed the telephones. I found out from Hamed that there was also a wireless set somewhere in the camp, but Jake had not seen it. Two trucks had collided at Sidi Rawi, and had to be abandoned, leaving us with thirteen vehicles.

I suggested to Jake Easonsmith that the presence of an Italian-Tripolitanian camp on our line of retreat called for a change of plan. I knew a track leading away from Barce from a turning on the El Abiar road, which would take us back to Benia, avoiding the Tripolitanians. He considered the plan but decided against altering his arrangements.

'A night operation must have a very simple plan. We may fall into some confusion in Barce; we shall be more likely to get our men out if they come back along a route they already know.' I know now that he was right in being more concerned about withdrawal than attack. After a night raid loss of control comes easy; try then getting your men together if they don't know the way to the meeting point!

We stayed at Sidi Selim in complete darkness till ten. I spent the time whistling like a wretched owl; no answer came to the call of the Buma, my Arabs never turned up and I don't know what happened to them.

At ten we drove off, Jake Easonsmith leading in a thirty-hundredweight, I second, then the remaining trucks and the jeeps of the Guards patrol, then the N.Z. patrol with four trucks and a jeep. The N.Z.

wireless truck with the doctor had been left near the tomb at Sidi Selim. Our route lay along the track coming from Jerdes el Abid which runs into the southern tarmac road from Derna to Barce on top of the escarpment six miles from Barce. In the darkness Jake ran off the track and we got involved in some difficult going. When he flashed on his headlights I had a vision of his truck crashing through a wooden gate into somebody's back garden, of a concrete one-storeyed house and of frightened silent people, Italian civilians, slipping out of a window on the ground floor. Then all was darkness again: we all drove over vegetable beds like stampeding cattle, followed Jake sharp left and back on to the track.

On the main road we turned on our lights, pretending we were an enemy convoy but feeling more like tourists in the unaccustomed glare. We wound down the escarpment; on the straight, in the plain, where the road runs on a low embankment, our lights picked out two light tanks with Italian markings, hull down, one on each side of the road. My heart gave a leap. Jake Easonsmith opened up with two guns: I saw his tracer bounce off the closed turrets. We did the same as we came within range: I expected to be blown up, for I fancied that the tanks' guns were swinging on to me, but they drifted past without giving a flash. A racket arose behind us as our trucks opened fire in turns, then silence: we drove on to Barce in the cool of the night.

When we stopped just outside the town only a few lights showed here and there, with the sleepy noises of a small town at midnight. Nick Wilder and his New Zealanders drove off towards the landing ground, avoiding the town, Sergeant Dennis took the Guards' trucks past the main square along the El Abiar road, Jake and his driver drove away in a jeep on a job of his own, I remained on the road with one thirty-hundredweight truck and five Guardsmen. They had got hold of a jar of rum and were already far gone; to my vexation they took no notice when I tried to stop their drinking. They drove their truck off the road and went on boozing, talking in hushed whispers. Their speech was rudimentary, propped up by an expletive every three or four words, such as: 'If a f— tank comes f— along the f— road; f— me if we can stop it with our f— guns.'

I stood on the road, expecting the tanks to come after us. There was a distant clatter of tracks, which came to nothing. Across the road, fifty yards away, a low hum came from a tall building. I walked over and peeped in at the door into a well-lit workshop: several Italians in overalls were at work on lathes; their faces were white, their talk in whispers; their hands were sluggish as if fighting an overpowering sleepiness. I returned to the road and sat down on a stone like an old man taking the cool of the evening on his doorstep.

A chatter of guns came from the far side of the town, a glow lit the sky, and suddenly the show started. Tracer flew, fires sprang up on the landing ground: the dispersed planes were being set alight one after the other, and, by the columns of red smoke that arose, I followed Nick Wilder's slow progress round the airfield. More distant bursts came from my left, where Sergeant Dennis had driven off, and, close at hand in the main street, I heard the small thuds of hand grenades. The lights snapped off in the workshop, the Guardsmen went on whispering in their foul gibberish. Elated, I made a note of the fires as they appeared on the airfield: I thought Nick Wilder would like to know how many planes he had set alight.

A vehicle approached from the main square, stopped, signalled with a torch and drove up. It was Jake, back from his games in the town; he had had a good time and chuckled contentedly, relieved of the burden of leadership. He was not sure he had spotted Headquarters, and he asked me to go back with him. We drove along the still deserted main street and pulled up outside the well-remembered 'hotel': H.Q. offices were on the ground floor and billets upstairs. We wanted to alarm the staff and make them look after their own skins instead of organizing a defence of the airfield, but we forgot a little our military purpose in a boyish enjoyment of a 'wild-western' stunt. We banged on the door; as nobody came we blew it open, went in and ran round till we found the signal office with a lonely signaller on duty at the telephone exchange. He went and sat down in a corner of the room while we put two hand grenades inside the standard: he beat a retreat with us, saluted on the doorstep and walked away down the street: having gone twenty yards he suddenly bolted. We then lobbed hand grenades through the first-floor windows and got a meagre reward of muffled shouts and dark shufflings. 'You would think a couple of hand grenades exploding under the bed would stir them up.' But neither the racket on the landing ground, nor our own efforts seemed to bring anybody out. Jake took me round to a little square behind the hotel where earlier he had found and damaged some parked trucks; we now set these on fire, and when the flames leaped up we went quietly to the far end of the long, straight main street and drove down again very noisily. We fired our machine guns into the houses, emptied our pistols into the doors and dropped hand grenades in our wake. On our second rush, nearing the main square, a small shell ruffled overhead, first response to our provocations. From the jeep parked in a dark alley, we peeped out and saw a tank lumber up from the El Abiar road and turn into the main street. This at last was what we had been working for, and with a little regret that our party should be over, we returned to our Guards' truck.

'Buffalo Bill,' I said. Jake nodded and gave a low laugh.

Just over half an hour after Nick Wilder had driven off I counted twenty-eight fires blazing on the landing ground, and there was apparently quite a battle on. The Italians had got a machine gun going on the roof of a hangar and a mortar thudded at intervals. At ten minutes to one I counted thirty-two blazes on the landing ground, and the streams of tracer thinned out.

On arriving at the landing ground Nick Wilder had opened an unguarded iron gate and driven his trucks through: his first target, as luck had it, was a petrol tanker, which went up in flames at once, and kindly lit up the scene. He then drove in single file from one parked plane to another as he discovered them, each truck in turn firing a few volleys as they went by. Their last truck carried incendiary bombs, one of which, if the plane was not yet on fire, was deposited by hand in the cockpit: the truck then caught up with the party. The landing ground was big and the planes widely dispersed: Nick led a leisurely procession round and round, meeting at first with no opposition. The Italians were in confusion, for, although they had been warned by their intelligence of our projected raid, they had not taken the threat seriously, and beyond posting perfunctorily on the road those two tanks we had fired at as we came in, had made no other arrangements to defend themselves. As I found out later, they had had too many scares passed on to them from Headquarters to bother much any longer.

After nearly an hour on the field, having dealt with all the planes he could find, Nick Wilder decided to return to the rendezvous, which was for one o'clock at the Guards' truck. There was now plenty of wild fire coming at him from heavy machine guns on top of a hangar, and also a mortar or two were flopping bombs here and there: neither men nor trucks had been hit. Driving out of the airfield gate he mistook the road somehow (I think he turned left when it should have been right) and a moment later he realized that instead of skirting the town by the way he had come, he was leading his line of trucks down the narrow main street of Barce; in his headlights he picked out three light tanks staggered across the street: the Headquarters defence which had been called up as the result of Jake's and my boyish pranks. The two rear tanks, in a grotesque eagerness to come forward both together, crashed into each other and went dead; the third one, dazzled by the headlights, started firing high. There was no room for the New Zealand trucks to turn round under fire, and they carried no weapon heavy enough to knock out the tank: they could thus neither withdraw nor fight it out with guns. Standing on the accelerator in the leading truck Nick Wilder gathered speed and deliberately rammed the tank head on. His thirty-hundredweight rose and crashed down on top of the tank turret, converting both vehicles into a mess of mangled metal; the New Zealand crew jumped down unhurt, and piled into the following trucks, Nick Wilder taking the lead in the gunner's seat of the jeep. The way was now clear right down to the station, from which fire was coming: down they charged, firing as they drove. At the station square roundabout, the driver of the jeep, blinded by the tracer Wilder was firing, hit the kerb and overturned the jeep. The driver was thrown out, but Nick Wilder, pinned under and soaked in petrol, passed out. The crew of the following thirty-hundredweight put the jeep back on its wheels, loaded poor Wilder — unconscious or dead — in the back, and a moment later I saw them arrive at the Guards' truck, in a jeep and two thirty-hundredweights. One truck had been wrecked on the tank and the other — the last in line — with Craw and a crew of four had been cut off and wasn't seen again.

As the petrol evaporated off him Nick Wilder recovered in a remarkably short time, and he told me his story in his usual clipped speech while we waited for Sergeant Dennis's Guards party to turn up. The New Zealanders sorted themselves out: one man, who had been wounded, suddenly collapsed and slid to the ground. As we stood in a bunch on the road round his body someone said:

'Poor Jimmy is dead.'

'The hell I'm dead,' said Jimmy's corpse. 'I was only resting,' and he scrambled to his feet, suddenly quite fit. We all laughed, feeling light and gay.

Dennis arrived a moment later, minus a truck and crew which had taken the wrong turning and got involved the next morning in a private battle, which was described to me five years later by an Italian eye-witness. I have given his account at the end of the next chapter.

Dennis had had a rowdy party in the barracks, driving round the huts, lobbing hand grenades and firing through the windows. He had been entirely successful in keeping the troops away from the main battle on the landing ground.

We had now done our job and we all drove back towards Sidi Selim where Lawson, the doctor, was waiting for us with the wireless truck. I thought the two tanks might still be watching for us in the dark, and rode rather gingerly till we reached the top of the escarpment having seen no enemy. Then we turned off the main road along the track leading to Sidi Selim, Jake Easonsmith pushing ahead to the wireless to exchange news with David Stirling's S.A.S. party in Benghazi. But the signallers had been vainly tapping their keys: we feared that things had gone wrong with our neighbours, as indeed they had.

While we waited in the dark at Sidi Selim for the tail of our party to arrive, Sergeant Dennis drove up at three o'clock with the news that the last Guards' truck had missed the track and turned over. 'They were drunk', I thought, 'and deserve what has befallen them.' I would have written them off, but Jake Easonsmith, quite unmoved by moral indignation, drove back with me to the scene of the mishap.

He knew, as well as I did, that if he chose to leave the careless crew to their fate and push on immediately with the rest of our party, we could in the remaining two hours of darkness be well away in the open desert to the south before the enemy got aircraft in the air (which would have to be called up from Benghazi to the ravaged airfield in Barce), and in the trackless expanses beyond the foothills planes would be hard put to discover our few remaining trucks. An hour's delay in getting started meant the difference between a sound withdrawal and probable disaster. Jake Easonsmith deliberately accepted the delay: alone I believe amongst us, he would not have been content to save his best men at the cost of abandoning a weak crew after it had got itself in trouble through its own incompetence. He had achieved against the enemy everything he had set out to do, but this success was far from enough for him: he would have considered his enterprise a failure if he had refused to give succour to the most inexperienced and most helpless of his men. His standards were not altogether of this world, and I acknowledged his greater rectitude with a certain humility.

We found the Guardsmen sitting sullenly by their overturned truck, amongst the litter which had spilled out. With a truck towing a rope passed over its belly the fallen lorry was hauled up to an upright position: it rocked back on to its wheels and settled on the road; equipment was piled in and back we drove to Sidi Selim, where we collected the main party and pushed on. The first grey light had already broken the deepness of the night when our column entered the rocky gorge near the Italian Tripolitanian camp at Sidi Rawi which Jake had shot up earlier in the night. As we approached the rocks I saw flashes on both sides of the road and heard the rattle of many machine guns: a few streamers of tracer converging, as it seemed, on to me made me duck in my seat (I was riding in a thirty-hundredweight with the driver on my right), but many more invisible bullets whined around me, which did not upset me at all. I was making a note in my mind of the psychological effect of tracer when I felt my left hand knocked off the side of the truck, where it was resting, as under a blow from a hard fist. A fraction of a second later a similar blow hit my left knee, and my driver gave a gasp. I looked at him: he seemed unmoved.

'Been hit?' I asked.

'Hit in the leg,' he replied.

'Can you drive?'

'I'm O.K. for the present,' and drove on with care.

I lifted my left hand: the little finger dangled, hanging by a piece of flesh, and there was some blood. For the first and only time during the war, anger seized me. I wanted to get even with the creature who had taken a liberty with my wholeness, who had broken off maliciously *my* finger. I seized the handle of the gun in front of me, swivelled it sideways and fired bursts and bursts in the direction of the flashes on my left. When I had emptied the pan a man sitting behind me fitted a fresh one for me and I went on firing with rage in my heart.

A little later I saw, in the feeble light, that the truck following us had stopped and we halted also, for it was our rule that if one vehicle stopped everyone did the same. There was trouble behind us and we waited, firing at the flashes, dim as they were in the growing daylight. Sergeant Dennis in his jeep appeared, left the track and drove in a wide curve to the left towards the enemy huts with both his guns spurting. The rhythmic buzzing of bullets slowed down, and we also held our fire to save ammunition. Jake drove up, stopped a moment to tell me that the wireless truck had had a tyre ripped open by a bullet. 'Never,' he said, 'have I seen a quicker change of wheel,' and he drove on smiling to himself. We followed in a straggled column, round a bend, which put us out of sight of the enemy ambush. By the side of the track two mounted Tripolitanians sat their horses, completely immobile, staring at me out of curiously grey faces.

I asked my neighbour: 'What have they put on their faces? Dust? Powder?'

'I think they are scared,' he replied. 'See, they can't move.'

Paralysed with fear, they waited for death, but my anger had passed and I let the helpless men be. I would have been better advised to kill them.

Another quarter of an hour's drive took us to the rendezvous, where Easonsmith waited and guided us to our position under a tree.

I limped a hundred yards over to a tree under which Lawson, the doctor, was opening shop, and waited with the others to be attended to. Although (as we made out) thirty-six guns had fired at us at close range for nearly fifteen minutes, my driver and I were the only casualties in the ambush: the others had been hit during the fighting at Barce, none of them much hurt. My driver, a tall Guardsman, had a neat bullet wound through the calf: his leg had stiffened and he could hardly walk, but he was quite unmoved, and we all sat on the rough ground smoking and joking, enjoying ourselves quietly. Dick Lawson, a cheerful young M.O. with a chubby face, made a quick survey of his patients: he took on first those who required least attention: thus I came last. I have always had a fondness for messing about with other people's wounds, and I proffered perfectly unrequired assistance to the doctor and his medical orderly. I realized that I was a bit of a busybody, but the excitements of the night were still in me and wouldn't let me remain inactive.

Bandaged up, the other men moved off, and my turn came. Dick Lawson injected anaesthetic into my hand, and said:

'I am going to amputate your finger. Don't look. It will soon be over.' Dutifully I turned my face away under the unreasonable impression that he would feel abashed if I watched him do something indelicate. I felt the bone crunch under his tool, then looked round to see him stitch the flesh over the little stump. It was done, without any real pain. My knee had only a few small splinters embedded in the flesh which he prised out with the point of a scalpel. It wasn't even stiff.

Meanwhile the fitters were busy with the two trucks which, damaged at Sidi Rawi the previous evening, had been recovered and towed in after we had come out of the ambush. Loads were sorted out and guns cleaned in a cheerful activity: we all thought we had done with fighting for this trip, and we prepared for the seven hundred mile run to Kufra.

As we were widely dispersed over rolling scrubby ground, where occasional trees grew, I could not see what was happening at every truck. When I heard a few bursts of one of our machine guns followed by several rifle shots, I picked up a tommy gun and walked over to find out the reason of this new disturbance. I was told that some Tripolitanian horsemen had been seen galloping in the distance and that Jake Easonsmith had driven off in a jeep to chase them away; the bursts I had heard were his. I had nothing to do and felt restless — I believe also that Lawson's injections combined with the fatigue of a sleepless night had slightly affected my judgment. I fancied I saw someone moving behind bushes and off I went, crouching low, stalking the enemy on foot, alone with my tommy gun. I crashed, a very noisy Red Indian, through the undergrowth, and uncovered one of our New Zealand trucks and its crew. A wave of self-consciousness swept over me: I saw myself as in a mirror, a stoutish, awkward man, with hand and knee bandaged, preposterously stalking his own men. I had been seen too, and the tale of the 'Old Major' chasing the enemy with his tommy gun entertained many simple souls for months to come.

CHAPTER III

THE ORYX

JAKE EASONSMITH returned after a while, having chased away the snoopers: as he thought that the horsemen's report of our position would be passed on to enemy aircraft he decided to move on. Repairs on the two damaged trucks were completed, we tidied up our leaguer and, as I was to travel once more in a jeep, I went over to collect my kit from the truck in which I had driven during the night. The men, busy and in a hurry to get on the move, had already piled some other stuff on top of the bed-roll and rucksack which held all my belongings: they persuaded me to let things be for the present, and to collect my kit at the evening halt. Back at my jeep I took stock of what I had left: the rubber-soled shoes, socks, slacks and shirt I stood in, a bandage and a sling on my left hand, a bandage on my left knee, an army belt with compass, revolver and ammunition, field glasses, a tommy gun, a copy of *Paradise Lost* and a water bottle. Because one of the few rules I kept was never to let myself be separated from my kit, I worried over my weakness in giving in to the Guardsmen — with good cause, as it turned out, for their truck was burnt out shortly afterwards.

Spread out over two miles of sparsely wooded hills so as to be less of a target to aircraft, our trucks and jeeps got under way, keeping parallel courses. The sun, well up by now, was kind to chilled limbs and weary bodies. Glad to be on our way home after the success of our battle, we rocked sleepily in our seats; now and then images of incidents of the previous night flickered through our minds, bringing a glow to sleepy eyes and raising self-centred chuckles: we were contented and at peace.

There is a satisfaction in being wounded and yet well enough to be no burden to anybody. My injuries were light enough to enable me to look after myself and to take a share of duties and I wouldn't have called myself a casualty: nevertheless I was well pleased with the blood-stained dressing on my hand, and I took an interest in the curious pain

I felt in the finger which Lawson had clipped off. I had seen it dropped into an enamel basin, but I could still feel a sting under the nail which wasn't there. A dim childish pride in cutting a fine figure no doubt, but the main pleasure I got from my wounds was that they were tangible and visible evidence to the reality of my previous night's enjoyable experiences. I was a little dazed with lack of sleep, slight shock and anaesthetic, but I had only to look at my hand to be assured that I wasn't living in a daydream.

We drove a few miles: at twenty-past ten we heard a noise of low-flying aircraft, and every one of our vehicles stopped in its tracks. Two C.R. 42s, old-fashioned Italian fighter biplanes, abreast and half a mile apart, flew over our vehicles dispersed in the low scrub, nearly disappeared over the hills, then banked and returned in line ahead. They flew directly over my jeep, disregarded it, but dived and clattered away with their guns at the Guards' wireless truck — the one that carried my kit — which I could see behind me stuck on the top of a bare hill. After the third or fourth dive I saw black smoke rise, thin at first, then a thick rolling column lit by the sharp reports of exploding ammunition and that was the end of the wireless truck. The crew got away and walked over to another truck unmolested.

The Italian planes (which, as I learned many years later, had been called up from El Abiar, as the thirty-two aircraft in Barce had been destroyed by Nick Wilder the night before) flew away to the north. When after a minute they had not returned we required no orders to thaw out and make for cover. There was not much of it: thin, isolated acacia trees, with little spread and transparent shadows, were our only comfort. Camouflage nets had been spread out when half an hour later the planes returned. They had landed at Barce, fifteen miles away, well contented with their success, but unfortunately for us, an angered commander, still smarting under last night's trouncing, had sent them up again to go and destroy every vehicle and kill every man of the English raiding party. They made for the beacon of smoke from our burning truck, now a couple of miles in our rear, and flew criss-cross over the neighbouring area, searching for our vehicles. They discovered another one of our trucks and machine-gunned it till it went up in flames. After fifty minutes they left to refuel and reload the guns, returned after twenty minutes and kept up this regular rhythm during the remainder of the day.

During the intervals of peace we hurriedly moved our vehicles to a new pattern and cached some petrol and some rations. Each time the planes returned we left the trucks and took cover. Wilder and I disagreed with Easonsmith about this, and suggested that we should man such anti-aircraft guns as we had and fire at the aircraft. He had been in similar situations before and objected that the only result would be to give away to the enemy the position of our trucks and add human casualties to our losses of equipment. Looking back on the events of that day, I think he was wrong.

Towards half-past one, I was sitting with my back against a tree trunk, reading book two of *Paradise Lost*. Ten yards away, on my left, Jake Easonsmith sat under another tree, also reading. From the hills around us rose five gigantic, spreading bushes of black rolling smoke, signs of our disintegrating military power. Overhead, now near, now far, the two Italian aircraft swerved and banked fussily, looking for fresh targets. The sound of their engines came in gusts, then died down to a faint purr.

Some change in the noise reached my mind through the baroque latin verbosity of Milton's verse and made me look up: I saw two thin parallel horizontal lines and the blurred propeller circle of a plane gliding down head on directly at us. 'In a few seconds,' I thought, 'I shall be full of holes,' and a mortal apprehension came over me. Jake Easonsmith under his tree also lifted his eyes from his book, watched the approaching plane for a while, then turning towards me, his bearded face broke into a humorous smile of tender understanding: he nodded twice pensively and resumed his reading. Thus, silently, he proclaimed the vanity of human fears and destroyed in me for ever the seeds of dread.

Until that day I had had to rely on a carefully cultivated enjoyment of risk to keep up my spirits; under the pleasant excitement of danger I succeeded in overlooking the threat of bodily violence, but an underlying fear remained: I was always happy in battle but often uncom-

fortable on night patrols which provide no excitement. Jake enjoyed
danger as much as I did but he had a serenity which carried a deeper
strength; in his contemplative mind he examined dispassionately the
threat of disaster and found it was of no moment: neither the prospect
of death nor of failure had the power to trouble him. The secret of his
strength became mine also the moment I saw him smile at the gliding
plane; it has remained with me ever since.

In wonderful peace I returned to my book. A few moments later puffs
of dust rose out of the sand around us as the plane fired and missed.
We went on reading, expecting another assault: which never came.
Either the Italian pilot had lost interest, or he was unable to find our
trees again in the featureless landscape.

On my right the scrubby stony desert rose slightly to a small acacia
tree a hundred yards away, then to another, then to a larger one under
which stood one of our trucks: beyond that the ground dipped out
of sight. The two planes reappeared and made for the truck: one of
our men, unrecognizable at the distance, scrambled to his feet from
under it and ran towards the dip: the planes opened fire, the man fell
to the ground, out of sight, and didn't get up again after the enemy had
flown over. Easonsmith put down his book and rose. I said: 'Don't
bother, I shall go.' He nodded and sat down again. The sky being
temporarily clear I walked briskly towards the first tree. Half way
over, a plane came, flying at no more than a hundred feet: I saw the
goggled face of the pilot looking over the side of the open cockpit.
He saw me too, fired two bursts at me, then drifted away. I picked
myself up and ran for the tree: I could see the other plane coming from
the opposite direction. I reached the tree in time to crouch on the
ground with my head pressed against the base of its trunk: it wasn't
more than six inches thick and I felt as large as a house; my position
was so undignified that I broke into a silly laugh; twisting my head
to one side I caught sight of the plane as it dived and spat bullets
at me. It missed, I got up, waved a hand at the pilot and dashed for
the next tree, chased like a rabbit on the way by the first plane, which
came up on my left. Its bullets also went wide, and I reached the second
tree with no holes in me. I stayed here a good while because the two

aircraft, taking steep turns, kept coming alternately from the right and from the left and hardly gave me time to squirm from one side of the trunk to the other. After each miss I waved an arm, a foolish thing to do, but the two big machines with their thundering engines and their guns chasing me around my puny acacia were too incongruous to be taken seriously. Suddenly all was quiet, the planes had left, their ammunition all wasted, for none of the pieces of metal they had thrown had torn into me. I got up, somewhat out of breath, and looked around: the landscape, surprisingly, was unaltered: smoke was still coming up from the five burning trucks; Jake Easonsmith in the distance lifted an arm in greeting; in front of me I could see our truck under its tree, but the man I had come to help was nowhere visible. I picked up my tommy gun and walked over a ridge into a shallow dry wadi: under an overhanging rocky ledge where the waters had scooped out a recess two feet high, I found my man lying, eyes closed, white and very shaken. I sat down in the sand and spoke to him.

'Not hurt,' he answered, 'just upset. I'll be all right in a moment. This is a good shelter. Stay here with me.' I did, because the planes, having rediscovered the truck on the bank above us, strafed it in end-less rounds for nearly an hour. One behind the other they roared across the wadi, firing as they flew, then turned round and did it again. During each assault thousands of bullets buried themselves in the sand and clattered on the rocks of our cave. It was rather unnerving. Across the wadi, on the upward slope, thirty yards away a hobbled donkey hopped about grazing on the bushes, untroubled by the noise.

His master appeared from up the wadi, a ragged Arab as unconcerned as his ass, and squatted outside the narrow cave where we both huddled and engaged me in a polite conversation in which reference was made neither to our strange position, nor to the bloody bandage on my hand, nor to the burning trucks, nor to the planes overhead, nor to the general hullabaloo. This battle of ours, which of course he couldn't help notic-ing as he was in the very heart of it, was no concern of his and he studiously ignored it. What he wanted to know, as it appeared in the end, was whether we would like to exchange a few cigarettes for sour milk which he offered to go and fetch for us from his tent. He departed on this errand, riding his donkey amongst the whistling projectiles.

When the planes at last departed I was much surprised to find our truck on the wadi bank still sound, and drove it into the wadi a few hundred yards below our shelter against a rock from which the westering sun now cast a shadow. The planes came back, failed to discover the truck in its new hiding place, and made for other targets. I stayed in the wadi, waiting for the planes to leave to join Easonsmith once more.

The afternoon wore on. A Tripolitanian horseman showed up on the skyline at the head of the wadi, then rode cautiously down. Crouched behind a bush I took a slow, careful aim with my tommy gun: slowly, slowly, dragging his feet it seemed, the rider came nearer. At twenty yards I fired one shot. The man started, turned his horse round and walked it away as slowly as he had come: when he had gone thirty yards, he tossed his head, rolled off the back of the horse and lay spreadeagled in the sand, his left foot twitching. When I got up to him I found him dead. The horse cantered away up the wadi.

Shortly before sunset I joined Easonsmith once more, and he gave me the news. Lawson, the doctor, had managed to drive away a truck with all the casualties and hide it in a deep wadi under a wooded hill two miles to the south. With the exception of two jeeps, all the other trucks, he said, were burnt out. Nick Wilder had bullets through both his legs and a slight face wound, two other men had been hit, making with the men wounded the previous night six casualties in all, including myself. I told him about the truck I had concealed in the wadi, which he had counted as lost: as soon as the sun dipped below the horizon we collected a few men and set ourselves to load it with the rations, and the petrol which had been cached. Dusk was thickening, we thought we had done with air attack: having still two thirty-hundredweight Chevrolets, two jeeps and plenty of supplies we could easily carry our thirty-three men to Kufra, seven hundred miles away only. Then came a set-back: in the failing light a slow heavy three-engined transport aircraft lumbered overhead. We didn't bother, for generally transport aircraft are not interested in the ground, all their attention is for hostile fighter planes. Unexpectedly this plane gave us

two bursts of its guns and went on its ponderous way, without looking round. It was as if a friend had suddenly slapped you hard in the
face. Unfortunately their aim was good and after they had gone, smoke
started pouring out of our truck. Hurriedly we pulled off what stores
we could before the whole load was sheeted in flames. We then found
that the jeep which had been standing by had a large hole through the
top of the petrol tank and a gashed tyre.

Easonsmith gathered his men in the thickish wood on the hill above
Lawson's truck, and took stock of the situation. He had thirty-three
men, of whom six were casualties, two of them serious: Nick Wilder,
wounded in both legs, and Parker, with a bullet through the stomach.
One Chevrolet truck in good condition, a jeep in good order, another
jeep with a punctured tank and a torn tyre. Enough petrol and water
for two hundred miles, some rations. No wireless, no spare tyres.

Forty miles away to the south-east, near Bir Jerari, he had left on
his way up to Barce a truck with stores of water, petrol and rations.
One hundred and forty miles further on was L.G.125, a disused R.A.F.
landing ground of the year before, used frequently by L.R.D.G. as a
rallying point; this had been given as a common rendezvous to stragglers
on the present operations. Five hundred miles again to the south,
beyond the Sand Sea, was Kufra, with the headquarters of A Squadron
L.R.D.G., and 216 Bomber Squadron R.A.F., and a garrison of the
Sudan Defence Force.

Jake divided his force into a driving and a walking party. Driving
in the Chevrolet were the six casualties, the doctor (Lawson) in
command, a driver, Wallbrook, a navigator Davis and a fitter. They
were to make first for Bir Jerari for supplies, then for L.G. 125, where
they might meet an L.R.D.G. patrol. If they didn't they were to push
on non-stop, skirting the Sand Sea, which was impassable for a single
truck with six cripples on board, slip through the Jalo gap (avoiding
enemy-held Jalo), and on to Kufra, a trip of some seven hundred miles,
which, all being well, could be covered in seven to eight days. Lawson
doubted that Parker, with his stomach wound, could survive that long.
One of the jeeps would travel with this party.

The remaining twenty-three men under Easonsmith, with the other jeep to carry supplies, would walk to Bir Jerari, collect the spare truck and push on to Kufra. I wanted to be included in the walking party, but Easonsmith determinedly over-ruled me, saying that my wounded knee, though it left me enough agility to dodge Italian C.R. 42s, would not stand up to the forty mile trek to Bir Jerari. I submitted because my knee was becoming really painful.

With the New Zealand sergeant, Easonsmith wrote out a nominal roll of each party: the men were called one by one and told to which party they belonged, everyone to report to the sergeant in an hour's time at eight o'clock, in the woods on the hill. We then got busy getting the trucks and their loads ready. It was quite dark under the trees: several Arabs from neighbouring tents turned up and provided us with milk, amongst them my friend the donkey rider. Hamed, the Tripolitanian lad captured by Jake the previous night, had now his first meal: we were in Ramadhan, and nothing I could say had induced him to eat before sunset. The Muslim custom exempts the traveller from the fast, but Hamed, about to set out on the longest trip of his life, didn't consider himself a bona-fide traveller.

At eight o'clock the sergeant called the roll and found two men missing: Jake's driver, Gutteridge, and another, both good men with a long experience in the L.R.D.G. They had been seen only a few minutes previously and somebody had heard them talk of going over to the Arab tents in search of eggs. I walked over in the dark to the Arab village and questioned the women: they had indeed seen the two men, given them eggs and seen them wander away in the opposite direction to our trucks. I called and shouted and got no answer: the two blighters had gone for a walk and could not be recovered. These two lads, eager and competent both, would never have been found missing from their patrol in the normal course of their journeys, but tonight, when their very life depended on being with their companions — a situation which they could appreciate as well as anyone in the party (one of them was a navigator) — they chose to stroll away and enjoy the cool of the evening. I have experienced a similar mental derangement in other men, so often that, in later years, I made a rule on such occasions as this to allow no one out of sight. We left without them.

We drove off in the moonless night, Wallbrook driving the Chevrolet truck and I the jeep, with Doc. Lawson in the passenger seat. Davis in the Chevrolet set the course. The going, up a rocky wadi, was abominable. We seemed to be going up steps, then hanging with two wheels on to a rocky ledge, then we got jammed between two large boulders. The front left-hand tyre of the jeep was flat, which didn't make the steering easy, and, with the jolting, the petrol splashed out of the torn tank and compelled me to add a gallon or so every ten minutes. My left knee was getting stiff and I found it increasingly difficult to press down the clutch for the perpetual changes of gears. After an hour's driving the walking party was still ahead of us. We caught up with them only when we came out of the wadi on to a plateau. At that moment the other jeep, which had been making no better progress, blew a tyre. I decided to abandon my jeep and to give two of its wheels to the walking party, who would thus have a spare. We pushed the doomed jeep on to its side, removed two wheels which we gave to Jake, set a time incendiary bomb over the tank, climbed on to the Chevrolet and drove on. For a while we could hear the voices of the men in Jake Easonsmith's party, but the going was better now and we left them behind.

Davis, our navigator, tried to keep a straight compass course and the driver did his best to follow his instructions, but the night was so dark that he could just see far enough ahead to avoid crashing into trees and boulders. Of the general lie of the land he could see nothing: he drove ahead in a straight line as long as he wasn't stopped by an impassable obstacle. We found ourselves, at one time, driving along the steep side of a hill at such an angle that we could hardly cling on to our seats and we expected the truck to topple over, but it righted itself; then, some time later, we stopped dead with our front wheels nearly over a cliff, a vertical drop of forty feet or so to a wadi below. We drove round, followed the curving cliff edge for a long time, found a way down, slid and skidded to the wadi bottom and started climbing up the opposite bank. Night was wearing out, there was no time to send a man on foot to reconnoitre ahead: if dawn found us anywhere near our starting point, the planes would soon be on us and our adventures at an end.

The climb out of the wadi proved difficult: it was steep and of screes, which had to be rushed, and protruding rocks, which should be taken with care. The heavy truck rocked and swayed, the uphill wheels on rock, the downhill ones on shingle in which they spun, digging a hole which slowly brought the truck to a dangerous angle: suddenly the wheels gripped (having reached rock I suppose) and sent us lurching forward, over boulders and through high bushes with a loud crash. We pulled up on a level keel, and while the fitter got down to inspect the damage, Lawson injected a dose of morphia to Parker, to whom the jolting was an agony. Surprisingly no damage had been suffered, and we continued on our wild, blind course, the driver muttering to himself over the wheel as he dodged and skirted. Later the going became better and finally at three-thirty that morning Lawson called a halt. He wanted to spare Parker, who was weakening. We had covered nearly fifteen miles: by stopping now and starting again at daybreak we could put at least twenty-five miles between us and our starting point before the planes got into the air: they would have to search an area of a thousand-odd square miles to find us.

Accordingly we stopped on a sandy patch, made tea and went to sleep for a couple of hours. The sand was soft under the truck, but the early hours of the morning were very chilly and I had neither blanket nor coat. I woke up with the first signs of dawn and stretched painfully a very stiff knee. I saw Lawson on the truck, bending over the still body of Parker, his chubby face ruddy in spite of fatigue and two sleepless nights. I grunted, he nodded cheerfully: against all the rules Parker was still alive. We drove off straight away.

Wallbrook, our driver, was a half Maori, with a black beard and an indomitable cheerfulness. He denied that he had nearly overturned the truck once or twice during the night drive: he knew exactly where he was going and all Maoris could see at night anyway. Davis, the navigator, was a short New Zealander, with a thoughtful disposition and a quick temper. Our lives were in his hands and he had a difficult problem: with a magnetic and a sun compass he had to navigate our truck by dead reckoning over seven hundred miles, making landfalls at Bir Jerari and at L.G.125 on the way. As he had neither theodolite nor wireless he couldn't check his position from the stars. His starting point after the night drive was doubtful, but his first landfall, the truck near Bir Jerari, should be fairly easy to make because it was in a wadi covered in thick scrub and bushes, quite conspicuous in the bare plain, and very familiar to many of us who had used it frequently as a lie-up for operations in the Jebel and on the Triq el 'Abd. Having found the truck, he would have a good start for his second lap, as its position had been determined by astrofix. Davis had not been able to save his theodolite but he had his log book and his maps.

We drove steadily the whole morning. When we halted at noon for dinner we had left the Jebel foothills and their trees behind us, and were in pleasant yellow hills of gravel and sand, the watercourses marked by heavy bushes. The sun was quite hot and we drove the truck in the shade of a particularly high bush. Parker was too ill to be moved — he was half stunned with morphia and not quite conscious — but his heart stood up well. Nick Wilder was taken off the truck and laid on blankets on the sand: when I went over to him he glared malevolently at me, as if I was the cause of his helplessness. He felt perfectly fit and resented not being allowed the use of his legs. His patched-up face gave him a comical appearance which caused half-concealed grins and increased his annoyance. While dinner was got ready I got him to tell me the story of his adventures on the landing ground and in the town at Barce. Generally a man of few words, he spoke now more in grunts than with his usual clipped New Zealand diction. From his account, or as much of it as I managed to understand, I have written the story I have given in the preceding chapter. His temper improved as he spoke, and when, as we were finishing eating, the distant engines of an aircraft were heard, he suddenly gave one of his irresistibly endearing half-smiles, as of a boy of eight, and chuckled:

'This time we fight. Old Jake is not here to stop us.' We did nothing of the kind because the plane, a mere speck high overhead, didn't see us and passed slowly out of sight. We pushed on and by four o'clock we were in Wadi Jerari. Davis, receiving unsolicited advice, shook his head as if throwing off raindrops, said nothing, steered a sinuous course down the wadi and finally halted opposite a great tangle of matted bushes, inside which we found, well camouflaged, the truck we were making for. Within an hour we had taken our load of petrol, water and rations, collected a spare tyre and left a note for Jake saying we had called at sixteen hundred hours on September 15th, 1942, and left at seventeen hundred hours for L.G.125.

We drove till dark and slept ten hours, our first real rest since the morning of the thirteenth.

Parker was still alive the next morning, September 16th, but in great pain. Morphia seemed to have lost its power to put him at ease; he was conscious and apologized for the trouble he was giving, though I have not known a quieter patient. He could not eat nor was he allowed to drink: all we could do was to try and make him comfortable in the back of the truck, where Lawson gave him a shot of morphia every few hours. The bullet which had gone in at one side and out at the other had made a long serrated gash in his stomach. Fortunately the going was becoming better as we progressed to the south so that the jolting in the back of the Chevrolet was less desperately painful.

The weather was exceptional: very clear with sparkling sunshine. We were now in the desert, not yet quite barren, but too far from water for any human beings or their cattle. The northerly breeze had lost the aridity of the summer blasts, touched for the first time with the approach of winter. The horizon expanded and contracted as our lonely truck rose and sank with the long yellow rolling hills, still and quiet but not devoid of life: under a bush in the very early morning I saw a huge hyaena turning round and round like a dog before settling down to sleep; then an hour later I saw a couple of oryx. The heavy beasts, the size of a large calf, their coats milky white, and with long curved horns, grazed on the sweet-smelling bushes. We stopped the truck for a while to look at them, for none of us had seen such animals in all our travels in the desert, nor did I see any again. We propped up Parker so that he too could have a look at the creatures: it seemed important that he should know about them before he died.

From first light until darkness we plodded along, slowly so as not to jolt too much, but steadily and with only short stops to ease the patients and for a very short meal at midday. We were trying to reach L.G.125

as early as possible in the hope of catching there one of the patrols which we thought would visit the place periodically. They would not, however, we imagined remain more than a few hours each time in the neighbourhood of the landing ground, for it was an occasional target for the Luftwaffe and it offered no cover whatever. If we met a patrol they could, with their wireless, get a plane sent up from Kufra in a few hours to take Parker to hospital in Egypt; if we met no one we should have to drive on to Kufra ourselves, and Lawson was positive that Parker could not survive the five hundred mile trip, some of which was very rough going.

We covered over a hundred miles on that day and I reckoned that when we bedded down for the night we were not more than thirty miles from L.G.125. I wasn't sure, however, because Davis was very jealous of his navigation and evaded my questions. L.G.125 was not marked on my map and I had to go by memory.

The next morning, September 17th, we travelled about two hours: then Davis, who had been watching the speedometer, told the driver to stop, climbed on to the back of his seat and looked slowly round the horizon: behind us stretched the tracks of our wheels like the wake of a ship — otherwise nothing was in sight but the smooth undulating surface of the desert, of flour-like dust strewn with hard shiny, grey stones. We had travelled one hundred and forty miles from Bir Jerari on a general bearing of 140° and according to Davis's reckoning we *were* on L.G.125. In fact we were not, nor did he expect us to be. But he knew he was only a few miles away. I looked round and, strangely enough, in spite of the emptiness of the barren landscape, I shared his confidence. Davis climbed down and said:

'We shall soon find it.'

'What do we look for?' I asked, for I had never been to L.G.125 before.

'The tail of a wrecked Hurricane standing on its nose.'

Davis took us slowly two miles due west, two miles due south, two miles due east, two miles due north: when we completed the square we had seen no Hurricane. Davis then started us on a four mile square: half way down the second side, I touched him on the head and pointed to the west where something showed which didn't seem to be desert.

'Would that be it?' Davis looked and said:

'Could be.'

We didn't know whether there might not be some Germans about, so we crept up slowly to the thing. It was the Hurricane on its nose all right, and other wrecked and burnt Blenheims and Hurricanes began to show up. As soon as we were sure, we took a wide detour and circled the landing ground out of sight, looking for fresh wheel tracks, but found none. We then drove boldly on to the far end of the landing ground, away from the wrecked aircraft, found some old covered dugouts and put the patients in one and converted another into a surgery for Lawson. Parker was very faint and the doctor wanted to look after him in peace.

There were no enemies on the landing ground, but neither were our friends at hand: it looked as if we might have to remain here a few days, in which case our rations and water would run out. I thought there might be some pickings to be found on the landing ground, which the R.A.F. had used for several months during the previous autumn — and then had left rather in a hurry: I took Wallbrook with me on a scrounging expedition. When we rejoined Lawson in the late afternoon we had found a hundred gallons of petrol (which we didn't need), seven dozen cases of army biscuits, twenty-two tins of bully and about twenty gallons of water. With these supplies we could, at a pinch, remain here five or six days and still have enough left for the trip to Kufra. Lawson decided to wait at L.G.125 as long as Parker lived: he was in such a state of exhaustion that there was no point in trying to make him travel by truck any further.

We collected our new stores and brought them back to the dugouts. The truck was then driven against the remains of a hut and camouflaged. Under the net, the fitter did his maintenance.

Just after sunset we heard the engines of several vehicles. We took cover and waited, while the unidentified visitors seemed to settle at the other end of the ground, out of sight. Later when darkness fell, we saw the glare of a fire they had lit. About half-past nine Davis crept away to reconnoitre. We waited, lying on the sand outside the dugouts, a long time. We waited an hour and more. Davis must have been captured we thought. Nick Wilder suggested that just before dawn I should take the men who could carry weapons and attack the enemy in their sleep. It seemed to me a sensible thing to do, and at half-past ten I set out with Wallbrook, in whom I had great confidence, to reconnoitre the enemy position: having got beyond the last dugout I saw a shadow walking towards me, swinging a torch. I challenged, the man shone the torch on his own face and revealed the features of David Lloyd Owen. It seemed that our troubles were over.

CHAPTER IV

RESCUE

WHAT had delayed Davis was that on approaching the leaguer he had heard the wireless which someone had tuned into a German broadcast and he had naturally assumed that the visitors were German. Only when the wireless was turned off did he hear and recognize the voices of his friends in Y Patrol.

I thought at the time that pure luck had brought Lloyd Owen and his patrol to L.G.125 a few hours only after we had arrived. I knew that he had been engaged in the operation against Tobruq and I assumed that he was now on his normal way back to Kufra. I never asked him because I wouldn't have expected him to give me an answer. We didn't ask questions about the movements of other patrols on the principle that 'Of what he has no knowledge a man can't talk'. We kept our counsel and achieved a high standard of security. As it is, for six years I have marvelled at the coincidence which saved the life of Parker and provided a dramatic anti-climax as a conclusion to our perfect adventure. But the coincidence was not where I thought, as I have just discovered. At dawn on September 17th, at the time we were watching the oryx, Jake Easonsmith's walking party had fallen in with Olivey's Rhodesian patrol — a coincidence no doubt. As a result, at eleven-thirty that same day L.R.D.G. Headquarters in the Fayum had received a signal, 'Jake and twelve men found. Doctor with one truck and six wounded may now be at L.G.125. From there head for Kufra. Get aircraft to search. Details later.'

Headquarters signalled to Lloyd Owen, who was lying up at Hatiet el Etla, seventy miles from L.G.125. He set out and a few hours later found us.

Many signals passed between L.G.125, the Fayum and Kufra during that night, while I slept like a beast and Parker moaned and fretted. The next morning Lloyd Owen warned us that a plane was due from

Kufra at thirteen hundred hours to pick us up. We knew enough of the difficulty for an air navigator to find our small landing ground at the end of a flight of four hundred and fifty miles over flat, absolutely featureless desert, to be sceptical about the time of arrival. It might be two or three days before the R.A.F. succeeded in finding the landing ground, we said, and went deliberately and unconcernedly about our business. At twelve-thirty we lit a smoke generator as a wind indicator — just in case. At twelve-forty-five some credulous fool reported a noise of engines and was laughed down, but three minutes later a fat Bombay bomber circled the ground and landed: I walked up and arrived just as the door opened and Bill Coles, an old friend of mine, climbed out of the cockpit. He commanded 216 Bomber Squadron and had flown the plane over himself, which was natural enough, but to me the apparition at that moment of an unexpected friend seemed to be an act of personal gracefulness of the Fates.

That night we slept in Kufra like children without a care in the world. On the next morning, September 19th, we were put on board a Hudson and flown non-stop to Cairo. It was a long trip and the sun was setting when our plane landed in Heliopolis: I was surprised to see two ambulances waiting for us. We had a long drive to the New Zealand General Hospital in Helwan: as I came out of my ambulance I saw Parker being wheeled away on a trolley. I followed, talking to him, as far as the door of the operating theatre, where a surgeon and two sisters waited ready for action. He had travelled for six days with a gaping stomach but now he would be attended to without a minute's delay. That was the way with the New Zealanders.

Though I was not strictly entitled to it, I was admitted to the New Zealand hospital along with my companions and I felt I was receiving a great favour. I was taken upstairs, where an orderly undressed me, put me in a bath, scrubbed my back, poured me out a glass of beer, lit me a cigarette and then put me to bed. It seemed a lot of attention for a little finger shot off, but it was done so kindly and I was so tired that I made no effort to defend myself.

But when I woke up next morning I found on my locker a flowered toilet bag labelled: 'With the compliments of the New Zealand Red

Cross.' In it were all the soaps and brushes a man can desire, two packets of cigarettes, a bag of sweets, writing paper and chocolate. This was too much: abashed I packed everything back and when the Sister came round I drew her attention to the mistake which had been made: I was not a New Zealander and not entitled to this bounty. She laughed and said the folks at home would be glad if they knew that their present had gone to a 'Tommy'. Sister Simpson was gay and kind and lovely to look at: I unpacked my treasures once more and started on the happiest five weeks in my life.

Before I left hospital Parker was up and about, the pride of the staff, who maintained that by all medical standards he had no right to be alive. He rejoined the L.R.D.G. and I met him once more in Wilder's patrol a few months later.

Nick Wilder also recovered perfectly, and the last time I saw him towards the end of the war, he was a lieutenant-colonel commanding Div. Cav., the New Zealand armoured regiment. He is now back in New Zealand, sheep farming as of old, and absorbed entirely in ewes and lambs, black faces and merinos.

Jake Easonsmith spent some days in the Jebel with Olivey's patrol collecting most of the stragglers, then returned to Kufra. A year later, on November 16th, 1943, a lieutenant-colonel in command of L.R.D.G., he was killed in action on the island of Leros and we lost a great man. He was then thirty-four years old. His upbringing had been entirely civilian, his pre-war career commonplace, nor had he given to his friends and relations more than a hint of the elevation of mind and the strength of character which were so apparent to all of us who fought with him. He was from Bristol, of a comfortable family, educated at Mill Hill; he took employment with a tobacco firm, which he left to become the representative of an Australian wine firm. For several years he toured the west of England selling Empire wines to pubs and hotels. His friends of that period remember with a mild amazement that instead of peddling around his case of samples in the ordinary way of commercial travellers he got himself a caravan in which he lived with his wife: a few days in Gloucester, then in Cheltenham, then in Torquay, Penzance or Tiverton, as trade directed. He also had a house that he built himself near Bristol. By all accounts he was perfectly satisfied with this low-level existence, pleased to be successful in his business, and with no more daring hobbies than a liking for motor cars. It is recorded that he had played rugger for Clifton — the town, not the school — and that he showed an interest in the Arts. The friends of his youth are quiet, unassuming and provincial: his success in the war, measured by them in terms of promotion and awards, for of his real achievements they heard nothing, surprised them to a degree of affectionate pride.

Out of this comfortable mediocrity he enlisted in the ranks in the 66th Searchlight Battalion at the outbreak of war, transferred as a lance-sergeant to the Tanks in 1940, went through a course and was commissioned as a second lieutenant in July 1940. At the end of that year he was drafted to the Middle East, where he volunteered for the L.R.D.G. very soon after his arrival. His active life lasted thus something under three years. In that short period of time he developed a new and powerful personality, as has happened to others in war time, and he learnt and perfected a type of warfare for which there was no precedent in military tradition. His most remarkable achievement was to create a standard of behaviour which came to be followed as a matter of course by hundreds of men who came under his influence.

I may seem to be unfair to Bagnold and Prendergast, greater soldiers than Easonsmith, who are the real creators of the L.R.D.G.; the fact is that I saw little of Bagnold, who had already relinquished command of the L.R.D.G. at the time I came to be its guest, and Prendergast had for me the unapproachable quality of the commander-in-chief, whereas I lived daily with Easonsmith, and he was the man who introduced me to the spirit of his exceptional unit. He remained for me a model commander, most of what I did when I got a command of my own was founded on his example, and my contacts with him have altered permanently my attitude to life in general, to risk and danger and to death. Had he survived, he would undoubtedly be much alarmed at the conclusions I drew from his unconscious teaching.

ACCOUNT

OF THE RAID ON BARCE BY LIEUTENANT PRIAROGGIA OF THE ROYAL
ITALIAN ARMY

Report concerning the British Raid to Barce (September 14th, 1942)

During the first days of September 1942 a secret information was brought to the Italian H.Q. in Barce that the British were preparing an attack against Barce. I don't know the reason, but no credit was given to that information.

My company was stationed three miles south of Barce. (Along the track going to El Bit, just before the first mountainous slopes of the Jebel, where the track takes on up hill. This location is about one mile from the road going to El Abiar.)

One night, I think it was about midnight, we heard loud shootings in Barce. Since we could see the luminous trajectories of the 20-mm. shells (being very high above ground level), firstly we got the conviction that the A.A. artillery was firing at some enemy bombers, carrying on a night raid on Barce, but after a short while it appeared quite clear to us that a heavy battle was being fought, not against bombers but against some enemy land unit.

We were connected by field wire with the H.Q. in Barce, so we were informed eventually that about twenty British trucks, coming from the southern Jebel highway (maybe Teknis), had got into Barce and were attacking the airport. Then we got orders to get ready in case the British had chosen to withdraw towards El Abiar. In the meanwhile the battle was getting to its climax: high fires were rising from the airport and the crackle of the shooting was deafening.

An hour or so later everything was quiet again, except the flames which were still raging in the airport.

We were informed by phone that the British trucks had taken the airport guard by surprise, started machine-gunning and destroyed thirteen bombers. It seemed they had tried also an attack against the Italian Q.M. Stores, then all of them had fled taking the southern Jebel highway, except two. These two trucks were reported to be trying to escape towards El Abiar, but, after having got out of Barce, the M.P.s' light tanks that were chasing them had lost sight of both.

All night we were on the alert, but we got no news of the two enemy lorries.

Just before sunrise we perceived the roar of an engine about eight hundred yards far from our outposts. It seemed to come from a deep ravine of the Jebel, hidden by thick bushes. The roar was intermittent and went up and down like the noise of an engine which is being started and does not start.

We made up our minds to send a patrol (an officer, four men, with a small truck and a machine gun) to see what was happening.

As soon as our patrol got within rifle range from the ravine, four or five machine guns, hidden somewhere amongst the rocks and the bushes, started blazing away. Our patrol, not being properly armed, was compelled to stop and be very careful in advancing further.

This situation lasted maybe an hour, until one of the M.P.s' light tanks, drawn by the noise of shooting, came up to help. At the sight of the Italian tank, the British crew set fire to the truck (evidently damaged and unable to move) and tried to take off through the Jebel.

The ravine was very narrow and the abandoned British truck was right in the middle of it. Now this truck was heavily loaded with pretty big mines, and, as soon as the fire reached the mines, these started exploding, hindering the pursuers from getting close. Furthermore the British, while they retreated, kept on firing backwards. Thus it took perhaps an hour or so before the Italian patrol could pursue the chase. But it was too late, since the British had enough time to run far away, and, as far as I know, only two of them have been captured during the following days.

[The British truck referred to in this account was one of Sergeant Dennis's Guards patrol commanded by Findlay. The men, helped by the Arabs, eventually reached Wadi Jerari and were taken up by Eason-smith and Olivey.]

PART FOUR

POPSKI'S PRIVATE ARMY

CHAPTER I

A LITTLE MAN WITH A CRAZE FOR P.T.

THE Barce raid was the last of my free-lance ventures. From the time I left the New Zealand hospital till the end of the war I was in charge of a unit of my own and the new responsibility weighed at first heavily on me, till many mistakes taught me the difference between the duties of a commander and those of a lonely adventurer.

My first three weeks in hospital were a holiday. I was very lucky that my knee healed after a few days and my hand, though slower in getting well, did not trouble me much. The only 'Tommy' in the ward I was treated as a spoilt child by the New Zealanders, patients and staff, and enjoyed many privileges, such as being allowed to leave the hospital in the afternoon and drive to Cairo, where I often spent my time in the N.Z. Club, or to Ma'adi where the N.Z. base camp was. In a way the pleasure I took in being admitted as an honorary member of the community was a peculiar form of snobbishness, for I consider the New Zealanders to be a superior kind of humanity, but my friendships were sure and easy, such as I have never experienced with other people. There was Isabel Simpson, the sister in charge of my ward, and her brother Ian, and Don Steele, one of the founders of the L.R.D.G., and Bob Elliot and his brother, both doctors, and Frank Edmonson, another M.O., and many others whom, though they have now drifted out of my life, I still think of as a group to which I belong.

On October 14th, 1942, though I had not yet been discharged from hospital, I thought I was well enough to discuss with Colonel Hackett his plans for my future employment. I called on him at Middle East Headquarters, where he told me, in veiled terms, that the battle of El Alamein was due to start shortly (in ten days as it turned out). During the battle itself, and even more so in the course of the pursuit which would follow, the enemy could be much hampered by shortage of petrol, the supplies of which were carried by road partly from Benghazi, partly from Tripoli, respectively six hundred and twelve hundred miles away. On the strength of our success in burning the dump at El Qubba I was docketed at Headquarters as a petrol destroyer, my knowledge of the Jebel Akhdar and the help I could command from the Senussi Arabs enabled me to get information and to reach places denied to our other raiders; for these reasons Hackett wanted me, as soon as I left hospital, to raise and take command of a small motorized force with which I would raid the enemy petrol line between Ajedabia and Tobruq.

I refused. We had already, I said, L.R.D.G., S.A.S., Adv. A. Force, G. (R.), and others unknown to me, all tripping over one another behind the enemy lines: it was bad policy to add to their numbers another small independent unit. Furthermore, to be able to carry out the task he wanted me to do I ought to be allowed to concentrate on the operational side and have my mind free from administrative duties. What I didn't tell him was that my ambition was to become a member of the L.R.D.G., the finest body of men in any army as I thought (and still do), and I was not going to miss my chance of getting in. I suggested that a new squadron be added to L.R.D.G., with special duties, under my command: in this manner, with the support of the best unit operating in the desert, I would achieve results far greater than if I was saddled with the responsibilities of a unit of my own.

To this Hackett finally agreed, subject to the consent of Lieutenant-Colonel Prendergast, commanding officer L.R.D.G., and on the understanding that I would recruit my own men and make no call whatever on L.R.D.G. personnel. I left Headquarters full of joy.

My personal prospects pleased me — also the new tone of confidence I had heard about the coming battle. What had happened to the army and to Headquarters, which I had last known so depressed, and so defeated? Previously all the talk had been of enemy offensives, and: 'When Rommel decides to walk into Alexandria, there is nothing we can do about it.'

In Groppi's I met McMasters, a former C.S.M. of mine in the Libyan Arab Force, and now R.S.M. of a Hussars Regiment, a hard-boiled regular of fifteen years' service, a man who naturally, and rightly, assumed that he and his fellow sergeant majors *were* the British Army, and who entertained an affectionate contempt for all officers. Over drinks he grew enthusiastic about the new commander-in-chief, Eighth Army. Since Wavell had left us, our C.-in-C.s had been so dreary that I hadn't bothered to find out the name of our latest acquisition.

'It's a general called Montgomery,' said McMasters, 'a short, wiry fellow, with a bee in his bonnet about P.T. The first thing he did when he took over was to order half an hour's physical training for Army Headquarters Staff every morning before breakfast. Tubby brigadiers came out in their vests and pants and *ran*. They heaved and they panted, shaking their fat paunches, for everyone to see, and when they couldn't make the grade, they got the sack. Sacked them right and left, he did, all the fat bastards.' McMasters chuckled ferociously.

'A few days ago he visited the regiment. Talked to the officers, then to the N.C.O.s. He told us everything: what his plan was for the battle, what he wanted the regiment to do, what he wanted *me* to do. And we will do it, Sir. What a man!' he concluded with unaccustomed emphasis.

A general who has the courage to sack brigadiers from Army Staff and who knows how to evoke enthusiastic devotion in the hearts of regular sergeant majors, will, I thought, have no difficulty in defeating Rommel — or even in winning the war. General Montgomery has had my devotion ever since that memorable conversation. He has met with no rivals, sad to say: I have known clever generals, but none, with the exception perhaps of Freyberg, who knew that battles are won primarily by the hearts of men, and that a few shy stuttered words are not enough to set hearts aflame. May Field-Marshal Lord Montgomery forgive me: the little fellow who took over a beaten army on August 13th, 1942, and led it to victory just over two months later, knew the tricks of the trade. The ludicrous downfall of the discredited brigadiers, the burning of withdrawal plans, the informal visits to the units, the personal contacts with the ranks, the brave flamboyant words, the hat with the two badges, the unorthodox clothes, the absence of ceremony, were as necessary to Eighth Army as the tanks, the guns and the aircraft which it received at that time: and nobody else but our little general seems to have thought of providing this kind of equipment. Whether he was deliberately 'playing tricks' or following unconsciously his natural inclinations does not matter in the least: armies are not led and inspired without a good deal of showmanship.

At Army Headquarters, which I visited a few weeks later, I took a personal pride in the disappearance of the 'old boy' nitwits and the rise to power of a small group of efficient, hard-working civilians. There was no nonsense about them, and they got the work done: when they relaxed they had, thank God, something to talk about. Their brains were furnished and didn't stoop to the ineptitudes of army gossip.

CHAPTER II

LOST

FOR seven days I remained a member of L.R.D.G. It appeared then that the war establishment of that unit did not allow for an extra squadron, and I was thrown back on my own. I grumbled and argued and threatened, but as I had no alternative to offer I found myself a few days later appointed commander to the smallest independent unit in the British Army. A war establishment, M.E. W.E. 866/1, was hastily drawn up: it allowed for twenty-three all ranks:

Five officers:	one major
	one captain
	three subalterns
Eighteen other ranks:	one sergeant
	two corporals
	fifteen privates
And six vehicles:	four armed jeeps
	two three-ton trucks.

We had no adjutant, no quartermaster, no tradesmen, no scale of equipment or weapons.

The provisional name of the unit was 'No. 1 Demolition Squadron'.

My instructions were to recruit the men, draw vehicles, equipment and weapons, and be ready to move to my chosen theatre of operations by November 15th, in twenty days' time.

We all treated the affair as a joke: not because the unit was so small (it was in fact larger than I needed for my immediate purposes), but because it was an independent command. I decided that if I was to be a fool, I would be a glorious one and behave in the grand manner. I wanted a name for the unit that would be short, fanciful, easy to memorize, and, for security, such as would give no indication of its nature. 'Desert Raiders', 'Jebel Rats' and many others failed to please. One morning in November, time getting short, Shan Hackett's patience failed:

'You had better find a name quick, or we shall call you Popski's Private Army,' he said with feigned ferociousness. Why not? The name fitted well with the farcical aspect of the undertaking.

'I'll take it,' I replied. 'I would like to be known as that.' Hackett stared at me, undecided, then grinned, jumped up, and led me downstairs to the office of the Director of Military Operations, Brigadier Davy, with whom rested the decision. A man of imagination and of humour, he agreed immediately, and undertook to square it with the War Office. We laughed and I rushed out to an Indian tailor in town to order shoulder flashes of dark blue with the letters P.P.A. in red. (Later I altered the flashes to white letters on a black ground.)

I had used as a book plate for several years a design of an astrolabe, several of my boats had been called by that name, and it seemed now a fitting symbol for a unit which would have to navigate its way by the stars, so I took my book plate to a Jewish silversmith off the Shareh El Manakh and got him to cut in brass a reduced and simplified design of this astrolabe, which we would use as a hat badge. (Astrolabe is a name given to several astronomical instruments formerly used to measure the altitude of stars, before the adoption of the sextant at sea and the theodolite on land. My design is taken from a sixteenth-century Italian instrument.) The first badges were cut and engraved by hand; they turned out rather too exquisite for the roughness of our manners; later we had a die cut and made the badges of silver, which takes the stamp better than brass. Our Cairo Jew provided us for a long time, till, towards the end of the war, we gave our custom to a silversmith in Rome.

I took a specially worked specimen to Brigadier Davy for approval, with some trepidation, as it looked more like a jewel than a cap badge, but he sanctioned it, to be worn on a black tank corps beret which I had chosen as the unit's headdress.

We had now:

A war establishment
A name
A headdress
A badge
A shoulder flash
One man (myself).

I had two officers in mind, both from the Libyan Arab Force. One of them, Captain Yunnie, from Aberdeen, whom I have mentioned earlier, was released straight away and joined me in Cairo. The other, Lieutenant Caneri, a Frenchman, was not immediately available, but the commanding officer of the L.A.F. promised to send him on to me as soon as he could be replaced.

I called on the commanding officer of the King's Dragoon Guards, the armoured-car regiment with which I had served for a short while a year previously, and asked him to spare me the services of Regimental Sergeant-Major Waterson from Glasgow, which he kindly agreed to do. Waterson, a regular soldier, was just out of hospital and temporarily unemployed in his regiment. I had met him in Abassieh Barracks, where I had set up my headquarters (in the L.R.D.G. quartermaster's stores!). He had expressed a great eagerness to join my newly-formed unit, and I thought that his experience of fighting in armoured cars, his general resourcefulness and his knowledge of the ways of the army would make him a useful recruit.

I set Yunnie and Waterson to draw equipment, and drove down to Ma'adi on a visit to the Director of Survey. Amongst his personnel Sapper Petrie, a young Scottish surveyor with considerable knowledge of practical astronomy and no battle experience whatever, volunteered to join P.P.A. I drove him back to Cairo to select a theodolite from the three instruments which were available in the Middle East, and left him at Abassieh Barracks, the fourth member of my squadron.

Two days later I flew down to Kufra via Wadi Halfa to make several arrangements with L.R.D.G.: a two thousand five hundred mile trip which brought me, amongst other things, one recruit, Corporal Locke, who had been for some time on their waiting list. Jake Easonsmith thought I would find him useful and he was right.

On November 4th I had two officers and three other ranks. The battle of El Alamein had been won and the pursuit of the enemy started. As I wanted to catch the Germans on my own battlefield, I had to hurry or they would have been pushed out of the Jebel before I arrived. I went on a recruiting campaign in the Reinforcement Depots of the Suez Canal area. My determination to keep our aims and our methods secret didn't make appeals for an unknown unit very attractive. Mystery, and the promise of adventure, were my only assets: it produced nine volunteers, mostly R.A.S.C. drivers whose only experience of warfare had been the driving of lorries in convoys in the back areas, and none of them as solid and purposeful as I would have wished. Of these nine, Driver Wilson, a Scot, remained with us till the summer of 1944, and Driver Davies, a Yorkshireman, was, with myself, the only original member of P.P.A. on the rolls when the unit was disbanded after the end of the war: I dropped the others.

With two officers and twelve other ranks, nine of whom were quite raw, I had to be contented. I took with me also three of my Libyan Arabs: Sergeant Mohammed Mustafa, Private 'Abdel Salam Othman and Private Yunes Yusef Abdallah. We all took a course in the use of explosives at the S.A.S. training centre at Kabrit, and by November 22nd I informed Middle East Headquarters that I would move out the next day.

Our equipment had been drawn on the L.R.D.G. scale, with, in addition, such items as fancy or experience dictated and could be coaxed out of complaisant quartermasters. We had over a ton of explosives, but only eleven days' rations, petrol for fifteen hundred miles, but very few spare parts for our vehicles, for they were nearly unobtainable. For the jeeps we had none at all, barring what Yunnie had succeeded in wheedling out of an American technical base.

Our vehicles were four jeeps armed with twin Vickers-K .303 machine guns (swivel mounted) and fitted with racks to carry twelve four-gallon cans of petrol, giving a range of six to seven hundred miles. These jeeps carried a gunner and a driver each and constituted our fighting force. To carry our stores we had two three-ton lorries, armed with one Vickers-K gun each, and manned by two men. My plan was to conceal the two lorries in the Jebel foothills and use them as a base from which we would raid in our jeeps. I hoped to be self-supporting for two months.

In the evening I called on my Belgian friends, Maurice Jacquet and his wife, who had been very good to me and had put me up each time I had been in Cairo. They both came down to admire my brand new jeep (these vehicles were still a novelty), its guns and its fittings. I said goodbye, raced the engine and drove off with a flourish. Round the first corner I had to pull up very suddenly with smoke pouring from under the chassis: I had forgotten to release the hand-brake.

On November 23rd, 1942, we left Cairo for Kufra Oasis, the first lap of wanderings which ended in Vienna three years later. Our route lay first along the main road up the Nile Valley to Asyut, then one hundred and thirty miles to Kharga Oasis, along a well-marked track. In Kharga began the desert trip of nearly six hundred miles to Kufra.

It had been arranged with L.R.D.G. that they would issue us with a wireless set (and an operator) when we arrived in Kufra: for the journey there we were out of touch and I hoped we would not get into trouble. The day before we left Cairo I had received from L.R.D.G. a signal giving me the route I should follow from Kharga: it was a number of astronomical positions such as 24° 16′N., 29° 32′E. and so on; between these points we were to make our way as nearly in a straight line as the ground permitted.

At Kharga we had filled up with petrol from an L.R.D.G. dump and we left at midday. Minding the limited experience of my drivers — we were driving jeeps for the first time in our lives — I led at a cautious pace. The going was good and by nightfall we had covered sixty miles. Bob Yunnie was in exuberant good spirits, so was Sergeant Waterson, and the men caught the infection. I was more subdued; the only one in the party who had ever travelled over the open desert, I felt the weight of my companions' inexperience and tended to expect disaster at every moment. Petrie did his first astrofix with assurance: I was relieved to find that it tallied with my dead reckoning. For his own satisfaction, for he was that kind of man, Petrie did another astrofix later that night, by a slower and more accurate method which kept him up till the early morning, when he was satisfied that he knew our position within a mile.

On the first day out I started worrying everyone into a meticulous routine and I went on doing this — with other men and in other places— till the end of the war. From now on the matter was never out of my mind: an endless conflict between my companions' longing for carefree adventure and my own determination to avoid disaster. Successful adventures, in our line of business, depended on a rigorous attention to detail, as seamen know well enough, but soldiers will not readily admit. I wanted my adventurers to be tidy and thrifty, proper misers chained to a perpetual repetition of tedious duties and piddling cares; they had to have minds like ants, stamp collectors, watch makers and accountants: orderly, precise, unhurried — at the same time I expected them to risk cheerfully the sudden loss of everything they had, to take chances, to make quick decisions, to keep their heart when fortune changed, and to carry out unexpected orders vigorously. I required of them to be both cautious and extravagant, matter-of-fact and imaginative, to plan carefully their enterprises and also to act on sudden inspiration: conflicting qualities seldom found in the same man. In my selection of men and in their training I put more stress on the plodding virtues than on dash, assuming (often rightly) that each one who had volunteered to join our parties cherished in his heart a boyish desire to take a hand in some fun (an understatement which described our more extravagant performances), and would, when the time came, rise to the occasion. My job was to see to it that on that occasion, often a very sudden one, my prospective hero's gun, having been kept clean and well oiled, fired freely, that his vehicle, well maintained, was fit for pursuit or for flight, that he could, without hesitation, lay his hands in the back of his jeep and bring out what he needed: a belt of ammunition or a hand grenade or a torch. I wanted him also to have made sure that petrol had not leaked out of faulty cans, that his emergency rations were at hand, and that his map case had not been torn off his truck when he had last forced his way through bushes. In action, untroubled with mechanical difficulties, my ideally-trained soldier would be free to apply his mind to the fundamental problems of his trade, and be ready with an answer to the ever-recurring questions: 'Where am I?' — 'Where is the enemy?' — 'Where are my friends?'

On that first evening halt I imposed only the most elementary duties, for my men were raw and could easily have been overwhelmed with instructions. I put first every one of the drivers, man or officer, to maintain his vehicle, and the gunners to clean their weapons. Only when these tasks were completed was the evening dinner cooked, after I had supervised the issue of rations and water. We all messed together and took an equal share of fatigues. The Arabs, however, cooked their own food from their own rations.

Petrie, the navigator, who was also gunner on his truck, then set up his theodolite and picked out his stars. Welsh, the fitter, went round the vehicles asking for a job. Sergeant Waterson checked the stocks of petrol and water, of which he brought me a daily statement. Dry desert bushes were collected for the morning fire. When all was done, we sat in the sand round the fire, and drank the Arab tea of our Senussis. Then one by one the men dropped out to roll themselves in their blankets alongside their trucks. Silence fell, the fire flickered out, and, as I fell asleep, I heard the pervading hum of the constellations overhead as they pivoted round the low-lying pole.

With the first lighting of the eastern horizon, I rose, folded my bedding and stowed it in my jeep. Chilled in my shirt and slacks I wrapped myself in a coat and waited for the flash of flames when the cook threw a live match on petrol-soaked branches. The dancing light showed up the yellow sands, the trucks and the still sleeping men. I wanted to make an early start, for I have an irrational belief that an hour gained in the morning is somehow worth three extra hours' driving before sunset, and everyone was so eager that we were on our way as the sun cleared the horizon. I set the sun compass for the first lap of the day's course, adjusted its dial for the time of sunrise, read the speedometer, set my watch for local time (another watch kept Greenwich Mean Time received on a small 'comforts' wireless set) and led off through hilly country. Petrie, following in his jeep, noted down the course followed: bearing, read on the sun compass, distance on the speedometer; then in line ahead, the two three-tonners, the third jeep and finally Yunnie in his jeep brought up the rear. To avoid the risk of vehicles going astray the rule was: if one stops everyone stops. On each truck the gunner was responsible for keeping a watch on the following vehicle, but he seldom did, and every hour or so I stopped the column and drove back to the tail to see that no one was missing.

The going was of softish sand between hills of crumbling rock, a desolate landscape. The trucks bogged many times, practice for us in the use of the steel sand-channels. I noted that all my men worked willingly: they might be inexperienced but they were keen and took their duties to heart. Nearly all Scotch or north country men, they had a natural stubbornness and quiet tempers: they struggled cheerfully to keep the trucks on the move, and delays did not make them lose patience. Yunnie and Waterson cracked jokes and gave to our desperate enterprise an atmosphere of Sunday picnic.

On the second day out from Kharga at about 15.00 hours, Davies's three-tonner stopped, its fan belt having snapped. Welsh the fitter drove up, and started fitting a new one. I waited, waited, went round to investigate, and found that our spare fan belts were of a wrong type, too short and too thin to fit our Chevrolet trucks: the passing incident had turned into a minor disaster. There was no question of towing a truck overloaded with five tons of stores; I wouldn't consider abandoning it, nor its load: if I had had a wireless I could have asked L.R.D.G. to instruct Nick Wilder and his patrol, who were coming up behind us, to bring the proper spares; but I had none and I cursed and blasted Captain Heywood, O.C. Signals, L.R.D.G., who had, unfortunately, arranged to deliver my set in Kufra and not in Cairo.

I had to send Yunnie and Petrie back to Kharga in their two jeeps with instructions to signal Cairo from the Egyptian post asking for the spare belts and ten days' rations for eighteen men to be flown to Kharga. I reckoned they could be back in three days. Petrie was confident that he would not get lost, and what I had seen of his navigation made me trust him.

I didn't mind the mishap about the fan belts, but I felt very badly a blunder I had made about the rations. What had happened was that before leaving Cairo I had estimated that P.P.A. would make the run to Kufra in eight days (against five days which was the L.R.D.G. record); I had then, without sufficient consideration, added a mere three days as a safety margin: a total of eleven days, which was the amount I had drawn. Now we had already eaten three days' rations, we would eat three or four days more before Yunnie came back and we got our men on the move, and we would then have over five hundred miles of difficult desert ahead of us, which, at our slow rate of progress, it might take us anything up to six days to cover — if we had no more accidents. Thus the minimum of food required, allowing no margin, was thirteen days: two more than I had. I had no choice but to publish my shame to the world. I never forgot this initial blunder; my former companions, when they read this, will understand why it was that I was always overloading their vehicles in anticipation of disastrous emergencies that never materialized.

While we were waiting for Yunnie to come back, Waterson and I got down to train our men in the elementary tricks of our trade. Few of them had ever fired a gun, and none of them could handle our Vickers-K machine guns. There was nothing for it but to go at the old rounds from morning till night: strip, put together, strip and once more put together. For variety we threw a few hand grenades and, as a reward for those who could strip and put together blindfolded, we staged a mock jeep battle which was designed to amuse them and no more, for battlecraft can only be acquired by surviving your first battles.

Corporal Locke stood out amongst our men. He was of a ferocious appearance, with a piratical black patch over an empty eyesocket, his face and indeed most of his body criss-crossed with scars and multi-coloured grafts. We had nothing to teach him about weapons or the driving of cars, and he seemed to have been through the most excruciating adventures. I say 'seemed' for I never got to know what his past history had been. Locke was imaginative; the tales he told were rich in detail and of a glorious inconsistency. When I first interviewed him he told me that he was of French birth — his name, he said, was really Loques, which he had altered to an English spelling when he joined the British Army — that he had studied chemistry for one year at London University, which accounted for his elegant, slightly bookish English, that he had an unquenchable thirst for German blood, that he had already killed several of the enemy with his own hands, and that he hoped, if I took him in my unit, to kill many more with a dagger he carried in his battledress blouse. He had served in tanks, but had come by his wounds in the course of hand-to-hand encounters with the enemy. Another version, which came out later, was that he was of British birth with parents in Leeds, and that he had studied chemistry for one year at the Sorbonne, which accounted for his very colloquial French. He had lost his eye on an occasion when he had jumped down the turret of a German tank and killed the whole crew with a spanner.

His French and his English were faultless — I could never catch him out in either language — and not only was he perfectly bilingual but he could behave like an Englishman or a Frenchman according to his company. He was very popular with our men, who never doubted that he was as British as they were themselves; on the other hand I have heard him exchange slangy obscenities in a greasy Parisian accent with French soldiers in Algeria, by whom he was accepted without hesitation as one of their own. His written English was terse with some literary elegancies, his French spelling was sometimes shaky, a contrast which after two years led me to believe that Leeds was more likely to be his birthplace than Reims, Villefranche or Paris.

Bombastic and bloodthirsty, he showed at times a disarming modesty as if asking that his tall stories, a failing which he could not help, should not be held against him. In action he was sensible and composed; although he tended to look for trouble when he was on his own, he took care when he had men in his charge, not to expose them to unnecessary risks. He liked to adorn himself with daggers and bludgeons and second-hand articles of clothing of enemy origin; he stated in refined tones his determination to bring back the ears (or the head, or the privy parts) of the German he would kill, but in fact he never carried out his beastly threats. Locke was a braggart, but a very unusual one, for he was not a coward, but a sensible, brave man; for this reason I kept him in P.P.A. for nearly two years, and released him only when the strain and one more wound threatened to overcome his overstrung balance.

Yunnie arrived back with the supplies a day later than I had expected because he had found the Egyptian wireless operator at Kharga willing but in fact incapable of sending his message to Cairo, and consequently he had had to drive all the way back to Asyut in the Nile Valley, where an R.A.F. camp helped him out. Yunnie was not on good terms with the points of the compass and though he affected an easy familiarity with the sun's azimuth, he had no idea of its relation to the plotting of a course with the sun compass; yet on their return Petrie told me that Yunnie had led all the way, following our tracks, to be sure, when he could see them, and going by remembered landmarks when he couldn't. His memory was uncanny and few could beat him at identifying a track.

We pursued our cautious way on a south-westerly course, our drivers learning a little more desert craft each time they got bogged till we reached a point 23° 11′N. and 26° 32′E., where my instructions showed that I should set a course due west. We had been travelling for the last twenty-four hours across a level plain, but now, barring our new route, a continuous escarpment stretched north and south along the western horizon. The maps of this part of the desert show few features, but even so, our new course would it seemed lead us directly against the eastern cliffs of the Gilf el Kebir. This is a triangular plateau which rises vertically fifteen hundred feet above the surrounding desert plain, like a large island from the sea. From its base, one hundred miles long, somewhere in latitude 24°N., where it emerges from the Egyptian Sand Sea, it runs south to its apex in latitude 22° 42′, presenting all along its odd ninety miles an unscalable obstacle to vehicles bound for Kufra from the Nile Valley. The only practicable route is round its southern tip and then north-east to Kufra; not quite round the tip though, for there is a kind of Magellan's Straits, narrow, tortuous and precipitous, but quite accessible to vehicles, which cuts off the mass of the Gilf el Kebir from its outlying southern extremity. These details didn't appear clearly on the maps; in fact, the main use of the map in these parts was that of a conveniently scaled sheet of paper on which we plotted the course we had followed, and the isolated features of which we had determined the geographical positions with sufficient accuracy. We navigated much like the medieval mariner with his Portolans — itineraries which told him what courses he should sail to get from Venice to Cyprus or to Sevilla, but showed no continuous chart of the coasts. In my present case the portolan (in fact, the signal I had received from L.R.D.G.) told me to drive west at this particular point, and I had no choice but to comply. So west we drove and got immediately entangled in a maze of valleys half filled with soft blown sand, amongst rocky crags which rose higher as we proceeded. The three-tonners were soon hopelessly bogged: pushing forward with two jeeps, then climbing on foot to the top of a scarp, I discovered a wild landscape through which the route I was intended to follow with my heavy vehicles could not possibly lie. I returned to the trucks and we spent the rest of the day in getting them back to the plain.

My portolan had gone wrong — corrupted in transmission — and I cursed once more poor Heywood, who had not delivered me a wireless set for the trip. I then sat down in the headlights of my jeep, with the maps, and tried to think of the right thing to do. Up to this point my job had been to take a party of vehicles on a routine trip from Cairo to Kufra. I found myself now unexpectedly in the position of an explorer in an uncharted country: all the information I had was that I had to get round the barrier of the Gilf el Kebir where it petered out somewhere in the south, how far to the south I had no means of telling. I thought, however, from preparations I had made for a trip to Oweinat before the war, that the tip of the Gilf el Kebir was not south of that mountain which I remembered stood in latitude 22°N. (on the boundary line between Egypt and Sudan). If my memory was right, as we were now approximately in latitude 23°, the furthest south I would have to travel would be about eighty miles. I decided to move roughly southwards over the plains where the going was good, keeping the cliffs of the Gilf el Kebir in sight if possible; and to stop every twenty miles and push a reconnaissance westwards to find what was happening to the escarpment.

I felt very acutely that overloaded three-tonners, clumsily driven, were not suitable for the work of exploration: the next morning at dawn, having lightened my jeep of everything it carried except some petrol, water and food, I set off to reconnoitre the route ahead, leaving Yunnie in charge, with instructions to take advantage of the delay and pump a little more weapon training into our men.

I set my gunner, a man called Hough, to log the route. With a bewildered look on his face he took up notebook and pencil and set himself to write down bearings and distances; as he was another of those men in whom the points of the compass arouse an uncomprehending hostility, the task made him very sad, and I am afraid his career in P.P.A. was doomed from that day. In contrast with his misery I enjoyed myself thoroughly. I liked the meticulous work of breaking a new route through unexplored country; gone were my haste and my impatience and I even forgot the war as I became immersed in delightful details. After two miles of sandy hummocks I came upon a dead level plain of yellow sand, a dry lake bed; its shimmering flatness reaching to the southern horizon invited speed: so smooth that, with the accelerator quite down, the jeep skimmed over its surface without a tremor. To the east white sand dunes, lifted above the ground by mirage, floated in the air like sharp clouds; on the opposite side the broken towers of the Gilf el Kebir, lit by the rising sun, rose in formidable black and white solidity.

After nine miles of dream-like gliding came the shore of boulders and sand, with outcrops of decayed rock, through which the going soon became heavy. When I judged I had gone twenty miles from my camp I turned westwards towards the Gilf, now out of sight behind some hills. Five miles onwards I topped a rise and discovered once more the line of the escarpment, a dull grey now under the higher sun and blunted by the midday haze. It fell off to the west, but, just visible, the line of cliffs turned south again in the distance: the passage was not yet here.

Instead of retracing my steps I drove down into a broad valley where the going seemed fair. I found I could make good progress on a bearing of 243° which slowly converged on to the distant line of the escarpment. After ten miles I emerged on to another level pan; just as I was slowing down for the far shore I cut across the tracks of a vehicle. I stopped, examined and came to the conclusion that not more than four or five days ago an L.R.D.G. type of thirty-hundred-weight truck had gone this way, travelling slightly north of east. As it did not take me much out of my way I followed the tracks, going in the direction from which the unknown vehicle had come, on a general bearing of 260°.

Less than a mile away two more tracks joined up with the first one, then two more, and a mile ahead the five tracks hopelessly intermingled where a defile between two rocky hills had compelled the trucks to travel in line ahead. Beyond the defile the tracks separated again, but kept roughly parallel courses on a bearing of 245°. At this point I told Hough we would have a meal, and after he had got the petrol cooker to burn and I had drunk my tea, I lay down on the sand to think. If the tracks had indeed been made by L.R.D.G. vehicles, it was likely that they were not a surveying party — which had little reason to operate in this area — but just an ordinary patrol on it way from Kufra to Kharga and Cairo. If such was the case I could stop playing the explorer: all I had to do was to follow the tracks all the way to Kufra. An alternative I thought of referred to a certain Count Almasy, a Hungarian German, well known as a desert traveller in Egypt before the war, who, it was rumoured, had started on the German side an organization on the lines of the L.R.D.G., equipped with captured vehicles. I dismissed for the time being the possibility that the tracks might be his, and decided to bring up my party and follow the tracks as long as they seemed plausibly to be leading to Kufra. I didn't doubt my ability to make the oasis on my own, but as I knew that the going between the Gilf el Kebir and Kufra was generally very heavy and that, after a good deal of research, L.R.D.G. had worked out a route which presented a minimum of difficulty, I thought I might as well take advantage of the work that had been done and waste no time floundering in morasses which others had found how to avoid.

I made my way back to camp by another route than I had taken going out, shorter and, as it turned out, easier. We reached the lake bed which I had crossed in the early morning: in the whole of its flat seventy-odd square miles there was one rock, in shape like a plough-share buried upright in the sand with its nose sticking out no more than three inches: I hit it at fifty miles an hour with my right-hand wheels, destroyed both tyres and buckled a wheel. Hough, who had become more and more despondent over his grubby notebook, jumped out and set about the jack and the spare wheels with an ostenta-tious heartiness which meant all too clearly: 'If I had been *driving* and not made to do bloody *sums* like a schoolboy, we would have saved two of the precious tyres you keep preaching about.' In which he was probably right. I would have liked to appear like a demi-God to my men, but I had been conspicuously unsuccessful so far: I had bungled the rations: as far as they knew, with all my pretences at scientific navigation, I had got them all lost in the mountains the day before and had found my way again only when I had got on to a track (which any fool could do), and now with my reckless driving I had lost two new tyres when no other driver had yet even had a puncture.

While Hough was driving me back to camp at a sensible pace I made two resolutions which I believe I have kept ever since: one was that I would preach no more, the other that I would publish my blunders widely and use them as demonstrations of the way things should not be done.

I saw so much gear unnecessarily unloaded, lying around in camp when I arrived that, although there was scarcely an hour's daylight left, I ordered an immediate move as a lesson in mobility. We camped again on the far shore of the lake bed.

The next day, the second of December, following the tracks we reached the entrance of the defile at the southern tip of the Gilf el Kebir: in the distance I saw some vehicles and, remembering Almasy, I moved up to attack with four jeeps, Sergeant Waterson, much more of an expert than I was, leading. At closer range the vehicles were seen to to be, not an enemy patrol, but part of a heavy supply column of the Sudan Defence Force on its way from Wadi Halfa to Kufra, where they had a garrison; we covered our guns and lashed them down before driving up. The cheerful black Sudanese led us to their British officers, with whom we exchanged the gossip of the desert.

On December 4th, eleven days out from Cairo, winding our way amongst decaying hills, we caught sight of the palm groves of Kufra, a low, dark line stretching across the horizon. When I reported to Lt.-Col. Prendergast, under whose command I now came, I submitted meekly to his banter about achieving the slowest journey on record from Cairo to Kufra and thus missing my last chance of fighting in the Jebel. Blundering commander of a half-baked unit, I had no wish to put on airs.

CHAPTER III

PROOF OF YUNES

O N November 23rd, the day we left Cairo, Eighth Army
in Ajedabia, south of Benghazi, completed the third (and
last) liberation of Cyrenaica. When we reached Kufra
the advanced units of the army were sitting opposite Rommel's
entrenchments at El Agheila between the coast and the salt marshes,
building up for the next assault. No more a battlefield, the Jebel had
become the playground of 'Occupied Enemy Territory Administration', and the purpose for which P.P.A. had been formed had ceased
to exist. An attractive objective for us lay now six hundred miles
further to the west, beyond Tripoli and well inside Tunisia, in the area
where the Germans were preparing a rather formidable defensive line
between Jebel Tebaqa and the sea coast. This 'Mareth Line', as we
called it, had originally been fortified by the French in Tunisia against
a possible Italian invasion from Tripolitania. After the fall of France
and the Allied landings in North Africa, the Italians, who now occupied
Tunisia, had turned the Mareth Line inside out to make it face northwards instead of to the south, so as to protect Tripoli from an eventual
Allied thrust. When Rommel suffered defeat at El Alamein, realizing that he might have to abandon Tripoli and be pushed back
into Tunisia, he ordered the Mareth defences to be switched
back to their original quarter, in the hope that he might contain there
the advance of Eighth Army and thus preserve Tunisia as an Axis
bridgehead in Africa. About the Mareth Line Eighth Army knew
little and counted on the L.R.D.G. to discover more.

For me this change of objectives brought up a ticklish problem.
I had been well contented to take my gimcrack unit, raw as it was, into
the Jebel when all I required of it was to provide me with transport, supplies, wireless communication and eventually an escort; with
Yunnie, Waterson, Locke — three good men — a few proved Arabs,

and the help of the whole population of my Libyan kingdom, I should have had a force quite large enough to blow up and destroy all the petrol dumps I could locate: the sneaking tactics successfully used on my previous expeditions would do the trick again. Operating in Tunisia, over unknown ground amongst a possibly hostile local population, was a different kettle of fish. Moreover my targets in Tunisia would have to be completely altered: to the enemy, with his line of communication measured no more in thousands but in hundreds of miles, petrol supplies would cease to be a vital problem; the topographical investigations so urgently required by Eighth Army would be done entirely by L.R.D.G.: they had the numbers and the experience, and I hadn't. I set my mind on harassing enemy convoys and on raiding headquarters and landing grounds: I would, I decided, employ my unit in spreading 'alarm and despondency', a much derided policy which I would turn into a grim reality. For this purpose I knew I had enough cunning and the ability to make use of local circumstances: I lacked a striking force and I set about forging myself one.

From Kufra, where we now sat, the nearest point at which the enemy line of communication on the coast could be reached was over seven hundred miles away, and a desert journey of about eleven hundred miles was required to get to the Mareth Line. I did not want to undertake operations at such a distance from my base as, if I did, I should have, on reaching my destination, barely enough supplies for the return journey. What I wanted was to establish a forward base where I could be self-supporting for two months and have leisure, first to investigate local conditions and then to carry out a succession of raids. I had consequently to remain with the L.R.D.G. until forward dumps had been established. This suited me well enough because I had made up my mind that the best means of training my men was to attach them to L.R.D.G. patrols and make them share their experiences.

Prendergast ran his unit with a business-like efficiency. Ignoring deliberately the glamour of his enterprises, he hated improvisation and organized his fantastic patrols on the solid basis of a railway service. The patrols ran to a timetable, and, however great the distance, reported twice a day on their wireless their position to Headquarters.

Quiet and matter-of-fact, when his presence was required Prendergast flew his own plane, a civilian Waco, to a pin point in the desert, and returned to Headquarters to take up the burden of routine administration. He spoke little and kept somewhat aloof from us all: yet he inspired us with enthusiasm — an improbable enthusiasm which had for its object punctuality, not adventure.

I foresaw some difficulty in persuading him to train my men as I thought he would (very rightly) be reluctant to burden his patrols with 'passengers'. There were, however, precedents: L.R.D.G. had in their time trained the wretched Middle East Commandos, and the very successful S.A.S., and they had given courses in desert navigation to many armoured units of Eighth Army, not to mention the innumerable lifts given to myself, to Advance 'A' Force, to G.(R.), S.O.E. and others on the Jebel bus line. I bided my time doing chores and running errands. On December 16th L.R.D.G. Headquarters moved up leisurely five hundred miles to Zella Oasis in the Fezzan, which had been partly evacuated by the Italians. Four days before Christmas I took a convoy of the Heavy Section up to El Agheila on the coast road for supplies: the enemy had been pushed out eight days earlier on December 13th, and Eighth Army had already established there a supply point and a NAAFI dump.

I made my way back to Zella, through the small oasis of Marada, beyond which, crossing a bumpy sandy plain, our trucks got rather dispersed on a search for easier stretches. Through some delay I fell to the rear; as I was hastening to catch up I saw a man waving: it was Sergeant Waterson, who had sent his jeep ahead and had remained behind to tell me of a more comfortable route he had discovered. He climbed on top of the load in the back of my jeep and I drove on, talking to him as I picked my way. Getting no answer, after a while I turned round and found him gone, thrown off the vehicle by a particularly vicious bump: we picked him up again trudging along in the soft sand, two miles back on our tracks, grinning. The accident was the origin of a game called 'jeep riding' which is played between a 'rider' and 'driver' in the following way: the 'rider' reclines, balanced on the jeep load, with his hands behind his head, his endeavour being to hang on till the driver stalls the engine, bogs the truck or is compelled to pull up; the 'driver's' aim is to throw the 'rider' by any means short of damaging his jeep. Waterson, short and lithe, won all his matches as a 'rider'.

Later that day I drove my jeep down an escarpment to the sandy bottom, pulled up, got out, and signalled to the three-tonners to follow in my tracks. Weldon took the plunge first, slithered down the nearly vertical stretch, reached the sand, went ten yards and stopped with a mighty bang and a burst of smoke and dust that hid his truck completely from my view. Weldon and Petrie staggered out shaken but unhurt though it was discovered six weeks later that Weldon had a ruptured ear drum. Waterson dug in the sand and uncovered across the track a line of mines, from which he removed the primers with great dexterity. This was a job he enjoyed, and he put in his pocket a complete detonating mechanism to take it to pieces later at leisure, thus ensuring for himself complete privacy for several days to come.

The lorry, its left front wheel destroyed and with a bent front axle, could not be driven or towed: I left one of our men with an Arab to keep watch on the load, and we proceeded to walk the remaining twenty-five miles to Zella ahead of our vehicles, searching for mines as we went, for most of the way was so rocky and steep that we couldn't drive off the roughly made track. One of my Arabs, Yunes, showed an unequalled gift for spotting mines. By a distortion of memory I see him, far ahead of the rest of us, poking at suspicious stones with an umbrella, shouting 'mina, mina', waving an arm without turning round, bending to mark the spot with a small cairn of stones and scurrying along. We lifted altogether forty-six mines on that stretch of track. A few miles out from Zella I came across the twisted remains of a jeep and a grave nearby with an Italian cross marked: 'Ufficiale Inglese – Novembre 1942', a grim testimonial to my luck in driving over a mine too deeply buried to be set off by the lightness of my jeep: for Weldon had been blown up exactly in my tracks.

In Zella I found everyone recovering from a colossal Christmas party. The next day I resolved to tackle Prendergast. Instead, it was he who tackled me: I possessed four little treasures which he coveted, four precious jeeps with which, at that time, he was but sparsely provided. These vehicles had more agility than the standard L.R.D.G. thirty-hundredweight trucks: for reconnaissance on mountainous country they had no rival. As a result of our arrangements Corporal Locke with two jeeps was attached to Hunter's Yeomanry patrol, which drove out from Zella on January 3rd bound for the Jebel Nefusa, the semi-circular range which covers the approaches to Tripoli from the desert, with the object of discovering an unguarded motorable pass leading from the Fezzan to Tripoli.

I left Zella on January 8th with my two other jeeps, accompanying Lazarus and his Rhodesian patrol, with the mission of reconnoitring passes across Jebel Nefusa further west than Hunter, in Tunisian territory. I took with me Petrie, our navigator, of whose abilities I had formed good hopes, the Arab Yunes, Sergeant Waterson, my mentor in many things, and an untried cockney. I left Bob Yunnie in Zella, sore and nearly mutinous, to repair our truck and complete our equipment from L.R.D.G. stores. Our trip which was to be topographical, turned out differently from what we had planned.

Whereas Hunter was searching for a pass through which Eighth Army could send an armoured force to outflank Tripoli and thus make easier the capture of this port by the main forces moving up along the coast, our objective was in a sense the opposite. When the army had taken Tripoli the next obstacle on their line of advance would be the Mareth Line, with its main defences lined up between Matmata on the Jebel Nefusa and the sea. West of Matmata very weak defences stopped the twenty mile gap between the Nefusa range and Jebel Tebaqa. Montgomery's intention was to threaten this gap with a very strong diversionary force, thus outflanking the Mareth Line proper and doubling the length of defences Rommel would have to hold. To achieve this 'Left Hook' it would be necessary to find a pass through which the diversionary force, issuing from Tripoli, would cross over to the west of Jebel Nefusa and then move northwards to outflank the Mareth Line. The discovery of such a pass was our objective. On January 8th, the day we left Zella, the attack on the Mareth Line was still ten weeks in the future, the enemy main forces were at Buerat on the Gulf of Syrte; Tripoli, the whole of its plain within the semi-circle of the Nefusa range, the range itself, and most of the Fezzan including Mizda, Shweref and Hon were still in enemy hands. In the southern Fezzan General Leclerc was moving up with his French force from French Equatorial Africa and had just captured Murzuk.

Captain Lazarus, a young New Zealand surveyor, had worked in Rhodesia before the war; for this reason he had been taken from his survey section and put in command of one of the two L.R.D.G. Rhodesian patrols during the absence on leave of Captain Olivey. The other one was commanded by Lieutenant Henry, whom I was to meet surprisingly in the lavatory of the Hotel Transatlantique at Tozeur five weeks later. With Lazarus, his patrol of five thirty-hundredweight trucks and twenty-five men, and my own little group of five men, we spent the night of January 12th in the upper reaches of Wadi Zemzem. We had met some friendly Fezzan Arabs who enter-tained us in the tent of their sheikh. With the help of Yunes, more at home than I was in the Fezzan dialect, I gave them a political speech. We were the first British troops they had seen, a momentous break in the monotonous round of their pastoral lives; the party went well and they told us that there had been considerable enemy traffic moving northwards on the Shweref-Mizda road, twenty-two miles to the west. I issued goodwill gifts and bought from them a couple of lambs for our consumption. The next morning we drove cautiously up Wadi Zemzem towards the road: the going was good but very tortuous between twenty-foot sandy hummocks covered in scrub, which gave no visibility. Towards ten o'clock, when by our reckoning we were getting very close to the road, Yunes told me he heard a noise of vehicles *behind* us. I laughed and said:

'You are wrong for once, Yunes. The road is *up* the wadi and the noise you hear surely comes from the road.' We stopped our vehicles, I climbed a hummock and, sure enough, there was the road a mile away crossing the wadi at right angles, and with a good stream of traffic flowing along it: elements of the Italian garrisons of the southern Fezzan withdrawing to Tripoli covered by an Auto-Saharan company with armoured cars. As our route was across the road and to the west-ward we had to wait for a pause in the traffic to slip across: knowing the Italian custom of a long midday halt and siesta, we thought our opportunity would come in two or three hours' time. Lazarus moved his trucks quietly one at a time to dispersed positions, from which, well-camouflaged amongst the hummocks and quite invisible from the road, they could fire on the enemy vehicles if the need arose. We would engage only if we were discovered: at the start of a long trip it didn't suit us to risk casualties in men or vehicles, and an eventual pursuit by aircraft, for the sake of destroying a few ramshackle Italian lorries; the successful issue of the reconnaissance we were to do for Eighth Army was much more important than the infliction of minor damage on the enemy. Having posted the trucks to our satisfaction, we drove forward three hundred yards in my two jeeps, Lazarus and I with Yunes, Petrie and one Rhodesian, to the foot of a specially high hummock, from the top of which we had a close view of the enemy: we took out our notebooks and set ourselves to take down the parti-culars of the vehicles as they streamed past us. We were well hidden under bushes, seated on comfortable sand and commanded a long stretch of road; of our own vehicles behind us we could only catch a glimpse of one.

We had been at work about half an hour when we heard close at hand the slow thudding bursts of an Italian twenty-millimetre gun. We carried one of these weapons, but so presumably did the enemy; in the maze of hummocks sound was so broken up that it was impos-sible to decide from which direction the gun had been fired. A column of black smoke arose behind us from, it seemed, one of our trucks; a moment later came the rattle of several machine guns. We could see puffs of dust raised on and near the road as our men fired at lorries, making them spurt along, but of the enemy which presumably had attacked us and set fire, by a happy hit, to one of our trucks, we could see nothing, though the noise of the battle increased and seemed to come from all sides. We decided that Italian armoured cars, unper-ceived by us, must have left the road, and, driving down the wadi, which was here half a mile wide between rounded rocky banks some hundred and fifty feet high, were firing at our men from the cover of some of the hummocks which filled the wadi bed. Leaving Yunes on watch on top of our hummock, and our two men manning the guns of the jeeps at its foot, I walked back with Lazarus towards our burning truck. To our bewilderment we found it exactly as we had left it, unharmed but quite deserted, and another unaccountable vehicle burning fiercely sixty yards further downstream. There was no sign of a struggle around the Rhodesian truck, no gear lying around, no paper, no clothing: our men had just walked quietly away. The firing died down, and all sound, excepting the low roar of the burning truck. We stood scratching our heads, thinking of the stories we had read of the *Marie Celeste* found abandoned at sea with her sails set and all in good order. On closer examination we thought that perhaps a half-hearted attempt had been made to drive the truck away, and that it had got bogged as the wheels were somewhat low down in the sand. Another of our trucks, which should have been visible from where we stood, had vanished. After a while I walked towards the mysterious burning wreck. Half way across, a wail of bullets around my head sent me flat on the ground, I crept along to take cover behind a hummock. Somebody was invisibly watching me, someone who wanted to kill. I made a cautious way forward, cleared some bushes and uncovered the source of the fire: a small armoured car with a black German cross on its side. Going back to the deserted truck by a roundabout route, I found Lazarus still figuratively scratching his head: I told him the identity of our blazing visitor and we concluded that Yunes had rightly heard a noise of vehicles *behind* us, that a German armoured-car patrol had been following on our tracks up Wadi Zemzem, the twenty-millimetre gunfire we had heard was ours and it had knocked out one of the enemy cars. Why, with such a nice initial success, our men had chosen to walk away, abandoning their truck undestroyed, we could not account for. It was a rule with us that a vehicle which had to be abandoned in a place where the enemy could possibly get at it should be set on fire, and an incendiary bomb fitted with a short time fuse was always carried under the driver's seat for this purpose. The remainder of the Rhodesian patrol and the Germans, we thought,

[*facing:*   *Top:* YUNES AND THE AUTHOR
        Bottom: SOME MEMBERS OF P.P.A.

YUNES AND THE AUTHOR

WATERSON, CURTIS, RICHES, YATES, DAVIES, LOCKE, WILLIAMSON, (?),
STEWART, BEAUTYMAN, CAMERON

were probably now playing a silent game of hide and seek amongst the hummocks, and as there was nothing useful we could do before we got more information, we ran back to our jeeps, half expecting to find them vanished. Petrie and the Rhodesian, however, were as we had left them: Yunes, they told me, was still on top of the hummock, firing his rifle they knew not at what. I climbed up and found the Arab enjoying himself hugely: in his high tower, from a glimpse here, a flutter in a bush there, a puff of faint smoke, the echo of a shout, the whirr of an engine, he had pieced together a plausible account of our little battle. Remembering no doubt my earlier snub, as soon as he saw me scrambling into his nest-like retreat he said:

'Let me tell you first, Major, what I have understood. A party of five or six German armoured cars and two small lorries, *which I heard this morning*, have driven up Wadi Zemzem, following our tracks. The leading car came unexpectedly upon that one of our trucks which carries in the back the big Italian gun. Our gunner was quick on the mark, he fired first and knocked out the German. That is his smoke there. Our men then tried to get their trucks together, but they were unlucky, three of them got stuck in the sand and were abandoned by their crews who walked over to the remaining two trucks. One of these I can't account for — the last one, with many men on board, is at this moment trying to get out of the wadi up the far bank. The German cars have spread out and are searching the hummocks: they have found one of our bogged trucks and are trying to drive it away. There, that is its engine racing. The German commander has parked his armoured car in that hollow, behind those bushes, and has climbed that hummock: he is now looking round with his glasses.' Yunes shouldered his rifle and fired carefully.

'A near one,' he remarked. 'He will now keep low for a little while. I don't want him to see that truck of ours on the far bank.'

With my own glasses I managed to pick out some of the details of Yunes's picture. One of our trucks with at least twenty men was struggling amongst the rocks half way up the south bank of the wadi half a mile away. I could also pick out the German commander's armoured car, about four hundred yards away, and I caught a glimpse of the man himself before another shot from Yunes made him duck.

I slid down the hummock to confer with Lazarus. Our two jeeps with their light machine guns could not engage the armoured cars: our only hope was in deception. We drove back to the Rhodesian truck, set the time incendiary bomb on the tank, and fired several bursts of our guns in the direction of the German commander to give him something to think about. We then drove a distance up the north bank where there was some cover of trees and scrub, poured petrol over dry branches and set it on fire, hoping to distract the attention of the enemy scouts from our truck and men on the opposite side of the wadi. Finally we returned to Yunes's perch and I called to him to come down. He refused.

'I have hit a man in the car,' he shouted, 'and with my next shot I shall get the commander on his hummock. He is now looking at your fires.'

'Come down, Yunes,' I cried. 'We are going.' I heard two more shots, then a muffled:

'Missed! I am going to get him though.'

Yunes's head appeared over the top:

'Just a moment, Major. I am going to get him now.'

Three more shots of the rifle but still no Yunes. I got very angry and started climbing up, when in a cloud of dust Yunes came slithering down.

'Got him. They are carrying him down this very moment. Let us go and get some more.'

His long, sinuous lips were twisted into a smile of austere enjoyment, his eyes sparkled, the whole of his dark scowling face was lit with satisfaction. He dusted himself, and, perching his long bony self on the back of my jeep, he said ecstatically:

'Major, this is war!' He was older than any of us, but as happy as a child. We were not enjoying ourselves at all: Lazarus had lost his patrol, temporarily he hoped, but the chances of being able to carry out his mission were slender. I was blaming myself for having left our men to themselves — we should not have gone forward together, Lazarus and I: two officers to the patrol and neither of them with the men in their trouble! Petrie, under fire for the first time in his life, was puzzled and missed the comfort of experienced companions on whom he could model his behaviour.

Seizing the opportunity of a gap in the stream of traffic, I led our two jeeps on to the road, turned right and drove leisurely northwards for a mile or so, as if we were part of the straggling convoy; then I left the road and drove parallel with it for another half mile — then half a mile once more along the road — then off again on the far side on a slanting course that took us gradually away from the road and finally out of sight behind a hill. From this point I doubled back in a wide circle that brought us back to a spot opposite the south bank of the wadi where we had last seen our truck. I intended by this manœuvre to lead anyone following our tracks to believe that we had driven along the road on to Mizda.

I left the jeeps under cover, told Petrie to clean our twin guns (to keep him occupied), and with Yunes climbed a low hill: at our feet a bare fifty yards away ran the road, now quite deserted; beyond it the hummocks of Wadi Zemzem, and up the hillside, four hundred yards away, our truck stuck at a crazy angle and apparently abandoned. I hoped I had turned the tables on our enemies — we were now on their flank, and if we engaged them we would be firing from the wrong, the unexpected quarter. I watched a long time through my glasses, Yunes beside me fingering his rifle. A few Germans appeared from the wadi bottom clambering on foot over the rocks towards the truck; a burst of small arms fire from somewhere above sent them to cover, but they soon renewed their advance. We brought the jeeps round the corner of the hill, from where we opened up with our four guns, then pulled back under cover. The Germans, however, never suspecting that a new enemy had joined in the battle, fired steadily uphill from behind their rocks, and never looked at us on their right flank. We repeated the game many times and kept the Germans moving so slowly that they were nearly two hours in reaching the truck. They brought two of their armoured cars to the foot of the bank to fire uphill with their guns.

The Germans finally reached the truck, bringing two machine guns with which, from under cover, they opened up on a position near the crest of the bank. A moment later I saw our men running out one at a time from a sort of cave, up the hillside and out of sight over the rim. In spite of the heavy fire none seemed to be hit. I counted twenty men, more or less, out of twenty-five to be accounted for. We kept up an intermittent fire to prevent the pursuit till we thought our men had enough advance to escape capture. It seemed incredible that the Germans never suspected that they were fired on from across the road. After our men's escape they must have realized that the fire was not coming from above; obsessed with the notion that we were all in the wadi on their side of the road, they searched the hummocks with their armoured cars, and never even looked westwards, where they could not have failed to spot us, for we had become rather rash and also the part of the wadi west of the road, where we were, was flat and offered only the inadequate cover of bare rounded dunes: the bushy hummocks all stopped at the road.

The sun was now setting: guessing that the Germans would leave before dark, we took a wide circle, and a few miles north of the wadi hit the road again, in which we hurriedly dug holes for all the mines we had, covered them up with gravel and gingerly rolled a spare wheel over them to obliterate the signs of our work. We then retired under cover, four hundred yards up the road, and waited. Dusk was gathering when the German column appeared: five armoured cars, two lorries and three L.R.D.G. trucks on tow, a heartbreaking sight. They passed slowly in front of us. Lazarus looked at me and said in a choked voice: 'I know.'

Then the leading armoured car hit one of our mines, lost a wheel and the convoy stopped. We drove up immediately, opened up with our four guns and dashed away madly, zigzagging down the road. It was over in thirty seconds — when the rear armoured car started firing we were already out of range.

The battle was over — we had now to tidy up. There was enough of a moon to light us amongst the hummocks. We drove across the wadi, calling for our men in case some had remained concealed or wounded in the wadi: but none answered. We then went up to the

truck on the hillside which the Germans had failed to remove and set
it on fire. Before starting homeward we crept along the road to where
the armoured car stood at a drunken angle, abandoned. We put an
incendiary bomb in its belly and we departed.

Our rule was that when a patrol got dispersed the rendezvous for
the next twenty-four hours would be at a point fifteen miles back on
its tracks. Shortly after midnight we started back with two jeeps,
following our tracks as best we could in the dark, Lazarus leading.
About three o'clock, having covered twelve miles, we saw a faint
glimmer of a fire amongst rocks on our right: we hailed — Sergeant
Waterson came out to us, genial as ever:

'All nice and snug, sir. Come in and have a look.'

In a natural cave nineteen men were asleep, comfortable on beds
of twigs and leaves, round a smouldering fire. Waterson told us
how, shortly after Lazarus and I had gone forward, the gunner of the
twenty-millimetre Breda gun was foraging in the back of his truck
looking for a book, when some noise made him look up, and he stared
at a German armoured car sixty yards away. He cocked his gun and got
the armoured car with his first burst. They tried then to get their truck
out, thinking of joining the others, but got bogged. The situation
didn't seem serious, so they walked over to the next truck, never
thinking that they would never see their truck again. Confused fighting followed, their position rapidly grew worse, with the enemy all
round them and invisible: they all got into one of the trucks which
they drove up the hillside, thinking of hiding it in safety and then
coming down for the others. Their truck got jammed against a rock,
the Germans had seen them, and they were under heavy fire. Carrying
their small arms (Waterson had a tommy gun), they made their way
to a cave under the hilltop, Henderson the navigator being hit in the
stomach on the way. There they lay for several hours, potting at the
Germans who were trying to make their way uphill. When the Germans reached the truck Waterson decided with the Rhodesian sergeant
that the time had come to get away. They had to abandon Henderson,
who was in great pain and couldn't move; Binney, our cheerful cockney, usually full of banter and brave words, lost his nerve and refused

to face the dash in the open to the hilltop under the German bullets: Waterson tried hard but didn't succeed in putting heart in him, so he let him stay with Henderson to become a prisoner-of-war. Waterson took the trouble to go through his pockets to make sure he had no document on him that would reveal the existence of P.P.A., then dashed out after the others and over the crest. No one was hit but three Rhodesians got separated as the party made its roundabout way over the hills back into the wadi and up our tracks.

The balance of the day's scrap was:

> Two enemy armoured cars burnt out.
> Enemy casualties (if any) unknown. (Yunes claimed two.)

and

> Two of our men captured (one of whom was dangerously wounded).
> Three men missing.
> Five trucks lost, of which three had been captured.
> Our trip to Tunisia cancelled.

I did not altogether regret the incident. Waterson had proved himself to be a tower of strength, Petrie had stood up to the ordeal, had learnt much and could be now counted an active member of the unit; we had got rid of a weak reed, Binney. Thus, by slow degrees, would P.P.A. be built up.

The next day I arranged with our Arab friends of the day before that they would search the hills for the three missing Rhodesians; and surely enough they found them and sent them back on camels to Hon a week later. We proceeded to Shweref, fifty miles away, where an emergency rendezvous had been previously arranged.

Henderson died on his way to hospital in Tripoli. Binney, though in perfect health, had also found his way into hospital, where he was found when our forces occupied Tripoli. He asked to be allowed to rejoin P.P.A. but I wouldn't take him.

CHAPTER IV

STRAFING OF BOB YUNNIE

W E slunk into the wadi at Shweref with our tails between our legs to find a kind of general assembly of L.R.D.G., which mercifully took little notice of us. Never had I seen so many patrols together in one place, some going out, some coming home to Hon, where Headquarters had moved from Zella.

Prendergast flew his Waco over on the second day. He listened to our reports and commented: 'It was rather unfortunate, wasn't it?' — a very strong rebuke from him. We had no time to cry over spilt milk for the war was moving on. Eighth Army was attacking Rommel at Buerat that very day, expected to be in Tripoli a fortnight later, and wanted urgently information about the Mareth Line. Nick Wilder, now on his way back, had signalled that he had found a pass through the Nefusa range suitable for Montgomery's left hook, some forty miles north of Dehibat, and now the ground leading north from Wilder's Gap to the Mareth Line had to be reconnoitred and a route found, not just for an agile L.R.D.G. patrol, but such as could be negotiated by an armoured division. The defences between Matmata and Jebel Tebaqa had also to be investigated: no time could be lost because in a few weeks, with Rommel's forces established in that desolate area, it would be awkward for us to move around.

Dumps of petrol had been established near the Tunisian border and also at Tozeur, an oasis in southern Tunisia, in the hands of the French troops of North Africa, who were now fighting half-heartedly on our side. Jake Easonsmith had flown over to the Headquarters of First Army in Algeria for this purpose, and had brought back a number of incredible tales. One of these, which never failed to raise incredulous laughter, was that the officers in First Army wore *ties*: 'Did they also carry swords and were their men armed with crossbows?'

With these dumps at hand we could now reach Tunisia with supplies to spare for operations: on January 18th, P.P.A., complete and all there was of it, set out in company with Lieutenant Tinker's New Zealand patrol. My orders were to proceed with Tinker to Ksar Rhilane, three hundred miles away, in Tunisia, to reconnoitre with him the going leading up to the Mareth Line; then to get information concerning the defences of the line itself between Matmata and El Hamma. When these reconnaissances had been carried out, my intelligence role would come to an end and I should have a free hand to operate in any area *behind* the Mareth Line and do what harm I could to the enemy according to the information I could collect locally. Thinking of eventual contacts with the officers in ties on the other side, I got these orders written down, stamped and signed (a most unusual procedure with us), and went off to consult my old friend, Bill Shaw, L.R.D.G. intelligence officer. Captain Shaw, a civilian like myself, archaeologist in the Palestinian service before the war, was a veteran desert traveller. He had started with camels, then had joined Bagnold in his early motor trips to Oweinat and the Gilf el Kebir. His name appears in many places on the maps of these areas where dotted lines marked 'Shaw 1935' are the result of his running surveys. In the L.R.D.G. from the foundation, he knew more about the desert, its topography, its inhabitants (present and past), and its military possibilities than any man alive, and he could tell what every patrol that had gone out from the first day had done, where it had been and who were the men on it. His memory was prodigious, and though lately he had no opportunities of going out on patrols, he had a gift of describing a route or the clues to a hidden dump as if he had just been there himself. His desert lore was superior even to the Arabs'; it extended to areas where no Arab had ever been.

I went to him to be briefed about southern Tunisia: of the topography he couldn't tell me much more than appeared on the map, for none of us had yet visited this area, but he advised me not to count on being able to penetrate the Grand Erg, the sands of which I would find much less accessible to my trucks than those of the Libyan Sand Sea, and he warned me against the Arabs of Tunisia, whom he believed to be largely disaffected on account of their long-standing hostility to the French. This was bad news to me; I had planned an impregnable and improbable base in the Grand Erg Oriental, and had counted on a network of Arab information similar to the one which had served me in Cyrenaica. I hoped he was mistaken.

A rendezvous was arranged with Nick Wilder on his way back; he would give us fresh information about the southern part of our area which he had just reconnoitred. I was warned that the S.A.S. would probably be operating in the same parts as ourselves, but their movements and indeed also their aims remained obscure, for David Stirling kept his own council and preferred not to disclose his plans to possible rivals.

David Stirling, young, tall, good looking and dashing, had become (much against his naturally modest disposition) the romantic figure of the war in the Middle East. He had raised his First S.A.S. Regiment and trained it, at first for parachute operations, then for land fighting in jeeps. With Mayne and a band of friends they had ravaged the German airfields before El Alamein and spread panic amongst the defeated enemy troops after the battle. With a light heart and a cool courage he inspired in his men a passionate devotion and led them to thrilling adventures. Where we plodded, he pranced.

He was captured near Gabes a few weeks later and spent the remainder of the war in captivity.

Yunnie had brought up from Zella the tail of P.P.A., and Hunter had also joined the assembly in Shweref, bringing back with him our Locke and his companions. In this way, by a succession of coincidences, my little band was reunited. I moved forward from Shweref, leaving no one behind.

We had lost Binney, captured in Wadi Zemzem, but we had received a powerful reinforcement which increased our officer strength by fifty per cent: Jean Caneri, our third officer, had turned up in Zella. At the time we left Cairo he was with Chapman, my former companion in the Jebel, engaged in sinking ships in Benghazi harbour. The method they used was to swim at night across the harbour carrying special mines (nicknamed Limpets) strapped to their chests. Having reached a ship, they unstrapped the mine and fixed it to the hull under the water line. The mine was fitted with magnets by means of which it adhered to the steel plates of the ship's hull. They then set the time fuse, swam back to shore, recovered their clothes and walked through the town and on to their hide-out ten miles out in the hills. In due course the mine blew a hole ten feet square out of the hull and the ship went to the bottom.

The liberation of Benghazi had put an end to these exhausting exercises. Caneri, fearing to report back to Cairo in case he should be snatched up once more by the decaying Libyan Arab Force, wandered forward instead and happened to be in El Agheila on January 8th when an L.R.D.G. heavy section convoy came up from Zella for supplies. Caneri had been attached to L.R.D.G. for several months and counted many friends amongst its personnel: he gossiped with these men, heard casually that P.P.A. was stationed in Zella, put his kit on board one of their trucks and reported for duty to Bob Yunnie two days later.

Caneri (we pronounced his name as 'Canary') was French. Posted to the French Army in Syria at the declaration of war as a gunner sergeant, he deserted at the time of the fall of France, and came to Cairo where he had spent part of his childhood and had many friends. He promptly enlisted in the British Army, and was commissioned and posted to the Libyan Arab Force after a period of service in the Abyssinian campaign. He had taken a law degree at the Sorbonne, but having served two years as a conscript he had had no opportunity of being called to the bar. He was twenty-six years old when he joined us, and at that time spoke in a rather broken English.

I had now two officers according to my heart: experienced and determined men tied closely together by deep friendship, mutual understanding and a common purpose. Our outlooks differed and were in a way complementary: Yunnie, matter-of-fact as he was, had a romantic side with a touch of flamboyant bravery which gave colour to our undertakings and inspired our men; Caneri, hard and somewhat cynical, had a cold-blooded courage together with a disarming ingenuity: he was both liked and feared — and obeyed. He had a passionate love of tidy details which put order in our affairs where my haphazard negligence produced an incredible confusion. I had imagination, a broad view of our problems and a certain flair for picking out men suitable for our purposes, but without this persevering pair to implement them, most of my plans would have petered out. We had all three of us an obstinate continuity of purpose which urged us on unceasingly and never allowed us to relax.

I could open my heart to them both and yet lose none of my authority: I was thus spared the loneliness which induces a dangerous autocratic pig-headedness in so many commanders incapable of choosing outspoken confidants. With them I was by no means 'always right'; I could not take their acquiescence for granted and I had to consider my decisions more carefully than if my orders had invariably been law.

As soon as we set out from Shweref I realized that the minor operations on which some of us had recently been engaged had borne fruit. Our men, no longer merely thrown together by the chance of recruiting, had now some common memories, excitements experienced together, private jokes, a certain pride in their achievements (somewhat magnified no doubt), a desire to do more, and the beginnings of confidence in their fellows and reliance on their commanders. Locke had distinguished himself in trying to drive his jeep down a precipitous face of Jebel Nefusa west of Nalut, where he had gone with Hunter and his patrol. The jeep had turned over and rolled down the slope, a total wreck, Locke and his companion being thrown out unhurt. Amidst Tripolitanian soldiers (in Italian service) who had turned up at this awkward moment, Locke had recovered his guns and all his equipment. To the Tripolitanians he had somehow conveyed that he was a German officer experimenting with a new type of car. Hunter and he had spent the next night in the comfort of an Italian post (January nights are bitterly cold fifteen hundred feet up the mountains) talking gibberish German to one another, and had slipped away quietly before breakfast. Strangely, Locke himself had given me a very sober account — Hunter had been more colourful in describing our pirate's exploits and gave him great praise for his resourcefulness and his presence of mind

— but I can't say what stories he told his companions, to whom he was now a bit of a hero, and something of a mascot.

Driver Davies, the Yorkshireman, a storekeeper in civilian life, disgraced himself during the trip from Kufra to Zella by whimpering over a bout of malaria, but after his recovery it appeared that his short illness had brought out a latent forcefulness: he bossed his companions, cheered us all in our days of adversity, and showed so much strength of character and so much fun that he had to be made a corporal, then patrol sergeant and finally quartermaster sergeant.

We had lost one jeep down Jebel Nefusa, leaving us with three only, but Prendergast had arranged that Tinker, on completing his reconnaissance, should hand us over one of his. The two three-tonners were in good order.

We set our course through the Hamada el Homra (the red stony desert), about ten thousand square miles of blank on the map, as yet uncrossed by any of our patrols, which we expected to find very difficult going as it had somehow got a reputation for frightfulness. We were agreeably disappointed: the going was quite good over a rolling plain of firm sand strewn with stones. Coming after the black basalt boulders of the Kharug surrounding Hon, where trucks had to travel snakewise, and, however carefully driven, had their tyres shaved off by the razor-like edges of rock, the Hamada el Homra gave us a holiday drive. The reputation for frightfulness came from the complete absence of vegetation: it is a very empty stretch of desert, without a single bush for a hundred miles, but very lovely, the sand a pearly grey, with red stones about the size of a hand, set in it vertically on edge. When the sun is low on the horizon each slope according to the incidence of light comes out in a different colour, shifting, as the traveller proceeds, from pale coral pink to dark crimson.

One morning I noticed along the top of a slope to my left a multitude of small serrations bobbing up and down. Puzzled, as I thought, by a peculiar form of mirage, I drove idly up the slope: my serrations were the heads, just visible above the skyline, of a herd of gazelle bounding along in the same direction as we were going and keeping pretty well the same speed. There were, we estimated, more than two thousand of them, in one compact mass bound on some migration of theirs across the inhospitable Hamada. Suddenly the whole herd took a right turn and joined the path of our trucks: in a moment the beasts were amongst us, so close that I had to brake sharply to avoid running one over. On every vehicle rifles came out, but such was the amazement of our men (to whom hitherto a dozen gazelle seen at one time had been a wonder) at the number and the fearlessness of the lovely animals that not a shot was fired. They ran with our moving trucks for a while, then another turn took the herd out of our path over the northern skyline.

Davies mused a long time over the incident. At our next stop he came over to me:

'They must have thought we were another herd of gazelle.'

Out of the Hamada we drove into rocky hills looking for the petrol dump. With the 'chart and the instructions' we discovered our treasure: cans spread out under rocks and covered with stones. While we were loading, the trucks of T 2 Patrol, with Nick Wilder, came lurching down the wadi, like small ships in a choppy sea with the wind astern. They struck their sails and we exchanged the news. Wilder had found the gap in the range which several other patrols had searched for before him, and was now on his way back to Hon to report, refit and set out again. Much of his reconnaissance had been done wearily on foot, but driving, he told us, had been even more exhausting than walking. The going in the corridor thirty-five miles wide between Jebel Nefusa and the Grand Erg sand dunes was the most exasperating he had ever been over, and he sardonically wished us better luck than he had had, for we were bound for the same unattractive parts. We parted the next morning in our opposite directions.

In uncharted country, each patrol endeavoured to break a new route and to cover fresh ground on each voyage: the information brought back was the material from which Shaw and his surveyors built up maps on which layers of colours denoted the nature of the going. These maps were used by Army Headquarters to plan their movements over the desert and were also issued to the units concerned. Thus it happened that the next day we were running along the edge of an unknown escarpment, searching for a gully down which we could drive our trucks into the plain three hundred feet below. The gullies were all found to end in vertical drops; in desperation we chose to build ourselves a ramp at a spot where the cliff face itself had crumbled down somewhat. For five hours we rolled boulders and carried stones, then drove the jeeps down, then the thirty-hundredweights and finally my heavy, overloaded, three-tonners slithered, lurched and bumped their way down. All the time Italian traffic was running up and down the Sinaun-Nalut track, two miles across the plain. We had a meal and after dark crept across the track and away to the west to rest under cover of very meagre bushes.

The next day we crossed the Tunisian border and immediately encountered the exasperating country Wilder had promised us. Our course lay to the west of his, skirting ochre-coloured dunes, outliers of the Grand Erg Sand Sea, over choppy, closely-packed, sandy hillocks twelve to twenty feet high, overgrown with repulsive bushes. The whole of Tunisia seems to be covered with the decaying carcasses of monstrous, dead animals. In the north, straight, broken-edged mountain ranges sticking out of the plains are sharp backbones from which the flesh has rotted away and flowed down in streams of pus to fill the cesspools of the 'shotts' (a shott is a salt marsh); in the south we travelled as on dubious pelts, firm on top but supported underneath only by sagging putrid entrails. In the tracks of our bumping trucks I expected to see oozing viscous purple projections. In my childhood I had one day slithered down a high bank and landed smartly on my bottom on a very dead sheep covered in grass and leaves: the horrible long-forgotten memory never left me as long as I stayed in Tunisia.

We struggled on a few miles a day. The long three-tonners alternately bellied on the crests and wedged in the troughs of the sand waves; when we struck easier patches of more undulating ground the brush, thick, dry and brittle, collected under the bellies of the jeeps, jammed the steering and caught fire over the exhaust pipes.

On January 24th we met human beings for the first time, a band of twelve Arabs with two camels, ragged, starved and diseased, sulky and suspicious creatures who accepted our hospitality but kept their shifty eyes averted. I took one of them, Abdel Kerim ben 'Ali el Bendiri, with us, nominally as a guide, in fact as a hostage. I had less difficulty in understanding their speech than I had expected, and our Senussis conversed with them quite easily.

The next morning I decided with Tinker to leave behind all our heavy vehicles and to carry out the reconnaissance northwards with jeeps only. We drove westwards under a hill called Qaret 'Ali, intending to establish our base a few miles inside the sand dunes of the Grand Erg, where it would be safe against surprise by enemy land forces. At our first attempt we realized that the technique which had taken us over the Libyan Sand Sea would not serve us here: the dunes here were made of dirty brown, powdery, silt-like sand, into which our steel channels sank as in water. We gave up the attempt and established our base on a long patch of hard ground, surrounded on three sides by high dunes, a position easy enough to defend as it could only be reached along a narrow neck. Vehicles trying to force an entry would have to negotiate this difficult gap under the fire of our trucks, well covered themselves by low hummocks. To make things more difficult we laid a few mines in the gap, leaving only a passage for our own use. We filled with water from brackish wells under Qaret el Jesseb, three miles to the south. I put Yunnie in charge of the party, handed him our hostage, wished him good luck, and left, to be back in four or five days.

Our reconnaissance party was made up of Tinker, his navigator, and two of his New Zealanders in two jeeps, myself, Caneri, Petrie, Yunes and one man in two other jeeps: a nice party to handle, small enough to keep easily under control; as each one of us knew exactly what we were doing I had no worry about a tail that might go astray. Our low vehicles were practically invisible: the only enemy we had to beware of were armoured cars, and as long as we kept off the tracks, which they couldn't leave in this difficult country, we were quite safe. The local Arabs had reluctantly told us that the only German and Italian posts in the neighbourhood were at Duz, Jemma and Kebili. Ksar Rhilane, an old Roman fort twenty miles north of Qaret 'Ali, was empty by their account. We first made sure of this, and found the only inhabitant within its crumbling walls an elderly Arab called 'Ali, a former sergeant major in the French colonial troops, who spoke French, and preserved in his raggedness remains of military swagger. He told us that a number of vehicles similar to ours had been at the fort a few days previously and had driven off northwards (an S.A.S. detachment we concluded), and that two of these men, their jeep broken down and mislaid, had been living at the fort ever since — but they could not be found before we left. Separated in two groups to cover more ground, we made, as nearly in a straight line as we could, for Matmata, two miles short of which we arranged to meet again in the evening. Up, down and round we switchbacked over the hillocks, stopping only to clear the brushwood from under the chassis. In the early afternoon we reached higher ground and better going. Two unknown jeeps came dashing up a slope behind us: I turned to face them and put out a yellow flag, the agreed recognition signal for all our troops operating in Tunisia, but they took no notice, and stopped only when I fired a burst over their heads. They were six hearty paratroopers of the French section of the S.A.S., who had had originally three jeeps (but had smashed one), and now in their eagerness they were rushing off to Kebili for some vague purpose of their own, and wouldn't listen to my warnings of enemy troops, but drove off at an unreasonable speed, waving and shouting excited farewells.

At four o'clock of the afternoon we pulled up in a discreet wadi within sight of Matmata, a small stone-built town perched on one of the last spurs of the Nefusa range. Less than ten minutes later Yunes, posted as a look-out on top of a hill, waved Tinker in. He and I immediately walked towards Matmata over rocks and grassy slopes — this corner of Tunisia was like a real country — and before nightfall we had seen as much as we needed to make a fair sketch of the western approaches to the town. We had even been near enough to look into the sleepy streets, where, apart from a few Arabs, we had only seen two fat German officers, a very different picture from what I had expected of the fortress which guarded the western end of the formidable Mareth Line.

The main defences of the original Mareth Line extended westwards from the coast to Matmata. The gap through which Montgomery intended to launch his left hook extended from this town to the Jebel Tebaqa range: it was the main object of our reconnaissance. We had that day examined the approaches and found a possible route for an armoured division: it remained now to reconnoitre the actual battle ground. We knew that the planners at Eighth Army Headquarters were waiting for the results of our investigations and we made all the haste we could.

During our absence Yunes had been gossiping with some Arab shepherds, to whom he had given out that we were German officers concerned with the building of the new defences, and had given them hopes of employment. He had heard that some of our supposed colleagues were indeed engaged in building strong points along a line extending from Matmata to the eastern tip of Jebel Tebaqa. This was precisely what we had come to investigate; during the next day, roaming gingerly in the twenty mile gap between the two ranges, we saw I believe most of the work being done by the Germans at the time, which was not very much. They were not taking too seriously the possibility of an attack in force west of the Nefusa range. We knew better and felt very powerful in our four little jeeps.

Tinker had a gravity well beyond his years — I believe he was only twenty-two — and a great big, black, bushy beard gave him an elderly appearance. I treated him as a man of my own age, and such was the assurance of his manner that I tended to take his advice in many matters. Several months later I called on the L.R.D.G. in Egypt, where they had gone to refit, and saw most of my friends. Left alone in the mess I went over in my mind the names of those I had wanted to see and found that Tinker had not put in an appearance. An unknown, slim, clean-shaven youth came in, whom I had noticed previously keeping shyly in the background as if he was a new recruit. I asked him:

'Do you know if Lieutenant Tinker is in camp? I particularly want to see him.'

Surprised, he laughed.

'I am Tinker. I wondered why you wouldn't speak to me, Popski.'

At the end of the fourth day of our reconnaissance we considered that we had the answers to the main problems set by Eighth Army: we had found a route – of terribly bad going, but just practicable, from Wilder's Gap up to the western end of the main Mareth Line; behind the line and as far as El Hamma we had found, with the exception of one wadi, the ground free of major obstacles, either topographical or man-made, and we knew the location of the defence works that were built at that time.

Six weeks later the New Zealand Corps, comprising the Second New Zealand Division, the Eighth Armoured Brigade and General Leclerc's force, reinforced later by the First Armoured Division, was to advance along the route we had reconnoitred and to attack Rommel's right wing on the ground over which we had just been wandering. They forced their way as far as El Hamma, outflanked Rommel, compelled him to withdraw his forces to Wadi Akarit and won the Battle of the Mareth Line.

Our share in the coming events was now to pass on our knowledge to Eighth Army, and accordingly we made for our wireless at Qaret 'Ali.

We separated once more: I took an easterly route along the Nefusa foothills, Tinker went zigzagging towards Kebili, and promised to join us at our base the next day, calling at Ksar Rhilane on the way. With Caneri we struggled on for hours in a maze of hillocks till we emerged on the Kebili-Fum Tatahwin road: it was lovely and smooth, the temptation great – we fell, and, ignoring the risk, whizzed along the road. I pulled up to ask a young shepherd how far to the water.

'Quite near,' he said, and went on to gossip of other things. As we were leaving he said: 'The two cars of your friends are at the well now,' and pointed to two Italian scout cars which – unnoticed by us – were drawing water from Bir Soltan a quarter of a mile to the right of the road. I had a hurried conference with Caneri: we were in great spirits, our reconnaissance had been more successful than we had dared to hope, forty miles away only, the comfort of our big trucks would be ours this very night, and we could now afford to enjoy a little fun. I decided to shoot up the Italian cars and investigate the wells. Water supplies, I speciously argued to myself, were a matter of vital importance to a large force moving in the desert: Eighth Army would want to know all about Bir Soltan, and my mission would be incomplete without a report on this water.

We cocked our guns and I led slowly along the road, looking for the turning which led to the wells. The plan was to drive our two jeeps abreast and thirty yards apart, straight at the wells, and open fire at a hundred yards range. Carefully — round a bend — and uphill. My gunner tapped my arm, pointed ahead and said: 'Do you see what I see?'

What I saw was the turret of a whacking big tank, hull down by the roadside a hundred yards away. I stuck out my arm for Caneri, turned sharp left off the road, put my foot down and went bouncing along the hillside out of sight. Caneri, who had seen nothing, had the sense to follow me and caught up when I had gone in a wide circle and crossed the road again three miles below the wells. The laugh was on us even more than we knew: I heard later that what I had seen of the turret was all there was — it had no tank underneath! Set up at some past time as a machine-gun post to guard the wells, it was not manned.

At another well five miles from Ksar Rhilane where we stopped for water, an ancient, toothless Arab, nearly unintelligible, made desperate efforts to warn us of some urgent danger. All we could gather was that something had been burnt and that the enemy was about. The poor creature could not know which of us was fighting whom. I thought there might have been a scrap between the French madmen and an Italian patrol from Duz. Anyway, it seemed reasonable not to drive into Ksar Rhilane without first making sure that the enemy wasn't in it: so two miles short of the Roman fort, we concealed our two jeeps in thick bushes, and while we waited quietly for the night to fall I told Caneri of plans I was making. That evening I would write my report to Eighth Army; the next day I would remain at Qaret 'Ali, waiting for Tinker's return. The following day Tinker and his New Zealanders would make for Hon and we would remain to start operations on our own account. I had noticed a telephone line connecting the half-built German strong points off Matmata: we would liberate a field telephone, tap the line, ring up Headquarters in Gabes and find the times of the supply trains running from the harbour in Gabes to railhead in Medenine. With this information we would arrange for a train to blow itself up, together with a bridge between Gabes and Katena. If the times turned out suitable, we might simultaneously make a noisy night display in the streets of Gabes as a diversion. I would arrange to give the Germans the impression that our raid had originated from French-held Tozeur, and we would then withdraw in peace for a while to a new hiding place south of Qaret 'Ali. For the next operation I was thinking of breaking past Gabes into central Tunisia. By the time I could be ready for it I thought Eighth Army would be on the Tunisian border, Gabes would be within fighter range of the R.A.F., and our place would be much further back in the enemy rear.

Night came. Caneri and Yunes walked away towards Ksar Rhilane. Busy in my mind with the details of my plans, I lay down on the ground to wait for their return. An hour and a half later the lights of a car showed below the skyline. We brought the guns of the jeeps to bear on the track and waited: I thought Caneri had been captured and that the enemy were now searching for us. Two headlights that might have been those of a jeep appeared over a rise. I made up my mind and flashed R — R — R on my torch. The headlights blinked T — T — T, an agreed reply, and we uncocked the guns. A jeep pulled up, Caneri climbed out, with him was the French lieutenant parachutist. I said:

'I am glad to see you are still alive and free.'

He laughed. 'I know. But we never got to Kebili. We smashed another jeep, piled the six of us on to the last remaining one and came back to Ksar Rhilane. Now it seems that the enemy has been active. I have heard rumours that three Messerschmidts strafed your camp at Qaret 'Ali yesterday morning and that some of your vehicles have been burnt out.'

We drove to the Roman tower. 'Ali, the friendly old sergeant major, late of the French Army, confirmed the rumour. Two of the Arabs we had met at Qaret 'Ali had ridden to the Italian post at Duz with the information of our leaguer.

I left Caneri and the six Frenchmen concealed outside Ksar Rhilane to intercept Tinker on his return and prevent him from falling into a trap, for if, as I expected, an Italian armoured patrol came down from Duz or Kebili to deal with the survivors of the Luftwaffe raid, the only track they could use ran through Ksar Rhilane. I drove off in the night, with 'Ali to guide me to Qaret 'Ali.

The jeep crashed through the malevolent, man-high Tunisian weeds with a continuous crackle. The glare of the headlights gave them repellent, unnatural hues of metallic green and white as they sprang at us out of the night and vanished under the car. 'Ali understood his job; after an hour and a half we turned right into the defile leading to our leaguer; as I drove through my lights suddenly picked out the skeleton of a three-ton truck standing gauntly burnt out amongst flung litter; I drove round the leaguer, counting the wrecks: every one of my trucks and those of the New Zealanders stood burnt to the ribs. There was a deadly hush and no sign of our men.

CHAPTER V

LIKE NEW ZEALANDERS

AT the far end of the leaguer we picked up footprints in the sand of many men, a trail leading into the highest dunes. I left the jeep and followed the trail on foot with a torch: up and up I trudged for a quarter of an hour, shouting my name, reached a crest, sank into a hollow, climbed another slope. I was challenged and shone my torch on a figure muffled in a blanket. Bob Yunnie led me to a hollow where his men were sleeping: they were all there, but two New Zealanders had limb wounds and couldn't walk.

He had saved a few pistols and tommy guns, some rations and a few blankets. Thirty cans of petrol which he had buried had been dug up by the Arabs during the night and stolen. All the rest was lost. The Arabs, including our hostage, had vanished.

The extent of my disaster filled me with sombre joy. My mind was swept clean of all the plans and the hopes with which I had been busy day and night during the last three months, and I had not even a flicker of regret for the strenuous preparations and the long efforts now suddenly wasted at the very moment they were about to bear fruit. From my long-cherished plans for defeating the enemy single-handed, my mind switched over in a moment to consider the new and desperate problems which I had now to solve. Exhilarated by the urgency and the difficulty of the task, my brain functioned with a delightful, effortless lucidity, which I had never experienced before, for I am usually a slow and muddled thinker, full of questionings and doubts.

Woefully cheerful, Yunnie told me that early the previous morning three Messerschmidts had dived from just over the high dunes which surrounded the leaguer. The rattle of their machine guns was the first warning he had had. Backwards and forwards they dived and machine-gunned, and flew away after five minutes, leaving his nine trucks ablaze and exploding. He had tried to save our wireless jeep, which had not been hit, but a burning petrol can, projected from one of the three-tonners, landed on the truck and put an end to it. Two New Zealanders had bullet wounds and several other men, including Waterson, had suffered superficial burns while they were attempting salvage from the blaze. Expecting an Italian motor patrol, he had withdrawn with his men into the dunes, where they could only be attacked on foot.

We sat talking in low voices, the men asleep around us. A fire had been kindled by our Senussis and they brewed us some tea, for they had salvaged, together with their weapons, their teapots and glasses. While I questioned Yunnie and listened to his replies, a picture of our situation formed itself in my mind with a clarity of detail that owed nothing to any conscious effort of mine. This picture in outline was as follows: the nearest spot at which I could expect to find help was Tozeur, the French oasis on the other side of Shott Jerid. The distance from Qaret 'Ali to Tozeur was roughly one hundred and ninety miles over unknown desert — probably very rough. The enemy, mostly Italian, had known posts along our route at Duz, Kebili and Sabria. They knew of our presence in the area. The nomad Arabs were miserable but actively hostile: they might fight us themselves, and they would certainly attempt to ingratiate themselves with their Italian masters by reporting our movements. Though they were few in numbers we couldn't hope to move through their areas without their knowledge, and we should have to rely on them to show us the wells, and probably for food. We had no wireless.

Our vehicles were five jeeps, with no more than fifty gallons of petrol between them: probably enough to take three jeeps as far as Tozeur.

Counting the Frenchmen and the two S.A.S. men stranded in Ksar Rhilane, our party numbered fifty-one men, two of whom were wounded and unable to walk. The others were ill shod (most of us wore open sandals or gym shoes on our bare feet) and untrained for long marches.

The food available was sufficient for five or six days, on very short rations.

My immediate tasks, in order of urgency, were:

Communicate the results of our reconnaissance to Eighth Army.
Get medical attention for the wounded.

Get our men out of the dunes at Qaret 'Ali, before dawn if possible, to avoid the risk of their being trapped by an Italian land force, and then march them to Tozeur to safety.

Warn Henry, who was coming up behind us with his Rhodesian patrol, of the danger he was in of being betrayed to the Luftwaffe by the local Arabs.

By the time Yunnie had finished his report I knew how I was going to set about my business. It was fascinating, I thought, to find all the answers without having to rack my brains; I hoped this unexpected power of decision would remain with me for ever, and I looked forward to the next few days with pleasure. I had all the men woken up and sitting around me; with fresh wood on the fire I kindled a bright blaze so as to light their faces for me while I spoke to them; and to give them time to collect their spirits I made the Arabs draw extravagantly on our meagre supplies of tea and prepare a powerful brew of Arab tea for everyone. I myself woke the two wounded New Zealanders and helped them to the fire: they had had a shot of morphia and slumbered heavily.

When I saw that I had everyone's attention I said:

'You may think that something has happened to Tinker that he is not here with me. Tinker is all right. He will be back tomorrow. While you were being strafed here we made quite a scoop, Tinker and I, and we want to get the news back to Army quick. We have now got no wireless so we shall go over to First Army to find one.

'Our mishap here was brought about by the local Arabs who betrayed us. I know the two who did it. The Arabs here are not like the Senussis; they are paid by the Italians and the Germans.

'The nearest place where we can get in touch with First Army is Tozeur, held by the French. We are going to walk one hundred and ninety miles to get there. We shan't all walk: Tinker and Caneri are going to drive in three jeeps carrying twelve men, including our two casualties. The rest of us will walk. If possible when the driving party reaches Tozeur they will raise transport and come back to collect the walking party. But we mustn't count on it. I reckon we can walk to Tozeur in eight days and we are going to start in two hours' time so as to get out of this place, which I don't like, before daylight. Also we haven't got much food and we don't want to waste it sitting on our bottoms.

'I shall drive the two casualties to Ksar Rhilane right now and drive back here in the early morning to collect the food and kit which the Arabs haven't looted. Sergeant Waterson will be in charge of the walking party from here to Ksar Rhilane, and Yunes will guide you by the shortest route, which does *not* follow the tracks of my jeep.

'Bob Yunnie, Sergeant Garven and Sergeant Mohammed will remain here for no more than seven days, in case Henry and S Patrol call here on their way to Tozeur. He is to warn them of the danger of betrayal by the Arabs. If Henry does not call they will make their own way to Tozeur.

'With a little luck we shall get out of this jam without any worse trouble than very sore feet. I want you all to keep close together and allow no one to stray. This is not the Jebel. A lonely man will not have a chance amongst hostile Arabs.

'That is all. Thank you very much. Waterson will now call the roll.'

My original intention had been to leave Sergeant Mohammed behind alone to convey the warning to Henry, but I had accepted Yunnie's offer to stay with him, and Sergeant Garven, a New Zealander, had also asked to be allowed to remain: he felt, I believe, that L.R.D.G. should be represented on this desperate rear party.

Yunnie, at that time thirty-three years old, was fundamentally a civilian. He held the methods and the discipline of the army in some contempt and preferred — passionately — to go his own way. He claimed now, as a privilege, to be allowed to remain behind on this risky mission: I thought it would compensate him, in a way, for his cruel disappointment at the loss of our equipment, for he, more than anybody else, had had the trouble of getting it together, and now it was all gone while he was still waiting for his first chance to use it.

He thought that, assisted by the craftiness of Mohammed, they would be able to survive in spite of the treachery of the local Arabs. Mohammed had been with him on the two hundred mile trek behind the lines, when his Libyan battalion had walked from Ajedabia to Tobruq nearly exactly a year previously: and from that time he had put great faith in his ability.

The two wounded New Zealanders were carried to my jeep, and I drove immediately to Ksar Rhilane, where I left them with Caneri; then back again to Qaret 'Ali to rummage for food by daylight. Waterson and the walking party had left at four guided by 'Ali, on whom Yunes kept an eye.

Bob Yunnie, Mohammed and two men of P.P.A. were collecting tins when I arrived. Fortunately the Arabs had no use for tinned food, and had overlooked it in their very thorough looting, which had even included the theodolite, after it had been salvaged and hidden under a bush.

On my way back for the second time to Ksar Rhilane with our small stock of supplies and my two men, I followed the tracks of the walking party and overtook them about midday as they were resting and waiting for their dinner to be boiled: a large kid which Yunes had bought from some Arabs. They seemed all in good spirits and Waterson particularly ebullient. I believe that, like me, he enjoyed disasters.

At Ksar Rhilane Tinker was very impatient to get our reports sent over to Eighth Army. We decided that he would leave the same evening for Tozeur and First Army, and that my walking party would follow in the tracks of his jeeps. After sending off our messages to Eighth Army, he would try to raise transport and come back along his tracks to meet us and give us a lift. We found that we had enough petrol to send three jeeps to Tozeur, with a few gallons left over for my jeep and the French one which would carry supplies for the walking party and give us the protection of their guns, as long as the petrol lasted.

My walking party consisted of thirty-seven men: seventeen New Zealanders, twelve British, six French and two Arabs. As we were practically unarmed, our chances of avoiding being killed on our two hundred mile march were slender. On our right, and no more than five miles distant from our route, stood the Italian posts in Duz and Sabria. On our left the sands of the Grand Erg prevented us from giving the enemy a wider berth. All along the first hundred miles of our route any Arab who decided to betray us would not have to ride his camel more than a few hours before reaching an Italian post where a reward would be paid for his information. I had no fear of a motorized column, as the Italians possessed no vehicles that could travel over the difficult country we would be crossing, nor could their aircraft hurt us much beyond compelling us to waste time under cover; but they had mounted native troops against which we would be quite powerless once they got on our tracks. And the nomad Arabs themselves with their antique muskets could well snipe us out of existence if ever they discovered how few weapons we carried. In the latter part of our march we ran the risk of encountering patrols of French Goums, who had a reputation for shooting first and asking questions afterwards, and for being rather indiscriminate in their choice of enemies.

My only chance of getting my men through alive lay in bluffing our enemies, Italians and Arabs, and playing them off, one against the other. This I proceeded to attempt without delay. The Italians first; though three days had now elapsed since the air attack, they had shown no signs of sending out a patrol to investigate. I assumed that the reports they must have received of vehicles moving around Ksar Rhilane made them shy of risking a scrap with an unknown number of heavily armed and highly mobile jeeps. I decided to give them a fantastic idea of our numbers. I got 'Ali to invite a few of the neighbouring shepherds to have tea with me at the fort: then, while we were sipping, Caneri drove smartly into the courtyard with two jeeps, came up to me, saluted, pocketed a document I handed to him, and departed with a great noisy revving of engines. A moment later Tinker repeated the ceremony with three jeeps, then the French lieutenant with two vehicles, and so on till, in the course of an hour, every one of the fifteen men we had with us at the moment had come up before me and our five jeeps had been displayed nine times over. Hurried alterations were made to the jeep loads between each scene, although I felt sure that to my untrained guests one jeep was as good as another. I knew that in the early hours of next morning an alarmed Italian commander in Duz would be pulled out of bed to listen to reports of fifty jeeps mounting six guns each, all passing through Ksar Rhilane in one afternoon. It would, I hoped, put him on the defensive, clamouring on the telephone for reinforcements from Kebili. A warning no doubt would also reach Sabria, further on our course.

The show over, I went into a huddle with Yunes and 'Abdel Salam to concoct a programme of deception for the use of the Arabs we would meet on our march.

Waterson and his party walked in from Qaret 'Ali later in the after-noon and that evening Tinker and Caneri, with the two casualties and eight men, drove off to Tozeur, taking with them by mistake two of the petrol cans which had been put aside for my use.

The next morning I called my motley party together, gave them my instructions successively in English, French and Arabic, and we walked off in good order for a well, Bir Haj Brahim, twenty-five miles away, where I wanted to spend the first night. Two hours later we were a straggling column stretched over a mile: Waterson and a group of enthusiasts led the pace at a rate that I found hard to keep up. Now and then I got into my jeep and counted the men as they went by, then drove up again, carrying the last stragglers to march with Waterson for a while. In this disorder we were lucky to gather all our men to the well at nightfall. The six Frenchmen insisted on riding in their jeep, and nothing I said could shame them into taking turns at walking and giving lifts to the more footsore of their companions. They were quite unconscious of the precariousness of our position and talked wildly of pushing ahead and clearing away the Arabs for us.

We found some shepherds watering their cattle at the well and tried on them the story we had prepared. Their acceptance gave us hopes that we would also succeed in deceiving warriors less obtuse than these simple-minded lads. The next day we kept better order, stopping every hour and collecting the stragglers each time, but we covered only fifteen miles. We saw no Arabs at all the whole of that day.

On the third day we again did fifteen miles. Some of the men were now going barefooted rather than in open sandals which collect sand between foot and sole and make walking very painful. But their feet were tender and they made slow progress. We camped for the night seven miles from Sabria in sand dunes. The night was so cold that I burnt a hole in my leather jerkin sleeping on the fire; another man burnt his socks off his feet. These comical mishaps considerably helped our morale.

We had seen no Arabs during the whole day, but two men came up to our fire after dark: it seems there was a feud between the tribe which pastured its flocks near Duz and that which kept near Ksar Rhilane and to avoid daily clashes they left an empty no-man's-land to divide their grazings; thus it was our good fortune that gossip seeped through slowly, and rumours of our identity had not reached them.

Like all the tribesmen in southern Tunisia these men were destitute and lived miserably off their thin cattle for which they had no decent grazing. The French, the Italians and also some of their Arab brethren settling on the land further north, had slowly squeezed them out of the rich pastures on which their forefathers had lived in plenty. Hence a surly resentment against all the people in the north, dull grievances which I intended to exploit for our own ends. 'Ali of the Roman castle, who was glib and politically minded as befitted a man who counted himself well travelled and enlightened, had provided me with a knowledge of local politics, sufficient, I hoped, for my dealings with the half-savage tribesmen.

I entertained my visitors as nobly as my means allowed and asked them to inform their sheikh, whose tents were pitched some twenty-five miles to the south-west, of my visit on the following evening. For their pains I gave them a present of money, generous indeed but not so extravagant (I had inquired from 'Ali the Italian rates of pay) as to excite their cupidity. I gave them to understand that I had matters of importance and secrecy to disclose to their sheikh, counting on the Arabs' love of intrigue to keep their mouths shut.

My big bluff had to be made on the next day or never, because after that time I would be out of petrol, and, without the prestige of a car, I couldn't hope to impress the intended victims of my deceptions with my secret importance. My visitors no doubt could not have helped noticing the scarcity of our weapons: so I hinted broadly that with us all was not as it seemed, as our common enemies, the French, would in due course find out to their grief. With this suggestion of secret weapons I sent them home.

On the fourth day we made an early start and walked over twenty miles following the tracks of Tinker's jeeps, to come to rest in the early afternoon two miles from a spring, 'En bu Rdaf. The going over choppy hillocks overgrown with bushes was tiring for the walkers and alarmingly heavy on petrol for the jeeps. We had all suddenly become extremely ragged; every semblance of military smartness discarded, our appearance was that of a band of refugees. The raggedness, however, was not in our hearts: shadowed the whole day by Arab horsemen, we moved in a close group, ready to fight at any moment, the few of us who possessed a weapon disposed at the head and at the tail of our column. My jeep drove a few hundred yards ahead, the Frenchmen in the rear, driving and stopping alternately so as not to outstrip the men on foot. During the afternoon more and more horsemen showed up on both flanks: with old French Chassepot rifles or long Arab muskets slung on their backs, they became bolder as their numbers increased and I thought that it was only out of respect for the twin guns on our jeeps that they refrained from falling on us.

At the evening halt I found that no more than a few pints of muddy petrol were left in the tanks. We drained and strained the last drops from the French jeep and poured it into mine, hoping it would last long enough to enable it to perform its last task. I got ready for a ceremonial call: as I had carried my kit with me in the jeep all the time I had not suffered to the same extent as the others from the disaster at Qaret 'Ali; I managed to dress with some appearance of decency. and strapped on to me a .45 pistol, field glasses, compass and empty pouches. Yunes and 'Abdel Salam had salvaged some of their kit together with their rifles, and we made them look spruce enough. They were the only ones in our crowd who wore army boots. I took Locke with me as my gunner and covered his nakedness — for he wore only a pair of khaki shorts — with my sheepskin coat and gave him my spare pair of desert boots, three sizes too big. I armed him with a tommy gun and an automatic — he had also saved his dagger — and briefed him in his new role. Thus arrayed, the four of us drove off to 'En bu Rdaf, the spring of water at which I had arranged to meet my visitors of the previous night. An Arab, impressed from the crowd of onlookers, guided us. At the spring, to my immense relief, I found both my messengers waiting for me: perched on the back of my jeep they escorted us to the tents of their sheikh.

A man of mean appearance with clever shifty eyes, he was sitting under a patched tent with the flaps up. As he rose to greet me I saw that he too had made an effort to smarten himself up: his threadbare burnous was white and fairly clean, but his followers were clad in the usual ragged brown homespun. Assuming my best party manners, I drew out as long as I could the exchange of courtesies, noticing hopefully some preparations for a meal. My host and his followers being unarmed, I unbuckled my belt and threw it in the jeep: my Senussis required no telling and had already placed their rifles under Locke's care. He remained sitting behind his guns and refused mutely invitations to alight.

We sat down under the tent on camel saddles covered with sheepskins: our host, a poor man, owned neither wooden sofas nor rugs. As we had arranged, Yunes sat next to me to help me in my conversation and interpret when the local dialect became too obscure for my understanding; 'Abdel Salam, a wizened old man of great cunning and sagacity, sat amongst the followers to spread calculated indiscretions.

I wanted to impress my host with the importance of my own person, as well as with the greatness of my condescension in visiting him. My aim was to make him feel flattered and eager to learn the object of my visit; never to suspect that I wanted favours from him. For this reason I dragged out the conversation interminably in polite courtesies and general gossip until the meal was brought in. Yunes, with whom I had rehearsed the proceedings, seconded me admirably, while 'Abdel Salam carried on the good work in the background. We talked and talked, on a multitude of subjects, but never mentioned our purpose. Beyond the fact that I was a high-ranking German officer, and my two friends Tripolitanian sheikhs of high standing, I told him nothing of our intentions and aloofly ignored his pointed questions.

The meal of boiled goat and kuskus was silent as good manners required. When water had been poured over our hands, I asked my host to let down the flaps of his tent and admit inside only his trusted confidants.

I started then on the evening's business. The German command, I said, had become equally distrustful of the Italians and of the town Arabs in the north. As things were going the only consequence of us Germans winning the war in Tunisia would be to replace greedy Frenchmen by even greedier Italians in the possession of the land. What we wanted was a Tunisia controlled by warlike nomads under German supervision, a military base for us in which contented tribesmen would recover the fat pastures which had been filched from them by the French and their scheming town-Arab friends. Truly these town Arabs had now turned against the French and started a Free Tunisia movement: but all they wanted was plunder. Our business was not to fight a painful war to the end that fat, deceitful, town dwellers should grow fatter and richer and finally turn us out of the land. Our friends were the faithful nomads, brave soldiers like ourselves; we intended that they should have a share of the rich loot of Gabes, Sfax, Sousse and Tunis, and then pasture their flocks in peace and amity on rich grass lands — no more on God-forsaken parched and barren sand dunes.

In this vein I talked for hours: I never knew I could say the same things in so many different ways. When I tired, Yunes took up the thread and described the fabulous wealth of Tunis (which he had never seen). In the gloom of the far end of the tent 'Abdel Salam murmured to a close circle of enthralled listeners.

What we wanted from the tribesmen, I told my host, was their help to evict all the settlers, French, Italian and Arab alike — when the time came, which was not yet. I had taken the opportunity of my present mission to call on him, a man of influence as I knew, to prepare him for the call. He would understand that the matter must be kept secret from our weak Italian allies. They had still their uses for us at the present time and should not be made suspicious.

Loot, intrigue, treachery, fat pastures, glory — I had exhausted the temptations I could offer my debased Arab host. Under his native composure I felt him excited; cupidity shone in his eyes. I thought he was ripe for further disclosures: I kicked quietly Yunes's leg to draw his attention to the change of subject and said, quite casually:

'I might as well tell you the truth about the occasion which has brought us here. The French in Tozeur have three companies of Tunisian Goum. We hear that the men are much disaffected to their French officers. We have got together the German soldiers I have with me, all picked men, and dressed them up as escaped British prisoners-of-war. In this guise we intend to drift into Tozeur, where the French, unsuspecting, will receive us well and quarter us in the barracks with the Goum. We will get to work amongst the men and one night the three companies will rise, cut their French officers' throats and seize the town. They will be led by my men, every one of whom carries a powerful German automatic pistol concealed under his clothes.'

I had done it! I watched Yunes anxiously out of the tail of my eye. He expanded my speech and added a few details. Our host leaned over and in a low voice asked Yunes some questions which I failed to understand. Then Yunes very deliberately lit a cigarette for the host — not from his lighter, but with an ember picked out of the fire. We had arranged this to be a sign that, in Yunes's opinion, the bait had been swallowed.

I went on: 'For the sake of likelihood we cannot take our cars into Tozeur. I would like to leave them here if you would care to look after them till I send someone back to collect.'

The sheikh agreed and I thanked him casually. Standing up to stretch my legs I heard Yunes whisper to our host:

'These Germans are generous.'

We talked of other matters, but I felt that he had something on his mind.

'Will Your Excellency walk with the men? I am very poor but I could provide you with a riding camel, not a good one, but still, one that would go.'

I looked at him dreamily, as if I was turning over in my mind vast problems of strategy:

'I leave such matters to be settled by Yunes,' I said, and strode out of the tent into the cold night.

When Yunes joined me later it appeared that we were to be provided with two camels, one intended for my personal use, the other to carry our stores. He had also obtained four sheep, one of which was being slaughtered at that very moment to provide supper for our hungry men. The three others would be carried on the camels. It was just as well that he had succeeded in refilling our larder, otherwise the next day would have seen the last of our rations.

Better still than transport and food, he had induced the sheikh to provide a khabir to go with us, a guide who would vouch for us and smooth out unpleasantness which might arise with Arabs of other tribes along our route.

I gave Yunes a gold coin for our deluded host, and I drove back to camp extremely weary and fighting down an unexpected urge to giggle. I said to Yunes:

'We have told many lies tonight. Please God we may be able to tell the truth sometimes after this.'

'God be praised,' he said piously. 'These Arabs are extremely credulous,' and he chuckled softly. I shook with uncontrollable laughter.

The next day, fifth out of Ksar Rhilane, we started late. We made camp for the six Frenchmen, who had long ago expressed their determination not to walk and who now asked to remain behind to guard the paralysed jeeps. Failing to convince them of the unwiseness of their choice, I arranged with the sheikh for food and warned them not to forget that they were supposed to be Germans. They laughed: 'Anything rather than walk!' They couldn't speak a word of intelligible Arabic so perhaps they couldn't give us away.

The khabir turned up with two camels and the three sheep, we loaded our blankets and few remaining rations, and walked away. We covered twenty miles before nightfall, one hundred and fifteen from Qaret 'Ali. The sixth day I estimated also at twenty miles. Waterson was like a bird, hopping about and cheerful. He had taken special charge of Petrie, who tended to brood but always kept in the van. Most of the New Zealanders walked with these two. They showed no signs of being upset. Some of my English lads dragged behind and required encouragement now and then. Locke, completely unperturbed, walked generally by himself, flapping his feet in my large desert boots. The Arabs were quite at home on the march and somehow their clothes suffered less than ours. The cold, sharp during the night, became unbearable towards morning, and as we couldn't sleep we walked away before dawn.

On the seventh day we saw several horsemen hovering about. The khabir grew nervous and talked of going home. During the afternoon we heard a distant noise of aircraft and we went to ground, dispersed amongst the hillocks, The noise grew and grew and suddenly one of my men stood on top of a hillock waving and cheering, and the next moment we were all doing the same: two hundred feet overhead, fifty R.A.F. bombers in close formation thundered over us on their way to Tripolitania. We still had our noses in the air when I noticed, on the ground this time, coming towards us, a school of jeeps wheeling up and down over the hillocks like porpoise in a choppy sea. Tinker, in a hurry as usual, drove up to me. He had four borrowed jeeps with him. Caneri with another four jeeps was searching for us along a shorter route, in case we had lost the original track. I sent Yunes to guide Tinker to the two jeeps we had left with the Frenchmen, and we all sat down and rubbed our feet; we had walked one hundred and fifty miles. In an incredibly short time he was back with our vehicles from the spring from which we had walked in three days. We piled in, six and seven to a jeep, and drove off. That night we slept on the shore of Shott Jerid. The next morning we drove like birds over the mud flats at the western tail of the Shott, fearful of hitting a quagmire and of being engulfed. At eleven o'clock we hit the tarmac road which runs from Touggourt to Tozeur, and a little after twelve we sat down to lunch in the gaudy dining-room of the Hotel Transatlantique in Tozeur. We looked very incongruous, sitting in fours at our tables, with white linen, an array of cutlery and three glasses to each of us.

The hotel had been built just before the war for tourists who wanted to experience in luxury the thrill of visiting a Saharan oasis. At this time we were the only guests, but a large staff was at hand who tried hard to treat us 'comme des millionnaires américains'.

After lunch I was shown up to my room: I opened the door and closed it again with an apology, for there was already a bearded old gentleman standing in the room in the gloom of the drawn blinds. I told the servant:

'There seems to be a mistake, the room is occupied. It belongs to an old man with a grey beard.'

The servant looked queerly at me, stepped forward and opened the door once more. I followed him in and gazed at my own unaccustomed reflection in a wardrobe mirror that faced the door. The unseen beard which I had grown during the last three months had turned me into a mournful replica of Great-Great-Uncle Henry, whose repulsive features appeared on one of the first pages of the family album. In our childhood, my elder sister and I had often praised our luck in being born long after the foul old man's death: and now he had come to life again with his dismal expression, his spaniel eyes, his untrimmed black beard with the white strip down the chin, his horrible stodginess.

I sat down in the darkened room and ordered the servant to fetch me a barber.

'Please tell my friends not to come and see me till I have been visited by the barber.'

What with the shock of discovering in myself the image of my loathsome great-great-uncle, and with the aftermath of my orgy of lying, I lived for three days in a daze. I slept, I ate, I joked with Augustine the housekeeper, I took short convalescent walks in the palm groves and the walled-in fruit gardens of the oasis where limpid green sunlight filtered through the leaves and brooklets chattered between overgrown banks.

Tinker had been up to First Army Headquarters in Laverdure to get our messages transmitted to Eighth Army: what he had seen there was like fairy tales, which agreed in spirit with the fantastic, unearthly softness of the warm oasis and the Western luxury of our new home.

Unknown eerie creatures appeared and went: war correspondents, the first I had ever seen, who filled some of my men with whisky and concocted incredible fables out of their drunken ramblings, an elderly Psychological Warfare Branch major who requested me to distribute tracts to the Arabs next time I went out — stacks of leaflets printed on strong soft paper which were eminently suitable for the use to which we eventually put them, and a romantic French officer of the 2e Bureau, Captain Révillon of the Spahis, who hid the flamboyance of his white and scarlet uniform under a putty-coloured cloak which swept the ground.

Caneri came back and left again for a place called Tebessa in Algeria, to return the jeeps he and Tinker had borrowed from kindly Americans for the rescue of our walking party. One day in the hotel lavatory, a noble room of silver and pink, 'un pissing palace' according to our French parachutist, I lifted my eyes to see that the occupant of the slab next to mine was Henry, Lieutenant Henry who commanded the L.R.D.G. Rhodesian patrol, for whose benefit I had left Yunnie marooned in Qaret 'Ali. We greeted one another over our unbuttoned flaps. Yunnie, Garven and Mohammed had come up with him: their warnings against the treachery of the Arabs had not been in vain for they had been sniped at all the way from Ksar Rhilane and had suffered some casualties. Knowing we had gone the same way on foot and unarmed, he had hardly expected to find any of us alive. On his way back Henry was wounded in the spine by a bullet from an Arab band, lingered on miserably for several months in the Scottish Hospital in Cairo and eventually died.

Yunnie treated his performance as a joke: he had enjoyed himself, for this kind of activity suited him better than the wheedling of equipment out of unwilling quartermasters. He had in fact done extremely well and I was very proud of him. Henry had not called at Qaret 'Ali but had driven straight on. Yunnie saw his trucks in the distance and decided to take a short cut across the dunes of the Grand Erg to catch him round the corner. He had previously provided himself with three camels against this very eventuality. With Mohammed and Garven he had then ridden non-stop in a straight line fifty miles from Qaret 'Ali to Bir Jabiar, south of Duz, where they had caught up early one morning with the Rhodesians, who, having taken a longer route to avoid the Sand Sea and travelling only by day, had reached the same well only the night before.

Yunnie was never much concerned about ultimate issues. To him action, the action he liked, was an end in itself. Going with him over the details of his perilous vigil at Qaret 'Ali and his dash across the Sand Sea, I was surprised to discover that he had already forgotten what the object of his enterprise had been. He remembered every minute circumstance, but he had lost sight of the fact that, originally, it was to warn our companions of impending dangers that he had volunteered to remain behind.

I had arrived in Tozeur on February 8th, 1943. Five days later we were all gathered there together and I decided, as everyone was well rested, that we would move to Tebessa in Algeria to refit. Tinker and his New Zealanders were about to fly back to the Middle East, and before they left they gave us at the Transatlantique a farewell dinner, memorable as much for the grandiose exquisiteness of the food and the abundance of the wines, as for the appropriateness of the speeches and the tactful art with which thanks were suggested and praise conveyed in matters so delicate that a direct statement would have been bombastic and brought embarrassment to all. New Zealanders are New Zealanders and there is no one like them.

CHAPTER VI

TAMING A RABBIT

BOB YUNNIE, Caneri and the bulk of our men drove directly from Tozeur to Tebessa. With four men in my jeep, I made a detour through Gafsa, the headquarters of an American Division, to get information. I spent the night in Feriana and reached Tebessa very early the next morning. The town lies on a plateau three thousand six hundred feet high: it was covered in snow when we arrived. Coming from the tropical heat of Tozeur, in our torn drill shirts and slacks, we froze stiff; teeth chattering, I walked into the office of the American Second Corps supply dump to ask leave to use their telephone. I wanted to get on to the Town Major and find where the rest of my party, who had arrived the day before, were billeted. My men remained outside, miserably huddled in the truck. I was a very long time telephoning: when I came out the men had vanished. I found them again in a shed, stark naked, revived by an enormous breakfast they had just put down, joking and yelling while clothing was flung at them. A benign Father Christmas, Colonel Myers, Second Corps quartermaster, beamed on his new-found children. Each one of us was issued with two of every article of clothing which the fatherly U.S. Army provided for its men: socks; woollen underwear; cotton ditto; boots long, short, brown, black; woollen shirts; slacks and jackets thin and thick; overalls; wind jackets and an amazing variety of headdress. We found our billets in a warm, dry barn with plenty of straw. Waterson exhibited the rations he had drawn for a week: coffee, grapefruit juice, milk, butter, spam, and, hanging from the rafters, whole sides of bacon and hams.

According to the rules I should not have stayed in Tebessa, but flown back with my men to the Middle East, to refit in Cairo and drive out again one thousand and three hundred miles back into

Tunisia, a matter of many weeks. However, as Headquarters Middle East had not bothered to recall me (or, if they had, the signal never reached me) having considered the situation of our two armies converging on to the German forces in Tunisia and made up my mind that our only chance of taking part again in the fighting in Africa was to refit quick on the spot and join in the battle before it was over, I decided to ignore Middle East and try my luck in Algeria with First Army.

Eighth Army had taken Tripoli on January 23rd (two days before the Messerschmidts strafed us) and was now on the Tunisian border building up for the attack on the Mareth Line. First Army from North Africa had moved eastwards up to a line extending a hundred and eighty miles north and south through Tunisia from the Mediterranean coast to Gafsa, with British elements on the left flank, French in the centre and American on the right. This front was now fairly static; by no means continuous, large stretches of undefended mountains stood between the valleys along which our forces had advanced; it petered out south of Gafsa, where Jebel Asker and Shott Jerid were deemed adequate cover for the American right flank. Von Arnim opposed us along this front, the Tunisian plains extending in his rear a hundred miles eastwards to the sea; Rommel with his forces based now on the Mareth Line and deployed from Jebel Nefusa to the coast, faced southwards towards our Eighth Army.

Both German armies were supplied by the Tunisian ports: Bizerta, Tunis, Sousse, Sfax and Gabes. The roads and the railways issuing from these ports presented good targets for small raiding parties. We could there inflict damage out of proportion to our numbers; and as a result of our activities some enemy troops might be diverted to escorting convoys and protecting railway bridges.

In the air the Germans were considerably inferior in striking power to the combined air forces of First and Eighth Armies, but they had an advantage in the possession of a very large number of airfields dispersed in the central plains of Tunisia. This scattering of small landing grounds presented difficult and shifting targets to our aircraft, but they were very vulnerable to land attack. I thought that the destruction on the ground of a few of the remaining Axis aircraft was within my means and well worth attempting.

To reach these objectives — road convoys, trains, railway bridges and aircraft on landing grounds — I counted on being able to cross into the enemy rear either through one of the gaps in von Arnim's front facing First Army or round the open flank south of Gafsa. The area in which we would operate was small by our desert standards, and the nature of the country, open and densely populated with hostile Arabs, excluded the possibility of occupying a hide-out for more than a day or two. Our raids consequently would be short, of no more than three or four days or even less, and our base would be kept in friendly territory, on our side of the line. We had no longer a desert open to us in which we could vanish. In our former warfare the enemy had presented an open flank over a thousand miles long: here he was besieged practically on all sides. To strike at his vital parts we would have first to find a gap in his defences, then slip through the gap, hit and run back, trusting that the gap had not closed behind us.

For this type of operation I could be contented with much less equipment than I had required in the open desert: wireless communications were no longer vital, petrol dumps were not needed, and, as my base would be established close to an army dump, I had no obligation to carry large sets of spares either for vehicles, weapons, equipment or clothing.

I decided that as soon as I could get five jeeps in fighting order, and weapons and equipment for their crews, I would start operations on a small scale, and build up in the meanwhile suitable reserves.

On arriving at Tebessa we had made a private arrangement with the officer commanding Corps Workshops to have our four jeeps overhauled. Two or three days later I heard that a senior British officer from First Army Headquarters, on a tour of the variegated units of which this composite command was made up, had established his headquarters in Tebessa for a few days. I thought this was a good opportunity to get the temporary attachment of P.P.A. to First Army sanctioned, and authority given to Second Corps to fit us out, and I

U

made preparations for the interview, my first with a British officer of First Army. Mindful of the tales I had heard, I took trouble over my dress, for, though I was not willing to make undignified concessions, I wanted to create a good impression. I carefully discarded all clothing of American origin (except for underwear) and made up my uniform as follows: crêpe-soled suède desert boots in good condition, white corduroy slacks, neatly patched and freshly laundered and pressed (a bit frayed at the ends but that could not be helped without cutting them down to shorts), the top part of a khaki drill shirt, over it, and covering its deficiencies, a grey New Zealand jersey, over that again a leather jerkin of great elegance (which I had exchanged for a pair of flying boots with a colonel in Tobruq eighteen months previously). The back of the jerkin had a largish burnt hole, as a result of sleeping on the fire — a matter of small importance as I need not turn my back on a senior officer. On my head a black beret, with a P.P.A. badge. As a point of honour I wouldn't wear a tie, even if I had one, but I was prepared to compromise: I knotted round my neck a brand new red silk scarf, a farewell present from Madame Jacquet in Cairo which had somehow survived, and tucked the ends neatly inside the collar of my shirt.

Thus attired and full of confidence I addressed myself to the senior officer's staff captain, explained that I was the commanding officer of the first Eighth Army unit to make contact with First Army, and asked to report to his commanding officer. This officer, a young man exquisite in a Sam Browne and all, asked:

'You want to speak to the senior officer?'

'I have just come through the desert from Eighth Army and I want to report. I always report to Army Headquarters when I come back from the desert. In fact I want to speak to your boss. Here are my credentials if you require any.' I handed him my roving commission, established by Lieut.-Col. Prendergast at Shweref, instructing me to harass the enemy at my discretion and according to my judgment in areas held by the enemy north of the Mareth Line (or words to that effect). He looked at me with amazement, incredulity and distaste.

'You want to speak to my commanding officer dressed as you are?'

It was too delightful to be true: I hugged myself and carefully noted every detail of the conversation for future reference.

'How else do you expect me to speak? To tell you the truth, I've got nothing else. I have just been three months in the desert. I have driven over three thousand miles from Cairo in a jeep. And owing to a misunderstanding with some Messerschmidts we ended up by walking one hundred and fifty miles. Please be a good lad and fix that interview for me now.'

The situation was beyond him: he limped across to the senior officer's caravan.

I was introduced to the presence, saluted smartly (I had made Waterson, late R.S.M. of the King's Dragoon Guards, put me through the drill), and stood at attention. The senior officer, I have no doubt, was a very brave man: it was his misfortune that, not only did he look like a rabbit, but he also behaved like one. He had his nose on his desk when I climbed into his caravan, and said without looking up:

'I understand you have had some trouble with your kit.' He looked at me then and his protruding eyes and puckered lips expressed pain, revulsion and anxiety. I got annoyed with all this fuss about dress.

'Not in the least, Sir. Your staff captain must have misunderstood me, Sir. These are the clothes I wear when I report to the G.O.C. in C. Eighth Army, Sir.'

'Well, and what can I do for you?' said the rabbit meekly.

'I want to carry out the instructions that you have now on your desk, Sir. It is a matter of some urgency, Sir, as you will appreciate. I have lost many of my vehicles and most of my equipment through enemy action, and I am not at present in a position to operate, Sir. I am sure General Montgomery will be very grateful to you, Sir, if you would instruct U.S. Second Corps to refit me, Sir. I have ascertained that the necessary equipment is available in their Tebessa dumps. All that is required is an order from you, Sir.'

It would be ungracious to complain of the rabbit. He asked no questions but granted me everything I asked for: we would be attached to Second Corps for refitting and administration, *not* for operations.

Our reports would be transmitted to Eighth Army. And we would revert to its command as soon as the junction of the two armies had taken place.

Eighth Army was not *liked* in North Africa. But its prestige was high and I believe that it was anxiously admitted that without its direct intervention on the Tunisian scene First Army, small and still raw, would be unable to force a decision — nor even to withstand the pressure if the Germans chose to strike.

Colonel Myers and Major Montgomery, O.C. Workshops, helped us enthusiastically. They were new to the war and as yet without experience: our small band took their romantic fancy, and we became, I'm ashamed to say, their spoilt children.

We had no fixed scale of equipment, no G ten ninety-eight to work by: from what was offered to us we took what we thought we could use. Second Corps Headquarters allotted us officially two jeeps, one of which had been earmarked for Myers's personal use, and we purchased another for a case of whisky. U.S. Army was 'dry' at that time, but we had the possibility of buying spirits. I drove a hundred and twenty miles to the nearest NAAFI in Constantine with Yunnie: I went in first and told a sob story which produced a case of whisky for O.C. Popski's Private Army; Bob Yunnie, a better liar than I, obtained two cases for second in command No. 1 Demolition Squadron. With the liquor we made ourselves popular with our American friends, and found we had something to offer in exchange for all the favours received.

We exchanged sten guns for U.S. carbines, and Sergeant Waterson's German Luger pistol for a pair of twin, quick-firing, Browning .30 machine guns off a slightly damaged Lightning fighter plane on Yuks-les-Bains landing ground.

I discarded our clumsy, obsolete Vickers-K guns, for belt-fed Brownings, sweet weapons which seldom jammed, easy to handle and little affected by sand or mud. I mounted on alternate jeeps a .30 and a .50 gun. The heavier guns could deal with armoured cars, a necessity I had learnt from my humiliating experience in Wadi Zemzem. We found later that, armed with a .50 gun, a jeep, low on the ground and agile, was more than a match for a slower-moving and half-blind armoured car or even a light tank.

I persuaded Second Corps to lend us a rocket-propelled bazooka, an anti-tank weapon they had just received for experiment, and undertook to give them a report on its performance under battle conditions.

So energetically did the Americans work for us that, nine days after our arrival at Tebessa as refugees, we had scraped together five armed jeeps and an assortment of small arms for ourselves, with which we mounted a raid on a landing ground near Bordj Fejaj, forty miles north of the Mareth Line, a target given by Eighth Army. Owing to German pressure, Gafsa, Feriana and Tozeur had been evacuated by the U.S. troops, and we had to go a roundabout way through Metlawi, a small French phosphate mining town of villas and gardens. Here I tasted the embarrassing fruits of glory when a fair French maiden exclaimed:

'Vous êtes de la Huitième Armée! Mais alors, vous êtes des héros!', threw her arms round my neck and kissed me on both cheeks.

We then crept between Kriz and Tozeur, both now in the hands of the enemy, and drove eighty miserable miles of truly Tunisian going between the deserted northern shores of Shotts Jerid and el Fejaj and the sharp-toothed crags of Jebel Asker, to find in the end only five aircraft on the landing ground. These we disposed of and we returned the same excruciating way. We found Tamerze held by a dispirited battalion of the French Foreign Legion, whining soldiers without discipline, who couldn't even find the heart to mount a guard at night. Their wine ration hadn't turned up, so they just sulked and quarrelled feebly.

In the mountains above Tebessa we ran into elements of the First U.S. Armoured Division on the move northwards to Kasserine. Their hundreds of vehicles had churned the road into a slither of mud; one of our jeeps, on tow with a cracked sump, skidded slowly sideways after we had stopped in a traffic jam. Nothing we tried to do could stop her and we had hurriedly to release the tow-chain and watch her go slowly over the side and plunge down the bank into the wadi below. During February and March we were never out of the mud in Tebessa. When it didn't rain, it snowed and thawed. Even the shores of Shott Jerid were less dismal than the Algerian mountains in winter.

I found Tebessa in a flap. Following on the attack which had pushed Second Corps out of Gafsa, von Arnim had now attacked the American position at Kasserine with strong forces of armour and artillery: the battle was not going well for Second Corps. Their armoured division, in action for the first time, had been beaten back, leaving some of its tanks in the hands of the enemy, who promptly used them against their former masters.

At three o'clock in the morning on February 24th I was woken up by a tap at the window: I opened and Captain Révillon, muffled in his cloak, climbed into the room. We had for some time arranged privately to exchange our intelligence (officially he was supposed to report only to the French General Staff) — a one-sided arrangement really, for I received many times more than I could give. Révillon (alias Blanchard, alias de Laennec — but I never learnt his real name) had spies everywhere. Long before the war he had taken charge of an Italian lad whose parents, poor Italian settlers in Tunisia, had both died of the cholera within a few days. He had sent the boy to a good school (at the expense of the secret funds of the French Military Intelligence service); his education completed, he had got him a job at a desk with a firm in Tunis, had found means to get him mixed up in an unsavoury case of embezzlement, had rescued him from the courts and had held him in subjection ever since, under the threat of being shown up, imprisoned and disgraced. In due course, under his suggestion, the weak-willed boy, who had now reached military age, enlisted as a volunteer in the Italian army in Tripolitania. Being clever, well educated, fluent in Arabic and in French as well as in Italian, and well briefed by the devilish Révillon, he eventually rose to be a confidential clerk in Italian Headquarters. From this post of vantage he regularly sent to Révillon, through secret messengers, copies of all the important documents that came to him to be typed or to be filed. What he couldn't lay his hands on in the normal course of his work he fished out of Headquarters' latrines at night, as the parsimonious Italians did not burn the contents of their waste-paper baskets but made use of them as lavatory paper. (I have now on my desk a document rescued in this manner, washed and ironed out, of which extracts will be found at the end of this chapter.)

This lad acted now as secretary to the chief Italian liaison officer on von Arnim's advanced headquarters at Sbeitla, and Révillon had woken me up in his dramatic way to tell me that he had just received information from his victim that, on receipt of an urgent request from his colleague Rommel, von Arnim had decided to call off the attack on Kasserine and send back south the Fifteenth and Twenty-first Panzer Divisions, the two armoured divisions he had borrowed for the operation. Ten days later, at Eighth Army Headquarters, I learnt that on February 20th General Alexander, who now commanded Eighteenth Army Group and co-ordinated the operations of First and Eighth Armies, had sent an appeal to General Montgomery asking him to worry Rommel so as to draw pressure away from First Army front. As a result of this appeal Eighth Army had immediately launched an attack with the only two divisions they had forward at the time, an operation of some risk (for their forces were very unbalanced at this stage of their preparations), by which Montgomery intended to compel Rommel to turn against him and recall some of the divisions which had been diverted from the Mareth Line to reinforce the attack against the Americans at Kasserine.

On this occasion Révillon's evidence was not of the unsavoury kind, but consisted of extracts hastily copied from the minutes of a conference held at von Arnim's headquarters on the twenty-second. I woke Yunnie and Caneri, told them to have six jeeps with petrol for two hundred miles of very bad going, eight days' rations, weapons and ammunition as usual, plus twenty-four anti-tank mines, ready to move not later than 06.00 hours, and drove off by myself to Corps Headquarters. At this early hour the whole staff was at work, weary and strained: the latest news from Kasserine was so discouraging that a withdrawal seemed inevitable, and the decision had been taken to evacuate the eight thousand tons of ammunition, petrol and general stores that lay in the dumps at Tebessa. The enemy was only thirty miles away and if he forced the pass down from Kasserine there was no natural obstacle to stop him from sweeping on to Tebessa and beyond.

I showed Révillon's minutes to the intelligence colonel: I agreed with him that the evidence was a little too flimsy to be acted upon, but, I told him, I would take a patrol to watch the Kasserine-Gafsa road, along which, being the shortest route, most of Rommel's armoured vehicles would probably drive, if indeed they were going south. If I saw tanks in any number heading south along that road, the presumption would be that Révillon's agent had been well informed, and there would be no need for Second Corps to withdraw, nor to evacuate the dumps in Tebessa. Finally I asked him, as I carried no wireless, to arrange for a direct link between his headquarters and the Derbyshire Yeomanry, a British armoured-car regiment in support to the American Corps, through whose advanced posts, at Bir el Ater on the extreme right flank, I intended to pass.

The poor intelligence colonel, harassed and sleepless, failed, though he tried hard, to make out why, unbidden, I was undertaking this reconnaissance, and by what means I would take six jeeps twenty miles to the rear of the enemy front line; he promised, however, to arrange the wireless link and wished me luck.

The distance as the crow flies from Bir el Ater to the Kasserine-Feriana-Gafsa road is only twenty-three miles, but it took a day and a half to cover. We drove through thick scrub which concealed every few yards a runnel roughly two feet deep and two across, at right angles to our course. The trucks advanced like jerky rocking horses. A jeep has six gears: we were most of the time in bottom and never rose above second gear. The mileage per gallon, which is sixteen on a road, and averaged ten on bad desert going, fell to six. It rained heavily all the time, but at this lower altitude the weather was appreciably warmer than at Tebessa. We spent a drenched night and plodded away again the next morning. One after the other the jeeps got stuck in runnels and had to be lifted out. Many times they got bellied with both front and back wheels in runnels and had to be dug out; and the ground was one soaked mass of matted scrub roots. The rain drenched the maps and got into the prism of the compass: anyway keeping a course on such a going was a matter of guess.

At fifteen hundred hours, when the road by my estimation was three miles away, I suddenly went into a secret panic: we would be attacked and overwhelmed as soon as we got in sight of the road: what escape could we hope to make over such a ground? Twelve good men who had trusted me blindly and had never questioned my word that our enterprise was a matter of importance would be killed or captured as a result of my foolhardiness. And if we did succeed in reaching the road, what of it? — the whole enterprise was pointless. Even if I saw some tanks the Americans wouldn't believe me, or if they did, the corps commander would refuse to take action. Could I hope to stop the withdrawal of a whole corps by providing a little piece of information? And if we succeeded in laying our mines on the road, as I had intended to do, and had given to my men as the main object of our enterprise, at best the result would be no more than a track blown off a tank: the damage could be repaired in a matter of hours.

I made up my mind to turn back before it was too late but, racked with fears and doubts I drove on: next time I got ditched I would give the order. I struck a runnel and I dared not look any of my men in the face while they lifted me out, but I drove on again in an agony of indecision. Then Locke, who was my gunner now, said he thought there was a line of telegraph poles ahead of us. I stopped: through my wet field glasses I made out telegraph lines two miles or so ahead: our goal was in sight and my panic melted away, leaving me in blissful contentment.

We struck good going on higher ground; I stopped our vehicles in a hollow and walked with Yunnie to the top of a rise from which we saw the road, the light railway and a building alongside it, the station at Borj Ma'aden bel Abes.

We stayed on watch a long time, waiting for dusk. I didn't expect the Germans would have any traffic on the road by daylight on account of our air patrols, and indeed we saw only two or three isolated trucks. What we did see at last was a long file of Arabs walking towards the station from their tents somewhere behind us, close to which we had driven earlier. No doubt but they intended to give us away and they were jostling one another to get in first for the reward.

We had with us on this trip two sergeants formerly of the S.A.S. with David Stirling, till he was captured at El Hamma, men of resource and determination, called Cooper and Seekings. Yunnie and these two, seeing that if the station held any troops or armoured cars these, being now alerted, might well chase our jeeps away before we could lay our mines, offered to lie in hiding till dark, then walk to the road carrying as many mines as they could, lay them and then walk back sixty miles to Tebessa over the mountains. These men, I realized, had no doubts of the urgency of our mission, for they were willing in order to carry it out, not only to risk their lives, which is easy, but to undertake, half exhausted as they were by their labours of the past two days, a tramp of sixty miles, in the dark and the wet, over vile, unknown country. In truth they had not bothered to study the importance of laying mines on the Gafsa road: an enterprise had been undertaken and it had to be carried out to the end. A plain, unquestioning tenacity forbade them to give up unless they had made their most desperate attempt. I recognized in them a strength greater than mine and I was about to consent, when, lowering my glasses from the station building, I perceived something which provided another answer to our problem. Between us and the road and running parallel with it, was a narrow, flat-bottomed wadi, the sand of which appeared broken up with many tracks. We drove into it and found the unmistakable marks of at least twenty tanks which, we reckoned, had passed this way towards Gafsa not longer ago than the previous night. Better even, we found a board on a post marked Gafsa with an arrow. A tank by-pass, we concluded, had been designed along this wadi, to avoid driving them on the hard tarmac. Hurriedly we buried two lines of mines across the wadi and withdrew in some haste because our look-out on the hill reported a line of armed men deploying from the station building and advancing towards us, like beaters at a shoot. Night was falling fast. I stopped after we had crossed two ridges and gave instructions for our night trip back to Bir el Ater: I intended taking a more southerly

314

route where I thought the going might be better. We formed up and started: Waterson, who drove second, pushed up alongside my jeep to say that he heard a vehicle behind us. I stopped, waved the others on, looked back, and, in the half light, saw two German armoured cars creeping on our tail; they halted one hundred and fifty yards away. At that moment tracers from Waterson's half-inch Browning rushed past me: his third or fourth burst hit the foremost armoured car, which seemed to give a shudder and then puffed out black smoke. I drove a little further away from Waterson and turned round to allow Locke to open up with my twin .30 guns, spraying both armoured cars. Waterson hadn't bothered to turn his jeep round, but, seated on the bonnet, fired over the stern.

The second car turned tail after firing a few bursts and disappeared over a hill. I was annoyed that none of my other jeeps had opened up: my men, it seemed, had not yet got much battle sense and presumably they waited for someone to point out the objective and give them the order to fire!

Sapper Curtis, a new recruit to P.P.A., who was driving a jeep with us for the first time, came trotting up to me: he had tipped his jeep down a steep, very narrow gully in the dark, and he didn't think it could be got out without much digging. His breath came short with anxiety:

'I suppose you will give me the sack now, Sir. I have lost my jeep — and not through enemy action.'

I told him to salvage his gun and as much as he could of his kit, set his incendiary bomb on the petrol tank and climb on to Davies's vehicle. We had to get back quickly with my information and I wouldn't spare the time to salvage Curtis's jeep; but I had no intention of dispensing with his services, as I believed he would turn out to be one of our outstanding recruits. I left him in doubt of his fate for the time being, which would do him and his companions no harm.

We went on in the dark over ground so bad that one of David Stirling's sergeants walked in front of my jeep to warn me of obstacles. For a long time we were accompanied by the noise of several armoured cars floundering behind us and we saw an occasional flash of a headlight. Then as we reached higher and better ground, they gave up the chase. I called a halt on a hill to the south of the morass in which we had struggled on our way out and listened: after a while a mighty rumble approached from the north, grew and resolved itself into the manifold clangings of tanks on the move, some more of von Arnim's armour slipping away to the Mareth Line. We drove towards home: on our way Locke, who had become fanciful with the excitement of our little battle, heard so many bangs behind us that by his reckoning each of our mines must have gone off twice over.

The southern route proved so fast that we arrived at Bir el Ater before dawn and we found there the troop of armoured cars of the Derbyshire Yeomanry ready to fight for their lives: they had been somewhat shaken by the glare of our five pairs of headlights.

From the Derbyshire Yeomanry H.Q. I sent two signals: one to U.S. Second Corps, the other, to be relayed from Laverdure, to G.S.I.1. Headquarters, Eighth Army, for the matter was really of more moment to them than to our friends in Tebessa who didn't have to withdraw after all and the position at Kasserine was restored.

A few days later I received a message calling me to First Army Headquarters in Laverdure. Thus I visited for the first time this scene of comedy and did not find it entertaining. I had no idea there could be so many bewildered, tired and querulous officers in the British Army. I found later, when I went to Allied Forces Headquarters in Alger, that there were many thousands more.

At Laverdure, a local spa where Headquarters were housed in hotels and villas, I was shown a signal from Eighth Army Headquarters, *fifteen days old*, requesting me to report. I flew over the next day, and arrived in the evening at the little tents and caravans of Eighth Army Headquarters, dispersed and camouflaged in a dusty plain south of Tripoli.

There was some joking at my fortnight's delay, for my assignment had now been given to someone else. It was to guide over the ground we had reconnoitred near Matmata some of the forward units of the New Zealand division, in preparation for the left hook at the Mareth Line. I reported to Bill Williams, the intelligence officer, then the next day I flew with him to Tactical H.Q. near Medenine to watch Rommel's attack, which had been threatening for a few days, and started on that morning, March 6th. By the evening three German armoured divisions had been beaten off and soundly defeated. (We had heard elements of two of these divisions moving south on the Gafsa road a few days previously.) The general who had directed it remarked that it was the first time in his life — and probably the last — that a battle had developed exactly as he had planned it. 'All I did was to sit and watch. From first to last I never gave an order.' This seemed to me all the more remarkable in that the action had been of Rommel's choice and it was he who had started it with an attack of his armoured forces. In the plane, on our way back to Tripoli, I told the general of my interview with the Rabbit: the moment seemed somehow appropriate.

When I came back the Americans were sitting once more in their old positions at Kasserine; they reoccupied Gafsa without opposition and pushed on eastwards up a deep mountain valley towards the coast and Rommel's only line of communication; but to my intense disappointment they were held at El Qettar and they failed to fall on Rommel's rear while Eighth Army attempted to force the Mareth Line.

Realizing they couldn't force the pass at El Qettar, Second Corps then pushed an armoured division down another valley further north and advanced as far as Maknassy where, just as they were about to debouch into the coastal plain, the Germans held them once more, and there the position remained for a while.

The road which supplied the American divisions in Maknassy ran in a straight line from Gafsa in a broad plain: it was covered on the right-hand side by one of the peculiar Tunisian mountain ranges, two thousand feet high and less than two miles across, rugged and serrated, uncrossable in most places except for a rock climber. On the far (southern) side of this range, in another broad plain, ran a road along which the Germans fetched up from the coast the supplies for their positions at El Qettar. Thus, side by side but separated, as it were, by a wall twenty-two miles long, the communications of the adversaries ran in parallel lines no more than two or three miles apart. Sitting on a crag on top of the range you could see on one side the German trucks making their dusty way west to El Qettar, on the other the American ones going east to Maknassy. Trusting the wall to be unscalable, neither side had bothered to put a guard on it.

Leaving my party in an olive grove on the American side, I set out in my jeep to reconnoitre every fold of the range, hoping to find an uncharted pass over which we would be able to take our jeeps into enemy territory. I had with me Jock Cameron, a new recruit to P.P.A., a gillie in civilian life, who understood mountains. After several unsuccessful attempts, we went up a wadi as far as we could drive, then proceeded on foot up a mule track which led us in less than an hour down into the German plain.

Examining the track step by step on our way back, we came to the conclusion that if we shoved stones, rolled boulders and blasted the rock, we could, with much work, make a very rough track for our jeeps.

On our way back home six German Stukas in close formation flew from behind us a hundred feet over our heads. I stopped the jeep and we sat frozen in our seats: we were in an absolutely bare, flat-bottomed wadi, with no cover for a cat. The evil birds passed on, unseeing, but ten minutes later came back, making directly for us: it seemed absurdly certain that we were the targets they were after.

This time I saw them coming and had time to drag away the unwilling Cameron, who had seized his guns, run a hundred yards and lie flat. Once more the creatures took no notice of us. When they had hopped over the hills, back in the jeep Cameron said:

'It seems a pity. So low, I couldn't have missed.'

'We hadn't a chance, Jock, with six of them they would have blasted us to bits.'

He grinned in his quiet way:

'It would perhaps have been better than losing the jeep and having to walk home.'

We built our jeep track and used it at night to let a few jeeps loose amongst the German convoys. For once in Tunisia the going was so good in the plain on the German side of the range that we could drive about in the dark: night after night we ambushed convoys on the two roads that led to El Qettar, shot them up, and, leaving the wrecks to burn out, got away across country to lay another ambush further along. Before dawn we slipped back through our secret door and rested in peace in our olive grove. The Germans must have been very busy elsewhere, or particularly dense: for a long time they took no pains to discover where we operated from; the only measure they took was to make their convoys travel in close formation, escorted by a few armoured cars, which really made our task easier by giving us bigger targets to fire at.

On March 20th Eighth Army forced the defences of the Mareth Line: I heard the news a few days later: assuming that Rommel would now be once more on the move, we took a patrol across the coastal plain, lay up a whole anxious day in a little wadi, and reached the coast road after dark. As I had hoped, we found here bigger game than we had stalked up to then: a battalion of lorried infantry of the Afrika Korps moving northwards. We opened up and did some damage, but, as soon as flames from the burning trucks lit up the scene and exposed us to the enemy, we had to beat it under heavy fire, with, as it seemed, several squadrons of armoured cars on our tail. We succeeded in shaking them off and got home, but they must have followed our tracks, for at ten the next morning Waterson, who was keeping watch from the mountain top on our 'back door', reported cars driving up to the foot of our private pass. The Germans established a post, mined and blew up the track on their side of the mountain and from that day the pass was denied to us. Two days later Waterson, while on a patrol with Yunnie and Dave Porter, a new recruit, amongst the wild rocks overlooking the new German positions, got separated from his companions and lost his way. To get his bearings he climbed a steep peak, pulled himself over the last rock and dropped inside a German machine-gun post manned by three surprised Germans, whom he immediately shot dead with his American automatic rifle. He stayed a good while observing the German positions at the foot of the pass, then gathered the documents of the dead Germans and their telephone, smashed the gun and scrambled back to our lines with his booty. I was in camp when he arrived, and he laughed, somewhat embarrassed, when I asked him where he had liberated a telephone, for, like many of our men, Waterson, enjoyed telling tall tales of his narrow escapes, but was singularly averse to admitting to an act of bravery. I got him a Military Medal for his misadventure — I hoped it would encourage some of our slow thinkers to shoot quick when the occasion arose. A few days later the Germans, informed of our position by Arabs from Sened, sent six Stukas to bomb our camp in the olive groves near a farm called La Maknassienne. They hurt none of us but got a direct hit on one of our jeeps, loaded with explosives: when the dust settled we couldn't find one piece of that jeep too heavy to lift with one hand.

At Sened, when we first came up, we collected about three hundred Italian prisoners who had been overrun and had taken refuge up a wadi with no exit. They had some vehicles with them, and, amongst others, one of the L.R.D.G. trucks we had lost to a German patrol in Wadi Zemzem. This was a trophy indeed, which I would have liked to send to Lazarus, but as he was now back in Egypt we kept it and eventually, shamelessly, traded it in for an American six-wheeler truck. We had in those days to live by our wits.

On April 6th Eighth Army defeated Rommel's rearguard on Wadi Akarit and debouched into the Tunisian plain. On the morning of the seventh we found that the Germans had decamped from the foot of our pass. By ten we had lifted the mines and the booby traps, cleared the track and we were driving south-east across the plain when we saw long clouds of dust raised by the advancing columns of Eighth Army. We fell in with our First Armoured Division and drove along with them. That night I disgraced myself by failing to find my own camp when, after dark, I came out of their H.Q. Mess, where I had dined with my friend Jock Barrow, at that time their intelligence officer.

The exquisite cooking and the wines of the General's Mess cannot have been the cause of my lapse, for Jock Cameron, who had dined with the drivers, proved equally unable, gillie as he was, to remember

where we had left our party. This is all the more strange as Cameron
was never known, before or after, to be in any doubt of his way,
however dark the night.

P.P.A. did a few forward reconnaissances for First Armoured
Division, but the enemy withdrew so fast that we caught up with him
only once, near Qairouan. We pushed on to Enfidaville: by that time
the enemy forces had all been penned into the tip of Tunisia, seventy
miles across; and there was no room for us to operate. On May
20th we pulled out and went to rest for two days on the coast, north
of Sousse, then drove to Philippeville in Algeria, to train and refit.

Tunis fell on May 7th and the remnants of the German and the
Italian Armies were rounded up in the Cap Bon peninsula.

TRANSLATION OF EXTRACTS

FROM AN ITALIAN MILITARY DOCUMENT RECOVERED BY CAPTAIN RÉVILLON

IN HIS PECULIAR WAY

H.Q. Armoured Division 'Centauro' (131)
To: Operation Branch, Intelligence Branch,
Units under Command.

February 4th, 1943 — XXI.
Subject: Acts of Sabotage by English patrols.

Sabotage operations carried out recently by the enemy with the use
of special vehicles reveal that this special form of warfare, highly
developed by the English, is being now used in Tunisia. Further undertakings of this kind must be expected.

In Libya these sabotage units have often appeared driving in German
vehicles and wearing camouflaged uniforms or even, sometimes,
German or Italian uniforms.

Their operations are directed mainly against fuel and ammunition
dumps, landing grounds, vehicle staging areas and lines of communication generally.

While one member of the detachment, who speaks correct German or Italian, endeavours to engage the attention of the sentries by some request, the remainder lay explosives at suitable points.

Whenever these patrols are in German or Italian uniform they also possess the relevant military documents. Consequently it is not sufficient, when dealing with suspects, to be satisfied with the sight of an Army Pay Book or of a Military Permit of any description. It has been proved that the most useful thing to do in such cases is to ask the suspected person questions concerning his height, his weight, or if he is an American, also his temperature. The suspected person will inevitably fall into a confusion because the English and the Americans normally measure lengths, weights and temperatures with units different from those in use in our country. . . .

The Chief of Staff.
(*signed*) L. Giaccone, Lieut.-Colonel.

CHAPTER VII

NO WAR IN THE GOBI DESERT

THE war was over in Africa; without an enemy at hand we felt strange, like boys kept at school after it has broken up, neither on a holiday nor at work. We very sadly realized that there would be no more deserts for us to fight in. We had had a foretaste in Tunisia of what war in inhabited countries could be like — and we hadn't liked it. In the desert we had fought a clean conflict between soldiers, with nothing to ravage. We had left no trail of piteous burnt houses and devastated fields; there had been few civilian casualties, no refugee women and children, no horrors and no misery. We had contended with one enemy we patronizingly despised — the Italians, and another — the Germans — whom we respected and, in a way, liked; our fighting had been set in a landscape which neither our explosives nor the messy litter which follows the battle succeeded in defacing.

Quite apart from the war, the arid beauty of the desert setting, its freedom and its naked cleanliness, had gone to our hearts. All this was over for us, unsavoury prospects loomed ahead, and moreover most of what we had taught ourselves during the last two years would have to be dismissed from our minds, and we should have to start afresh on the next stage, beginners inventing new methods. Yunnie wanted to start a war in the Gobi Desert, but there didn't seem to be an enemy for us to fight in those distant parts, so I told him sternly that he had better put all thoughts of desert warfare out of his mind and wait till I came back from Alger, where I hoped to hear of the future plans of Allied Forces Headquarters. We would then, I told him, make our choice amongst the countries where the next fighting would take place and train and equip ourselves accordingly.

The centre of our world was now no longer in Cairo, suddenly turned into a backwater, but in Alger, where the Allied Command was, and the planning staff and the supply centres. I drove there and looked for a roof. There were two hotels in Alger: the St. George in gardens on the hillside, old fashioned and comfortable, which was entirely taken over by the officers of Allied Forces Headquarters (A.F.H.Q.), and the Aletti down by the harbour, in the style of the Cumberland at Marble Arch; this was reserved for 'full colonels and above', and I had been pushed out of it on a previous flying visit. I didn't want to suffer the same indignity again, but called on an officer temporarily in charge of accommodation. This sanctimonious sour-puss (a *faux Jésus* Caneri called him) sent me to his newly-opened officers' transit hotel, where, he assured me smugly, I would find every comfort. The address given led me to the dark doorway of a leprous building in the old French quarter near the docks. I felt my way up an obscure and slimy staircase, oozing with the filth of a century of neglect, and debouched on the third floor into a cavernous hall, glaringly lit night and day with a multitude of bare electric bulbs. The partitions had been knocked down in what, at some remote period, had been a vast *appartement*, leaving the ceiling to be supported by cast-iron pillars, painted a muddy red. The walls, peeling and sticky, had originally been of the same colour. Wooden cots, roughly made from the dismantled planks of packing cases, stood dispersed about the cavern, the only furniture there was. Along the far wall, in a kind of huge recess, was a line of chipped wash basins with rusty, leaky, taps and three very public *cabinets arabes*, squat-down lavatories with two cement slabs protruding from a low, square pan full of excrement. Basins and lavatories leaked hopelessly and overflowed on to the un-even tiled floor, which was covered ankle deep with a loathsome wash and a dubious scum. Lines of wobbly bricks served as stepping-stones leading to the cots. The stench was peculiar. At a table on a wooden platform, close to the entrance, sat a depressed corporal, sole represen-tative of the 'management' of the hotel. Incredibly, most of the cots showed signs of being occupied, the officers' valises bathing in the muck on the floor and their garments hanging on ropes tied between the pillars.

Used to sleeping in the clean desert, I left these officers, fresh from England, to the unprotesting enjoyment of their squalor and beat a cautious retreat down the slippery stairs. On the ground floor, under the archway, I put a few questions to the Arab concierge: he explained that our 'hotel' had been a café and unlicensed brothel till, a few years ago, the French police had condemned it as insanitary and had expelled the tenants.

I had strong words with the faux Jésus, who turned nasty, claimed that the accommodation in the transit hotel, which he visited daily, had never provoked any complaints, and threatened to have me expelled from Alger. I heard later that he had been removed — I hope as the result of my report.

The next day I got myself attached to the planning staff of A.F.H.Q., which was housed in a former *Ecole Normale* at Bu Zareyah on the crest of the hills outside Alger. I was allotted a bed in one of the dormitories, decent and comfortable indeed, but, shy of communal living, I took an unofficial room at a small hotel up the road. More of a *guinguette* than a hotel, it served exquisite meals under the trees in the garden, and a rich variety of drinks in the *bar Américain*, a crowded, noisy and cheerful room opening on the street. On the first floor there were a dozen small rooms, designed originally to satisfy the simple requirements of Sunday couples, but occupied now by Allied officers, and, rather incongruously, by a large French family consisting of elderly females in deep mourning and several subdued children. The incongruousness resulted from the fact that whereas the officers' transit hotel by the docks had long since ceased to be a *bordel* my hotel was very much a *maison de rendezvous*. To be sure I chastely shared a room with George Jellicoe, the commander of another Private Army called the 'Special Boat Section' which operated at sea somewhat on the same lines as our own P.P.A. on land, but every night through the thin partitions of the other rooms came cheerful noises which pointed unmistakably to honeymoon activities: girlish giggles, rustlings and sighs, and bare feet padding along the passage to join the queue outside the only bathroom.

During our long chaste months of desert wanderings amorous visions, recollected or imagined, filled many hours of day dreaming — indeed one young man in the L.R.D.G. confided to me that he thought of nothing else — but when we came back to civilization and feminine company we found that desire had outrun performance: a little satisfaction went a long way. Things were very different with the men who had just left home to take up staff duties in Alger: thrown out of balance by new surroundings, unwonted leisure and the exhilarating feeling of personal importance that overcomes soldiers in an occupied country, they lived in a state of continuous erethism and sought out the girls unceasingly. The Americans confining themselves to essentials, were generally contented to employ the services of the professionals, but the British aspired to more elevated unions, leading to a grumble:

'*Les Américains sont putassiers, avec eux on sait où l'on est, mais allez satisfaire les Anglais: ils voudraient tous coucher avec des jeunes filles du monde!*'

By a strange misapprehension of the plain facts of life, the older the men the more they aspired to awaken in their partners feelings of tender love, as if the red band on their hats made up for the lost attractiveness of their forgotten youth.

Wenching was not the sole occupation of the staff: for a great part of each day they sat in their crowded offices in the St. George and wrote notes and memoranda in septuplicate which they exchanged with their colleagues. Though they had not yet, in those early days, risen to the splendour they achieved later in Caserta, when the strength of A.F.H.Q. exceeded twenty-seven thousand (the equivalent of two divisions), they were already then several thousand strong and overflowed from the main building to huts and tents in the gardens.

A very young brigadier in Operations Branch, who had wisdom beyond his years, revealed one of the processes through which this inflation of staff was achieved:

'Eight months ago,' he said, 'I was appointed G.3 in charge of a newly-formed Camouflage section. I was then a captain; I shared a desk with another officer in a crowded room and had a one-tenth share in a typist. I set out to send a questionnaire to every section of each branch in the Headquarters: the replies, which I received in due course — for in the army every communication receives an answer, or at least an acknowledgment — piled up in my "In" tray. To be sure, these replies were all of a kind — "Does not concern this section", or "Nil — nil — nil", but that's beside the point. I sent out further notes and received further replies. When the brigadier came round with my C.O., on a tour of inspection, he found me toiling away. To his kind inquiry I replied: "I am doing my best, but you can see for yourself, Sir," and I pointed helplessly to the tottering mass of documents rising from my tray and overflowing on the desk. Before I knew where I was, I had been promoted to major with a captain under me and two clerks in an office of my own. And now I am a brigadier with two lieutenant-colonels, five majors, and six captains under me, twelve clerks, a staff car and billets in a villa.'

I was accustomed to the austerity of Eighth Army Headquarters (no more than two hundred strong I believe), where a handful of hard-working officers each had a job to do and knew how to do it (if they didn't they got the sack), and where a caller received a friendly reception and effective help because it was taken for granted that his problems were genuine and required a quick solution; here, on the other hand, a herd of splendidly-dressed nitwits sent the visitor packing without troubling even to find out his business. God knows what they were supposed to do — they certainly didn't: an obscure fear of being found out was at the root of their surliness.

A.F.H.Q. was not alone on the job. Under them worked Eighteenth Army Group, with a staff of well over a thousand, then under them again the two Army Headquarters, and, looking after supplies and the troops in the rear, District and Area Commands. After the liberation of Rome I learned that Kesselring, the German commander-in-chief in Italy, had run his show with a staff of about forty, 'but then, of course he had been beaten'.

The Planning Staff up on the hill, 'Force 141' as it was called then, of which I had become a very temporary member, were a different kettle of fish. Gifted with brains, some of them brilliantly clever, their experience was not limited to office work: they had planned operations as well as taken part in the execution; they had in the past been responsible for the raids on Dieppe and St. Nazaire, the destruction of the Mohne dam, and many combined operations by sea and by air, of which I had, till then, not heard. Their knowledge, the sources of information at their disposal and the method of their work were of a standard with which nothing in my experience could compare: I had found my masters and I set about to pick their brains.

In Constantine I had met David Stirling's brother, Bill, who had raised in England and commanded now in North Africa the Second S.A.S. Regiment, a formation trained on the lines of the First S.A.S., which had performed brilliantly in the desert. He had helped me out considerably with men and equipment while the fighting lasted in Tunisia, and I had now arranged with him that P.P.A. would be attached to his regiment and go into training near Philippeville on the Algerian coast. I had left my men camped in sand dunes, overlooking a beach, in what we thought then a nice salubrious spot, put Yunnie in command and dismissed them from my mind for the time being. Caneri had driven to Cairo to straighten out our administrative problems which had got into a muddle, a job which kept him busy for nearly six weeks of hard work.

Ian Collins, the publisher, was the officer who introduced me to Force 141. He was one of the best brains on that brilliant staff and the hardest worker. On my first day he gave me to read, fix in my memory and return within two hours, a file entitled 'Operation Husky': the outline plan for the invasion of Sicily. The invasion of the mainland of Italy was to follow in due course. Knowing now what I had come to Alger to find out, I could have gone back to Philippeville and trained my men for operations in Sicily — and subsequently on the mainland of Italy. Instead of which I discovered I was in need of a holiday and stayed on in Bu Zareyah to work long hours at the Ecole Normale. The particular section I worked with was responsible for the planning of small-scale raids: eventually as a result of our labour the S.A.S. landed a party at night under Geoffrey Appleyard on the island of Pantellaria from an M.T.B.; George Jellicoe's S.B.S. landed from a submarine on the west coast of Sardinia, walked across the island, raided two landing grounds on the way, and were picked up again (some of them) on the east coast; parachutists were dropped

behind Genoa and blew up a tunnel; and a large party of the Second
S.A.S. were parachuted on the slopes of Mount Etna to spread alarm
and despondency in the rear of the Germans who faced our main landing
in southern Sicily. Some of the raids we planned were carried out —
many more, after several days' work, were found impracticable and
given up. Force 141 was very business-like and left nothing to chance
that could possibly be foreseen, a far cry from the haphazard, home-
made planning which had led to the failure of our raids on Tobruq
and Benghazi from the Middle East the previous autumn. Security
was of a high order — not on account of special measures but because
the members of the staff were sensible and didn't talk: they seldom
left the grounds of the Ecole Normale; when they did they drank
little and held their tongues.

Once admitted to the staff and known personally to my colleagues,
I found that there was no restriction on the exchange of information
between the sections: whenever possible I went round to those who
were working on bigger stuff than our piddling raids, and learnt.

I had reserved for my own unit a sea landing from a submarine on
the north coast of Sicily: my party was to walk across the north-eastern
tip of the island and attempt to blow up a railway bridge between
Messina and Catania, a line which, as soon as our main forces had
landed in the south, would become the main enemy line of communication. This expedition, however, was not to take place, for I discovered,
after I had been working for several weeks at Force 141, that as long as
any knowledge I might have acquired of the Allied plans could be of
use to the enemy I would not be allowed to take part in any operation in
which I ran the risk of being captured by the enemy. I couldn't deny
that this decision was 'good security', but it precluded me from taking
an active part in any operations till after the invasion of Sicily (and I
wouldn't consider sending some of my men in and not going myself).
I hastened to leave Force 141 before it started work on the plans for the
invasion of Italy proper, lest too much knowledge on my part tied me
down for another period, and I rejoined Philippeville and my men.

Very soon after our arrival in Tebessa we had started weeding out:
we sent back eventually to the Middle East all our original men with

the exception of Waterson, Locke, Davies and Wilson, Bob Yunnie's gunner. Petrie would have have stayed with us had not the Director of Survey insisted on his return. Meanwhile I never stopped recruiting: one night in Gafsa, in the confusion of the withdrawal, I found, wandering around, Sergeant Curtis, a sapper who, with his officer, had been lent to the American command to carry out demolitions and lay mines to cover the retreat. While they were in no-man's-land Arabs had fallen on them: his officer was murdered, and Curtis, when I found him, was trying to find a vehicle with which he could go back and complete the job. The moment was not auspicious to bother the American command, who were busy carrying out, for the first time in their lives, a withdrawal under enemy pressure: I took him round myself. Back in Tebessa he refused to rejoin his unit, insisting that his vocation was to fight with P.P.A., and I took him on. Much later and with great trouble, his position was regularized with Second Echelon, who had posted him 'missing'. Sergeant Curtis was an estimating clerk in Oxford in civilian life, a short, stocky fellow of twenty-four years of age, with an irrepressible gaiety. He became very rapidly one of the pillars of P.P.A. The ranks I mention of our men are those they eventually reached with us: for they all automatically reverted to private on volunteering for the unit and got no extra pay.

Corporal Cameron, whom I have mentioned before, came to us from Second S.A.S. I took him as my gunner from the day he joined us and he remained with me till he was killed by my side in our jeep a year later. He was a gillie by profession and his age was thirty-three.

When we met First Armoured Division after the break through of Eighth Army at Mareth, I lost no time in worrying them into letting me pick three volunteers from one of their tank regiments — from the Derbyshire Yeomanry I got two, and from L.R.D.G., when I visited them in Egypt in May 1943, I got five: Sergeant Mitchell, a Welshman, Sergeant Beautyman, M.M., Yorkshireman signaller, gunner and driver, a man of infinite resource and varied accomplishments, undaunted and reliable, whom I put in command of our headquarters on one occasion when none of our experienced officers was at hand. Beautyman was a restful character: whenever we involved ourselves in a really sticky mess he could be relied upon to come forward with some imaginative but practical scheme to get out of trouble. If we found ourselves in a pretty desperate position, with our jeeps stuck in mid-stream between high wooded banks and tracer coming at them on two sides from an unseen enemy, he would suggest something that sounded as flat as: 'It seems to me, Popski, that if we turn now first left and third right, we shall come out opposite South Kensington Tube Station,' but was in fact an ingenious way out of our troubles. Eventually he was put in charge of our Signal Section, where he undertook elaborate responsibilities with more success than I can describe without entering into technicalities.

He was only twenty-three when he joined us, and having enlisted at eighteen he hadn't had time to get a civilian job.

Sergeant Sanders, M.M., a New Zealander, and a merchant seaman in peace time, also came to us from L.R.D.G., where he had distinguished himself on several occasions, and had got an M.M. Short and spare, his speech was even more clipped than usual for a New Zealander and practically unintelligible. He was twenty-eight and went about his job with a gravity and a self-centredness which made him seem older. In his cool way he was a man of extreme audacity, but so matter-of-fact that he never got into serious trouble.

Corporal McDonald, an Irishman of twenty-seven, became our chief mechanic (he commanded the M/T section). His gift was to 'saw with an axe and file with a spanner'.

Mee and Williamson, an inseparable pair of north country men, came to us also from L.R.D.G. They were slightly younger than the average of our men and tended to get into wild trouble when not on operations.

Sergeant Porter, a glass worker from Lancashire, a sapper, broad and tall, with a round, smiling face, came to us from S.A.S. He became our expert on demolitions and was the most popular man in the unit. With him came Sammy Barnes, a metal worker from Nottinghamshire, a rather frail man of twenty-eight, very blond and shy, who really had more stamina than most of us; and Jimmy Hunter, a baker from Perth. Sergeant Riches came from the K.D.G.s, one of the very few regular soldiers who found themselves at home in the unit. An American officer had been attached to us for a while and took part in a few raids: the intention was that he should gain experience and eventually raise an American force to operate on the same lines as P.P.A. He was unfortunately withdrawn very soon and I haven't heard from him since.

With these and some others recruited in the same manner from these units, the K.D.G.s and the Greys, our numbers reached about forty other ranks and four officers of an average age of twenty-seven when we left Tunisia in September. We were of course wildly over strength, but our establishment was in the Middle East, and our numbers were still so minute that nobody in A.F.H.Q. bothered to inquire. In fact our strength was no greater only because I had been unable to find more men available who suited my fancy. I was determined on no account to lower my standards, and with the only method of recruiting open to me at the time, which was to go begging from friendly commanders for permission to call for volunteers within their units, the output was small. There was, even at that time, no dearth of volunteers; but a large number of these I judged unsuitable on interview, and amongst the few I selected a large proportion were, all too often, not released by their commanding officers, who, not unnaturally, were loath to let their best men go.

All members of P.P.A. were volunteers and it was understood that I had the power to return any one of them to his unit whenever I chose — conversely if any man got dissatisfied with us and asked to be returned where he came from, this would be done at the earliest opportunity. In fact, the latter eventuality seldom occurred because, if a man came to be dissatisfied, we generally knew it before he was aware of it himself, and we released him without giving him time to ask; we had no use for discontented men.

I was lucky (or wise) in the selection of men I made at that time: six of them were killed in action, but the remainder stayed with us till the end of the war, or, if a few of them left before, it was because the strain had been so great that I judged they needed a change. They formed the nucleus round which our unit was built when we expanded later; they trained the newcomers, and it was these men who created and maintained the standard of behaviour which came to be specifically ours.

We had no more use for our Arabs, and we arranged for them to be discharged from the army and returned to their homes in the Jebel. Yunes would have followed me to Italy — or anywhere — but I considered it unfair to keep him on, now that his war was over, and I overrode his wish. I felt his departure sadly, for it left me rather lonely. Our relationship of master to follower, friendly and confidential, allowed me to discuss with him private matters which could not be taken up with anyone else, and his advice was helpful, for he was shrewd. Humorous also and invariably cheerful, he was regretted not only by me.

When I returned from Alger to Philippeville I was uneasy in my mind about the future employment of P.P.A. Assuming that we got a modicum of support from the local population (of which there was a possibility according to our scanty information), I had no doubt that behind the lines in Italy, as we had done in the desert, we could manage to be useful in collecting intelligence, inflicting actual damage to the enemy and spreading alarm and despondency! (This last was more than a moral satisfaction, for we had evidence that during the German withdrawal from El Alamein the equivalent of approximately two enemy divisions had been diverted to guard the line of communication against the depredations of desert raiders.) The puzzle, however, was to get behind the lines in sufficient strength.

The two methods I had seen used while I worked with Force 141 were not satisfactory; they were: landing on the enemy coast in a canvas canoe from a submarine or a fast surface craft, or dropping by parachute. Both methods led ultimately to a small group of men trudging on their feet, each carrying a load of over sixty pounds, of which a small part only could be used against the enemy, for it included small arms and ammunition for personal defence, food, bedding and such items as wireless sets with their heavy batteries: little room was left for explosives and no heavy automatic weapon could be carried. This was unsatisfactory: the damage that could be done to the enemy was negligible in proportion to the expensive equipment used — and lost — on each raid, and of the highly-trained men who, except in the most favourable circumstances, had to be considered as expendable. Also the formidable physical strain involved led to the selection for these raids of men notable more for their strength than for their brains: and, consequently, the chances of their being able to survive in enemy territory long enough to carry out their mission were infinitesimal. In plain words, these enterprises seemed to me not worth undertaking.

I wanted to take behind the lines patrols of five jeeps, each carrying a ton of supplies, mounting between them ten heavy machine guns — the fire power of a battalion — and with enough petrol for a range of six hundred miles. I didn't know yet how to do it, and until I had found a method, the training I gave my men was bound to be irrelevant. The men felt it and there grew up amongst them a certain amount of bewilderment and some discontent. I tried to fob them off by providing entertaining forms of training: I got them folding canvas canoes and rubber dinghies to practise landings with, we paddled and we swam: nice holiday sport but no preparation for desperate enterprises. There is no more disheartening form of activity than training for an object which is not clearly conceived; when it became known that our neighbours in the sand dunes, the S.A.S. parachutists, were about to be engaged on operations and that we were doing nothing, I very nearly had a mutiny: in succession — Yunnie first — every member of P.P.A. came to me to ask to be given parachute training. I thought it would do them no harm and made the arrangements. Then the first heat of summer stimulated the mosquitoes in a nearby swamp, and we all went down with malaria.

When a sufficient number of our men came out of hospital I moved the unit to 'en Draham in the mountains on the Tunisian border, told them to be good boys and recover their strength as quickly as they could, and left for Msaken between Sousse and Qairouan, where our First Airborne Division was encamped. The S.A.S. parachutists were to be flown from here: I had undertaken to look after their signals for them for the duration of the operation and having helped with the plan I thought I might as well help with the execution.

They took off and were dropped at night in the foothills of Mount Etna, against all the rules, with no more damage than one sprained ankle. With the exception of one stick of men which dropped plumb inside a P.O.W. camp, they all came back eventually, having done much damage to the enemy communications. On this operation Geoffrey Appleyard, the officer who had led the raid on Pantellaria, was lost. He was, for the same reasons as myself, forbidden to take part in an operation; but he had flown out with the dropping party to reconnoitre the ground, and his plane crashed on the return trip. He was one of the few officers who had developed the technique of the small-scale raid: the care he took of his men made him stand out amongst brother officers who were too excited by the prospect of adventure to think much of anybody but their own selves.

Three nights before this operation on July 9th, I had watched the take-off of the glider-borne troops of First Airborne Division, who were to land on the Sicilian beaches ahead of the main assault by the sea-borne forces. I had never seen gliders before and knew nothing about them: for some reason one of them got in trouble just after the take-off, released its tow cable and landed in the dark amongst trees close to where I stood. I drove over, expecting to find a crash, and the mangled remains of the fourteen men it carried, instead of which I found the undamaged glider level on the ground, jammed between two trees, and the crew standing around preparing to walk back to camp. I was much impressed by this performance; the glider pilot showed me over his machine, an American Waco, and mentioned casually that it was designed to carry a jeep: there at last was the answer to my problems.

Three weeks later P.P.A. was camped at Msaken, attached to First Airborne Division and training hard. I had talked over my plans with General Hopkinson, who commanded our airborne troops. Once convinced of their feasibility, he grew enthusiastic, for he was that kind of man, and he and his staff helped us to the limit of their power.

Roughly, the plan for my first operation was to land six gliders on a deserted plateau in Calabria — five gliders carrying each an armed jeep with a balanced load, two men of P.P.A. and one pilot from the

Glider Pilot Regiment; the sixth glider with just a pilot, carrying supplies to be distributed amongst the five jeeps after landing. The gliders would be destroyed and the party, consisting of ten men from P.P.A. and six glider pilots, would drive away and do their business. For the return trip, when our petrol and ammunition would be nearing exhaustion, I counted on lying in hiding till we were overrun by our main forces advancing up Italy, or, alternately, arranging on the wireless for an M.T.B. to pick us up (without our jeeps, which in that case would have to be destroyed). As the glider pilots would have to share our fortunes it was decided to attach twelve of them to P.P.A., and we started straight away to train them in our craft. Conversely, I learnt to pilot a glider, in which my previous experience in flying helped.

With the help of Airborne workshops we equipped our jeeps in a manner which, with some later minor improvements, we maintained till the end of the war. Our vehicles were uncovered and carried no windscreen: they mounted on swivels fore and aft, two Browning belt-fed machine guns, one of .30 the other .50 inch calibre, firing in succession tracer, armour-piercing and incendiary ammunition. In racks outside the jeep we carried seven four-gallon jerrycans of petrol, which, with the tank, gave us an approximate range of six hundred miles. Ammunition, spare parts, tools for the truck, for digging and for felling trees, two boxes of compo rations, a towing cable, two spare wheels, a cooker (altogether over two hundred items), made up the standard jeep-load of approximately one ton. For the personal use of the crew (two or three men to each jeep) we carried a .50 automatic pistol each, plus a carbine (U.S.) or a tommy gun. Each patrol of five jeeps (later the number was brought up to six) carried two wireless sets, a three-inch mortar, a hand winch, a Bren gun with an infantry mounting, land mines and explosives.

I encouraged a certain diversity of clothing with the reservation, strictly enforced, that every garment outwardly worn should be a British Army issue. As a special exception Sergeant Curtis was allowed to wear a U.S. knitted peaked cap. Civilian and enemy clothing was banned, with the exception of dull silk scarves worn *under* the shirt collar, which could, if they so fancied, be worn by men who had taken part in at least one operational patrol. At that particular moment a camouflaged jumping jacket over K.D. slacks and shirt was much fancied by most of us: with its many pockets it was a handy garment, but being neither waterproof nor warm it came to be less favoured in the rigorous Italian winter. Headdress was the black beret, worn without a badge on operations, or more commonly the nondescript cap comforter. Sergeant Waterson still wore a stiff Kiwi hat. When I got my glider-pilot wings, I started wearing a red beret, but later, feeling it made my head rather conspicuous, I discarded it. Beards were still unregulated: eventually they became the privilege of the old hands with at least five operations to their credit, and were subject to my approval as to density of growth: no tufted fungus growth could be passed off as a beard!

On the whole we were still quite tidy — it was our first Italian winter that turned us into a band of scarecrows (and also the wider range of army issues of clothing).

Our bedding was of quilted sleeping bags and a ground sheet. Later we got issued with arctic eiderdown hooded sleeping bags, so warm that we slept in comfort in the snow.

Caneri loved order: mainly under his pressure I had now given some shape to our originally amorphous unit. We had two patrols (later the number was brought up to four) of fifteen men each, 'R' and 'B', of which I commanded one and Bob Yunnie the other. In each patrol a commander, a sergeant, a corporal, a wireless operator and a fitter had their appointed duties. Caneri was in charge of Headquarters with a wireless section and an M/T section. He had acquired a wonderful knowledge of army administration, and from that time we put in all the returns required of a regular unit. In later years I could boast that our administration was tidier than in most regiments. He started at this time keeping a War Diary and all the proper records.

The glider operation of the Airborne Division at the invasion of Sicily had been somewhat of a failure owing to faulty navigation of the towing planes. The gliders had been landed far from their objectives — many of them in the sea — and one of them, after flying for several hours, had finally sighted a coast and, the landing signal being given from the towing plane, had released their cable and come down on the Tunisian coast south of Gabes, one hundred and thirty miles south of their starting-point, instead of two hundred miles east of it as they should have been, had this coast been Sicily as their towing pilot fancied. This made me think that on our operations our six gliders might well come down in other places than had been planned: the crews of the jeeps would then have to find out their real location and make their way to a common rendezvous before dawn. With practised navigators on the planes I assumed that the error would not exceed thirty miles, and to train our men to find their bearings quickly in such a situation I devised an exercise in which two men composing a jeep crew were told that their objective was the railway bridge over the road one mile north of the town of Beja in northern Tunisia, but that their actual landing would take place at some spot unknown within a circle of thirty miles radius centred on Beja. They had the whole day to study the map: at nightfall they were blindfolded, put in the back of a covered truck and driven across country to a high valley in the chaotic group of mountains near Jebel Abiod, eighteen miles north of their objective. There they were released and put into their jeep, which had been driven up for them: their job now was, by the lie of the land obscurely seen against the starlit skyline, to find out their position, work out a route to their objective and reach it before dawn. The area chosen being deserted, and the hour late, they had little chance of getting information from a local inhabitant, even if they could have made themselves understood in the barbarous dialect of the mountains. Other parties were dropped at the same time at points up to sixty miles apart, and then we went to wait for them at the rendezvous. We repeated the game all over Tunisia and found, as could be expected, that practised crews often found their bearings in the mountains after no more than ten minutes' driving, but in the plains and the olive groves they often roamed for an hour or more.

Although we practised the same exercise with actual moonlight landings in gliders, there still remained a large element of unreality. All I hoped to achieve by this training was to give confidence to the crews in such a manner that, when they found themselves up against the real difficulties, the knowledge that they had done all this before would help them to avoid getting flustered. I remembered Bagnold's advice in the desert: 'When you think you have got lost, stop, smoke a cigarette, take a short nap and then start working out where you went wrong.'

I also wanted each crew to be self-supporting: if a patrol lost its leader or got dispersed, the survivors should be able to carry on by themselves.

Much of our time was taken up in flying in gliders, mostly by night, and trying, generally unsuccessfully, to check up on the route we followed as we flew.

We went on in this way till the first days of September 1943, when a decision of the Allied High Command, suddenly made known to us, altered our plans.

PART FIVE

ITALIAN PARTISANS

CHAPTER I

COGNAC FOR MAJOR SCHULZ

THE occupation of the whole of Sicily concluded, Eighth Army crossed the Straits of Messina on September 3rd, unopposed (or nearly), and advanced into Calabria. Meanwhile negotiations with Badoglio came to a head, and the Italian Armistice was signed but not yet published.

Ignorant as yet of these developments, the Airborne Division was, on September 1st, put on a week's notice to embark at Bizerta. I was told that P.P.A. would provide five jeeps and their crews to land (wherever it was) with the first wave of troops — the remainder of the unit to follow later. The operation was to be sea-borne, then land-borne, and we put gliders out of our plans — as it turned out — once and for all.

We got ready. I recruited Sergeant Brooks, an L.R.D.G. signaller, who had somehow got stranded in Msaken with his wireless truck. The arrangement was purely private, concluded in two minutes' talk (to be straightened out afterwards), but he stayed with us until the end of the war. He was a Londoner aged thirty-five, of extreme deliberation in his speech; a great reader of books with a thoughtful turn of mind and a gift of clothing common sense in expressions of crystalline originality. Conversing with him was a pleasure that I sought whenever I had an opportunity.

McGillavray, a young officer who had been seconded to us from the Derbyshire Yeomanry through the friendliness of its commander, Lieut.-Colonel (as he was then) Payne-Gallwey, rushed away to Alger to collect six new jeeps and came back having travelled over a thousand miles non-stop in his eagerness not to miss the embarkation. By the time he came back we were at twelve hours' notice: without troubling to get any sleep he prepared his jeep for action with his gunner, Gaskell, and drove away with us at sunset in a long, slow convoy which was carrying the first elements of the Airborne Division to Bizerta. When we arrived at the port at dawn he was not with us. We got on board the U.S. cruiser *Boysey*, and watched our vehicles as they were swung on deck. McGillavray appeared on the quay, riding a motor bicycle: the engine of his jeep had passed out half way between Msaken and Bizerta. In the middle of the night he had stolen a motor bicycle, found and woken up an American workshop and had so well succeeded in convincing them of his urgency that they were at this moment putting a new engine into his truck. He rode away to collect it, promising to embark on our cruiser, if he came back in time — if not, on one of the other ships of the convoy.

We sailed without him, but when we had been at sea a few hours, I got a signal from H.M.S. *Abdiel* saying that he and Gaskell were on board that minelayer with their jeep.

We sailed on September 7th. The next day the Italian Armistice was announced to us and our destination given: Taranto, the naval base under the 'heel' of Italy. According to the terms of the armistice our landing should be unopposed, but we were warned not to place too much reliance on this promise. On the afternoon of the ninth we caught sight of the Italian coast; then we saw the low shapes of naval vessels steaming out of port: the Italian fleet on its way to surrender at Malta. We entered the outer harbour and stopped. A launch flying Italian colours came alongside *Boysey* — and the commander of the naval base, an Italian admiral, in white uniform, gold braid and medals, came up the gangway and stepped on deck; an Italian officer, yet neither an active enemy nor a prisoner-of-war, which seemed strange. Night had nearly fallen when we moored at a quayside: to starboard stood a row of gaunt, bombed houses, silent and dead; to port, under the glare of our ship's searchlights, a company of our red-bereted troops formed up on the quay and marched off to the harbour gates.

The winches lifted our five jeeps ashore, we got in, and, leading our small company, I drove out of the harbour, past the guard, through the deserted rubble-covered streets of Taranto into the sleeping countryside, alone with my nine men in the dark, hostile continent of Europe.

A landing at Taranto had been considered, with several others, at an early stage of the planning of the invasion of Italy, but the decision to carry it out had, as I believe, been taken at the last minute when it was realized that the main landing of our Fifth Army at Salerno would be opposed by powerful German forces. The object was to link up with the Italian forces in the Puglie, and having stiffened them by our presence and our example, create a diversion on the German left flank which would induce them to divert some of their troops from Salerno.

A.F.H.Q. were so doubtful about the fighting power of the Italians that all they had told us was that Badoglio had 'promised the co-operation of his troops'. Indeed the extent to which we counted on this co-operation of the Italian forces went no further than the hope that we should be able to lift from them transport and petrol, for we needed them badly as the cruisers which carried our division to Taranto had room on their crowded decks for no more than a few jeeps and motor bicycles.

About the situation ashore A.F.H.Q. had been unable to tell us anything either of the numbers or the location of our new allies, or of the strength of the German troops — if any — which might oppose us.

From the Italian admiral who came on board I had learnt that an admiral commanded at Brindisi, that there was an Italian infantry division with its headquarters at Francavilla, and that a Corps Head-quarters was at Bari, which, he supposed, might have been informed of the terms of the armistice. The Germans, he said, had troops in various localities of the Puglie,[1] though some of them might have been withdrawn recently: more than that he wouldn't say. Being of a surly disposition, he made it clear that it was no business of his to give us information. This was all the knowledge I had of the situation when I landed from U.S.S. *Boysey* and drove out of Taranto in the night. My orders were:

> To contact the general commanding the division in Francavilla and give him verbal orders from my general.

[1] This region covers the Adriatic watershed of the Apennines from the Gargano Peninsula in the north to the tip of the 'heel' in the south.

To contact the admiral commanding in Brindisi and give him his orders.

To inspect all the landing grounds dispersed in the flat country between Brindisi, Lecce and Taranto, and report on the facilities they could offer for prompt use by the R.A.F.

To get intelligence of the German forces in the area.

Though it was not later than nine o'clock when we started, the whole population seemed to be already in bed. We saw no one in Taranto, then drove through San Giorgio Ionico and saw no one still. Half way to Grottaglie a flickering light zigzagged across the road: a cyclist, too drunk to understand my questions — my first contact with the Italian civilian population. Before entering Grottaglie we stopped a good while because of a convoy we heard driving somewhere beyond a railway embankment. When they had driven away along a side road, we pushed on without meeting a soul. In Francavilla I discovered, with difficulty, a military office: a sentry seated on the steps outside the door slept with his rifle between his knees. Woken up and disarmed, I put him next to me in the jeep, while Cameron in the back kept him covered, and under his guidance we drove to Divisional Headquarters. Bob Yunnie having placed the jeeps to cover the approaches, I drove up to the door of a villa where the general lived, and entered bravely the lion's den. I stated my business to a sleepy corporal, and ten minutes later a captain walked in and said in English:

'Good evening, Major. I *am* sorry I kept you waiting while I shaved, but this *is* a pleasure *indeed*. Won't you sit down and have a drink? I have warned the general, who is now getting up and won't be a moment: he *is* looking forward to meeting you, I know.

'I do hope you have had a pleasant trip. What kind of sea did you have for the crossing? The weather at this time of the year is generally good, though perhaps a bit hot.'

There were no lions it seemed in the den, only lambs. The general's moment was a long one: in the meanwhile I pumped the young man. Despite his silly prattle he was no fool: I would find the army and the air force very eager to help us — the navy was different, snooty

fellows, he said, but they would have to toe the line. With great satisfaction he rang up Naval Headquarters in Brindisi, and had the admiral
brought out of bed to be told that a British representative would call
on him at three that morning.

The Germans, he thought, had pulled out of the province by now,
but I had better be careful on the way to Brindisi not to fall in with
their rearguard. They had a large technical staff who had been
working on the airdromes, but few fighting troops. Somewhere in
the north was the German First Parachute Division, perhaps in Bari,
with which town telephone communication had been interrupted
earlier that day.

He was happy and excited. The war was over – the bitterness of
defeat had been swallowed, and he saw opening up a delightful era of
collaboration with English gentlemen: he was a bit of a snob.

We talked a long time of the campaigns in the desert. He was the
intelligence officer I have mentioned before who gave me the Italian
Staff's views of our raids on Tobruq, Benghazi and Barce. He knew
much of our plans for these operations, and even pretended he remembered my name. I brought a bottle of whisky from my jeep and
we shared it with his commanding officer when he at last turned
up. The general, having been given his instructions by me, said he
would call on General Hopkinson first thing in the morning, and would
arrange straight away for his divisional transport, such as it was, to
report at Taranto during the day. (As to bringing his troops to fight
with us, his only answer was a hopeless gesture of the hands.) Walking
out of Headquarters I was met by the sentry I had disarmed: with tears
running and heavy sobs he begged me to return him his weapon or
he would get into trouble.

Back with my men, I got Beautyman to put up his aerial and try
to get in touch with Brooks at Divisional Headquarters. I enciphered
a message giving my first scanty intelligence – then we had a meal.
Beautyman was a long time tapping his key before he got a reply, so
that, with one or another delay, when we finally reached the outskirts
of Brindisi the time was, not three, but six o'clock in the morning.
The few people about fled when they saw us, and we drove along the

347

streets preceded by a clatter of shutters hastily pulled to. The experts had promised us a friendly welcome from the population, but it was through a hostile, surly and silent town that we drove to Naval Headquarters.

Grimy and unshaven I padded in my slovenly desert boots up a marble staircase into a vast and noble room: through six crimson curtained windows the rising sun shone from over the harbour on to a tubby figure standing alone in the middle of the floor in gimcrack finery. The admiral wore a sash, a sword and many medals; he stared peevishly out of a yellow, puffed face, for he had been standing there three hours, and his first words were a complaint about my delay.

I called to the orderly who had showed me in:

'Bring a seat for the admiral, immediately. Can't you see that His Excellency is falling with weariness?'

The poor admiral, his surrender scene utterly ruined, declined the chair, but led me into an office where he sulked, puffed and objected while I talked. His head ached, he said, and he would attend to business later in the day, but I was in no mood to humour him, and twenty minutes later we were driving out to view the harbour, the seaplane base and the airport. By nine we had finished, had dropped him at his headquarters and drove off through the town on our way to Lecce.

Brindisi had in the meanwhile undergone a peculiar transformation: Union Jacks, Italian flags, and carpets such as are used for religious processions, had been hung from the house windows, stalls in the market square sold small Union Jacks (some of them rather queer), and red, white and blue cockades; the streets were so packed that we could hardly drive. Waves and waves of cheers enveloped us: men climbed on to our jeeps, shook us by the hand and kissed us in ecstasies of enthusiasm. It seemed very odd: two days before we had been still at war with these people, and now they gave us a welcome that could not have been exceeded had we been their own victorious troops returning home after the utter defeat of the enemy. They longed desperately for a hated war to end, and they cared not if their country's military disasters were the price of the peace we brought.

To their simple minds we were allies and friends, who had fought to deliver the suffering people from their wicked rulers and to put an end to nightmares of apprehension and terror: they loved us, their deliverers, hysterically. They were not, as some may think, trying to propitiate the new master, for their joy was uncalculating: obscurely, in their poor hearts, they felt that we had won the war for them.

I realized later that at our early arrival in Brindisi we had been mistaken for a party of Germans.

In every village that we passed that day events developed along a similar pattern: as we reached the first houses a wave of panic spread ahead of us, women gathered their children and bolted for their houses, slammed the doors and banged the shutters, carts backed up side streets, men on bicycles slipped furtively away, and the main square was empty when we arrived, except for two or three small boys who, curiosity having overcome fear, remained to watch us. As we drove by, their faces registered comically in succession surprise — incredulity — hesitation and then, suddenly, decision: off they darted, like mad, from house to house; bang, bang, bang, on each door, piping shrilly:

'Inglesi, Inglesi, Inglesi!'

As if they had been massed behind the closed doors waiting for the signal, crowds poured into the square and the streets: we were enveloped, submerged, cheered and kissed. If we stopped long enough, and often we had no other choice, locked as it were in the crowd, men of importance forced their way to my jeep and delivered speeches of welcome — offerings were brought: baskets of grapes, almonds and apples emptied over our knees, eggs, cheeses and loaves piled in the back of the trucks. Bottles of wine reached us, from hand to hand, over the heads of the people, glasses were produced and toasts proposed. In one village an old woman came forward with a pitcher of cool water and an egg, all she had, she said, for she was very poor. I took a long draught of water and, not knowing what to do with the egg, sucked it then and there. Everywhere the 'Americani', elderly men who, having worked in America for a term, had returned to their native village with a small hoard of dollars, came up, called ''Ello, Boy' and then stood mute, for they had forgotten the few words of English they had ever learnt.

The people who greeted us were all of the poorer kind, peasants and labourers, for in these parts the landed gentry and their satellites of the professions, doctors, lawyers and suchlike, don't mingle with the vulgar. The priests also kept aloof.

So much kindness might have overwhelmed us, but we managed to keep our heads, and during that day, our first in Italy, we visited all the landing grounds in Lower Puglie. From them all the aircraft had been removed and attempts had been made by the Germans to destroy the ground installations, but they had left in a great hurry without achieving much damage. The Italian Air Force officers in charge fell over one another in their eagerness to help us, each commander endeavouring eloquently to persuade me that *his* landing ground was more suitable than any other to be occupied immediately by the R.A.F., and they made a great show of starting repairs even before we had left them. The keenness of these fighting men was different in my eyes from the single-hearted enthusiasms of the poor people and left a bitter taste: they showed, to my liking, too much eagerness to fall on their former allies, the Germans, now that we had proved to possess the greater strength. They liked to think that their behaviour would commend itself to us, but I couldn't help feeling that their sudden change of face stank of treachery.

Towards evening, I reached an airfield, near San Pancrazio Salentino, with which my review of the landing grounds south of a line running from Taranto to Brindisi would be completed. Thinking of my job for the morrow, I asked the local commander for information about the installations further to the north, in particular about the airdrome at Gioia del Colle — the only one of importance, according to my knowledge, for the ground becomes rough and rocky as you proceed north from Taranto and is generally unsuitable for landing aircraft. He described the facilities at Gioia and said:

'As to the present state of the ground I am not informed, but if you don't mind waiting a moment I shall ring up my colleague at Gioia and find out from him.'

This very simple method had not occurred to me, as I had assumed, without giving the matter more thought, that all telephone lines to the north would be cut off. The colleague in Gioia said that German troops had occupied his airdrome early that morning, coming from Altamura, their headquarters. A little later we heard German voices and he rang off. Encouraged by this success we telephoned to various other places, talking either to the local Italian military commander, or simply to the postmaster. Many of the telephone exchanges were still functioning with their civilian staff, and so little were they adapted to the new situation resulting from the armistice and our landing, that no one questioned our business in asking for information: they had not realized yet that we had brought war to their peaceful backwater. I was enchanted by this easy method of getting inside the enemy camp. In less than two hours, just by sitting in an office and listening patiently on the phone over very faulty lines, I had been able to put the enemy on the map where before I had only a blank.

As a result of the talks, I had gathered that there were German troops to the north of Taranto and that they were concentrating in places of which I knew three: Gravina, Altamura and Gioia del Colle. Of their numbers, units and resources I was still completely ignorant.

By one in the morning on September 11th I was back in Taranto, twenty-nine hours after I had left it. Division Headquarters were now in a building in the town; such troops as had so far disembarked held a perimeter round the town and they had been in contact with enemy patrols on the main road to Gioia. I gave verbally the general information I had collected, dictated a report on the aerodromes, told the general that I would try to reach Bari in the morning and thence go to the rear of the German positions on the Gravina-Gioia lines, and went to sleep for a couple of hours on the roof of Headquarters building.

My heart was heavy with sad news: early on the tenth H.M.S. *Abdiel* had foundered in a few minutes after striking a mine in the outer harbour; there were few survivors of the crew or of the troops on board, and neither McGillavray nor Gaskell was amongst them — our first death casualties in P.P.A.

I had placed great hopes in McGillavray: gifted with courage, imagination, singleness of purpose and tremendously active, he was, I think, the most promising young officer I ever recruited for P.P.A. I was fond of the man and it was the friend that I mourned, not the loss of a useful officer. In our tense little world affection developed quickly, went deep and lasted; unexpressed ties of friendship held us together, a band of brothers who shared a taste for strenuous action, and our allegiance was to each other, more than to a wider community; the inspiration of our enterprises was our common wish to perform well the difficult tasks which we set ourselves. As the general military situation became less acute the need to keep our country free from a foreign domination receded more and more into the background of our consciousness.

In our hazardous pursuits we suffered death and the loss of friends with an even mind, but it grieved me that this man should have been killed before he had given his measure, at the very moment when his toilsome preparations would have begun to bear fruit.

Early that morning our five jeeps were once more on the road, which climbed first to the top of the watershed and then looked down on to Locorotondo and the Adriatic. The houses here are made of stone; circular and domed like beehives, they are spread over the countryside under clumps of trees. The landscape of grey rock and red soil adorned, but not clothed, with wild vegetation and very ancient olive trees, is so beautiful that driving down towards the Adriatic I fell into a dream and saw the whole of Italy stretched out before me.

'Jock, four hundred miles up this coast lies Venice, an island town of canals and narrow streets, where no wheeled vehicle has ever been seen. One day we shall land our jeeps on the main square, which is called Piazza San Marco, and drive them round and round, a senseless gesture no doubt, an empty flourish — but it has never been done before and at that time we shall be able to afford showing off because the war will be nearly over.'

Cameron, who was watching the map, replied:

'No doubt indeed. The village we are coming to now is Fasano, on

[facing: Top: LOADING A JEEP INTO A GLIDER
Bottom: L.R.D.G. LORRIES IN THE SAND SEA

the main road. Hadn't we better slow down and inquire, or we may run into a German post? The war isn't over yet.'

Fasano turned out to be unoccupied, and nobody stopped us till we reached the outskirts of Bari, where an Italian guard on the road provided, at my request, a guide to Corps Headquarters. I left my men in the street and walked in to see the corps commander.

He was a fat, fussy little man in a state of considerable agitation. He said:

'I want immediate support from your troops. You have got a wireless, haven't you? Then signal your headquarters in Taranto to send up immediately five squadrons of armoured cars, ten batteries of field artillery and two battalions of infantry. We have had a battle with the Germans in the harbour yesterday' (a scuffle, as I found out, with some German engineers who wanted to blow up the port installations). 'We beat them off — but this very moment they are coming back along the main road from Trani.'

The poor man had in Bari three infantry divisions with their artillery and several squadrons of tanks, but he hadn't the faintest notion how to employ troops. He had not in his life held an active command, and was in fact no more than a depot commander, who had overnight, so to speak, found himself in command of front-line troops — he was in a panic and his headquarters, having none of the organization required for battle, couldn't help him at all. The whole staff was scared of the Germans. I refrained from mentioning that our forces in Taranto had no armour, no guns heavier than four-pounders and no transport, but I agreed to refer his request to my headquarters and infuriated him by declining to give him any information.

'You are worse than the Fascists,' he sneered. 'How can we collaborate if you mistrust me and tell me nothing?'

Mistrust him I did indeed — and he fared no better with those who came after me; he ended as a war criminal before a tribunal for ordering the execution of escaped British prisoners-of-war, and was eventually (years later) shot by a British platoon.

He had no intelligence organization whatever, but acted impulsively on market-place rumours. In his panic he had ordered his own telephone lines to be cut, so even this means of information was denied to us.

As a compromise I agreed to go out with his chief of staff, a weedy old man with the mind of a gendarme, to visit the outposts that had hastily been disposed outside the town, and advise him on defence. When we came back to Corps Headquarters a message came through that the German command in Foggia, eighty miles to the north, was on the telephone of the Water Company. A private company runs aqueducts all over the Puglie, and they have their own telephone lines which had been overlooked and had escaped destruction. We went round to the company's offices: the Germans, it seemed, in their ardour of destruction had blown up a conduit at Cerignola, intending to cut off Bari water supply, instead of which, by some mistake, they had cut themselves off at Foggia. They now wanted the Italian commander in Bari to order the aqueduct company to send their engineers to repair the damage. I took the receiver and gave my German colleague in Foggia the equivalent of a German raspberry — not before, however, I had got from him some information about their forces and their intentions. At the end of our talk I let out that I was the commander of the British armoured forces in Bari, which, I hoped, would spoil his night for him. In those early days after the armistice, the Germans were nearly as much upset as the Italians by the sudden change from peace-time to front-line activities, and in their agitation they had a tendency to speak freely on the telephone. Later that evening I rang up several places on the aqueduct line and got a sketchy picture of the position north of Bari — but nothing at all to the south, excepting that the Germans there were supplied from Foggia.

My task now was to find out the strength of the Germans in the Altamura area because our weak division in Taranto was condemned to remain on a fruitless defensive until they knew what enemy forces opposed them. The object of our landing in Taranto was to attract German forces away from Salerno on the other side of Italy, where our Fifth Army were finding themselves hard pressed: Airborne Division could achieve nothing by sitting on its perimeter round the town, and on the other hand, few in numbers as they were, with neither artillery nor air support and little transport, they couldn't risk annihilation in attacking blindly an enemy whom they suspected to be three or four times stronger than themselves. The matter was of some urgency because, if they waited till shipping became available to bring in reinforcements, the position in Salerno might, in the meanwhile, deteriorate a little more and Fifth Army might find themselves thrown back into the sea. To be sure, our small effort at Taranto was not the main diversion threatening the Germans: Eighth Army, having crossed the straits of Messina from Sicily, was moving northwards through Calabria, but they had still two hundred miles to go over difficult mountain roads, interrupted every few miles by the destruction of bridges and tunnels, and we couldn't guess how soon they would be able to make their power felt.

I had spent the remainder of September 11th, after we arrived at Bari, pumping courage into the Italian garrison and putting some order in their military dispositions, hoping they would find the heart to hold the place against an eventual German attempt to recapture it: it was of some importance for our future operations that we should find the harbour and the landing ground in good condition when we had built up enough strength in Taranto to move up and occupy Bari. There was also an appreciable amount of transport and large stocks of petrol which I didn't want to fall into German hands. I hoped that, as a result of my indiscretion on the telephone, the Germans, believing Bari to be now in British hands, would not attempt to re-occupy it before they had got together a fairly substantial armoured force, and we should be spared the mortification of seeing the place fall to a mere troup of armoured cars — for the Italians were so jittery that no reliance could be put on them.

Night had now fallen, and, urgent as it was that I should proceed with my reconnaissance, I found it necessary to give ourselves a night's rest: we had slept no more than two hours since the morning of September 9th, three days and two nights ago.

We had a fine meal at the Albergo Imperiale, all of us at one large table, rather upsetting an officer from Italian Headquarters who had come to see if we were comfortable, for he was not in favour of officers and men feeding together. Beautyman, as usual with our wireless operators, worked most of the night getting my messages across to Taranto, while we all slept.

Putting together the meagre information I had, and looking at the map, I worked out a provisional picture of the German dispositions: they had forces based on Gioia del Colle, Altamura and Gravina, holding the crests of the hills, with a good lateral road. This line possibly extended to Potenza in the west and on to Salerno. The forces with which I was immediately concerned were supplied from Foggia along the road running to Gravina. As Bari was in Italian hands and the first place held by the Germans on the coast, to my knowledge, was Trani, they had from Gioia del Colle to the coast an open left flank forty miles long, which I presumed they guarded in some manner, either with detached posts or with patrols.

I made a plan to slip through this guard with my small party the next morning, cross by night the Gravina-Foggia road, the main enemy lines of communication, and establish myself to the west of it, in what looked, on the map, a fairly remote hilly area. Being there well in the rear of the enemy and on the opposite side to his open flank, I thought it unlikely that we should be bothered by his patrols, and I hoped I should be able to investigate his positions in peace. I say in peace, for on this trip, I was out to obtain information, which might prove to be a slow business, requiring care and cunning, and I had no intention of giving myself away by indiscriminate shooting. We had larger issues at stake than the killing of Germans or the destruction of a few of their trucks. Consequently my orders were that once we had passed into enemy territory there would be no shooting except in self defence and when flight was impossible.

We left the Italian lines at Modugno and proceeded along the main road to Bittetto, ten miles from Bari. We were greeted by the usual crowds and pinned down in the centre of the village. Picking out from amongst the frantic cheerers a man of more sober appearance, I asked him whether he had any knowledge of German troops.

'Of course,' he replied, 'there are two German armoured cars in the village now,' and laughed. What joke the yokel saw I don't know: we were caught in a compact mass of men, women and children, and if it came to a fight, God help us.

We discovered the two German armoured cars in the southern outskirts and chased them in the direction of Altamura. Where the road widened I spread out my jeeps to give a free field to each of our ten guns, and we let go with everything we had. One of the German cars stopped, but I let the other one go — it suited me well that the rumour should spread in the German camp that there were strong British forces in Bari.

I then retraced my way into Bittetto and left the village again to the west along a cart track. For two hours we wandered in a maze of tortuous lanes between high stone walls built to keep robbers out of olive groves. The map didn't help me much in this labyrinth but finally, unseen, we emerged where I wanted, in the foothills of the Murge, a barren plateau, forty miles by ten, stretching between the coastal plain and the valley in which runs the Gravina-Foggia road. Rising to fifteen hundred feet above the plain, its rocky, broken surface intersected by low stone walls, fit enough for sheep, would normally be considered inaccessible to any vehicles, but, as I expected, we found no great difficulty in driving our jeeps across it. When at last we could see the German road, we had not been detected and I felt that first the olive groves and then the rocks of the Murge were, between them, a discreet back entrance to enemy territory.

The road ran along a broadish valley, a thousand feet below the edge of the Murge plateau where I stood. On the far side rose the hills into which I wanted to go. Nearly opposite me was a hilltop village — Poggio Orsini, in which through my glasses I could see signs of military occupation. Between the foothills and the road there was a flat stretch of dark green vegetation, suspiciously swampy, which would have to be avoided. A mile down the road, towards Gravina, I spotted a small track leading off across the suspected bog into the hills: this track I decided to attempt after dark. The danger spots were: Poggio Orsini on its hilltop across the valley, Gravina ten miles down the road on our left, Spinazzola ten miles on our right, and of course the road itself with its German traffic. I called the men together, each one with his maps, explained the situation and told my plan. I then sent them in pairs to an observation post on the edge of the plateau to have a good look with their glasses at the country we were going to enter.

When darkness fell we eased our jeeps down a very rough gully into the valley, struck the road and turned into it, making for the side track. There was a little light from the stars and we crept along, hugging the verge, showing no lights whatever. Cameron, who was watching the speedometer, warned me when we had covered a mile: a moment later a high tension pylon loomed out of the dark, a landmark which I had seen from the top of the Murge, and I realized that I had overshot the mark: the turning into the track must lie a couple of hundred yards behind us. I stopped, warned the next jeep and started turning round: I was half across the narrow road when I saw the dark form of a truck bearing down on me from the direction of Gravina. I straightened out immediately and pursued slowly along the road in our original direction: there was no time to give a warning and I had an anxious moment wondering if the rest of my party would guess what I was doing and follow me quietly, or if they would carry on with the original purpose and get entangled with the German convoy while they were turning their vehicles round on the narrow road. A moment later Cameron reported the jeeps following on our tail and all was well. Twenty-eight ghostly German five-ton trucks crawled past our five jeeps, but their drivers, straining to keep on the dark road, took no notice, and our men had the sense not to open fire. A clash would probably have gone in our favour, but would have wrecked my chances of snooping into the German camp and discovering the information I required, for there would have been such a hue and cry the next morning that we should have had to leave the area.

When the convoy was past and out of hearing we turned round, undetected, found the side track and drove into it. I carried in the back of my jeep a man called Liles, a new recruit to P.P.A., whom I had taken with me on this operation for training, to give him experience of our ways. Now Liles fancied himself as an expert on all types of military vehicles, and after a while he said:

'I thought those trucks might be German five-tonners.'

'So they were, Liles, you are quite right.'

'What, all captured vehicles?'

'Not captured,' I said. 'That was a German convoy. I told you this road was German. We are now on the main German line of communication.'

Liles adjusted himself to a new situation with a sharp gasp. At the same time I learnt the lesson that infinite patience is required to make every man in a patrol listen to what he is told. We discovered that several of our new recruits were 'followers' who drifted along, trusting that when the time for action came they would be told what to do: the army had trained them too well in unquestioning discipline, and we had to break them into a more lively awareness. Liles, by the way, was not a *congenital* 'follower'.

The side track took us to a deserted farmhouse, then petered out. A moment later we had two jeeps wallowing in a morass. While we were pulling them out, Sanders wandered off, and came back having found a firm route across the hidden stream: at the top of the rise we came upon a country lane, then upon a rural road which I identified on the map. We left Poggio Orsini on our right at a safe distance. I pushed on into the heart of the hills, along winding lanes, up and down, from crest to crest. At two a.m. I called a stop, after crossing a stream which I took to be the Basentello; according to the map we were now near the centre of a group of hills and well away from the main roads. There was nothing more we could do before daylight, and having found in the dark a gully just deep enough to conceal our jeeps, we drove into it, set two men on guard to be relieved every hour, and went to sleep.

At five a.m. I was called to take my turn of guard duty: I posted myself under a tree with my glasses and waited for dawn to break. I had succeeded in getting my patrol undetected into enemy territory: the coming day would be the test of my ability to put this achievement to a practical purpose. Between me and our division in Taranto stood an unknown force of German troops: my object was to discover how many there were, and to do so I should need help from the local civilians, because, though undoubtedly I could, by surprise, fight my way into the rear enemy formations, such an action would in no way give me the information I required. From my experience of the previous days I knew that the peasants were favourably disposed towards us, but unlike the Senussi Arabs they were not a warlike people. During the next few hours it would be my business to find out: firstly, if they had enough self-control not to spread the news of our presence so widely that the rumour would reach the Germans, secondly, whether I would find a single individual amongst them with enough guts to give me practical help, and lastly, if their untrained minds would grasp the nature of the military information which was useful to my purpose.

My assets were: an imperfect command of the Italian language (but none at all of the local dialect), a certain confidence in my powers of persuasion born of past successes with other people in another land, and a long, long patience. Intensely curious about the way events would develop, I was looking forward to a test of my wits.

The sky lighted and I began to see the landscape: our gully was slightly above the Basentello: further away from the stream bare fields rose to a crest on which I discerned a large group of buildings with a few big trees. Dim human shapes moved backwards and forwards from the buildings to a nearby field, but it was yet too dark to make out who they were or what they were doing: perhaps troops digging. The buildings, a large farmstead or a monastery, being on the skyline, seemed hardly suitable to be used as a strong point, but even Germans make mistakes, and I looked round to consider an eventual line of retreat for my party. There was time yet, however, and I waited for more daylight.

The troops digging turned out to be women, dozens and dozens of them, coming out of the farmstead for their morning squat. I could see them quite plainly now in my glasses, with their skirts up and gossiping, I guessed, actively. I made a note of this interesting local custom, and turned to other matters. I flicked pebbles at Bob Yunnie, who was sleeping below me in the gully, and asked him to rouse the men: I wanted them to wash leisurely and then to cook breakfast, without, however, showing themselves outside the gully. We still kept our desert habit of carrying our own water, so there was no need to go down to the river.

A small boy trotted past us, along a track that led from the farmstead to the road along the stream: I beckoned, he came over, I made sure he saw our company in the gully, gave him a piece of chocolate and finally dismissed him with a message for his father (whoever he might be) asking him to come and talk to me. The die was cast, I had made my first contact.

The boy's father drove down in a trap: he was the tenant of the farm, a middle-aged man of sober demeanour and good understanding, courteous but shy. I told him that we were an advance patrol of a large force of British tanks which would move down later from Bari to wipe out the Germans in Gravina. He saw our men stripped to the waist and washing — I hoped that the sight of our composure would banish the alarm he might have felt at our arrival.

I mentioned no more military matters for the time, but put him on to local gossip; he fell in readily with my lead and told me how, German troops having occupied Poggio Orsini the day before, the inhabitants had fled in fear: in his own farm up the hill he had at present over one hundred and forty refugees, mostly women and children. I told him not to worry, that we would clear the Germans out of the area in a few days — in the meanwhile how was he for food? He was all right he said, the refugees having brought some food with them, and his farm was well stocked.

Would I not, he asked, move up to the farm with my men and accept a meal?

I declined this offer; it might give him too much trouble, and if ever the Germans came out and fought us, I didn't want any of his people mixed up in the clash.

'It is better,' I said, 'that the Germans shouldn't know yet that we are here. The crowd up at your place might gossip.'

He laughed. 'We know how to keep our tongues. This is Basili-cata, not the Puglie. It is not such a long time ago that we had the bandits.'

I offered him a packet of cigarettes, but he only took one, which he lit.

'There is some information I should like to have,' I said. 'If you have got any friends who would like to talk to me, please ask them to come down.' He departed to reassure the crowd at the farm that we were not Germans.

The cat was out of the bag, there was no reason why we should hide any longer, so we moved out of our gully up the slope to a more open space among trees, where I thought we couldn't be surprised, and where we had room to manœuvre, and an open field of fire if ever the Germans heard of our presence and became inquisitive.

The farmer's friends soon came down in droves. They were very excited and all thought they had vital information to give me. I interviewed them in turns and spent hours listening to fatuous gossip. I heard the story of the occupation of Poggio Orsini ten times over, and what the grandfather had said, and what the sister-in-law had seen. My difficulty was that these farmers didn't know their area. Apart from their own farms, and the towns of Gravina and Irsina where they went to market, they knew less than I did with my map. They couldn't tell me who lived over the next ridge but one, and none of them had ever been to Genzano, five miles away. I got the most fantastic accounts of the troops in Gravina: two hundred tanks, guns larger than a railway train, seven generals and so many soldiers that they couldn't be counted. 'Two thousand or thirty thousand, perhaps a hundred thousand!' Patiently I asked questions and listened: too often the talk digressed on to family matters and genealogies: these people were all related.

Still, a bit here and a bit there, I increased my knowledge — but by mid-afternoon I had a very poor showing for nine hours' work. I called to a little man who had been standing by for a long time waiting for his turn to speak, shy but less dim-witted than those other boobies. The first thing he said was:

'I know the quartermaster officer in Gravina, Major Schulz, the one who buys the supplies for the officers' mess. His office is in the piazza, the third house to the left of the trattoria, the one with the double brown door. My name is Alfonso.'

His words gave new life to my poor brain, dazed by so many hours of fruitless gossip.

'Alfonso,' I said, 'please tell those people who are still waiting that I shall talk to them tomorrow.' I took him by the arm and we sat down side by side on a stone. Alfonso had sold cheese, eggs and wine from his farm to Major Schulz, he had been in Gravina the day before and had noticed many things; he offered to go again and try and find out what I needed. Eventually we evolved another plan. First Bob Yunnie with four jeeps set off to watch the Potenza-Gravina road. He found a suitable hide-out on a height opposite the small mountain-top town of Irsina, close enough to the road to read the number plates of the passing vehicles. He organized the familiar routine of road-watching, and I pulled back three miles to a deserted railway station on the Potenza-Gravina line. From the station telephone I rang up Major Schulz: I had a long struggle to get through but eventually I got on to him. Speaking Italian mixed with a few words of German I told him, with a great show of secrecy, that I was the quartermaster sergeant of an Italian headquarters in a town which had recently been evacuated by the Germans, I had, I said, the disposal of eight cases of cognac which I would like to sell if he would offer me a good price. We haggled a good deal about the sum. When we had finally come to an agreement I said that for obvious reasons I didn't care to deliver the goods by daylight. If he would wait for me in his office that night at eleven o'clock I would drive up with the drink in a small captured American car. Would he give the word to the control post on the Spinazzola road to let me through without asking questions?

Major Schulz was a simple soul: he may have had scruples about buying stolen goods, but he wanted the cognac badly for the general's mess, and I had made free use of the name of his predecessor, Hauptmann Giessing, with whom, I said, I had in the past made several similar deals. (The relevant information came of course from Alfonso, a good schemer with an observant mind.) He agreed to my dubious request and promised to wait for me that night.

With Cameron we stripped our jeep and loaded in the back some compo-ration boxes, weighted with stones. At ten to eleven the guard on the road block lifted the barrier for us and waved us through, and at eleven exactly we pulled up on the piazza opposite Major Schulz's office. Cameron and I grabbed each end of one of our cases, went past the sentry, up the stairs straight into the office, where Major Schulz dozed at his desk. Woken up by the thump of the case on the floor, he opened bleary, drunken eyes and gazed at us uncertainly. Cameron didn't give him time to wonder at the nature of our uniforms, but hit him smartly on the head with a rubber truncheon — a gift to us from S.O.E. Schulz passed out and slumped in his chair. Cameron went down the stairs for another case — while I went through the papers in the room. By an amazing stroke of luck, open on the desk lay the ration strength of the units of the First Parachute Division and attached troops which were supplied by the distributing centre in Gravina, dated September 12th, 1943. While Cameron brought up the remaining cases I collected more documents out of the files. We placed a quarter-full bottle of whisky, uncorked, on Schulz's desk (the poor man deserved a reward), and walked out into the street. The German sentry was idly examining our jeep — moved by an impish gust of Scottish humour, Cameron, the sedate, shook him by the hand, pressed on him a packet of 'V' cigarettes, said:

'Good night, good German,' and we drove off.

Two hours later, from a fold in the hills, Beautyman tapped out:

POPSKI TO AIRBORNE STOP TOTAL STRENGTH ENEMY FORMATIONS OUT-SIDE TARANTO 12 SEP ALL RANKS 3504 RPT THREE FIVE ZERO FOUR MESSAGE ENDS

On the 0900 call I received:

AIRBORNE TO POPSKI STOP PLEASE CONFIRM TOTAL STRENGTH ENEMY FORMATIONS TARANTO PERIMETER NOT MORE 3504

I knew that Intelligence had put the figure much higher. Slightly piqued, I fell to the temptation of showing off and, having by now sorted out the papers I had stolen from the unfortunate Schulz, I composed a lengthy signal which ran to four or five messages and took the rest of the day to encipher and to transmit. It went something like this:

POPSKI TO AIRBORNE STOP CONFIRM TOTAL STRENGTH ENEMY 12 SEPTEMBER ALL RANKS 3504 RPT THREE FIVE ZERO FOUR INCLUSIVE OFFICERS 441 STOP LOCATIONS FOLLOW GINOSA OFFICERS 61 ORS 500 MATERA OFF 72 ORS 570 ALTAMURA OFF 83 ORS 629 SANTERAMO OFF 58 ORS 469 GIOIA OFF 92 ORS 755 GRAVINA OFF 75 ORS 140 STOP ORDER OF BATTLE FOLLOWS ONE PARACHUTE DIV 19 RGT D COY O.C. LT. WEISS INITIAL W.G. GINOSA B COY LESS ONE PLATOON O.C. HAUPTMANN SCHWARTZ INITIAL ILLEGIBLE GINOSA. . . .'

and so on: Major Schulz had filed his strength returns with care.

With this flourish I considered that my first mission was completed, and I turned my mind to investigations much further afield.

CHAPTER II

IVAN AND NIKOLAI

Two significant facts had emerged: one, that the Germans were weak — not more than half their small total strength belonged to fighting units (of the First Parachute Division), the remainder being technical and administrative staff withdrawn from the landing grounds and the harbours of southern Puglie; and the other, as our road watches indicated, that they were not being reinforced. It seemed, therefore, likely that their intended role was no more than to keep a watch on our landing and that they would have to withdraw as soon as we had gathered enough strength and mobility to press forward. That they might take the initiative and attempt to push us back into the sea appeared to be highly improbable: thus, although hampered by lack of field artillery, transport and air support, the positions of our First Airborne Division which was still skirmishing precariously on the outskirts of Taranto, was virtually secure. Seaborne reinforcements were landed daily, Eighth Army, pushing up from Calabria, was expected to link up in a matter of days, when they would be able to set the enemy on the run.

In the circumstances I didn't see that it lay within my power to give much more direct help to Airborne Division. The only aggressive action I could have taken was to harass the German communications, but it seemed wrong to waste the opportunities offered by the fluidity of the German front (which I didn't expect to last much longer) for the sake of destroying a few vehicles — an entertaining occupation but a piddling target; and I decided to part company quietly with my present masters, the Airborne Division, to push forward and investigate the main German forces further north.

The German First Parachute Division had its headquarters at Foggia two hundred and fifteen miles to the north-west: the importance of this town lay in the fact that it was the centre of a large group of airfields spread in a plain. I knew that our command was anxious to secure possession of these airfields as a base for strategic bombings of south-eastern Europe, and more particularly of the Rumanian oil-fields, and I expected that the Germans would put up some resistance and try to deny us the use of the area. The next battle, I thought, would be around Foggia, and I wanted to investigate the place before the trouble started. The objective might seem a little remote to my friends in Taranto and beyond their scope — so, to avoid arguments, I resolved to keep my own counsel.

There was, however, a snag which prevented me from immediately undertaking a long reconnaissance: we were using Italian synthetic petrol, and we had already found that with this fuel the performance of our jeeps was very poor and consumption thirty per cent higher than it should have been. I decided to return to our lines, fill up with our own brand of petrol (there would by now be sufficient stocks landed at Taranto) and load an Italian lorry with three tons of the stuff to make a few dumps in enemy territory.

The night after my visit to Schulz, I said farewell to my peasant friends and to Alfonso, told them I was going to Potenza and on to Salerno, and we started off along a country road leading to these places but, ten miles on, I cut northwards across country in the dark, drove through ploughed fields, circled a village, climbed a hill, discovered a ruined castle and spent the rest of the night there. At first light we started off again, drove down into a valley and found a convenient leaguer for the day in a small wood. My idea was to create such a mass of conflicting rumours that the Germans would conceive an exaggerated opinion of the large number of enemy troops reported in their rear. In this I succeeded in a way other than I expected: for the local peasants reported to me that during the previous night the Germans had hauled up their heavy guns into the ruined castle (where we had slept) and that their tanks had been heard — and seen! — in several villages.

Two men came up to me while we were waiting in our grove to resume our wanderings after nightfall; they were dressed as the other peasants, but with an outlandish air that proclaimed them of some different race: squat and strong, with rugged features, tousled blond hair and tranquil blue eyes, they stood before me, not to attention, but yet with a nonchalant hint of military smartness. One of them did the talking, in broken Italian. They were both Russian soldiers, captured together at Smolensk. They had been first held in a P.O.W. camp in Germany, then made to work with the Todt organization in France and later in northern Italy, from where, having escaped, they had found their way to the far south. They had worked in the fields with the Italian peasants who treated them kindly, but, now that we had arrived, they wanted to be allowed to join us and share our fortunes in fighting the Germans. The speaker's name was Ivan, his companion's Nikolai. I replied with a few Russian words to the effect that I was glad to have found them; in a few days' time our troops would liberate this part of the country and would look after them and send them back to their own people, but I had no room to carry passengers on my small jeeps.

'But we are soldiers,' urged Ivan, using now his native tongue. 'We want to fight with you now, and we can go back to Russia later. Please, please, take us with you: you speak Russian and you can give us orders which surely no other English officer could do. Please do not leave us with these peasants.' Nikolai never said a word, but grinned and nodded in violent agreement. My words had been cold because Russian came with difficulty to my tongue: I had to choose what I said according to the words I could remember, but I was much shaken by the encounter; the two men were lovable and I could imagine only too well how they felt. It broke my heart to refuse them but I thought it would be inconvenient to carry them if we ran into a scrap, and also I was a little afraid of what Sergeant Waterson would think: there had in the past been much joking at my tendency to collect 'pets'! Finally I compromised and agreed to take Ivan: Nikolai, I said sternly, would remain behind. He walked away dejectedly like a beaten child. Ivan went and collected a little bundle of his possessions; I told him he would ride on the back of my jeep — Liles moved elsewhere. In the late afternoon we drove out: passing a field where some men were working, Nikolai came running alongside us, saying goodbye

368

to Ivan: tears were running down his face as he trotted to keep up with my jeep. I realized that, unless I relented, these two friends would never meet again, so I made a sign with my hand. Nikolai gave me a smile, slowed down till the second of our jeeps came bumping along; then he took a flying leap and settled on the back of the truck.

These two served with us until well after the end of the war and became the mascots of the unit.

So far, our first trip behind the lines in Italy had for me personally been satisfying: I had begun to learn how to handle the Italians and I had made a scoop that exceeded my hopes; for all the other members of the party (excepting Cameron) it had been dull and disappointing. I wanted to give them a reward for their patience and keep up their enthusiasm, as I could now afford to do: instead of just crossing the main road after dark and disappearing immediately into the wilderness of the Murge, we stopped at a cross-road and laid an ambush; Bob Yunnie and Waterson posted one on each side of the main road, the remaining three jeeps strung out along a track which ran at right angles from the road over a railway line and away into the Murge: thus all our guns could fire on to the road together. I let Yunnie make the dispositions and he worked with so much certitude that I realized I had been wasting his talents dragging him around with me. I resolved to give him a patrol and let him operate independently as soon as the remainder of the unit had landed in Italy.

We were, however, out of luck that night for not a vehicle came our way. At three in the morning, with just time enough to cross back to Bari before dawn, we laid mines across the road, and, so that the Germans should not put the blame on the local civilians, Sanders, our New Zealander, who had a passion for heights, and, having served in sailing ships, climbed well, swarmed up a telegraph pole and tied a Union Jack to the top crossbar. I then pulled away my reluctant men and we drove up a narrow valley rough with boulders: we were half way to the top of the plateau when, from behind us, came a flash and a report, followed later by the red reflected glare of a fire. When at a later date we revisited the spot we found the burnt-out remains of a petrol tanker and trailer and two German graves by the roadside. But we got little satisfaction from this achievement at second hand.

In this matter we were not consistent with ourselves. The manner of it was that we were opposed to any enterprise that smelt of glamour; out for results, to hurt the enemy and help our side, we disclaimed any ambition to provide ourselves with exciting adventures. We took pride in our business-like methods, expected a good return from each one of our operations, and did not give a damn whether we cut a fine figure or not. According to our standards of business, mines on the road should have been considered a sound investment: they caused the enemy to lose lives and equipment, shook his morale and gave us no risk whatever; and yet, in the perversity of our natures, we didn't care to use them. We had little scruple in shooting up unsuspecting soldiers if we chanced to surprise them off their guard, but we found something mean in leaving mines to do their beastly work for us after we had gone: there are fine points of etiquette in the conduct of the bloody business of war, and this was one about which we had strong feelings. I can't remember that we ever used mines again, except as a protection.

We made use, however, of gadgets which we had christened: 'Turds mule, Calabrian', perfectly imitated turds made of painted plaster which concealed a small explosive charge. Strewn over a road they were indistinguishable from the real article: a truck driving over one of these set off a detonator, and, the charge exploding, blew a large hole in the tyre.

A little later that same night Cameron taught me another subtlety of good fighting manners: when we reached the top of the Murge plateau, deeming myself out of any possible contact with the enemy, I turned on my headlights to help me pick my way among the rocks and the stone walls. The figure of a man appeared in my lights: at first I thought he was a shepherd, but getting nearer I recognized a German soldier standing with his rifle at the ready against a low wall. Cameron, in his seat next to mine, cocked his gun and waited. At fifty yards I stopped, saw dim figures moving behind the sentry, and ordered Cameron to fire. He didn't. I looked at him, thinking he had not heard but he only shook his head ever so slightly, kept the man covered and said nothing. I changed my mind, swung out of the jeep and walked up to the German: he swayed slightly, stared, and let me pick his rifle out of his hands without resisting. Behind me I heard a slight shuffle: it was Ivan, carrying a tommy gun, who had come up. He looked at the German with good-natured ferocity, but never used his weapon. I asked the German how many were with him: eight, he said, and he would call to them to surrender with him. As in a trance he called out, but all the response he got was a scamper of hob-nailed boots over stones. We let off a few bursts but made no attempt to round them up in the dark. I entrusted the prisoner to Ivan on the back of our jeep, which pleased him as an auspicious opening of his association with us, and he chatted to his man in broken German. He, however, was so much shaken by his downfall that he mutely refused a cigarette and even a drink of water: he had been puzzled by our lights, for he didn't think cars could drive across the Murge; as, however, we came from the direction of his own lines he had assumed till the very last moment that we were a German patrol, and it was only when I walked up to him and he recognized my uniform that he realized his mistake: the shock had been so great that not till the next afternoon did he recover enough composure to take some food. This behaviour distressed us all; we would have liked him to enjoy the breakfast we gave him, a very good one too, we thought, of scrambled eggs. We liked our first prisoner taken in Italy, a pleasant young man whom we were quite prepared to adopt, but we handed him in a few days later. We always had a friendly feeling towards our prisoners, particularly those we captured in battle, as if our recent endeavours to kill each other had created a bond between us.

We reached the coast shortly after dawn, slept for a few hours in an olive grove, then drove to Bari where we found a few of our troops, odd specimens like ourselves: Hugh Frazer with his 'Phantoms' and also a detachment of Second S.A.S. under Roy Farran, who had driven up brazenly through the German positions in a train from Taranto. They could deal with local reconnaissance and this confirmed me in my resolve to penetrate deeper to the north. I requisitioned a lorry from the Italian command, sent it with Waterson to Taranto and got it back loaded with petrol the following night. While Waterson was on this job I established a rudimentary base in Mola di Bari in a farm and country house, where I left Brooks with his wireless set, two men and Nikolai the Russian. Ivan, dressed up as a British soldier and armed, I took with me, third man on my jeep.

Early the next morning we set out once more for the Murge: we had just crossed the Altamura-Ruvo road, which was occasionally patrolled by German armoured cars, when Beautyman's jeep's steering snapped. This accident, the only one of its kind we had ever suffered, caught us unprepared: I wanted to jettison the truck but Waterson would have none of it; he drove back to Bari, requisitioned a second Italian lorry, lifted two stout wooden beams from a builder's yard, rejoined us in a small grove of evergreen oaks (from which, thinly hidden, we had been watching the Germans go by), and proceeded ardently to load the disabled jeep into the lorry. He drove it in reverse up a precarious ramp, the wobbly front wheels held by two men on each side. He then drove the lorry back to Mola di Bari, and rejoined us — and we proceeded across the Murge. Our Italian petrol lorry took some coaxing, but we finally got it to Alfonso's *masseria*, near which we dumped some of the load. From there we pushed on by night along small roads well up in the mountains, lying up by day, and dumping petrol at intervals for future use. In this way we reached the neighbourhood of Bovino, ninety miles north-west of Bari and only ten miles from Foggia. From our mountain top we had a good view of the main German lateral road running from Foggia to Salerno in the valley at our feet, and in a village nearby I had the use of a telephone. The peasants were helpful: they had a very old tradition of conspiracy, banditry and secret societies, which made them fall in readily with my spying schemes. Exploited for centuries by the landowners and the Church, they were accustomed to hold together in a dumb, resentful opposition to their oppressors: the mass of the peasants on one side, the landlords with their scanty, middle-class followers on the other, lived in separate worlds with contacts so restricted that they might have been inhabitants of different countries. Thus it came about that although several thousands of peasants knew of our presence, and scores of them were actively working for me, no information ever leaked out either to the local gentry or to the Germans. In the ignorant minds of the poor peasants the landlords and their bailiffs, the priests, the lawyers in the small towns, the German command, their own Government, all belonged confusedly to a class of people to be feared and mistrusted, natural enemies, too powerful to be openly fought, on whom it was praiseworthy to play secret tricks. They had no personal hatred for the German soldiers and maybe they would have helped them as well as us, if they had come as friends, for they had no idea of the wider issues of the war. Restricted by their wretchedness and their ignorance, their knowledge was limited to their own villages of starvelings and to their heartless overlords: beyond that familiar circle stood an obscure and hostile outer world.

I had not to dissemble to pass myself as their friend: I liked the kind creatures. In spite of our rollicking assurance, they pitied us — weren't we poor soldiers torn away from our homes to fight a cruel war? — and they endeavoured to comfort us with food and hospitality. Furthermore I cared little for their gentry, fawning and yet insolent, intolerable in their assumption that their possessions made us of one family, they and I. The war, the sordid extravagances of the rascals they had helped to power, and now forsook shamelessly, were mere accidents which should not be allowed to come between gentlemen: cynical, cowardly, vain, selfish and futile, they had the impertinence to treat me as an equal!

The enemy in Foggia turned out to be much weaker than I expected, and having got the news on our wireless that contact had been made with the Canadians of Eighth Army, I returned to our lines to talk to them about it. We followed much the route we had come up by, crossed once more the Murge and arrived in Bari. We had found on the roads long columns of refugees. They were peasants dislodged by the recent battles, and many thousands of people of all conditions displaced by the Fascist Government, who now foolishly thought that, with the armistice, the time had come to regain their homes. They went in families, four generations together: great-grandmamas carried in chairs by their grandsons, sucklings in arms, tramping, tramping day after day, loaded with the bundles and the pathetic bursting suit-cases which we came to recognize in time as the mark of the refugee all along the roads of Europe. The compassionate peasants fed them as they could, but, poor themselves, they had already been eaten out; in every tumbledown farm hosts and guests starved together, and such was the press that many families had to camp out in the fields. The sudden impact of this misery shook us as the bloodiness of battle had never done, and we soon found ourselves out of rations. We gave a few lifts on our small jeeps, but the acts of mercy we could afford were of no avail in the immensity of the catastrophe. Distressed at my im-potence, I thought of enlisting the help of someone better equipped to provide relief, and, on our way to Bari, I called at Andria on Conte Spagnoletti.

This nobleman had given us hospitality on a previous occasion when Andria was still in a dubious no-man's-land. He had put us up for one night in a country house of his just outside the town, and I had appreciated his pluck in taking the risk of being found out by the Germans at a time when, though they didn't actually occupy the town, their patrols visited it daily. This time, Andria being now in our hands, I called openly at his town residence, a large flat in the thirteenth-century family *palazzo*. Young, handsome and wealthy, recently married to a very beautiful girl, Spagnoletti had notions of domestic comfort far beyond the modest requirements of most of his friends. His flat contained two bathrooms, one of which, done up in black marble and filled with gadgets, was as impressive as any I have seen, and, furthermore, was perfectly functional. In a part of the world where a W.C. is considered an amusing toy, where indeed even outdoor sanitation is deemed superfluous when a garden is available, my host certainly possessed a progressive spirit. We drank cock-tails, ate a five-course lunch served by two footmen in livery and white gloves (to be fair, this is not, in Italy, the sign of opulence that it would be in England), followed by coffee — real coffee — got up, crossed three drawing-rooms filled with gilt and scarlet Neapolitan furniture, and came to rest in a more intimate *salotto*.

I told the Conte about the destitution of the refugees: kind-hearted, he was shocked and expressed his compassion for the° unfortunate creatures.

'Beyond giving away our rations I can't do much to help,' I said. 'I have got my duties and they don't leave me much spare time. When our military government arrive in Italy, no doubt they will take the question in hand, but in the meanwhile it is a matter for people of good will. Your tenants are doing their best but, as you know, their means are small: they have no transport and, as to food, they are nearly starving themselves. Now you and your friends of the Landowners' Association — of which you are, I believe, president — if you get together . . .' I expected him to respond; to my dismay he only put on an expression of deep puzzlement and he said with hesitation:

'But — what has it got to do with me, or my friends? Surely it is a matter for the Government?'

'Look, Spagnoletti,' I replied, 'you know perfectly well there is no Government here at the present moment — neither Italian nor Allied. These refugees are of your own people, they are starving, dying of exposure and exhaustion on your land. Surely, now that you know the facts, you will want to help. In an emergency, such as the present, I would have thought that people of importance and power, like yourself and the other landowners, would like to come together and run the show for a while, till conditions get settled again.'

Poor Spagnoletti was very upset. 'We don't want these refugees here, they only bring trouble — why don't they stay at home? And there is nothing we can do, we have no petrol.'

'You have got horses and carts, haven't you?'

'We need them all for the work in the fields.' He grew peevish. 'I have got trouble enough of my own. Last year's crop of olive oil hasn't been all taken away yet. Where shall we put the new crop? And oil, which is worth twelve lire here, fetches eight hundred in the south, but we can't get it over. That is an urgent problem.'

I gave up. After the war, I thought, the miserable people of this land will settle their accounts with their masters. Let us go now and beat the Germans.

The Germans by now had been pushed back, but they were by no means beaten. Eighth Army, coming up from Calabria, had linked up with Salerno bridgehead on the left and Taranto on the right, and on the Adriatic side it was moving up towards Cerignola and Foggia. General Hopkinson, who commanded First Airborne Division, had been killed at Massafra, outside Taranto, on a visit to his outposts. He was a man who couldn't bear to remain behind when he had ordered his men forward, and a sniper shot him through the head. A well-beloved leader in his picked division, according to his men he was just what a general should be. It might seem a pity that he should have been killed, not on one of the airborne operations for which with great fervour he had prepared himself and his troops, but on a humdrum routine tour of inspection of his grounded troops; but it is a fit end for a soldier to lose his life in the punctilious performance of his less spectacular duties.

That was the way I hoped death would come to me — towards the end of the war preferably, as I wanted to see it through — for I never really expected to survive the war. (Even now, three years and more after the victory, I am still mildly surprised to find myself alive.) I didn't want to die, but, when I considered the matter — which was not often — it seemed unreasonable to expect my luck to hold through an indefinite succession of narrow escapes. This prospect didn't bother me at all but I preferred the end to be seemly and I often thought how annoying it would be if I got killed in a car crash, or, worse still, if I got caught by a bomb during an enforced visit to A.F.H.Q.

The days of our precarious isolation in Taranto were over; on every side the land was full of our troops (or so it seemed in contrast with our previous scantiness), the Germans in Altamura had been pushed back without great effort by the First Airborne and First Canadian Divisions; elements of Seventy-Eighth Division and Fourth Armoured Brigade, landed in Bari, were moving up the coastal plain.

All was a-bustle and it seemed for a while that we were going to push the Germans right back to the Alps; but I was never very happy in a crowd and I longed to get back to the dangerous peace of our lonely operations.

Jean Caneri having landed in Taranto with the remainder of P.P.A. and all our vehicles, I could now give Yunnie a sensible job: we sorted out our men, he took command of the patrol he had trained in North Africa and, at the request of Fourth Armoured Brigade, he set off immediately to reconnoitre the Gargano Peninsula on the right flank of our advance. Bob Yunnie was remarkable, even in our very informal little group, by his complete rejection of the commander's aloofness: he lived with his men more intimately than any of us, shared their jokes and their escapades, and in return received their unreserved devotion: they called him Skipper and took the cue from him in everything they did. Ruthless in discipline, he never overlooked a fault, and yet, without effort, he created an atmosphere of adventure and high spirits. Where I was calculating he seemed impulsive: although he laid his plans with care his mind worked so swiftly that he appeared to make his decisions on the spur of the moment and dashed into action with a flourish that concealed his Scottish craftiness.

Although, with his patrol, he was engaged more continuously than any other, and only once did he fail to achieve what he had set out to do, he suffered fewer casualties than any; himself, with a charmed life (bullets he said bounced off his spare, bony form), he never received a scratch. In the selection of his men he was incredibly hard to please; he rejected the reinforcements I offered him with an exasperating regularity with the bare comment: 'I don't like him', or 'He doesn't fit in the patrol', and preferred to go into action undermanned than carry someone who didn't suit his fancy. From the first his 'B' Patrol became a closed world, a crack unit, intolerable sometimes in their assumption of superiority, and so pleased with themselves that I could, at times, have wished that failure would teach them a fairer appreciation of other people's achievements.

They enjoyed themselves so light-heartedly that no one bore them a grudge for their occasional boastings; rather, I think, the men who served under more sedate leaders, such as myself, envied the privilege of those who were admitted to 'B' Patrol. Inspired with a sense of fun, they enjoyed the travelling, the fighting, the unexpectedness and the hazards of their roving life; as to hardships, they were generally so clever at making themselves comfortable that when by some chance they had to skip a meal or to sleep a night in the mud, they could afford to laugh at the mishap and treat it as a joke. Bob Yunnie knew that to himself and his men danger and labour were stimulating; but that hunger, cold and monotony (in that order) would inevitably get them down. Thus it came about that it was usual to see fowls tied to his jeeps: sometimes bought, more often 'they had rushed under the wheels'; and on one occasion at least that I know, leaning out of his seat, his corporal, Ben Owen, had caught a goose by the neck as he drove by, an achievement we all tried vainly to emulate. Whenever possible each meal was made a festive occasion: bellies were filled and at the same time minds were diverted from the boredom of waiting and watching.

Avoiding draughty castles on hilltops they put up for the nights in a country house, if they could find one, or perhaps only in a peasant hovel, or if nothing else was available they would build themselves shelters, never contented to lie in the cold and the rain if, exerting themselves, they could keep warm and dry. Thus if they hadn't that day fought the enemy, they had at least defeated the weather, and they could slip into their sleeping bags with a sense of achievement. In this manner they endeavoured to solve the problem of keeping the soldier comfortable and fit without pampering him, and they entirely succeeded in maintaining their keenness.

What was this keenness about? They didn't know, or at any rate if they did, they couldn't express it. Their standard answer was that they liked being with the boys and wanted to enjoy some fun, a statement which begs the question, as it does not explain the attraction of our peculiar form of fun. Considering that I have selected each one of our men, watched over them and nursed them for years, and cast out so many whom I considered unfit, I fancy I know more about their motives than they ever did themselves. They will no doubt laugh at my presumption and affirm once more that they 'liked being with the boys and wanted some fun and that was the long and short of it', but I think there was more to it and they can't prove me wrong.

I should say at once that each one of us had a set of private reasons for enjoying the continuous toil of our lives in the patrols: maybe escape from a domineering mother or an incapacity to submit to the formal discipline of orthodox units; with these incidental motives I am not concerned at the moment for I am trying to disentangle the common fundamental impulse which urged us all increasingly to greater exertions.

At the beginning of the war when we rushed into the army, peril threatened our land: we wanted to help, to lend a hand in the common danger, to follow our friends, to be active instead of sitting and waiting for disasters; some of us felt moral indignation against the Germans and wished to punish them for their wickedness, perhaps a few dreamt of cutting a fine figure. This original impulse sank rapidly into our subconscious mind; after two years of soldiering we had stopped bothering about the broad issue; we had forgotten the time when we had been anything else but soldiers: our life was in the army and our business to remain in it until the war had been won. But obscure duties which had satisfied us at first were no longer enough; a sense of unreality crept over us and bred in our hearts a desire to assert ourselves, to meet the enemy face to face, and to reach at the inner truth of a conflict, in which, although our uniform proclaimed that we were participants, yet we ever seemed to be hovering on the outer rim. We felt like a man in the back rows of a crowd watching an exciting game: he hears the cheers and the whistle of the referee but can see nothing; he presses his way forward and at length reaches a position where, through the eddies of the crowd, he can catch now and then a glimpse of the players; with effort he reaches the front row and he can now follow the game. But he is still unsatisfied, he feels the pride of his strength and of his skill, and, not content to remain a spectator, he will have no peace until he can also take a hand in the game.

From the moment a volunteer had been accepted into P.P.A., had passed his tests and had been posted to one of our patrols, he was one of the team and out with the players. He had now to prove himself or his place would be taken by another and he would find himself back among the audience. More and more, as he got absorbed in the skilful practice of the game he ceased to be troubled by the confusing issues of the war. The vague, world-wide conflict had been brought down to his scale, to a manageable size, to something he could apprehend entirely: no more an obscure individual in an army of a million men, but one of a team of fifteen, he could apply himself to problems within his understanding; failure or success depended on his own efforts and those of his few fellows. Thus he achieved a double satisfaction: he was at the very heart of the fight and he could affect the success by his own private exertions; the prize was well worth the risk and the effort.

Because fundamentally we considered our job to be a complicated, highly-skilled game rather than a duty, we could afford to take it seriously without being self-conscious. It is permissible to be in earnest about football, cricket or rock climbing, and to pursue these activities with a zeal which would be ridiculous and embarrassing if applied to business or the service of the Government. The risks we ran (there were ugly prospects for any one of us who got seriously wounded) and the help which our achievements, such as they were, could bring to our main forces, saved us from a feeling of futility, and thus it came about that we slaved away at our self-imposed tasks, and that, when circumstances forced us out of operations, we felt no peace till we had found some means of getting back to the battle. Twenty-nine months passed from our first starting from Cairo till the end of the war. During this period the time we were engaged in active operations totalled one year and eight months, the longest uninterrupted stretch being seven months. And we had no reserves — when the unit was engaged, the whole of its fighting strength was at work.

Our reward and our incentive were not so much our military successes — there is something deceptive about success so that somehow it fails to fill the heart — but the pleasure and the pride we took in the skilful performance of self-appointed and difficult tasks. We liked to think that not only were we good at the game, but we had invented it ourselves and that only a few choice spirits, besides our favoured companions, even knew the rules.

CHAPTER III

SHEPHERD AND DOG

THE Gargano Peninsula — the spur on the Italian boot — is a blob thirty-five miles by twenty-five, rising to three thousand four hundred feet from the sea on one side and the low Foggia plain on the other. Partly covered with chestnut forests, dissected by precipitous valleys, full of crags, cliffs and gullies, it was a bit of a job for ten men in four jeeps to go and winkle the Germans out of it. There was an idea that strong enemy forces might be entrenched in it — which could have made the position of our troops in Foggia mighty uncomfortable — but Bob Yunnie, Riches, Porter and their men grinned right round their heads when they left to undertake this rather forbidding assignment, as happy as birds released from their cage. They drove to Manfredonia on the coast, then hairpinned their way up two thousand eight hundred feet to a village called Monte Sant' Angelo, entirely peopled by tall, fair, blue-eyed Albanians, the Germans just pulling out on the other side. Here they started their inquiries: with them was Gino Missiora (battle name Mifsud), an Italian anti-Fascist captured in Abyssinia and now serving with P.P.A., a brave man and cunning, who was their go-between with the local population; in those early days no one in that patrol spoke more than a few words of Italian. From crest to crest and village to village they followed on the tail of the Germans, pressing them so hard that they couldn't stop to blow up the crooked road. Right across the lovely mountains, down on to the coast road, past the seaplane base on the lake of Varano, through Sannicandro, Poggio Imperiale and Lerina (in the malarial plain), on to Ripalta Castle, where a golden-haired English girl of unearthly beauty gave them a guide to a ford across the Fortore. Here they caught up with a German rearguard of engineers who were setting about to mine the crossing and engaged the battle straight away. The Germans had a field gun in the hills beyond the river; Yunnie's four jeeps dodged about to avoid the shells and kept up in the meanwhile such a fire that the engineers, leaving their dead and their unused mines behind them, withdrew into the hills. Very gingerly Bob Yunnie took his jeep to the river bank and drove it into the water: the flood came over the floorboards but the engine kept running and the jeep pulled up the far bank. The others followed him, up the road to the first rise, where, seeing a staff car approaching, they lay in ambush. They got the car, but the men escaped and must have spread alarming news: the field gun ceased firing, all went dead and quiet, and darkness coming on, Yunnie recrossed the ford, left two jeeps to watch it, and with the two others retired to Ripalta Castle and its fairy queen for the night's rest. By the next morning he had got a message back to Jean Caneri in Mola di Bari, who forwarded it again to Fourth Armoured Brigade, that he held a ford on the Fortore. During the following days he skirmished on the north bank of the river and kept the ford clear till our tanks came up from Foggia, crossed the river and fought their way into Serracapriola and on to Termoli.

In the meanwhile I had left Caneri to establish our base in Mola di Bari. He had done so well in Tunisia during the ten days he had remained behind that we were now completely self-supporting, with spares and supplies to refit our patrols when they came back from their operations, and heavy transport to carry the lot.

Before I left, Waterson had come to me with a request, very reluctantly made, to be left behind. He was, he said, war weary and felt he would not pull his weight on a patrol. In fact his health had given way and his old wounds worried him. I didn't try to dissuade him; I knew the symptoms well: when a man of his toughness lost his nerve after a long strain he could not be laughed off. Rest was the only remedy and probably a complete change. I told him to remain at base and make himself useful till I returned. We would then come to a final decision.

I promoted Sanders to be sergeant of my patrol, and we set off for one more deep penetration into German territory. I expected some difficulty this time in getting across the German lines: the numbers of the enemy had increased considerably with reinforcements brought down from the north; they had now, not scraped-up units as in Altamura, but a number of regular divisions strung across Italy from Foggia to north of Salerno, and it was likely that all the roads leading north would be too well guarded to allow us to slip across. The enemy forces, however, were concentrated on both coastal plains, leaving the central mountains lightly held. I was faced with the problem of taking my jeeps across country over the mountains.

Since the later years of the Western Roman Empire, the shepherds of the Puglie have been in the habit of taking their flocks of sheep to graze in the Apennines in spring and bringing them back to the lowlands in the autumn. In the course of centuries these yearly migrations have cut broad, ill-defined tracks across the forest; scorning contour lines they stretch for many miles in a nearly straight line, avoiding only the most rugged obstacles. Many trees have been felled so as to make place for grass and provide the slow-moving flocks with grazing on their way, but enough remain to make the mile broad tracks hardly noticeable to the eye, and they are marked on no map. In the local dialect such a track is called a trattúr. On my previous trip, I had noticed such a thinning of the forest near a village called Accadia, and had learned its use from the local peasants. It was unlikely, even if the Germans had noticed the existence of the trattúr, that they would have troubled to guard it, and I thought that where the sheep could travel our jeeps would be able to follow. So to Accadia we went: well behind the furthest advance of the Eighth Army, on its ragged left flank, where a shifting no-man's-land lay between it and Fifth Army as it moved more slowly north from Salerno.

The trattúr served us well. We had some difficulty when it branched out into smaller tracks leading to local pastures, but we kept on our way and found the going tolerably easy, the weather being still dry. We had to travel by day only, for in the dark we would have wandered helplessly off the track, but we met no Germans and very few of the peasants who live in fortified mountain-top towns, and our trip was quite uneventful. We crossed the main German lateral road between Savignano and Ariano Irpino, and then, finding ourselves well within enemy territory, we took to the roads, travelling by night now, and lying up during the day.

We thought at that time that Fifth Army would be able to liberate Rome within a few weeks, an objective pursued for reasons more sentimental than military, and the advance of Eighth Army up the Adriatic coast had as its main purpose to outflank the town and make its capture easier for the army on its left. At Army Group Head-quarters I had heard the view expressed that the Germans would fall back rapidly on to prepared positions in the Alban Hills, a group of extinct volcanoes immediately to the south of Rome, and there, in this last bastion, make a desperate stand to cover the city. A study of the map would, I am sure, have convinced me that such a course of action was too childish to commend itself to the German command, for the high mountains further south, extending as they did down to the coast, offered considerably greater facilities for defence than the hills of Albano. However, in my presumption I had not taken the trouble to examine the matter and I had given myself for this trip the task of investigating the formidable defence works which, I felt sure, were being carried out in the Alban Hills. From Cassino northwards we drove along Route Six; it was nearly deserted, which troubled me. Two hours before dawn we turned left and drove gallantly towards Velletri and Genzano: in these places undoubtedly German engineers would be working day and night. I would soon find out, but I didn't think we had more than a gambler's chance of coming back to tell. Round every winding of the mountain road I expected to fall into a hubbub; we were high up in the hills and on our left the ground fell sharply to the plain, to Anzio and the distant Mediterranean; on the slope where they should be building concrete gun sites, shelters and trenches, strangely we saw and heard absolutely nothing. The autumn night was soft, crickets were busy, an immense peace was on the world: something had gone wrong with my appreciation of German intentions.

Apart from a few sentimental tourists I don't believe there was a single German in the whole of the Alban Hills, and the latest fortifica-tions had been built in 1487. We spent the day in a vineyard and talked to the peasants. We saw a little military traffic on Route Seven, which runs to Naples, but the supplies for the troops in the south were carried by rail mostly and we found no occasion to break the peace. Towards sunset I climbed a hill to have a look at Rome on the horizon, then after dark we drove to the eastern side of the hills, where all also was peace.

I fancied I had discovered an important secret which might hasten the fall of Rome and shorten the war, but all it amounted to in fact was that the German command, at a time when it was still fighting to defend Naples, had not foreseen that we would land at Anzio four months later. Even for that operation my knowledge proved useless: for the planning staff, too timid to take advantage of the German unreadiness, sent our troops to a lingering stalemate which was not broken until after four months of bloody fighting.

Pleased with my illusory success and happily unconscious of its futility, but finding little more to do in this remote area, I took my patrol back into the Apennines, to the mountainous area bordering on the left flank of Eighth Army. Travelling fast I had no time to make inquiries from the peasants: I followed the smallest mountain tracks on the map, thinking that the Germans would not bother to use them when they had the freedom of the main roads — our air force being still too scanty to worry them much. Very early one morning we started winding up the narrow road that leads to Castel Vétera in Val Fortore and stops at this small town, two thousand feet up the mountainside. To the north of this road the map showed a patch of green, a wood, off the beaten track, in which I hoped we could shelter for a few days, make inquiries and lay plans for the future. The forest ran up a steep mountain and we could enter it nowhere, till we found a broad patch of fairly level ground; here we plunged into the undergrowth and concealed our jeeps in a dark thicket between the hillside and a large boulder four or five hundred yards from the road. Day came, Sanders reconnoitred the neighbourhood and found a mule track which climbed down six hundred feet to the valley bottom. I interviewed a few peasants, dull-witted boobies who helped me little with a confused (but alarming) story of German vehicles going up to Castel Vétera and back on the previous day.

We were all in our bower eating our midday meal, when we heard in the distance tanks coming up. We put out our fire and waited.

There was nothing else we could do: our fortress had no back door and we were trapped. Two German scout cars showed on the road and pushed on towards Castel Vétera. Ten minutes later they returned and stopped opposite our level patch of woods; one remained while the other drove down. Meanwhile the tanks had stopped out of sight; half an hour later we heard them grinding up. Time dragged on; a first tank came into view and was waved off the road into the wood by the men in the scout car; others followed clanking, to be dispersed to cover under the trees. By nightfall we had a squadron leaguered, somewhat uphill from our position, between us and the road. Just after dark more tanks arrived and these leaguered below us.

These elements of Sixteenth Panzer Division moving over from Salerno to the Eighth Army front, had, with motives similar apparently to our own, chosen this remote spot, well covered from the air, to leaguer in peace while the rest of their division moved to its concentration area.

The whole of that endless afternoon we kept ready to bolt up the mountainside, our weapons and emergency packs at hand, an incendiary bomb laid out on the seat of each jeep, but when darkness fell not one of the enemy had troubled to poke his nose behind our boulder; hours of waiting in our trap, coming after all those days of snooping and hiding, had put us in a savage mood: we longed senselessly to hear loud noises and to feel our machine guns rattle in our hands — unfortunately, though our half-inch bullets might knock chips off the armour of Mark IV tanks they couldn't penetrate it. We should have to use our wits and lay in turn a trap for the enemy who had so stupidly failed to catch us when he had us in his hand.

The position of the German tanks in two leaguers — one on each side of our way to the road — made me think of a possible deception; I conferred with Sanders, then called the men together, and we laid our plans. We divided all the explosives we had — about sixty pounds — into four lots and fixed to each one a long fuse. At one in the morning we crept out and placed two charges about fifty yards apart towards 'A' Squadron on our left and similarly two charges near 'B' Squadron on our right. At one-thirty the fuses had been brought back to our leaguer and five minutes later we detonated charge one. When the report went up and reverberated from the hills we started our engines and drove out between the trees towards the road, leaving one jeep behind to detonate the other charges at twenty seconds' interval. I intended thus to cover the noise of our trucks and to distract attention from us altogether. Charge two went off, and as it had been laid at the foot of a tall, slender tree, brought it down crashing near the foremost tank of 'B' Squadron. Charge three, on the other side, projected a clattering load of stones over a tank of 'A' Squadron, then number four went off and brought down another tree. We had reached now a position midway between the two squadrons, and while we waited for our last jeep to catch up we fired our only bazooka in the direction of 'A' Squadron. The small rocket-propelled shell described a lovely parabola of fire and landed in a bush. Now at last, the enemy on both sides began to wake up: we heard shouts and the noise of a tank engine starting: but, puzzled as they must have been, they were not going to rush into action before they found out what was happening. We staggered our jeeps and fired a broadside of our ten guns towards 'A' Squadron, then we moved on fifty yards and served 'B' Squadron, moved again and sent streams of tracer towards 'A' and 'B' simultaneously. Most of our rounds hit the trees, a few reached their objectives, a lucky burst of incendiary hit a petrol can and lit a dim glare in the lines of 'A'. Then at last coming from my left I heard what I had been hoping for, the short, deep report of a seventy-five millimetre. Somebody in 'A' had lost his temper. We concentrated our pinpricks on 'B' till they also let off, and after that all we had to do was to poke the fire. After ten minutes 'A' and 'B' were at one another good and proper and we edged off towards the road, splinters and branches showering down on us as shells — which were not meant for us — hit the trees overhead.

I fired a German signal cartridge which I had carried many months with me: it generated a lovely shower of purple and silver stars, and was followed immediately — which rather startled me — by the deafening report of a seventy-five fired, it seemed, at point-blank range from an unnoticed tank. I thought it was time to say goodbye, and I led my little company down the road, leaving the battle behind. Alas, round the first bend, we came upon a tank broadside-on across the road: two men were at work on a sprocket by the light of a repair lamp, quite uninterested in the noise round the corner. Ivan shot one; the other surrendered and climbed on to the back of my jeep in charge of the Russian. We could neither get round the stranded tank nor move it, so we had to go back near the battlefield to reach Sanders's mule track and slither down to the valley bottom. A reflected glare from a fire above helped us to reach the river bed without mishap; we crawled upstream over gravel and round boulders in the lowest of low gears. Fortunately the rains had not broken yet and the flow was only a silly little trickle, otherwise our jeeps would still be in the stream. Our obliging prisoner jumped down and pushed of his own accord whenever our wheels began to spin in the loose gravel, and then jumped on again as soon as we got a grip.

We struggled up the stream for three hours, the valley so deeply encased as to forbid any attempt at getting out; when dawn broke I stopped to make the morning call on the wireless. I had something urgent to tell the R.A.F.; fortunately, though I was quite vague as to my present position, I knew exactly where the two squadrons of the Sixteenth Panzer were: I gave the map reference and a conspicuous landmark of forest jutting out, like a nose. Beautyman was in luck that morning: he heard Brooks as soon as he opened up; in an hour he had done, and once more we struggled up the stream. Later in the day I was surprised to see our bombers on their way to the target we had given them, for it was but seldom that the R.A.F. could give priority to casual targets at short notice. We had made so little progress since the preceding night that we heard distinctly the thud of the bombs.

Late in the afternoon our position was peculiar: the valley had become even narrower and on each side of it ran a road, several hundred feet above us, carrying some traffic of which we could see now and then the tops of lorries over the parapets. If they saw us, they didn't bother, thinking probably we belonged to their own side — but our guilty conscience made us expect a hue and cry at every moment and we plunged noisily along with our hearts in our mouths. Getting tired too with the strain and lack of sleep, we tended to exaggerate our danger. For the first time I took a tablet of benzedrine, a drug which had been issued to us in North Africa by a medical officer of the Airborne Division: half an hour later I had recovered my composure, I faced our problems with light-hearted confidence, and my brain was lucid. The effects of benzedrine vary, however, from one man to another — most of our men having been made to try it once, hated it and refused to use the drug any more: it made them dopey and miserable; Ben Owen even maintained that it sent him to sleep. There is of course a great amount of moral prejudice against the use of drugs, a weakness from which I am not immune: but benzedrine has done me a good turn more than once.

About five o'clock the valley opened up, the shingle river bed widened and gave us better going; in the distance we saw the two roads sink down and meet on a low bridge across the river, which, identified on the map, showed that as the crow flies we had covered five miles in twelve hours. Because an enemy convoy was crossing the bridge, I stopped our jeeps under a bank and we cooked our evening meal, then going with Cameron to examine the bridge, we found that on the right-hand bank we could, without too much trouble, build a ramp to take our trucks from the river bed on to the road. Back at our camp, Ivan had removed his prisoner's boots, and, for good measure, also his slacks: with German convoys passing three hundred yards away, he was taking no chances.

After dark we took our jeeps under the bridge and started work on the ramp. We didn't let the passing convoys interrupt us for we were in a hurry; by midnight our five jeeps were on the road, and before dawn we had found our trattúr and left behind us the main road from Foggia to Naples. The position had rather changed since we had gone through, but we made Accadia without much trouble. I sent Sanders and the patrol to Cerignola to rest, and pushed on to Eighth Army Headquarters with Ivan's prisoner.

I wanted to find out what was happening: I had received daily on the wireless a short situation report, but I felt that events were running ahead of me. I also wanted to meet my friends, whom I hadn't seen since I had visited Eighth Army in Gabes six months previously, and talk of subjects entirely unconnected with the war. With a feeling of coming home I found Headquarters in new surroundings, to be sure, but looking much as they used to in the desert. Right through the Italian campaign they stuck to their caravans and their tents; unlike other headquarters which liked to spread themselves in châteaux, there was no nonsense about them; unlike these others, too, they were happy and singularly free from bickerings, jealousies and intrigues. A happy mixture of regular and war-time officers gave them breadth of outlook, freedom from prejudice and a kind of universal competence: 'Operations' and 'Intelligence' were manned mainly from Oxford University: pure civilians. I noted with some regret that my own Cambridge had not, it seemed, produced in that generation a similar body of men of general excellence — or were they all at home engaged on scientific research?

Bill Williams, an Oxford history don, was head of Intelligence: he was interested in my Sixteenth Panzer Division, not because I had played tricks on them but because so far, in Italy, Eighth Army had not encountered any enemy armour. He wanted more information about them than either I or Ivan's prisoner could produce, but he was grateful at having been forewarned of their arrival on his front in time to avoid an annoying surprise. I undertook to try and find out more about their strength and their intentions.

Business concluded we talked on other subjects: I had been so immersed in my own schemes that I had completely lost sight of the war as a whole — there were no newspapers for me to read and I seldom listened to the B.B.C. news. I was shocked by his opinion that the war would not be decided in Italy: at that early date he already foresaw the long stalemate and the repeated battles for river crossings. I was even more surprised to hear him talk of home politics and of the Labour landslide which he hoped would follow on victory. Such matters had entirely fallen out of my range of vision and I was glad to feel once more a citizen of the world.

In the meanwhile, even during the two days which I spent at Army,

First Canadian Division, moving up on the left, had reached the Foggia-Avellino road, so that my trattúr, shorn of its mystery, now led to our own lines. Our troops on the right, advancing rapidly in the coastal plain, had overrun Foggia and were making for Termoli; the Canadians on the left, entangled in the foothills, had not got further north than Bovino: between these two staggered front lines lay an open flank completely unguarded by us. For all I knew the Germans also might have neglected to occupy this stretch, and I attempted to reach the concentration area of the panzers by a short cut across the range of mountains bordering the plain west of Foggia.

I collected my patrol, we passed the outposts of Fourth Armoured Brigade and drove into no-man's-land on a sunny morning along a country road bordered with hedges. The mountains here rise abruptly: two miles ahead of us and twelve hundred feet above the plain stood a small town called Alberona. We were carefully rounding a bend, when a funny little man with a big moustache, driving a trap, recognized us for British, and madly shouting and gesticulating warned us of a German post at the end of the straight stretch of road that opened before us. To avoid being seen we crashed through the hedge into an orchard on our right and took counsel with our new friend. Calmed down, he proved sensible and helpful: under his guidance we reached a farm track, then another and landed well behind the enemy road-post in a wood in the foothills, where we spent the following thirty-six hours. Our plucky little friend walked into Alberona to get the town surveyor to come and see us, a man of character, he said, an artist, and a great enemy to Fascists, Germans and all tyrants; he promised to be back with his hero at midnight.

Our wood was on a little knoll to which no one could come without being seen for quite a distance: we posted our jeeps to cover the approaches, set a guard, and spent the day in leisure. I examined the range through my glasses for a possible way over, and then slept till evening: I had long formed the habit of sleeping whenever I had a chance, were it only for half an hour at a time; that day I had five hours of delightful peace. At the end of the afternoon some peasants came with a gift of eggs, a ham and a large pitcher of wine: they told me that staying with them

[facing: JEEP PATROLS IN ITALY

was an escaped British prisoner-of-war — could they bring him along after dark? I invited them to do so, but they came back later saying that the prisoner was suspicious and would like a token of our being really British. I gave them a two shilling note of army money, the brown cover of a Field Pocket Book with its black elastic and a piece of the red-striped white flannel provided by the army for the cleaning of rifles. With these they departed.

Since our landing in Italy, indeed for the last six months, we had not seen a drop of rain and we had completely neglected to equip ourselves against it. That evening clouds gathered, and shortly after dark the weather broke in a steady, tepid, tropical deluge. My only protection was a jumping jacket, which is by no means waterproof. In the darkness somebody came splashing: I shone a torch on the ham, eggs and wine peasant: the British prisoner, he said, was standing outside the wood and would I come *alone* to meet him. The poor man had much suffered and was very, very suspicious.

On the edge of the wood I picked out a tall figure, with a peasant's jacket over the remains of a uniform, streaming with water. I shone the torch on to myself, then went forward and shook hands with a few words of greeting.

'You *are* British, are you?' he asked.

'It's all in order,' I replied. 'My name is Peniakoff, Major Peniakoff. I command' — what could I say that would seem plausible? — 'I command a reconnaissance unit of Eighth Army. Come along to my truck and have a drink.'

I took him by the arm and he yielded. Cameron produced some whisky and we took nips from the bottle in turn. We managed to light cigarettes, soon put out by the warm rain which poured over us, down our necks and out again at the boots.

'My name is Klopper,' he said, 'of the South African Division. You may remember that I was the general in command at Tobruq in forty-two.'

I remembered only too well how the fall of Tobruq had sent us hiding behind hedges; I remembered also much gossip about the surrender, but not a fact, not a single authentic fact. I had taken for granted — very unfairly — that things had been mismanaged by the man now talking to me in the rain, a fugitive, who had taken the trouble to escape from, I supposed, a quite comfortable imprisonment. It was embarrassing, but, in that rain, to observe the niceties of tact would have been absurd:

'I have heard a lot of gossip,' I said, 'mostly malicious. You will soon realize that many uninformed people like me are under the impression that you surrendered too easily.'

It was surprisingly easy to get to the heart of the matter, standing in the dark.

'I know,' he replied. 'I want to get back to the Union as soon as I can. There will be a court of inquiry.'

After that the ground was cleared; we gossiped a long time in an intimacy of friendship, and I did most of the talking, for he had been cut off for a year and a half and wanted to catch up. Finally I arranged to send him to our lines the next day, and we parted.

At midnight the surveyor arrived from Alberona, a fierce, restless man with an urge to help. He told me that the Germans had a small garrison in Alberona, and another in Volturino three miles to the north. Between the two towns, which were not connected by a direct road, the mountain range was free of enemies. He had brought with him a plan of Alberona, beautifully designed, with the German defences accurately marked. The road to the town crossed a stream in a gorge: the bridge was mined ready to be blown up, and it was covered by machine-gun posts sited high up in the left bank of the gorge.

He thought perhaps it might be feasible to drive our jeeps over the range between Alberona and Volturino, but he doubted it. He knew only one possible route and that would require digging at one spot. On the far side we could reach down fairly easily on to a road. He suggested that I should send someone on foot with him the next day to survey the route he had in mind. With a blind prejudice against splitting up my patrol, I made the mistake of refusing his sensible suggestion; instead I asked him to come the next evening and guide us up the mountainside in our jeeps; I would take the risk of the route turning out impracticable. He agreed eagerly and promised to have a party of men with picks and shovels at the critical passage to help us across.

We started off the next day immediately after dark. A day of sunshine had dried up the ground, but there was mud under the dry layer. We tackled the slope half way between the two little towns, driving up an old cutting in the forest; the surveyor had a party of men chopping down the undergrowth ahead of us. The climb was slow but presented no serious obstacle till we reached the bank the surveyor had warned us about: we were then level with Alberona, a mile and a half on our left, but still well below Volturino, the same distance on our right. We imagined the Germans in the two villages safely in bed (the time was half-past eleven), the night was very dark and the forest thick: secure and forgetting about the enemy, we set about cutting a path through the bank. With our men and ten of the surveyor's I reckoned we could not complete the work in less than two and a half hours; if another such obstacle appeared ahead, we would not be able to get over the ridge before dawn. Leaving Cameron to supervise the work, I pushed on on foot with Sanders and a guide provided by the surveyor to reconnoitre the route up to the ridge. We walked along a footpath, the guide and his white dog ahead, Sanders and I abreast. Short, spare and light of foot, the New Zealander flitted along; he was never much of a talker and on the trail he clamped down completely; I was a bit exercised to keep up the pace and spared my wind: very few words passed between us — comments on the practicability of the path and no more.

The path ran out of the forest over the open grassy hillside. From ahead of us came a tramp of horses' hooves: shepherds, I thought, who quite commonly ride in these mountains. Then a loud laugh rang out and an exclamation in German; at the same time two horsemen loomed out of the darkness and were on us.

'I have no weapon,' I whispered to Sanders. 'What have you got?'

'I know,' he replied. He drew his pistol and moved into the path of the riders, waiting for them to come abreast: his hand was lifted to shoot them point blank in the belly, when five more riders appeared behind the first two. I held my breath. Sanders's hand fell down to his side, the first Germans brushed past us, then stopped, the others came on.

'Buona sera,' I muttered, and walked on with Sanders. One of the Germans called out in pidgin Italian: 'Strada per Alberona?'

I grumbled something in gruff dialect-sounding gibberish, whistled for the white dog gambolling behind me and slouched steadily on. The German made a remark to his companions about surly bumpkins; they remained for a while, turned in their saddles and peering back at us, then, without another word, they rode on; thud of hooves and creaking of saddlery died out in the distance. It was over — we were once more strollers at ease on a deserted mountain. The path showed white against the darker grass — the silence was stupendous.

'Those were Germans,' said our guide when we caught up with him.

'So they were. Your dog saved us,' I replied, and with no more words we walked on towards the crest: from the bank which had stopped them the path up to the top was easy for the jeeps.

Over the ridge we peered into a black void; after a long while a faint light moved at a great distance, a car on the road down in the far valley. We walked back to our jeeps, vaguely expecting a burst of fire if the mounted patrol came upon them — there was nothing we could do about it and I wasn't worried: our men wouldn't be such fools as to neglect carrying their arms.

We came back to the cutting in the bank, where nothing had been seen of the German patrol. The work was not going well: the under soil was very wet and when the first jeep attempted the climb, its wheels sank in the mud. We tried and struggled till most of the night had been wasted and I resolved to turn back.

I didn't discuss our narrow escape from the German riders with Sanders till a day or two later: only in retrospect did that short incident take significance. It has been a bond between us to this day: not so much because we shared the danger, but on account of the perfect silent understanding with which we had acted: he had realized in the same second as myself that it would be a folly to shoot two riders when five more were coming on us; his hand with the pistol had gone down as if obeying an order of mine; then, without faltering, he had joined me in my impersonation of a shepherd going about his business with his dog. Without giving thought we could apparently read each other's mind.

I related the incident to Cameron. I had provided pistols, carbines, tommy guns, hand grenades, daggers and truncheons for the lot of us and then I must go and blunder into a German patrol without as much as a penknife in my pocket. But level-headed, the Scot would not sympathize.

'It has all turned out for the good,' he replied, 'hasn't it? If Kiwi and you had both been armed you would probably have taken on the seven Germans, and in that case where would you be now? But let it be a warning to everyone by all means, and don't leave your pistol in the jeep next time you walk away.'

Jock Cameron knew my mind all too well: I used the story in innumerable lectures on over-confidence.

The surveyor was chagrined. I consoled him by putting the blame on the previous night's downpour; he suggested several spots further south where I could make other attempts to cross the range, and departed home, leaving his plan of Alberona with me. I didn't expect to see him again in my life, but the very next day we dined riotously together in circumstances which I shall now relate.

We drove southwards along country lanes in no-man's-land following the foot of the hills. In a village near Troia I was told that some British armoured cars had been seen that morning. We nosed around till we found their leaguer in a wood: they were a Canadian armoured-car regiment, cheerful men, moving up ahead of the Canadian Division. I called on their commanding officer, who gave me without hesitation the information I wanted on the situation in the mountains: it was not encouraging for my plans as it appeared that the division had been everywhere in contact with the enemy and was pushing him back steadily: my useful open flank was dwindling.

In the Canadian mess over a drink the colonel mentioned casually that his task for the next day was to take a village called Alberona.

I said I knew the place, I had been there early that morning. The colonel looked at me queerly. 'How could that be? Isn't it held by the enemy — ?'

'It is held all right,' I said. 'I can show you where their defences are.' And I pulled out of my pocket the surveyor's beautiful plan. The colonel looked round with some alarm. The bravest man — and this colonel was exceedingly brave and wise — feels uncomfortable in the company of a madman. I felt the need to explain myself and the nature of P.P.A. — not with complete success. I'm afraid I wasn't quite honest and did not disclose in detail how I had come by my information. I had suddenly thought that it would be amusing to go in with the Canadians the next day and fight, for once, in an orthodox manner. I was on my mettle, and I offered to guide his regiment to Alberona and to show them a track up the mountainside leading to the top of the village — to the back door, so to speak. The front door, I said, that is, the main road, it would be useless to attempt, as we should find the bridge blown and we would only be machine-gunned, down in a narrow gorge. 'From here,' and I pointed to the surveyor's plan. The colonel was a little uncertain; not being a man to hesitate long, he said:

'O.K. you lead, but along the main road. If the bridge is blown we shall see.'

The next morning, to my immense vexation, we were five minutes late at the rendezvous and we didn't catch up with the head of the column till it had stopped at the last turning on the road before it entered the gorge. As we passed the colonel's armoured car he said with a grin:

'Oh, there you are. Range up behind the first troop of "B" Squadron. They go in first.'

In we went, head to tail, on the narrow road. The gorge deepened as we wound forward. We drove three hundred yards and stopped. German machine guns high above us in bushes on the left bank (where the surveyor had marked them on his plan) opened up and sprayed our column. Cameron examined the wall of the gorge and spotted an enemy post by the twigs which were broken off by their fire. He took a careful aim with his gun (a half-inch Browning) and let off slow bursts, methodically. I pointed out the target to our other jeeps, walked on to the leading armoured car and found it halted by the steep river bank, where the blown bridge had been. They were reporting on their wireless to the tail of the column, and the order to withdraw came through. I walked back to my jeep and waited for the jam to be cleared in the rear as the clumsy cars manœuvred to turn round on the narrow road. The armoured cars couldn't elevate their heavy B.S.A. guns high enough to fire at the German post, and they had to man the piddling Bren guns which they carried outside the turret — thus their gunners had no more protection than we had in our open jeeps. Three American fighters swooped down from the blue sky: we followed them, amused by their antics. Then suddenly they came lower and sprinkled us neatly. A man in the armoured car ahead of us fell, hit in the thigh: his companions dragged him out of the turret and laid him in a culvert under the road. Cameron pointed to the planes, then to his gun, and asked: 'Next time they come?' I nodded, and passed the word down the line. The planes came back on a second round and our ten streams of tracer curved after them: they flew off and bothered us no more.

The Germans turned their attention from the leading cars to our jeeps, and there was quite a patter of bullets on the road and the rocks of the cutting on either side. Cameron's gun jammed — he pulled the cocking handle once, pressed the trigger and when nothing happened, didn't try again but set himself quietly to take down the mechanism; he worked unhurriedly amongst the whining bullets with an amused smile on his face, whistling softly one of his weird Scottish tunes, laid the parts methodically on the jeep's bonnet, and never looked up. His ruddy, bony face gave no sign of concern. The man in the culvert groaned: I went over and found him bleeding. I got the first-aid case from my jeep and bound him up: 'Are you going to give him an injection, Sir?' said a voice. I looked up surprised, for I had lost the habit of being addressed in this way (it was generally 'Popski' or 'Skipper' with my men). Two Canadians were by the roadside, watching me. 'It might be a good idea,' I said, and gave the man two shots of morphia.

Cameron got his gun together again, tested it and looked up for a target. He was a deer stalker and noticed small details. This time he spotted a second machine-gun post, higher up and to the right. His bursts had a good result it seemed, for we suddenly found that we were no more under fire.

Meanwhile the jam behind us cleared. Sanders turned his jeep round and pulled out, we all followed in turn, and drove back to Squadron H.Q. at a cross-road, a mile back. From this cross-road the track which I had mentioned climbed up the hillside through vineyards and eventually reached the road on the ridge where it ran out of Alberona on the far side. According to the surveyor a small anti-tank gun was sited there, at the corner of the cemetery, but there was room to deploy and to manœuvre.

I asked the squadron commander if he would send someone to go with our jeeps up this track. He detailed four scout cars and off we went. It was a stiff straight climb and we had to stop on the way to cool the engines. The slower scout cars caught up with us and passed us — I was surprised to see them climb so well; with them we topped the rise, spread out on each side of the cemetery, made the road and overpowered the anti-tank gun before it could fire. We then drove down towards the village, which lay now below us; the Germans, seeing that we had got behind them, broke and took to the hillside: it only remained to round them up. The squadron followed up, puffing, the way we had come with the scout cars, and the Battle of Alberona was over. We had no casualties, but a number of bullet holes in our jeeps, a subject of competition between the crews.

We took up our quarters in the cemetery; surrounded by a high wall and closed by a gate, it was easy to defend, and I made myself a comfortable bed on a marble slab in the mortuary.

Before going to bed, however, we drove into the town: there was a very excited crowd in the streets. The surveyor was the hero and I greeted him publicly as the deliverer of Alberona. It ended, as it should, with a banquet, which rather astonished the Canadian officers.

Early the next day we set off over the rounded mountains towards

San Bartolomeo in Galdo. I had managed to ring up the telephone operator the night before; from him I had heard that there were still a few Germans in the town, but they were withdrawing across the valley, where many tanks were reported. Rain made the grass slippery and we skidded our way down into the outskirts of the little town. We exchanged a few shots with some Germans and settled down for the night in a slaughter-house, while I sent a foot patrol across the valley to investigate the tanks. They also belonged to Sixteenth Panzer, and I got their numbers and their markings quite accurately. The next morning the Germans' field guns started shelling us.

Having received a message from Bob Yunnie that his work was done and that he was looking for a job, I signalled him to join me in San Bartolomeo. We cruised about together for a few days trying to find a way through the German lines, without success, for they were too thick on the ground. We then separated: he went north with his patrol and I went south, following the German front line and probing it as we went.

We had a brush with a German rearguard at Noiano, then we had to walk eight miles lifting the mines the creatures had left behind them. We drove another five miles to Pescolamazza; on the further side of this small town we came upon a mile long column of American infantry marching out in single file, rifle in hand, to meet the enemy. Their faces were white, distraught with homesickness and misery. I stopped one of their officers and, hoping to comfort him, told him that I had passed the last of the enemy thirteen miles back. He gave me a look of suspicious incredulity and marched on.

I was shocked that these unhappy men should exhaust themselves so unnecessarily, and I drove on to their H.Q. in Benevento to tell them where the enemy really was. The staff officers, haggard and broken-hearted themselves, listened to me courteously and were at great pains to hide their conviction that no one could possibly have the knowledge to which I laid claim. Obviously, they thought, I was a case for the psychiatrist, and as I returned the compliment in my heart we parted good friends.

Benevento was my first experience of a bombed-out town: seen from across the river it showed nothing but piles of rubble and was horrible. I was surprised that we should do such things to a town whose inhabitants were obviously friendly; I put it down to a mistake and resolved to inquire into the circumstances which had led to this ghastly error.

From Benevento I pushed north once more towards Boiano and Vinchiaturo, where we came once more upon the Canadian Division fighting its way to Campobasso. Lieutenant-Colonel Harding, our friend of the battle of Alberona, was in temporary command of the division; calling at Divisional Headquarters I had been told that a message had just come that he had been awarded the D.S.O. When I met him at a forward post, later in the day, I told him the good news and produced a bottle of whisky. This coincidence, coming after the former one (at Alberona), gave him the unjustified impression that my sources of information were universal.

There was here an unguarded flank all along the eastern slopes of the Matese mountains: if I could but drive my jeeps over these mountains I would find myself once more comfortably in German territory. We made a first attempt south of Boiano; while we were crossing the plain towards the foothills, we got caught in rather heavy shelling by long-range German artillery. We took what cover we could and lay down waiting for the nastiness to die down. An old peasant made his way from his cottage amongst the shell-bursts to where we lay and stood by me gossiping or rather grumbling.

'I would have liked, Sir,' he said, 'to ask you to my house and offer you a bottle of wine and a meal. But I can't: the Germans, the scoundrels, have robbed me of all. They have taken my wine and killed my pig, the ruffians.' There was something irresistibly comical about the old fellow ranting about his pig and his wine, while shell-bursts sprouted all around him — and he wouldn't even sit down! I couldn't help a smile, at which he took offence.

'You laugh, Sir — there is nothing to laugh at. The murderers have plundered my house.'

I apologized for my levity, saying to soothe his feelings: 'At any moment now, by misluck, you may lose much more than your pig —

maybe your house or even your very life. Please lie down on the ground, do. You make me nervous standing up thus under this shelling.' He would have nothing of it — he ambled off towards his cottage, babbling of pigs and wine.

That first approach to the Matese proved fruitless: the mountains rose in a nearly vertical cliff. We made another attempt further south at a village called Guardiareggia, tucked up into the mountains, only fifteen hundred feet below the ridge. The local doctor, who was also an amateur geologist, promised to show us a way up: 'I know the jeeps,' he said, 'they can go anywhere. And I know the mountains, every inch of them.'

We made an appointment with him for the next day, and that evening I went to dine with an odd group of people who had been consigned by the Fascist Government to this isolated mountain village — rather than to a concentration camp. They were a middle-aged Yugoslav couple with a girl of twenty attached, four Jews and three persons whom nobody took the trouble to explain. They spoke several languages, mostly French and were well travelled. Surprisingly they seemed to have plenty of money and lived in some luxury in a large, ramshackle house. The dinner was good, the drinks abundant and varied, the atmosphere dubious, the clothes too elegant, the mood hysterical. We drank much and quick. Half way through the meal the girl who sat next to me laughingly drew my attention under the table to the fact that she wore nothing under her dress: she then suddenly threw back her head, vomited gorgeously and fell down in a drunken sleep.

We spent the next three days with the doctor geologist, driving our jeeps alternately up mountain torrents strewn with house-size boulders, and through stone walls. Having suffered much minor damage we finally came to the conclusion that either the doctor had grossly over-estimated the capacities of our vehicles or that we were not clever enough to drive to the top of the Matese, and we made our way home, temporarily defeated.

CHAPTER IV

RECRUITS

C ANERI had transferred our base to Lucera and there we all gathered. No more fortunate than I, in his attempts to cross the lines in the northern sector Bob Yunnie had found his progress stopped on the roads by demolitions, and across country by the weather. Half an hour's rain was enough to make even a moderately steep grass slope inaccessible: with no grip on the slippery surface the wheels spun, cut through the turf and churned the greasy loam underneath into mud. True a few hours' sunshine set it right again, but, until the following April, the sun seldom shone in the mountains for several consecutive hours. By the beginning of November the weather, the mountainous country and the increased enemy resistance had nearly brought the battle to a standstill. The Germans, reinforced to about twenty divisions, now held a line practically continuous across Italy from the Volturno River on the Tyrrhenian to the Sangro on the Adriatic coast.

For two months, since our landing at Taranto, a fluid military situation and dry weather had presented us with golden opportunities for worrying the Germans inside their own territory, but I saw unmistakable signs that this period of easy chances had now closed down and that in the future we should find our work tougher than any we had done either in Italy or in the desert.

I had no doubt that we should still be able to outwit the Germans, but, faced with a situation entirely new to us, until we had invented fresh tricks the obvious move was to pull out from the line for a while, sit back and cudgel our brains. I feared a little that Eighth Army might not share this view and assign us to routine duties for which we were unfitted, but I need not have worried. Major-General de Guingand, Chief of Staff of Eighth Army, had apparently reached the same conclusion as myself, but, in his pleasant manner he didn't wish to force a decision on me: he called for me a few days after my return and asked what were my plans. I had to tell him that, unless the weather improved, I saw no possibility of crossing the German lines by land, nor indeed, in the present static state of the battle, could I think of anything very useful we could do even if we managed to get ourselves behind the German lines by air or by sea. (If I had known then that some Italians were building up a partisan movement my reply might have been different.)

De Guingand then suggested that I should withdraw my unit to the rear and take advantage of the respite offered by the lull in the battle firstly to get a larger establishment sanctioned for P.P.A. and then to recruit, equip and train additional men. I fell in with this plan and didn't tell him that if my men were to remain out of active operations for any length of time I would be hard put to keep them happy and in good spirits: that was my responsibility and I didn't expect him to alter the course of the war to suit my convenience. Even during our busiest periods some of my men felt that I wasn't giving them enough to do or that their tasks were too easy and not up to our standards, nor was this opinion always unexpressed. Yunnie, Curtis, O'Leary, Porter, Cokes, Cameron, Owen, Sanders, seem to me, in retrospect, to have been much of the time hinting at the inadequacy of the opportunities I provided for their ambitions. Caneri, in closer touch with me, better informed of the general situation and with a Frenchman's acceptance of facts, took a more sober view. I had my share of frustration and in common with many of us, I reached the end-of-the-war feeling that we had not really given our measure.

Bob Yunnie found us billets in seven villas on the Adriatic coast north of Bari, at Bisceglie, and we all moved there in the middle of November 1943.

I sat down with Caneri to work out a new establishment. I had long ago fixed in my mind an upper limit of one hundred and twenty, beyond which I didn't care to expand our strength: the reason being that I wanted to know the character, the capabilities, the background and the personal history of each one of my men and to watch how he developed under the influence of his companions, and my brain was so made that I could not build up and keep in my mind a satisfactory picture of more than one hundred and twenty men at a time. Only thus could I maintain the high standard of the individual members of the unit, and the quality of their team work, in which lay our distinctive character and the justification of our existence as a unit; I saw no excuse for locking up in a specialized force more men than could be kept up to its highest standards. Furthermore, our *raison d'être* was that we achieved results out of all proportion to our numbers: this aim was furthered more by improving the quality and the experience of our men than by increasing their number. If, after we had done our best, it appeared that there was room for more work than we could do with a hundred men, let other troops follow in our footsteps and take on some of the jobs (they were welcome to our experience); we would remain free to lead the way in changing circumstances. Neither my ambition nor my inclination was to command large numbers, but to labour for perfection in a limited, pioneering field.

Yunnie and Caneri shared my views. When we were together most of our time was spent discussing our men; we took infinite care over the composition of patrols, promotions and dismissals, and over the training and testing of recruits. My two friends knew our men as I did and in a way, between the three of us, we ran P.P.A. as a family business. I reserved to myself the duty of recruiting — inconvenient as it was that I could, as it were, do it only in my spare time (when I was not engaged in planning or on actual operations) — not that I mistrusted the judgment of my companions, but I found that their tastes differed from mine and the only way I could find of developing P.P.A. the way I wanted was to select the men myself. Yunnie, I thought, was too apt to be influenced by wayward feelings; Caneri, on the other hand, tended to disregard intuition and to judge a man according to his written record.

In December Caneri and I flew over to Alger to put our case before the Establishment Committee. This ferocious body, we had been told at Army Group, cut down savagely all requests for increased establishments or even dismissed them flatly if they suspected that exaggerated claims had been made. Cautiously we asked that our original strength of twenty-three should be increased to seventy-odd (determined to go, in practice, well above that figure), but I found the devouring lions sweet and reasonable — to my amazement they pointed out that my figures were too low, particularly in signalmen and tradesmen (rare birds on the market in those days) and should be amended.

We returned with an establishment (NA/229/31) providing for eighty all ranks, including six officers, two warrant officers, four sergeants, five corporals and five lance-corporals, fitters, wireless operators, wireless mechanics and armourers. The total strength was divided into four fighting patrols: 'B', 'R', 'S' and Blitz (H.Q.), administrative headquarters, signal section and M/T section. We made the necessary promotions to provide the cadres for our new organization (Caneri became second-in-command and adjutant), and then I set about recruiting to make up our numbers.

The times were over when we had to live by our wits: we had now authority to draw volunteers from all units in the Central Mediterranean Force; in theory every commander could be compelled to hand over as many of his men as wished to join us and I was willing to take. In practice, I never drew a man from a *fighting unit* in this dictatorial manner, which I considered unfair and which would have given me a bad name with commanders with whom I had every reason to remain on friendly terms: as in the past, transfers from fighting units were made only under amicable arrangements with the commanding officers. With base formations I had no such scruples, but my main source of supply was found in the reinforcement depots which had recently been transferred to Italy from the Middle East and North Africa, and held a large number of men who had fought with Eighth and First Armies. Another useful privilege we were granted at that time was that those of our men who went on leave or were admitted to hospital had to be returned to us in due course: in this way we suffered none of that draining away of experienced men, the plague of the ordinary unit, which breaks the heart of every company or squadron commander, liable as he is, at any moment, to lose his carefully selected N.C.O.s as a result of a minor sickness or the normal rotation of leave.

I signalled the training depot newly established near Taranto asking them to call for volunteers amongst their men for fighting service with Popski's Private Army, a 'special service' unit, and to have them ready for interview in a week's time. For reasons of security I could give them no other indication of the type of men I required (beyond the fact that they should be physically fit and experienced drivers with, if possible, battle experience), and also because I knew that the officers in the depot could have only a scanty knowledge of the big floating population that passed through their hands. When I arrived I found that one hundred and thirty men had put their names down. I got them together in an olive grove and addressed them in my loudest voice:

"The unit I command is rather secret — most of you will have never heard of it before — and I realize that you have volunteered mainly out of curiosity and because you are bored with life in the depot. A few of you, however, may have heard rumours about us: before we go any further I want them to know that everything they have heard is untrue. We do not go dashing about the streets of Rome kidnapping German generals right and left, we have not been parachuted in our jeeps into a P.O.W. camp in Germany, I am not an eccentric Polish millionaire, we don't get treble pay, in fact the men who join us drop their rank and their pay suffers accordingly; our other ranks are not privileged to dress up as officers when they go on leave, they are not even allowed a tie.

'For reasons of security I can't tell you as much about my unit as I should like you to know before you make up your minds, but I shall tell you this much: our service is mainly behind the enemy lines; it is not too uncomfortable but very, very tedious. Most of the time we wait and hide — often we have to run away. The virtue we require most is patience, patience and steady nerves. There are risks, of course, but I assume that you wouldn't mind that. I want you, however, to realize that if one of us gets wounded it is just too bad: there is no medical officer to look after him and no hospital to take him to.

'I have known very brave men, men who were never upset in an ordinary battle, and yet they could not stand the strain of our operations. If a man does not care for that kind of life he can't possibly be blamed. I want those who feel that our type of service is not in their line to stand down. The men who don't want to press their applications, please stand down.'

Nobody moved. I did a little prodding: two or three overcame their self-consciousness and fell out — thirty other doubters followed the lead.

This preliminary weeding-out completed, I told the remaining ninety-odd men that the men I selected would first undergo training, and then be tried out on an operation before becoming full members of P.P.A. At any time during that period, as well as later, they were liable to be dismissed if I thought fit 'and no blame attached'. Conversely if for any reason they wanted to leave the unit they would be released at the earliest opportunity.

Sitting at a desk in a tent I then saw the candidates individually. Having made a note of name, previous service, driving proficiency and knowledge of weapons, I put away notebook and pencil and started a conversation. I took my time, for the best candidates and the most eager to be accepted came to the interview tongue-tied and in a state of nerves. When I felt the man had eased up I asked:

'Why do you want to join us?'

The replies I got fell into four categories. Many were diffident. 'It might give me a chance to get on with the war.' 'I don't like to sit back and let the others do the fighting.' 'I am not particularly good at anything special but I should like to have a try at something difficult.' These were the answers I liked best.

Then we had the glib and flattering replies which brought the interview to a sudden end. 'I have an urge towards high adventure.' 'I hate the Germans.' 'I would consider it a great privilege to serve under such a distinguished officer as yourself, Sir.'

Some were sullenly aggressive and said: 'I am browned off. I want to get away from the depot.' A very feeble reason I thought, and generally sent them packing, though Ronnie Cokes, a thirty-year-old

R.A.S.C. driver and one of my best recruits, gave me this type of reply with so much vigour and such a wealth of invective that I accepted him on the spot and made a damn good bargain.

Lastly, I got the fanciful replies. 'Because I couldn't get on with the Guards officers in the Commandos,' or 'Because I want to learn Italian,' or 'My grandfather was an admiral'. These in most cases I dismissed on the spot, although I accepted the man with the grudge against the Guards and he showed up tolerably well.

This concluded the preliminaries, and if I thought the candidate was worth the trouble I got down to business. I told the story of one of our operations — or of a blunder, such as my encounter with the German riders at Alberona — produced maps and exposed problems of topography and of supplies. I talked and waited for questions and comments: when I got response I could build up in my mind a picture of the man's personality; when I didn't I cut the interview short: whatever his hidden virtues, a fellow with no imagination could be of no use to us. The interviews were enjoyable for me: they required mental agility, for I couldn't afford to spare much time on each candidate: my judgment proved right for roughly half the men I selected; how many good elements I summarily dismissed I cannot, of course, tell.

On the third day I had interviewed everyone and made my selection. Out of a hundred applicants I had picked fifteen, and seven of them eventually remained in P.P.A. A good haul and above the average, for over the whole of our time we didn't retain more than three and a half per cent of the men I interviewed. I don't think I was too fussy: for one thing, we couldn't afford to take on any but talented drivers. As it was, they required four or five months' training before they reached the proper acrobatic standard of driving over mountains, across rivers, in mud and snow. Fundamentally, success depended on our ability to take heavily-armed jeeps into improbable places — we could make no concessions on that score. Then our men had to have topographical intuition and the gift of finding their way in the dark. From amongst the men with the technical qualifications we had to pick out those who possessed the fundamental qualities of character, who were brave, sensible, patient, cool, resourceful and determined.

And if the poor blighters turned out to be real angels of virtue, still it wasn't enough: they had to fall in with the humours and the conceits of fourteen men in a patrol, who considered themselves the best men in the army and were not prepared to welcome newcomers except on their own terms.

Most of our men had a secondary-school education, none had been at a public school or a university. With two or three exceptions they came from working-class families, mostly with an urban background; in politics they ranged from Tories to Communists (only the latter held their political convictions more than perfunctorily); according to the religion duly registered in their pay books, a majority belonged to the Church of England, with Roman Catholics, Presbyterians, Methodists and Baptists following in order of numbers, also one Jew and one Atheist; none of them, however, as far as I could find out, had any strength at all of religious feeling; neither in behaviour nor in argument did anyone ever display any interest in matters of faith. They were not ignorant, for they all had had a religious upbringing, but so completely unconcerned that they could not legitimately be described as Christians.

We got on very nicely without religion. We preserved the decencies through the violence and the licence of war: raped no women, tortured no one, looted in moderation and only from those who could well afford to lose, drank decorously (by soldierly standards) and refrained from bullying, went wenching only with the best, and, when we could, we looked after the girls we got into trouble.

As a matter of course, we helped a companion in trouble, took our duties to heart, looked after our men, loved our enemies (in the persons of the prisoners we took), and laid down our lives without making a fuss. Our behaviour was modelled on that Victorian ideal of a gentleman, which has, in the course of time, drifted down from the class which first formed it (but has long since discarded it) to the bulk of the people for whom it is now the naturally accepted standard of conduct. There occurred many misdemeanours — mostly of a technical nature — for which I had to take sanctions, but the men themselves always saw to it that there should be no stealing, no lying, no quarrelling, no bullying, no disloyalty, no cowardice, no shirking of responsibility, nor any of those monstrous ill-defined crimes which come under the heading of 'letting down the boys'. I was well rewarded for the trouble I took in selecting our recruits and weeding out misfits.

By the end of December, after more recruiting trips, our numbers had reached a figure slightly above our new establishment, and Bob Yunnie got busy with the training. At the end of the war our numbers, exclusive of recruits in training, were one hundred and eighteen.

Sergeant Waterson had not recovered his 'battle nerve'; he might have been useful to us in running our headquarters and supervising the training of recruits, but he felt uncomfortable in the unit now that he was unable to fight and asked to be released. I let him go.

I took our two Russians, Ivan and Nikolai, off battle duties because I thought they had done enough and I didn't doubt that they would receive bad treatment from the Germans if ever they were captured; it was unfair that they should run greater risks than the rest of us. Nikolai became cook to the unit and fed us remarkably, Ivan looked after me when I was at Headquarters, where he had many other duties. They both learned Italian, but no English, worked all day and were never at a loss. When they ran out of firewood they took a few sticks of gelignite and blew down a tree. Ever smiling and ready with a joke, they became the pets of our men, who took a pride in their strength and their peculiar achievements. One of these was to drink at one go two gallons of wine out of a can.

I don't know why the British have a reputation for being bad linguists: it certainly did not apply to our men, who all learnt Italian after a few months. Their grammar no doubt was sometimes atrocious but they had got well beyond mere cookhouse talk, and when we had been in Italy a year I could pick out any man at random, send him alone to the next village with a complicated message for the head partisan and be sure that he would bring back a complete and accurate reply.

I was less successful in recruiting our officers. Our unit seemed to have a fatal fascination for a type of officer whom Bill Stirling described as 'Café gangsters'. The rule to which I stuck, that every new officer should revert to his war-substantive rank, was a great stumbling block. While the other ranks forewent their stripes cheerfully, the officers clung to their rank; they had climbed to the dignity of temporary captain or major, and the prospect of going down again upset them. At any rate they wanted the assurance of quick promotion, which I couldn't give, as my only vacancies were for lieutenants. And most of the lieutenants who offered their services were little idiots — or had something wrong with them: they drank, or they lost their memory or they suffered from delusions. Yunnie thinks that I set an impossibly high standard: but when our sergeants were more efficient than most majors, how could I put a pup of a lieutenant to command them?

The sober, competent officers whom I required existed no doubt, but they were all employed in fighting units, where they were quite happy, and anyway their commanding officers took good care that they shouldn't leave. On the other hand the depots bulged with thousands of nitwits who had been turned out by the Officer Cadet Training Units, and were quite unemployable. Nor did they want to be employed — not in a fighting unit. They dreamt of a staff job and promotion; or, if they had not enough pull, they would be contented with a job as a town major or with A.M.G.O.T. (the Allied Military Government in Occupied Territories) where they could look forward to comfortable billets, an obliging girl friend and reasonable profits on the black market. The initial mistake was in the selection of candidates for the O.C.T.U. Such was the snobbishness of the army in the early days of the war that the ordinary ranker, who hadn't been to a good school and hadn't got a middle-class background, was reluctant to apply for a commission. 'I shall never feel comfortable in an officers' mess,' he said, and remained in the ranks. But feeble youths, out of schools where the main knowledge they had acquired was that success comes to those who can pull strings — ignorant, lazy, greedy, selfish, without pride or ambition, without responsibility, without honesty and without honour — got commissioned in swarms, grew little moustaches, tucked their handkerchiefs up their coat sleeves, and intrigued ferociously to get a good posting.

Three officers I acquired at that time did not belong to this unsavoury crowd. They were: Reeve-Walker, a South African mining engineer; Rickwood, a British tank officer, and a strange character named Dick Talbert, a short, ugly man, scruffy and long-haired, with a clever, mobile expression. He was a trained engineer, a brilliant mathematician, a good musician, with a lucid mind, a sense of realities, and an ambition to be a success in P.P.A. He had seen service in Special Forces in the Middle East and though aged thirty was only a lieutenant, which he accounted for by the fact that he had never desired promotion but preferred jobs to his liking. I put him, after a few days, in charge of the newly-formed 'S' Patrol, where he was immediately a success with the men. I took him and his patrol on a training trip across southern Italy, and I was impressed to see how easily he acquired the tricks of our trade; indeed, I felt he would very soon teach me a trick or two. He was the man I had been looking for: no mere follower, but a leader, he would bring me new ideas and invent new methods. I enjoyed his company, for his conversation ranged over many subjects and he had the confidence that goes with a well-furnished brain.

We returned to our base at Bisceglie, where Talbert devised a gadget to lock the differential on the wheels of a jeep so as to double its power of pulling out of mud. On Christmas Eve we made a successful trial of the modified jeep, which we tried hard to bog, but in vain. We had a little celebration, and I went to bed. On Christmas Day we had arranged a dinner of some excellence for the whole unit. Talbert could not be found for a long time, till he was discovered lying in a stupor in a garret. Roused and brought down, he drank a little, made an incoherent speech, and had to be carried away, dead drunk. It appeared that on the previous night, after I had retired, he had gone on drinking till morning. The incident was unfortunate, but I thought no more of it, till, the next evening, I found that Talbert was still drinking and had not sobered down for forty-eight hours. On the fourth day he came to me, very repentant, promised wildly never to drink any more and asked to be given another chance. But the unfortunate wretch was a dipsomaniac; with all his brilliant talents he couldn't keep off the drab fascination of alcoholic joys, and after several relapses I had to break his association with P.P.A. The last I saw of him was in 1945, on a road in Austria, looking very wild, still a lieutenant and seeking a job.

On that same Christmas Day, after dinner, everyone having gone to rest, I was half-dozing in a chair in our mess, feeling a bit heavy, when in walked, very carefully, a large young fellow (one of my new recruits); he saluted and asked permission to speak to me. I was a little surprised at his solemn manner — if a man wanted to speak to me, he didn't usually make a fuss — but I realized he was half tight, as was everyone else in the unit at the moment, and I told him to carry on.

'It is like this, Sir,' he said. 'I have decided to kill myself. However, as it is Christmas afternoon and all the lads have enjoyed their dinner so much and are so happy, I wonder if it would be a good thing to do it today, or should I put it off till tomorrow? Perhaps, Sir, you would be good enough to advise me on the matter.' I woke up completely on hearing this strange speech; before I could speak he went on.

'I have wanted to die for a long time. As you know, I joined the S.A.S. in North Africa: I hoped I would get killed, but I didn't even go into action. Then I tried to jump out of a plane without a parachute, but the door jammed and I couldn't do it. After I had got the sack from the S.A.S. I heard about your unit, Sir, and I thought: in P.P.A. surely I will get killed. So I applied to volunteer and you very kindly took me on, but when I reported here I found that you were off operations and my chance had gone once more. This can't go on for ever and now I am going to blow myself up with a hand grenade. I have it here, Sir.'

He pulled a bomb out of his pocket and swaying gently he started toying with the pin. I got a little alarmed. There was nobody but the two of us in the house — I had given leave to Ivan to go and see some Russian friends of his in Bisceglie — and here was this madman pulling at the pin of his hand grenade. I talked and talked, keeping an eye on his hands, but he wouldn't be persuaded, so finally I said: 'All right, Richards, if you want to kill yourself on Christmas Day, I can't stop you. But you had better make a good job of it. You wouldn't like to miss yourself and become the laughing stock of the unit. Neither would I. I like neat jobs. If this bomb of yours came out of our stores, it is practically certain that it is not primed. You would look an ass if you tried to kill yourself with an unprimed bomb. Let me have a look.' I put out my hand. As in a trance he obeyed my suggestion and handed over the weapon. I unscrewed the cap, removed the detonator, put it in my pocket, screwed back the cap and gave him the harmless toy. I then walked out of the room and roused Dave Porter and Bill O'Leary, the two strongest men I could think of. But Richards put up no resistance, and he marched out between those two like a lamb. Less than six weeks later we got a signal from a hospital in Alger to the effect that Trooper Richards was now cured, and with reference to G.R.O. requesting all General Hospitals to return to unit P.P.A. personnel on discharge, he would be put on a plane to Brindisi at the earliest opportunity. Somehow we didn't share the optimism of the psychiatrist in Alger; we warned the Military Police in Brindisi and all over Italy that a dangerous lunatic was about to land and — so far — I have managed to dodge Trooper Richards.

Reeve-Walker took over 'S' Patrol from Talbert, Rickwood 'R' Patrol from myself, and more will be said of them both later. But neither of them had a very long active career with us: Rickwood was shot in the stomach six months later, and though he recovered eventually and came back to us, he was never really fit again for strenuous duties. Reeve-Walker had a meteoric career at the head of his patrol, cut short by a request from the South African Army that he should be returned for duties with one of their units. Though we had several other officers posted to us, two of whom were brilliant, I made up my mind about that time that we would be essentially an 'other ranks' unit; this we remained, till the end of the war, and gave little employment to gentlemen's sons.

CHAPTER V

'THE GUARDS'

I N the first days of January 1944 our four patrols were out in the mountains, training fiercely in the snow; I was in Caserta, trying to understand the unhappy minds of the men whose job it was to plan a landing at Anzio. Fifth Army, part American, part British, with also some French Moroccan troops, moving up Italy from Naples, was held by the Germans on the Garigliano and at Cassino, where the spine of the Apennines spreads mountainous branches down to the very coast. To overcome these obstacles by a frontal attack would be costly. It was planned to land from the sea a force at Anzio, on the far side of these mountains, sixty miles in the rear of the line and thirty miles from Rome. From Anzio onwards to Rome stretches a level plain, the reclaimed marshes of the Campagna Romana; from Rome north-westwards to Pisa (where the high mountains once more reach to the coast) two hundred miles of plains and hills: it seemed that if only we could put behind us the mountains and defiles between Cassino and Anzio, there were no natural obstacles to stop us till we reached northern Italy. If by then the enemy was sufficiently broken up by the chase, we might take the Apennines in our stride, cross into the Po Valley and reach up to the foothills of the Alps, liberating the whole of Italy and bringing the war to the very borders of Hitler's domain.

Fifth Army Headquarters shared with a small detachment of A.F.H.Q. the thousand rooms of the evil palace of the Bourbon kings, and overflowed into tents and caravans in the gardens, an awesome extravagance compared with the purposeful sobriety of Eighth Army. The mood was of the death-bed in an ill-conducted household. Surely somewhere behind closed doors, in the heart of the noisome palace, a foul creature was lingering over a too-long-delayed end. A white-haired general described to me the plight of his men: 'What can our poor American soldiers do? No equipment and no clothes, nothing suitable for this frightful weather.' Tears came to his eyes.

All day long British and American officers squabbled over precedence. Each morning I found another branch in control — working out a new plan. With the date of the landing less than ten days ahead the scope, as well as the object of the operation, were still debated. I tried to keep up my spirits, thinking 'On the eighteenth, on the eighteenth at dawn we shall drive our jeeps up the beach at Anzio, a tiny spearhead, make for the Alban Hills, and be free.' I kept my counsel: it was sufficient that they had been instructed to include us in the first wave. All I wanted was to be landed in time and to get away. I knew what we would then attempt to do on the two roads which fed the German positions on the Garigliano and on Monte Cassino. On the eighth our patrols were loading at Bisceglie, on the tenth I called them in: in the evening they came racing down the mountains on their way from the other side of Italy. On the eleventh, all previous plans of landing a mobile force of armoured cars, tanks, self-propelled guns and lorried infantry were scrapped, and the building up of a strong beach-head decided instead. On the twelfth they reverted to the old notions. On the fourteenth the Quartermaster Branch, following on some obscure palace revolution, seized control of operations, and, playing for safety, resolved on the slow beach-head build-up. On the sixteenth I extorted our embarkation orders from a harassed colonel. On the seventeenth at dawn, while we were mustering before driving down to Naples harbour, I was handed a signal cancelling our participation in the landing. That night the force sailed without us, landed at dawn on a deserted beach and never saw an enemy for two days.

Four months later, having missed their opportunity, they were still fighting on the open coastal plain, dominated from the hills which the quartermaster had failed to give them as their first objective.

There was at first some hope entertained that the German line, threatened from the rear by our newly-landed forces and assaulted in front from the sea to Cassino, would break: P.P.A. were invited to wait for a chance of slipping through, and we sat for a few days with a British division on the Garigliano. The river was forced and our division stuck in the mountains on the far side of the river: for the enemy had been able to contain our beach-head in his rear without weakening much his forward position.

My men, after great hopes disappointed, were very unhappy; when I was asked to provide a foot party to blow up a bridge on the enemy lateral road, a mile or so behind the forward position, I accepted the job more for the sake of raising our spirits than on account of any great faith I had in the usefulness of the undertaking, for the bridge was small and low and could be by-passed with no great trouble. The event proved different from my expectation.

I set forth with Yunnie to reconnoitre: at a Guards Brigade Head-quarters we waited a long time outside the brigadier's caravan for the row inside to subside: two voices, one shrill, one piping, were slanging each other with boyish fury. Micky and Sandy were having some disagreement and didn't mind who heard them. They came out and down the steps; Micky, our middle-aged brigadier, and Sandy, a scraggy chit of a subaltern, still quarrelling furiously. What it was about I couldn't say for the argument ran according to a primitive pat-tern: 'I told you.' 'No, you didn't.' — 'I tell you I told you.' — 'And, I tell you, you didn't. — If you had told me, I wouldn't say you didn't tell me.' — 'It is no good saying you are sorry, Sandy.' — 'I never said I was sorry, Micky, and I won't.' — 'Yes, you will.' — 'No, I won't.' Then suddenly Sandy saluted grandly, about turned and marched away straight into a cloud of dust and smoke raised by a sudden shell-burst, and the brigadier turned to us with a grin. He arranged for us to visit two of his battalions whose forward positions would, he thought, give us a good view of the objective. As we took leave: 'I'll go with you,' he said impulsively, but someone called from inside the caravan: 'Micky, you are wanted on the line,' so he corrected himself: 'No, I won't. Good luck to you.'

We went first to the position of a battalion of a county regiment. The colonel was a short, plain man, with the looks of a country solici-tor; outside his headquarters, in a group of small dugouts on a bare slope facing away from the enemy, he had mustered his clerks and cooks and addressed them with great vigour, exhorting them to take a hand in the defence in case the companies forward failed to hold the next enemy counter attack. 'Leave your typewriters and your pots and get your rifles — if you know where they are. The Germans are not going to break through *this* battalion.' We had arrived, it seemed, at a time of crisis. He directed us to the position of 'A' Company: 'Over the crest — be nippy, it's under fire — bear left in the dip, up the next slope, past a stunted tree, along a goat track still to the left, and there you are. Don't go over the top of the slope — it is in full view. Things are quiet just now but since last night when we took these positions we have had three counter attacks and we have not had time yet to dig in properly. Barker is the name of the company commander.'

Captain Barker was lying in a shallow slit trench, smoking a pipe. He grinned: 'You will have to wriggle on your tummy, one at a time, to the crest of the slope to have a look at your bridge. Better wait a moment, I think another counter attack is brewing. We have one platoon on the forward slope, the two others are here, right and left.'

We settled to wait in a very small slit trench out of which we heaved a limp corpse. Mortar shells were peppering the stony hillside, uncomfortably close. At first we sat up in our trench, then, observing the behaviour of the others, we hugged the earth. There is an etiquette for visitors to positions under fire, and it is seemly to be neither more nor less cautious than your hosts. A moment later a rattle of machine guns from over the ridge announced that the fourth counter attack was on its way. We expected at any moment to see Germans running on the skyline over the crest, and we felt as if we had wandered, hands in our pockets, on to a playing field between two furious rugger teams. Bob Yunnie took out his pistol, cocked it and laid it beside him: 'What do we do now? I suppose we can always run with the others.' The men of the two platoons around us, dispersed amongst the stones, lay beside their guns in small scratched trenches. The din increased and came nearer — but we saw nothing. Then it slowed down and died out. The business of the war had gone on, another attack had been held and the Germans pulled back to their lines.

We wriggled in turns to the crest and had a look at our bridge. We saw no Germans but could make out the forward platoon of our troops under some bushes. The approaches to the bridge were hidden; it seemed that from the next ridge on the left we would have a better view. So we left Barker to prepare for the fifth counter attack. and strolled back down the slope amongst the popping mortar shells.

The Guards Battalion on the left were a much grander affair. They had put their headquarters in the houses of a village on a hilltop, in full view of the enemy under a cross fire of artillery, mortars and machine guns. Whereas our friend, the county solicitor, seemed to run his battalion single-handed, the Guards had a full staff: the C.O. in one house, the adjutant in another, the officers' mess across the street, the quartermaster down the road, the intelligence officer, the signallers, all accommodated in billets. The rickety houses were crumbling down and the blast of each shell-burst sent stones crashing through the ceilings. You couldn't move in the streets without being picked out by a sniper and the enemy seemed so near that everyone spoke in whispers. We found the colonel in his office storming in a hushed voice at a dead telephone: the lines had been cut by shell fire, the linesmen had suffered heavily and couldn't keep up repairs. Three hundred yards to the rear we had come up a gully completely concealed from the enemy where Battalion Headquarters could have worked in comfort, but for an obscure reason they preferred to be in billets. Grandly we declined the offer of tin hats (for this seemed to be an occasion when the rules of etiquette had to be broken) and I was not displeased to give mild annoyance to our hosts — at the risk of a broken head from a falling stone. With many stops under archways the colonel and the intelligence officer took us to a house at the top of the village from which, under showering bricks, we got a view of the whole approach to our bridge. A narrow valley dotted with trees ran out of the Guards' position down to the road and bridge, which could thus be reached all the way under cover. The colonel pointed out the positions of 'C' Company through which we would have to go; the location of the enemy posts he didn't know, but he thought they were thin enough. I asked him about minefields, of which, he assured me, they had laid none. 'C' Company commander, whom we visited later, confirmed this information. We were having a drink in the battalion mess when a large piece of the wall collapsed on to the table — but we saved our glasses and departed.

In the early afternoon Bob Yunnie took his party of six to look at the ground they would have to walk over at night. They inquired again about the mines and were assured that none had been put down. They made arrangements to be let out of the company lines that night and to be let in again in the early morning.

After dark Caneri and I drove the demolition party as close as we could to 'C' Company lines. They were: Bob Yunnie, Curtis, Owen, McAllister, Locke and Hunter, six black-faced devils moving silently on rubber soles. We had a meal and then they shouldered their packs of explosives, picked up their carbines and moved out into the night. Their spirits were high, more so than ours that stayed behind, awaiting their return. Neither Caneri nor myself liked this operation: its object was futile, and, if we didn't expect much trouble at the German end, we were not so sure of the reception our party might get on their return, from a dull-witted Guardsman. I decided to stay where we were till the men came back; uneasy in mind, we had no wish to talk, and sat on the ground each one by his jeep. We were in a narrow valley which the Germans were plastering leisurely with one of their six-barrelled mortars which we called at that time (wrongly) a nebel-werfer or more commonly 'Sobbing Sisters'. The bombs came over in broken volleys of six with a peculiar slow, sobbing wail, weird but not displeasing, multiplied by a very good echo. I amused myself for a while puzzling out the relationship between flash, sob, crash and echoes. Then I dozed off. I was woken up by a sound of voices whispering on the other side of the jeep: it was Curtis talking to Cameron in his usual slightly breathless way. The time was one forty-five. He was sorry, Curtis told me, to have had to come back so soon, the job not done. The fact was they had run into a spot of trouble, not too bad really, but they had only two fit men left, Bob Yunnie and himself, and, having tried, they had found that two men could not possibly carry enough explosives to blow up the bridge. Next night they would take out another party by another route, for in the valley they had followed they had run into a minefield forward of the Guards' outposts. Hunter had been killed, his throat cut by a splinter, McAllister badly injured and couldn't walk, Locke and Owen hurt, but could move on their own, though with difficulty.

Caneri and Cameron went back with Curtis. They got a stretcher party of the Guards and brought back McAllister, but they had to leave Hunter's body behind while they chased some of the Guards who had got lost and were found wandering bravely into their own minefield.

The next day Bob Yunnie got up a party to recover Hunter's body. I stopped them as they were about to set out, for an attack was planned which in a few days would give us the ground where the lad lay, and much as it went against the grain to leave our dead behind, I was not willing to suffer more casualties to bring him back.

McAllister was a long time in hospital and when he came back to us was still too weak to rejoin his patrol, and he was employed as storekeeper at our base. Locke recovered fairly quickly, but this last experience added to so many others proved too much for his nerve, and a few months later our pirate, black eyepatch and all, sailed for the Middle East, where we had arranged a job for him. Owen also was not too long in hospital and came back to be one of our star turns.

We collected a hundred pounds in the unit for Hunter's widow and baby. His death, unimportant in itself, had upset us considerably, for Hunter was liked and he had lost his life, not fighting the enemy, but through the negligence of our own people.

I had made a mistake in consenting to organize the raid and resolved never again to engage our men in close contact with others of our troops. A few days later, giving up the hope of a speedy break-up of the German line, I withdrew my men and took them back to a mountain village sixty miles north of Naples — to prepare for other plans I had conceived.

CHAPTER VI

A SHIPWRECK

IN the desert, where we had learnt our trade, our operations were all of a pattern, in this manner: we raided the enemy-held coastal area out of the inner desert (of which we had the freedom and the enemy had not) — we hit and hit again — then, before our supplies gave out, we vanished back into the waste and returned to a base securely held and supplied from our lines.

I had used the same pattern in our early operations in Italy, and successfully for a time, but the desert pattern was applicable only under freak circumstances, and both the topography and the shape of the Italian country were against it: if I persisted I should run into a dead end. So I had to set about to unlearn lessons and forget mental habits before I started on new plans.

I eventually decided to establish mountain bases well in the rear of the enemy line, supply them by air, and operate from them without attempting to bring my patrols back to our lines, either for supplies, refit or reinforcements.

To bring my men with their jeeps and their supplies to the bases, the overland route being impracticable, I should have to fly them in gliders or land them from the sea. It appeared that all gliders had been moved to England from the Mediterranean, in preparation for the landing in Normandy, but that a few landing craft were available: the sea route thus became the only possible choice. Once the bases were established and held, reinforcements and supplies could be dropped by parachute. This programme involved the co-operation of the Navy for the landing; of the R.A.F.; of No. 1 Special Force, a secret offshoot of S.O.E. which dropped supplies to partisans in northern Italy; of 'A' Force, another secret society, which rescued escaped P.O.W.s from the region of central Italy where I thought of making my landing; and of the Italian partisans to guard my bases. I didn't like to be dependent on so many bodies, but I had no choice and I hoped that once I had bases established and well stocked, I would be my own master again, and so it turned out in fact.

Preparations for this operation, which received the code name of 'Astrolabe', took three months, and involved much travelling between our base, Army Group at Caserta, the Navy at Taranto, Advanced 'A' Force in Bari, No. 1 Special Force at Monopoli, Eighth Army at Vasto and the Parachute School at Brindisi. The work fell mainly on myself, who did the general planning and the sales talk, and on Jean Caneri, who translated it all into practical arrangements. Caneri had a tidy mind and an unquenchable thirst for good administration: he had organized our headquarters on the best army model and made a point of carrying out all administrative orders, of which I had only a dim notion. The forms required were filled in and returned at the appointed intervals: he claimed that no division in the army had better-ordered affairs than P.P.A., of which I am no judge; but considering that I had no complaints from the men and few major 'rockets' from our administrative masters, I presume that Caneri was not doing too badly. Strangely this passion for order and legality went with an uninhibited gift for scrounging. He turned up at District Headquarters and called on the A.Q.M.G. (for his method implied striking at the head), very business-like, with a briefcase full of documents and a deliberately assumed French accent, to complain of the delay in delivering our 399 Mobile Wireless Station. The A.Q.M.G., slightly taken aback, for these stations were scarce and only allotted to Army Headquarters and above, protested that P.P.A. had no authority.

Said Caneri: 'But, Sir, you 'ave given us authority yourself, 'ere is your letter, and 'ere is the authority from A.F.H.Q., and 'ere is our establishment and 'ere is G.R.O. 18/44 of last February; paragraph 9, as you know, deals with the allocation of W/T Stations, and if you please, Sir, you will sign 'ere and I can go to the Signal Stores and draw the set.' And the A.Q.M.G., shamed by a display of erudition greater than he possessed himself, signed.

In one of the men I had recruited Caneri discovered qualities which suited his purpose: he promoted Private Moss to be squadron quartermaster sergeant, then sergeant-major, and this man took to heart his job of fathering the unit. His ambition was to foresee all the needs of the fighting patrols and provide for them in advance. Ceaselessly at work himself, and a hard taskmaster, he directed his own efforts and those of the few men working under him with intelligence: as a result, although the unit was completely self-supporting and provided its own maintenance for the elaborate equipment it employed, we never had more than three men on administrative or technical duties for every seven fighters. With few exceptions, the whole of our base staff was drawn from the patrols: men who were recovering after being wounded, or resting after a long period on operations. Thus I could draw on base to reinforce a patrol, and, conversely, I always had employment for a man who had to be temporarily relieved from fighting duties.

Moss was helped by Corporal Snape, a quiet man and the perfect clerk, who worked apparently day and night. I took him out on several operations as a patrol corporal, a role in which he enjoyed himself immensely. Between operations he returned to his clerking; equally a success in either capacity. He was killed at the end of the war.

Bob Yunnie remained at home and trained the men. Our base at that time was up a nearly vertical three thousand feet high mountainside. The access, the road having been blown, was either by a goat track, or by a funicular belonging to a hydro-electric plant, on which we managed to balance a jeep. When we chose we could cut ourselves off from the outer world, and enjoy as our own a hundred square miles of mountains and lakes, and a peak six thousand feet high. In March there was plenty of snow: Eighth Army provided ski-ing equipment for every man in the unit, and we recruited four instructors from an *Alpini* battalion; later, when the snow melted, we practised rock climbing, at which a few enthusiasts amongst our men became fairly expert; useful accomplishments as they proved more than once, but mainly intended, in my mind, to develop self-confidence in the men and to keep them interested and fit during the period of preparation. We practised also other exercises which had a more direct bearing on our military activities.

One evening I came home from a trip to Caserta and found waiting for me a young captain, John Campbell, who had come from the I.R.T.D. (Infantry Reinforcement Training Depot) to offer his services. For the occasion he had put on his best clothes; apart from the hair, which hadn't been cut for six months, he looked neat enough in a tunic, trews (his regiment was the Argyll and Sutherland) and rather dainty shoes. Tired, hungry and a little short in temper, I was not impressed; Campbell was tongue-tied, said the wrong things, and I turned him down. Caneri took me aside and said: 'I would give him a try. I have talked to him this afternoon, he seems all right. You have frightened him.' I looked again at the big awkward lad in his tight clothes and told him: 'We have an exercise starting in an hour's time. Without going into details now, it involves finding your way across country with a companion and walking about sixty miles carrying forty pounds in a pack and your weapons. The trip has to be done in record time, as it is by way of being a race. Go on the exercise – if you come back in good time I shall take you in P.P.A.'

Later that evening Campbell, in borrowed boots and battledress, climbed into the back of a lorry with the other competitors; I had softened to the extent of giving him as companion my gunner, Jock Cameron the gillie, of all our men the cleverest at finding his way over mountain ranges. They were driven out in the dark; in the early hours of the morning the pairs were dropped a few miles apart, given an escape map printed on a handkerchief, told hurriedly where they were and they pushed off to make their way back to our base in San Gregorio in the Matese Mountains. They were to avoid highways, assumed to be enemy-held, and to have nothing to do with the local population, assumed to be hostile – which they had no difficulty in doing as they were mistaken by the peasants for German parachutists and created quite a scare. They carried their own food, escape rations; their only compass was of the kind that can be hidden in the stem of a pipe.

Cameron and Campbell arrived first, thirty-two hours after they had been dropped and two hours ahead of the next pair. The last pair, Duggan and a companion, turned up on the fifth day, having walked all the time and crossed the Apennines three times. Duggan lost whatever chances he may have had to serve in a patrol, but found a job in our headquarters as a cook — his companion, having failed again on another exercise, was dismissed.

Campbell remained with us till the end of the war and rose to be the fourth of us 'Big Three'. But he had a long way to go before he took command of 'S' Patrol, made a name for it in cloak and dagger operations, and got himself two Military Crosses. I gave him first to Jean Caneri, for whom he ran errands for several months; following the example of his boss he developed a masterful manner with reluctant quartermasters. Thus he got his first training fighting, not the Germans, but our rear headquarters in Italy, where he came to be known and feared for an awesome obstinacy. He mastered a crippling inferiority complex impressed on him in childhood, and when later I put him in charge of a patrol he developed into the most daring of us all.

At the end of May 1944 many of our men, but not myself, had graduated from the Parachute School in Brindisi; we had acquired the technique of receiving parachuted supplies at night (which had first, I believe, been developed in supplying resistance movements in France and the Low Countries), and we had learnt to play with that coy pair, Rebecca and Eureka, who between them, in awful secrecy, guided planes on a radio beam towards the dropping zones where we waited for the containers and the men they would drop on us from the sky.

'A' Force had on three occasions taken off escaped prisoners from a beach near the mouth of the Tenna River on the Adriatic coast, sixty miles behind the German front line as it now stood near Pescara. The naval craft they had used had taken soundings, from which it appeared that there was just enough water to sail a loaded L.C.T. over a sand bar five hundred yards off shore and beach her on the coast. From the beach there was easy access for vehicles to a road.

No. 1 Special Force was in intermittent wireless contact with an agent they had staying with Italian partisans at Cingoli, a town in the mountains thirty miles inland where a hide-out could be arranged for us in the woods for our first day ashore. These considerations made me pick on the mouth of the Tenna as our landing point, the Navy agreed, and it was arranged that the operation would take place during the 'no moon' period in June, between June 12th and 17th, three days each side of the new moon. I should have liked to land on the twelfth, but there were several delays, and the date finally agreed was June 15th at 2300 hours.

I should in fact have liked to land very much earlier, at the beginning of June, but the Navy, having first agreed, discovered a ruling that vessels should not be exposed on an enemy coast except at night and during 'no moon' periods, and none of the arguments I put forward could prevail. Meanwhile the main battle, which had started round Cassino on May 11th, had succeeded in breaking the German resistance; on May 23rd the Anzio force broke out from the beach-head in which it had been fighting since January 18th; on June 4th Rome fell and Fifth Army pursued the Germans in disorderly retreat beyond the Tiber. On the Adriatic side of Italy there had been less activity, but on June 10th Eighth Army took Pescara, an advance of ten miles which might be the first sign of a German collapse in this area. Much greater actions were taking place in Normandy at the same time, but, absorbed in our own affairs, we took little notice of the opening of the Second Front.

The earlier we got into our positions, the greater advantage we should be able to take of the German withdrawal; for a retiring army was one of our natural targets — more important still was it that we should land before our beach was overrun by our own advancing forces.

On June 12th I sent an advance party to our landing point. They sailed in a naval M.L. which made a landing at midnight one thousand yards south of our beach. Bob Yunnie with Gino Mifsud, the Italian anti-Fascist who had been with us for over a year, and accompanied by a local partisan leader known under the battle name of Quinto, whom I had seen at 'A' Force Headquarters, went ashore and walked away inland. I wanted Yunnie to get in touch with the partisans and obtain from them a picture of the situation from the coast up to Cingoli. Three days later, unless in his view the situation was such that an attempt to land the main party could only end in disaster, he was to come down to the beach and signal the L.C.T. carrying me and the main party to the landing point. If on account of the weather or for some other reason we were unable to reach the landing point at 2300 hours on the fifteenth, or if we didn't see Yunnie's signals, it was agreed that we would repeat the attempt on the sixteenth and the seventeenth. Quinto was to provide the contacts, Gino, in civilian clothes and with faked documents, was to tour the countryside on a bicycle and check the information given by the partisans, whose judgment I didn't trust too much. Sergeant Porter of 'P' Patrol landed with Yunnie to reconnoitre the beach and its exits; he sailed back the same night on the M.L. to make his report to me on what he had found. Two naval officers landed also to reconnoitre the beach from the naval side. They were all back the next night in the port from which they had sailed, where a jeep waited for Porter and brought him to me. He had drawn a sketch of the beach: one hundred yards of firm sand led to the beginning of a good dirt track, which, passing under the railway, joined six hundred yards further on with the main tarmac coast road. He had found neither mines nor vehicle obstacles and during the hour or so he had spent ashore he had seen no more than five or six German vehicles driving along the road.

The naval officers had taken some further soundings and reported everything in good order. They had made a note of landmarks on the coast which would make our approach from the sea foolproof.

This first success was a good omen. I still saw a number of possible snags for which I endeavoured to make provision, but on the whole I thought the odds were in our favour: if Bob Yunnie had landed without trouble on the twelfth, we stood a good chance of doing the same three days later. I trusted the Navy entirely to see to their side of the undertaking: I stood in such awe of them that I wouldn't have dared to make a suggestion even if any had occurred to me.

I collected my party and on June 14th we drove to Manfredonia, a small port south of the Gargano Peninsula. After dark we moved into the harbour and drove our twelve jeeps in reverse up the nose ramp into the L.C.T. Four rows of three jeeps fitted snugly into the 'Landing Craft Tanks', and this consideration had determined my decision to employ twelve jeeps. Having got them in, we drove them all out again so that, each man knowing when his turn came and where he had to drive, there should be no confusion at the actual landing. Sergeant Porter had paced out on shore a replica of our beach and the track as he had seen them. He and Corporal Owen directed the vehicles and got them lined up in the proper order. We repeated the process a second time, then re-embarked and the L.C.T. sailed.

H.M. L.C.T. 589, commanded by Lieutenant H. Dale, R.N.V.R., carried a crew of eleven. The strength of my party was thirty all ranks; myself with Corporal Cameron, Sergeant Beautyman, Sergeant Mitchell and Signaller McCulloch forming Blitz Patrol in two jeeps; Captain Rickwood, Sergeant Sanders (the New Zealander), Sergeant Porter and eight men — 'R' Patrol in four jeeps; Lieutenant Reeve-Walker (South African) with six men of 'S' Patrol in three jeeps; and finally Sergeant Curtis with Corporal Riches and five men of 'B' Patrol in three jeeps, of which, after we had landed, Bob Yunnie would take command. We couldn't fit more than that number into twelve jeeps — the L.C.T. could not take more vehicles, and the Navy couldn't spare a second L.C.T. — for the time being I had to be contented with this small party.

We carried in addition a detachment of four officers and sixty-nine other ranks of Ninth Commando. They had offered to hold the beach-head for us while we landed, and although I didn't think I needed them, I hadn't liked to refuse them a chance of taking part in an operation; for the poor lads had been sitting inactive for over eight months. They were to re-embark and sail back with the L.C.T. after seeing us ashore.

Our total complement thus was one hundred and fourteen.

Our craft was only a floating box, an unarmed, rectangular, flat-bottomed hull with the engine room, the tiny bridge, the chart-room-cum-ward room, the ratings' quarters in the stern, and a swinging ramp in the bows, over which, when let down, vehicles could be driven. She was escorted by two naval vessels of another kind: one was an M.F.V. — a Motor Fishing Vessel; deceptively in appearance like a wooden sailing craft, with stumpy masts and a dirty grey deck house, it could travel at a fair speed, carried a Bofors in the deck house and was fitted with some new navigational device which computed, so I was told, a dead-reckoning position unaffected by drift or current. The other escort was an M.L., a Motor Launch, which looked quite openly like a tiny destroyer.

My men, happy and excited, lay on deck between their jeeps and talked in whispers throughout the night while our ship plodded over the quiet sea. Their time for the last two months had been full of new activities, followed by a week of ceaseless work, to get themselves ready for an unspecified expedition in which, as they feared in their hearts all the time, their place might be given at the last moment to a more lucky companion. This night, for the first time, they had nothing to do or to worry about till the morning, when I would tell them where we were going and what I expected to do. Meanwhile they floated in a void, suspended between the world they had left behind and the strife they would face the next day. For a few hours they were free to dream of adventure.

I was in the same mood, but before letting myself sink into blissful inactivity there was one more little job I wanted to do. Two photographic reconnaissances had been flown the day before by the Desert Air Force to cover the various roads we could follow between our landing point and our first hide-out in the woods near Cingoli, and the photos had reached me just before embarking. In the chart-room, as a last and rather superfluous precaution, I set about checking my maps by the air photos, in case they were inaccurate in some detail. As I did so I noticed that one of the bridges we would have to cross appeared on the photo to be destroyed. A shadow of anxiety disturbed my inner quiet. Then I discovered another bridge, unmistakably blown. As there were no signs of bomb craters it could not be the work of the air force — who anyway had agreed to keep off our area till we had gone through (except for the main coast road). I concluded that the partisans had been active — were probably active again this very night — and the peace of my mind went like a soap bubble. My trouble was that if, starting from the coast at about midnight, we did not succeed in reaching the mountains before dawn, our presence would be discovered by the Germans before we had time to get organized, and my

432

long-range schemes would fall to the ground. Three rivers stood across our way: if the bridges had gone the streams would have to be forded, not an impossible task in June, but a slow one that I could not hope to complete in time with twelve jeeps, at night and in a hurry.

I succeeded in working out two routes along which, according to the photos, the bridges were intact. They were longer by half than my original one, running to about sixty miles of tortuous going: I marked them in blue and yellow respectively on twelve sets of maps, then I tore up the photos and threw the bits overboard.

As there was nothing more I could do, I dismissed my plans from my mind and walked out on to the bridge to talk to our young, black-bearded skipper. Sailors have a serenity denied to ordinary men; in the company of Dale the last vestiges of concern evaporated and I lightly laid aside my responsibilities until the time came to land.

Dawn found us sailing north-west by north up the Adriatic, out of sight of land, a clear sky and no sea.

After breakfast I gave out my instructions, to each patrol in succession:

'Tonight at 2300 hours we shall make a point on the coast, one thousand yards south of the mouth of the Tenna River. Bob Yunnie will be on the beach from 2200 hours to 0100 hours. If conditions are right for us to land, he will flash at intervals the letter R, dot-dash-dot, on a red torch, during the whole of that period. If we don't pick up his signal we shall put out to sea and try again on each of the two following nights.

'Our landing point is sixty miles in the rear of the German line. According to my latest information there are few German forces inland, though they have some military traffic on the coast road, and they may have control posts on the roads and guards on the bridges. Bob Yunnie will give me fresher information, as it is possible that the situation has altered during the last few days.

'There are some friendly partisans in the area of whom we shall get to know more than we do now. Our code name with them is supposed to be "Banda di Pappa". I am not very sure that they know it.

'My intention is to establish a base in the mountains, supplied from the air, from which we shall operate as long as conditions remain suitable. When necessary we shall move to other bases, always keeping in the rear of the enemy.

'As soon as we touch ground the ramp will go down and the Commandos will disembark to form a beach-head for us. The jeeps will not land till I give the order.

'Our objective tonight will be Cingoli, which we shall reach before dawn, following the route marked in yellow on the map.'

Technical details on disembarkation and the mode of travel followed.

'You will all memorize the yellow route and be able to follow it without reference to the map — as we have done on exercises before. It is a long route, over sixty miles, with forty-four cross-roads, and it goes through four small towns, of which I have made sketches from the air photos.' I explained about the bridges which compelled us to take a devious route. 'If the bridge over the Tenna near Fermo has been blown since my photos were taken, we shall follow the blue route, which you will also memorize. This evening you will hand over the marked maps to me to be destroyed.'

I fixed the rendezvous in the woods north-west of Cingoli, about which there would be no difficulty, for however well we might be hidden from the Germans, every peasant would know where we had gone.

'The main point to remember is that we must be well clear of the last main road south of Cingoli before 0500 hours, lest all our future plans go by the board. We shall travel fast and anyone who takes the wrong turning will be R.T.U. the next morning.' (R.T.U. stood for 'Returned to Unit' — dismissed from P.P.A. — our one and only punishment.) 'If we meet resistance we shall fight our way through, and all the Germans we may meet will be killed. This means that we shall take no prisoners and we shall finish off the wounded. Thank you very much. Good luck to us all.' This was as much feeling as I dared put in my speeches, anything more would have been considered incongruous by my audience.

It was a long route to memorize, but we had done more difficult than that on exercises more than once.

I then made arrangements with Captain Long of the Ninth Commando for guarding the beach-head. We had Porter's sketch to work on and we marked out the posts. I asked his permission to say a few words to his men: I put them in the general picture, told them what was expected of them, and, in a more florid speech than I used with my own men, thanked them for their help. I then stood by while Long and his officers briefed their N.C.O.s.

I spent the remainder of that day in a delightful stupor although I came back to the world twice to rehearse my route. I would be leading the party and I didn't care to disgrace myself, but in fact I relied entirely on Jock Cameron.

Before sunset we changed our course to the west and the mountains of Italy rose out of the sea. Before leaving port the skippers of our three ships had decided that, disregarding the Admiralty instructions not to come within sight of the coast by daylight, they would make sure of their landfall before dark. I liked to see that the Navy had as few scruples about disobeying orders as we had ourselves.

At dusk we hove to, with the M.F.V. standing by; the M.L. opened up her engines with a roar and sped towards the coast. An hour later a dark smudge appeared on our port bow, the launch back, having picked up her landmarks. The M.F.V. parted company and with three hours still to go we started the run-in, dead slow, without a ripple. At 2200 the coast showed up. At 2230, watching through the glasses to pick up Bob Yunnie's red signal, I saw uncanny lights flitting here and there over the beach. I couldn't account for them; car headlights couldn't move that way! Could they be hundreds of men brandishing torches, excited partisans come down to meet us? Blast them, blast Bob for letting them come! At 2245 I ordered all jeep engines to be started up. At 2250 the skipper by my side said: 'Look, exactly over our bows.' In the glasses I saw a small red glow, strangely immobile and dull amongst a myriad darting points of greenish fire, blinking slowly dot-dash-dot, pause, dot-dash-dot, pause, dot-dash-dot, pause. There was nothing in a silent world but those weird lights and the friendly red torch. On the deck below me Owen muttered 'Bob is still alive.'

The L.C.T. put on speed, lurched, scraped the bottom, pulled herself off. We were over the bar, in clear water; then another lurch on an uncharted sand bank, and clear again. At 2330 the anchor chain rattled down, the bows slid up the beach, the L.C.T. stopped with a jerk, and the ramp went down. Below me on the sand stood Bob Yunnie, in a cloud of fireflies.

He came on board as the Commandos filed out without a sound. Leaning against the bulwarks we stood talking in whispers: the situation ashore had deteriorated during the last two days. The German Army was in retreat, its transport covered the roads and there were troops in the villages. I went down to the beach and talked to Gino, who had cycled half way to Cingoli during that day: he had seen long traffic jams on the roads inland and machine-gun posts on the bridges, but no preparations yet for demolitions.

I had to make a decision and I turned arguments in my mind while Bob Yunnie talked: I was tempted to let my twelve jeeps loose amongst the German Army, but I didn't want my men to lose their lives in one silly blaze of glory.

Perhaps the next day the troops would have moved on and we might be able to nip in before the rearguard came up — a very long chance, if it was a chance at all. I walked up to the main road, six hundred yards away, and saw a convoy of trucks, armoured cars and guns in a jumble creeping along head to tail. I came back still undecided: I had but to lift my hand to Porter, waiting at the foot of the ramp, and the jeeps would drive up the beach. If I didn't opportunity might never come again. The temptation was great, but common sense prevailed in my mind. Our chances of fighting our way to the mountains before dawn were slender; caught by daylight in the plain we would have to abandon our vehicles and slink away on foot — a band of refugees. I said to Porter: 'Landing cancelled. Pass the word along,' and walked aboard to warn Dale, our skipper. Bob and his party came aboard also; the Commandos were called in, the ramp went up, the engines started astern and the L.C.T. prepared to put out to sea.

Fast aground, she didn't move. The crew hauled on the anchor cable astern and using the engines alternately, then together, the craft backed two yards, then stuck with the stern slowly swinging to port. Dale tried vainly to check the drift with the full power of his engines. At 0045 hours he reported that he was aground, his anchor had dragged, and a coastal drift, helped by a northerly breeze, was gradually bringing the L.C.T. to broach to. Apologetically, for I hated interfering but after all Dale was very young, I suggested that he cast another anchor — if he had one — some distance out to starboard. 'I know,' he replied, 'I have got an anchor all right, but no boat to take it out.'

I went into the bows and had the ramp let down again. It now ran parallel with the coast and five yards off it, into five feet of water and a soft bottom. The two girders we had brought with us could not help us to land the jeeps now. We might drive one jeep into the sea, perhaps two, to lighten ship, but lying on the bottom they would prevent any forward movement of the L.C.T., and astern we were against a shallow sand bank.

At 0100 hours Dale with a lamp signalled the M.L. which was standing out at sea, invisible in the dark, asking her to come in and try and tow us off. He got no reply. The M.F.V. had left us, bound for the Dalmatian coast, two hours previously.

At 0115 hours, wrecked on an enemy coast, with our escort out of contact, we decided to abandon ship and take our men ashore. My men could look after themselves, and I trusted the naval crew to be just as good, but I had on my hands seventy-three Commandos; tough fighters as they were, they would be a raw crowd to take across forty miles of open plain, filled with enemy troops, to the comparative safety of the mountains. They were not trained for such an expedition. The prospects of survival were unpromising; I had no choice but to make the attempt. Sitting in the tiny ward room with Rickwood and Long, Bob, exhausted, asleep on a locker, with the nominal rolls before me, I split up the one hundred and sixteen men we had to get off into twelve groups, each one including three members of P.P.A., one of whom would be in command. I appointed myself commander of a Commando group and put Rickwood in charge of the sailors. My plan was to put the parties ashore at intervals, and walk them inland along three separate routes, lie up during the day, walk again at night, and so on until we reached the mountains, to wait there for Eighth Army to come up.

I detailed Sergeant Curtis to lay demolition charges on each jeep, and on the engines of the L.C.T., and called for the leaders I had appointed to the escape parties to come with their maps for their instructions: meanwhile Long got his groups of Commandos organized. Weapons and ammunition to be carried — no food except escape rations.

At 0135 hours Dale, who had been on the bridge, reported signal contact made with the M.L., which, coming in to us had run aground on the sand bar, five hundred yards out at sea. I allowed for seven more men to be taken off: the crew of the M.L.

At 0200 hours the M.L. signalled that she was afloat once more, to seaward of the sand bar, and that she could stand by till daybreak to pick up as many men as could be ferried across to her. I decided to take my chance of a sea rescue, cancelled the landing parties and asked Lieutenant Dale to attend to the ferrying, for this was a naval matter. The order of evacuation was: Commandos, then P.P.A. less rear party (Cameron, Curtis and myself), lastly the crew of the L.C.T.

I woke Bob Yunnie and asked him if he would care to take ashore a small foot party with a wireless set and remain in the area to give Eighth Army general intelligence and bombing targets until he was overrun or I succeeded in joining him overland. His reply was: 'If you say so, Popski,' for he never expressed any approbation of the nice jobs I selected for him, and he went off to select his party. He intended to take two men only; after some argument, finding that every man in his patrol wanted to go with him, he took four: Sloan wireless operator, Owen, O'Neil and Gino. They took a wireless set, batteries, their weapons and ammunition, slid overboard, waded ashore and out of sight, accompanied by Quinto, the partisan. In my present position there was nothing more I could do to take advantage of our presence on the flank of the enemy.

The skipper of the M.L. paddled across to us on a Carley float to discuss the position. The draught of his craft being too great to allow her over the sand bar, our men would have to cross somehow the five hundred yards of water that separated us from the M.L. Between us we had one rubber dinghy carrying six, and two floats carrying three each: allowing for one man to bring the craft back, we could ferry eleven men across on each trip. A first batch of eleven Commandos turned up in battle order, carrying weapons, ammunition and full kit. My orders had been 'Bodies only to be saved', and we had to strip them before lowering them overboard on to the flimsy craft. Later on a few Commandos succeeded in slipping away in full kit, with a disastrous effect on the overloaded floats — the only acts of indiscipline which occurred.

The position of the Commandos was trying, for apart from waiting to be carried off they had absolutely nothing to do, and most of them didn't know what had happened. My own men were busy and several of them secretly hoped that, not being taken off in time, they would have a chance of joining Bob Yunnie's shore party. The crew of the L.C.T. worked quietly, cheerful and absolutely unmoved.

On first coming on the coast, being very conscious of the enemy on the road a few hundred yards away; we had talked in whispers and moved on padded feet. While Dale tried to wrench his craft off the sand banks the roar of the engines made us forget caution, and while the first party was leaving there was even some shouting over the dark water. At that moment a British plane flew overhead and dropped flares half a mile away, pulling off our blanket of darkness. Bare and exposed, we froze in our places: a hush fell over our company, and in the sudden silence the hum of the traffic and the German voices on the road appeared to be heading directly at us. Without a word our men picked up their weapons and manned the port bulwarks — the L.C.T. was too deep for us to use the jeeps' guns. Nothing happened. (I heard later from Bob Yunnie that when the flares dropped the Germans abandoned their vehicles and took cover off the main road.) We waited for an eternity till the whine, the crash and the boom came of bombs dropping on the road and rail bridges over the Tenna, a thousands yard away. Then the flares floated down to earth and darkness fell over us once more.

The Commandos were awkward on the water and few of them

could swim. Finally the dinghy towing the two floats with their human loads vanished in the dark and we settled down to wait for their return. I distributed to my men and to the crew the contents of two boxes of cigars I had — a gift from Egypt — and went into the ward room where Dale was tearing up documents and charts. I felt the same elation of spirits I had experienced while we were extricating ourselves from disaster at Qaret 'Ali, and not a shadow of regret.

A simple calculation showed that ferrying eleven men at a time we could not possibly take off everyone before daybreak: on the suggestion of Sanders I set our men to extract the inner tubes from our twenty-four spare wheels and inflate them to make life-buoys.

The dinghy did not return for an hour: the Commandos, attempting to get out of it in military formation, had stepped together on the gunwale and capsized it and the crew of the M.L. spent much time fishing them out of the sea and bailing out the dinghy. The time was three in the morning: with two hours to go till dawn when we should be in full view of the Germans on the road we had still one hundred men to take off. We made ten Commandos slip an inflated inner tube under their armpits, tied the men on to a line and lowered them into the water. As none of the Commandos could paddle we had to put a rating on each float and off they went: the dinghy and the two floats towing the men on the line behind them; nineteen Commandos ferried over at each trip.

With a glow of dawn showing in the eastern sky, the dinghy and floats came back for the last batch of Commandos; I saw them go without sorrow. We had still on board nine of the crew and twenty-seven of P.P.A. — they would have to swim for it. Rickwood stripped to the skin, sprang on to the bulwark and with a 'Yo-ho' went into the sea head foremost. The others followed yelling and laughing —their bobbing heads disappeared towards the small light which the M.L. showed over her side. Sanders, a pistol belted around his bare body, swam carefully on his back in the quiet water, smoking a cigar. Only our rear party remained on board. With Curtis I went round the charges he had laid and we poured petrol over the jeeps and the torn-up papers in the chart-room.

We gathered on the bridge waiting for the dinghy. Lieutenant Dale said:

'Never mind my L.C.T. She is expendable. But all those nice jeeps!' We had spent much labour and much love on them and I felt a pang.

'Don't worry,' I replied. 'War is wasteful. We shall get some more.'

But although we equipped many more jeeps before the war ended, we never brought them again to the same pitch of perfection.

Darkness lifted. A bank of white mist spread over the sea, hiding the M.L., but to landward we began to discern through the trees the slow-moving column of traffic on the road. The dinghy bobbed up. Curtis having set the delayed fuses, we climbed down into the small craft and threw in the clothes left behind by the swimmers. Sitting on the bow thwart I picked up my sculls, a rating sat in front of me, Curtis and Cameron in the bows. We held the stern of the dinghy against the side of the ship for Lieutenant Dale to come in. Erect in the stern, his log book under his arm, he saluted his ship: then he turned round and sat down, and we pulled away.

We floated a long time in a milky whiteness. A voice hailed us impatiently: suddenly we came out of the mist and there was the M.L. above us. It got under way as we were pulled aboard. The skipper was in a hurry: he had heard a train coming up the line and didn't want to miss it. He sailed a quarter of a mile along the coast, then stopped; the train came into view, and he opened up with the Bofors. The tracer curved towards the land — after a long while there was a cloud of steam and the train stopped. Bob Yunnie, sitting under a haystack two hundred yards from the railway line, cursed us abundantly.

Stern down and bows out of the water, the M.L. made for home with a roar of her twin engines. She rolled abominably. One hundred and eighteen men on board a craft designed to carry seven in very moderate comfort were somewhat cramped. Somehow the sailors managed to give us all hot coffee and whisky, which made us very brave for a while — then we began to fight seasickness. I held out till I saw Dale go under; my honour safe, I pushed my way through the crowd and was gloriously sick overboard.

We reached Manfredonia that afternoon at four. Our only casualty was a Commando who, having been ducked when the dinghy capsized, was feeling a little drowned, but the N.O.I.C. entertained us as genuine shipwrecked mariners. On landing I signalled instructions to Jean Caneri: he wasted no time and early the next morning we were on our way to San Gregorio in our own three-tonners which he had sent for us. At our base I found everyone a-bustle equipping the ten battle-worthy jeeps which remained to us. The whole of that day we worked and through the night and through the next day. At 0315 hours on June 19th, seventy hours after abandoning the stranded L.C.T., we were on the road with much the same party, in ten jeeps, driving northwards in an attempt to take advantage of the German confused withdrawal and cross their lines in the mountains. None of us had had time to brood over our ill-luck and our spirits were high.

Yunnie's wireless had opened up at ten o'clock on the sixteenth from a position in the Tenna Valley, and every few hours since then he had been giving bombing targets. So good was the co-ordination with the air force that he was able, after giving the new target, to report on the results of the bombing of his previous one. His messages were received by our wireless station in San Gregorio, and retransmitted to our station at Eighth Army where our liaison officer, Lieutenant Costello, then rang up Headquarters Desert Air Force, who got on to their bombers.

I signalled Yunnie that we were on our way and would pick him up. I considered he had a two to one chance of remaining alive till that time.

At dawn we stopped on a mountain pass and looked once more on the Adriatic. We bought a basket of seventy-two eggs from an old woman and finished them off on the spot between the nine occupants of the three leading jeeps. For my share I sucked twelve.

At Chieti we entered no-man's-land: the Germans were on the run, and when we bedded down in a wood that night, sixty miles further on, they were still two days ahead of us.

442

The next morning, outside a mountain town of the Abruzzi, we were met by strange creatures riding thunderous motor tricycles: they wore shiny black satin slacks and blouses, pink caps and orange neckerchiefs, and suspended about their persons were hand grenades and daggers. They dashed about in a frenzy, yelling orders at one another, and did nothing — with hysterical earnestness: my first experience of 'partisans of after the liberation'. By a precipitous diversion, which hundreds of their more sober companions in ordinary peasants' clothes were digging out of the mountainside to by-pass a viaduct blown by the Germans, they led us to the town hall, where I found their head man. His name had been given me by my friends in 'A' Force — he was a man who had helped many hundreds of our escaped P.O.W.s to rejoin our lines. A little, round man with an earnest countenance, he had appointed himself mayor and was furiously signing passes as I came in. He dropped his pen, came up and embraced me; he had obviously not slept for three days but his mind was clear. The Germans, he said, were somewhere beyond Sarnano, a town fifty miles ahead, and he gave me the name of a partisan friend of his who could help me. We drove out of the town through a dense crowd who did their best to induce us to stay with them and celebrate.

In the next town we met more fancy dresses, and as we were jammed in the crowd a man sat himself on the bonnet of my jeep, took my head between his hands, kissed me on the lips and exclaimed in English:

'Oh lad, I am glad to see you.'

'And who the hell are you?'

'3528957 Lance-Corporal Wilson, W. L., R.A., captured at Gazala.'

'Wilson, I am bloody glad to see you,' I said, wiping my mouth, 'but you should know better. Now please get off my jeep and get your friends to make way for us.' There were many more escaped British prisoners in the crowd and we didn't get away easily.

In Sarnano by four o'clock the crowd was even more excited than usual as the Germans had left only the day before. My partisan friend was not in town but at a small village eight miles further on on a side road. We pushed on until I found him, dour-faced and hard-eyed; I didn't like him much, but he seemed more business-like than his fancy-dress companions. He undertook to send men to Tolentino, a town on the river Chienti fourteen miles forward, to see if they could confirm the rumour that it had been evacuated. Travelling in a cart they would be back by ten o'clock that evening. Would we accept, all of us, to dine with the partisans in the village inn, while we waited for his patrol to return?

We were all pretty well done in: I had pushed on since early morning without stopping for a meal (for every hour counted), and the excitement in all the towns we crossed had been exhausting. I accepted the offer. On the evening call we had news from Bob Yunnie. He was now five miles inland, not more than twenty miles due east from us — as the crow flies — and doing well. His area, still congested with troops, was much harassed by our air force, which, guided by his messages was doing useful damage. He stated that the German rearguard was thirty-five miles to the south (as we were level with Yunnie's position it seemed that the withdrawal inland, where we were, had been more rapid than on the coast). The intention of the Germans, he said, was to make a stand on the river Chienti, the one I intended to cross that night. If his information was correct, I hadn't got a chance.

The partisan dinner was slow in coming. At ten we had not yet sat down and I got very impatient with the partisan leader, who, very apologetic, remarked that, as his men had not yet returned from Tolentino, nothing was lost. When it was served the meal turned out to be worth waiting for. Cameron, sitting next to me, put down huge helpings, against his habit, for he was a very abstemious man. Although he didn't drink he became unusually talkative and told the company the story of Lance-Corporal Wilson's effusive greeting.

The leader of the partisan recce party came in at last: he had been right over the river into Tolentino with his cart and had not seen a German till he had reached the market square. He offered to guide us into Tolentino along country roads, and would be ready as soon as he had had a bite.

At midnight, with the partisan guide on the back of my jeep, I led our column in the dark. As our forward troops (along the way we had come) were still one hundred and fifty miles behind us, I thought that the Germans, lulled into a false security, had failed to organize their defence of the river. If we succeeded in crossing it, by the morning we would be deep in enemy territory.

We were coming down the hills into the river valley about a mile and a half from the bridge, when a burst of automatic fire came from a farmhouse on the left, my side of the road. Some bullets hit the floor of the jeep between my legs and drew sparks: I wondered how they had got there without first going through me. I stopped the jeep to give Cameron, who was sitting on my right, a chance of answering the fire with his gun, and at the same time I turned round to warn the following trucks. Sergeant Mitchell, who was next to me, opened up, and Sergeant Beautyman, who drove the third truck, did the same. More bursts came from the farmhouse but the half-inch gun on my jeep didn't fire — surprised, I turned towards Cameron to see what stopped him, and found he wasn't there.

I walked round and found him lying on the road, wounded and unconscious, where he had slipped out of his seat. With Sergeant Riches, who had some understanding of first aid, I laid Cameron in the ditch, undid his clothing and began to dress his chest wound by the light of a torch; but he was far gone and after a few rattling gasps he gave a deep sigh and died in my arms. Meanwhile our men had stopped firing from their jeeps, and, led on foot by Beautyman, had entered the farmhouse and were apparently clearing it with their tommy guns. A moment later they reported two Germans killed and some others escaped.

We put Cameron on the back of my jeep (from where our guide had vanished). I sent for Corporal Taylor to be my gunner and we drove on. Less than a mile down the road we drew heavy fire from the bridge, and I turned back. The Chienti was guarded and my second attempt to cross the lines had failed.

We stopped outside a graveyard, where there was a plot of level ground, and bedded down. I stretched myself in my sleeping bag,

Cameron alongside me, and woke up at dawn, holding his cold hand. I rose covered in white down from my bag, torn by bullets where it had lain in the back of my jeep. Twenty rounds or more had hit my car and apparently had travelled round me to go and hit Cameron on the far side. He had been killed by bullets meant for me, who had led him into the ambush. The kind wife of the grave-digger stitched up my kit, while her husband dug my friend's grave. He made me choose a plot, offering me the best of his lovely graveyard, on a slope looking on to soft hills. I strolled round, looking at the tombs; in the mortuary I saw a body laid out. Coming round once more to the grave-digger I found him making a wooden cross, and he asked me what inscription I wanted painted on it. Having written it out, I talked with him for a while, then said idly:

'You have, I see, another body waiting to be buried.'

'It is my son, Sir, he was with the partisans; the Germans killed him yesterday morning.' He said no more; I fell silent, wondering at the humility of these people who took trouble with our dead and never mentioned their own so much more grievous loss.

I refused the offer to have a coffin made, for a soldier should be buried with no other covering than a blanket, in the bare earth on which he died. Thus we lowered Cameron in the grave, our men standing round and a detachment of the partisans. I read a short service and said:

'I want no other end than Jock has had: a quick death under the sky, with no fuss and no tears, amongst the friends with whom he has toiled for so long. Let us now carry on with our work.' 'Amen,' said Sanders, and we filled the grave.

I sent Rickwood and Reeve-Walker separately with their patrols to reconnoitre fords across the Chienti, and I drove westwards with 'Blitz' to find a way over the five thousand feet range which ran north and south on our left. The partisans had tales of a band established in a mountain valley on the other side of this range, but they knew of no path leading to it; in this part of the Apennines there is still little travel between the valleys where small communities live without contact with the world.

Towards evening I discovered a valley which seemed to afford a possible access to the ridge. It was too late, however, to press on and I returned to our camp. 'S' Patrol with Reeve-Walker returned, having found several fords too strongly guarded to be attempted. Later 'R' Patrol turned in: they had run into trouble and Rickwood had been shot through the body. Our rough knowledge of practical surgery was of no help in such a case: we covered him up, injected as much morphia as we dared, laid him on a stretcher and drove him to the village doctor, who suggested, not hopefully, that we try the hospital in Sarnano. Unless he was operated on within two hours, he said, he was lost.

Morphia did not relieve his great pain: he grinned and joked when he could, but mostly his jaws were locked so as not to cry out. The hospital turned out to be a broken-down, one-man institution, run by a dejected surgeon-cum-G.P.-cum-obstetrician, with a diffident manner and a Sicilian accent. One of the three nuns who helped him to run the hospital combined the functions of anaesthetist and operating-theatre assistant. I gave the doctor some ether and sulfanilamide, for he had no drugs. We had to wait three desperate hours while, judging by the noises I heard, the surgeon was attending a confinement. At last, in his spotted black coat, he came to fetch Rickwood and wheeled him into the theatre himself. The operation lasted two hours – he had to open the abdomen from the navel to the pubis and patch up eighteen perforations of the intestines. When it was over he wouldn't say more than that in three days' time he might be able to judge if the patient had a chance of surviving. He seemed so unsure that I gave up all hope. He refused to take a fee but accepted the few drugs and rolls of bandages that I could spare and some tea for his patients. 'There is so little a man in my position can do to help,' he said, and added: 'Don't worry, if the Germans come back while you are away they won't get him,' and his dour face painfully cracked into a smile.

I left Rickwood (with Riches) in the care of the brooding old man, certain that I wouldn't see him again. And yet he recovered, and our surgeons, when eventually he came into their hands, said that the operation had been brilliantly performed. And – as in a tale – the dejected village doctor turned out to have been a well-known surgeon and a professor at Palermo University, until the Fascist Government had exiled him to a mountain village.

The next day Sergeant Sanders, now in command of 'R' Patrol, found a way across the range. Having climbed four thousand feet up rocky stream beds he was stopped, six hundred feet below the ridge, by a grass slope too steep for his heavy vehicles: he unloaded, dismounted the guns and, everyone pushing, succeeded in driving the empty jeeps in reverse to the top of the pass. They ferried up the loads on their backs.

Summoned by two of his men, who walked all the way down in the night, I joined him on the ridge the next morning with 'Blitz' Patrol. On the far side we slithered down screes and terraces, that put a return journey out of the question, to the head of a secluded valley and an Alpine village of wooden chalets such as I had never seen in the Apennines. A track led us down the valley to a larger village: here we were stopped by a powerful middle-aged man of a rugged countenance, armed with a German automatic rifle and wearing a German camouflaged jacket over his homely peasant clothes. He saluted, introduced himself as a detachment leader of the Brigata Sparsico and said that his orders were to lead us to the brigade commander, Major Ferri. By the roadside six of his men stood in silence. Although their arms, clothing and trappings — all taken from the enemy — did not match, there was about them an air of subdued soldierly alertness which I interpreted hopefully as a sign that the enemy was still with them, and active.

448

CHAPTER VII

DECEPTION OF A DIVISION

MAJOR FERRI confirmed my hopes. His mountain valley ran northwards ten miles to debouch through a narrow gorge into the valley of the Chienti. Down to the gorge was his secure domain, his little liberated kingdom — beyond it and across the Chienti German reserve troops were stationed with a divisional head-quarters in a town six miles north of the river. They had built no defensive positions and it seemed that they had not realized that with their armies retreating along the coasts on both flanks, they, in the centre, might soon find themselves in the front line.

I had got at last what I had been seeking: a mountain fastness opening into enemy territory, and (an unexpected blessing) I found myself also provided with a force to defend it, for Ferri and his brother Giuseppe, formerly Professor of History at Pisa University, commanded three hundred men whom they had collected round a nucleus of re-fugees, escaped internees and soldiers who had taken to the mountains after the Italian Armistice nine months previously. The peasants of the valley fed them as a matter of course; from the Germans they had captured arms and ammunition and even two cars; some of the supplies dropped by No. 1 Special Force had also found their way into their hands; thus equipped, they had been raiding German road traffic and damaging bridges and railway lines, always at some distance from their valley.

The Germans knew there were 'bandits' in the valley, and a few months previously had attempted to round them up. They had suffered heavy casualties forcing the gorge, and when they were finally let through and they drove up the valley, they found the villages empty, partisans and civilians having taken refuge in the forests. The Germans burnt several houses, looted the others, shot an old man and his wife who had refused to go into hiding, and withdrew. The inhabitants came down again, counted their losses, painfully set their houses in order, and gave more support than ever to the partisans, for such is the spirit of the Italian peasants. Tenacious and long-suffering, they never blamed the partisans for the reprisals they brought upon them — besides, many of their own youths had taken arms with the bands.

Totally different from the hysterical popinjays in their fancy clothes on the other side of the range, Ferri's men lacked experience, to be sure, but they were fighters. Their administration was adequate: the troops were fed regularly and well; discipline, though quite informal, was such that each man, having received orders, carried them out to the best of his ability, but cadres were weak and the lower formations too fluid for really efficient operations. Subordinate commanders, instead of being in charge of units of their own, were liable to receive an order such as: 'Go up to Fiastra, pick out ten men and take the bridge.' Enthusiasm had to supply the lack of efficient team work. In his planning Ferri, in common with most partisan leaders in those early days, made the mistake of overestimating the possibilities of his troops: engaging them in pitched battles, he had suffered heavy casualties with little compensating advantage, but at the time I met him he had already realized the value of hit-and-run tactics and of small night operations in which knowledge of the terrain and ability to fade away and regroup elsewhere gave his men a marked superiority over the more cumbersome regular troops of the enemy. The majority of his men were recruited locally and knew from childhood the ground on which they operated.

I suggested to Ferri that joining forces we could, between us, achieve great things. He agreed with enthusiasm: and that afternoon we drove together in a civilian car down the valley, over the Chienti (at last) and reconnoitred the ground. Ferri's intelligence was well organized: he had several small detachments posted far out, watching the Germans. We went round his posts, collected information and when I returned after five hours' driving I had in my mind a fair picture of the situation over one hundred square miles.

That evening I called for 'R' and 'S' Patrols and sent out two signals: one to Jean Caneri to send up supplies for ourselves and bren guns,

stens and ammunition for Ferri; the other one to Yunnie in the Tenna
Valley to join us as soon as he considered his job completed, for I had
work for him. The rendezvous was at the foot of the range, from where
we could ferry them across.

By crossing the range I had not only secured at last a base in enemy
territory, but I had at the same time found on my doorstep an enemy I
could worry. A weak German mountain division (without artillery)
was stationed a few miles away in a small town, surrounded by
fifteenth-century stone walls, rising on a knoll in the centre of
a cup-shaped circle of wooded hills. Under cover of the trees we
could, without being seen, bring our guns within range of the city
walls along nearly the whole of their circuit. To the rear, the Germans
in the town were linked with the outer world by a single precipitous
road over the mountains; to reach their troops on either flank the
only road at their disposal followed the Chienti, a mountain torrent
which here flows through narrow rocky gorges both up and down
stream.

We mined these gorges and set partisans high up in the rocks;
having lost several vehicles and a few men, the Germans gave up the
daily patrols they had been running along the river road, and restricted
themselves to the use of their line of communication in the rear. Then
one night we switched over to this road and blew up the bridge over
the river Potenza seven miles to the rear of the town. Deliberately
we did no more damage to the bridge than could be repaired in a couple
of days so as to give the impression that the demolition was the fumbling
work of partisans — we wanted the Germans to get worried about
their communications, but not to the extent of building a diversion, for if they took the trouble to dig approaches they could ford the
river two hundred yards below the bridge.

The bridge was duly repaired and two nights later we ambushed and
burnt a ration convoy three miles from the town. To make the supply
position more alarming, I set Ferri's men to harry the German foraging
parties who went out daily into the countryside for cattle, pigs and
poultry. All the time I took care that none of my men should be
seen by the Germans and that no weapons were used but such as

could normally be in the hands of partisans. In my mind the knowledge of the presence of British troops should come to the Germans
only as an unexpected and overwhelming blow, which would
induce them to withdraw.

The day after the ambush we opened up with two wireless sets,
giving the call signs of several of our armoured units. By the next
night we had six sets each sending spurious messages at the rate of two
or three an hour. The range of our sets, reduced by the high range,
was too short to interfere with the real communications of the units we
were impersonating, but we hoped that to the Germans it would seem
as if all these British tanks and armoured cars had moved up the coast
and had overrun their left flank.

Ferri was an exceptionally humane partisan leader. Although the
best his men could expect was a swift death if they fell in German
hands, he had captured a number of German prisoners and kept them
in a cave up the mountainside. Most of these men were Austrians of
an unwarlike disposition; being well fed and well treated they showed
no inclination to escape. Amongst them, however, we discovered two
N.C.O.s, fanatical Nazis, who I hoped would serve my turn. The first
one proved a failure: in spite of his high talk to his companions, he
declined the opportunity of escaping to his own side when it was
offered him. The second fell into my trap in this manner: he was
brought to me after dark to be interrogated in a room where I had set
up a faked office (I preferred to have my real headquarters in the open).
While we talked in English, two of our signallers came in and set
about marking unit locations on a map on the wall, from a situation
report they were supposed to have just received from Eighth Army.
When they had finished the map showed our forward positions running from the coast to some distance inland along a line well in the rear
of our friends in the town. The signallers went out and, as arranged,
I was then called away, leaving the German alone in the room with
the map, under a partisan guard. I came back after ten minutes, and,
being unable to get any information out of my pig-headed customer,
I pretended to lose my temper and said that I would take him with me
over the range the next day to our headquarters, where means would be

found to make him talk. He was then marched out and locked in a room downstairs for the night. There he found he could slip through a small back window and he disappeared in the night. In the early morning the partisan guard on the Chienti bridge heard someone splash through the stream, and, in spite of heavy but deliberately erratic fire, scramble out on the far side and away through the woods.

While we were playing these games Yunnie and his four men were completing a much tougher work in the Tenna Valley. Behind hedges, under haystacks, lying in the standing corn, in the midst of the retreating German army, he had missed little of what was going on on the two roads that crossed the Tenna. The enemy, fearful of our aircraft, lay up during the day; but however carefully they camouflaged their positions, our planes, guided by Yunnie's messages, always seemed to know where to drop their bombs and which woods they should spray with gun fire. When our troops got nearer he concentrated on saving the bridges: when the German sappers had laid their charges he opened up on them and with the help of a handful of half-hearted local partisans, whom he had somehow goaded into action, chased them away before they had set their fuses, and held the bridge till the first Polish armoured cars rumbled over. He then packed himself and his men into a captured German car and joined me where I was waiting for him at the foot of the range. I don't suppose I said a word of praise, for such was not our way, but when I saw his bony frame and his thin, dirty, weather-beaten face tumbling out of the car, and Owen, Sloane, O'Neil and Gino following, I felt a relief and a pride that I should have been embarrassed to express. I believe I said something like: 'Come in, you bloody ghosts, and have a drink,' and we walked silently into the village *trattoria*.

We got more talkative after dinner: of all their achievements the one that struck them as being worth most recounting was how they had induced a German sergeant not only to exchange their exhausted wireless batteries for fresh ones, but also to carry them to their hide-out where they then held him prisoner. Fooling the enemy was a legitimate subject of boasting — of danger and fighting little was said, nor indeed, I believe, remembered.

453

I gave them one night's rest and then we crossed the range together: the prospect of being once more with their friends and of fighting in jeeps, in the proper manner, instead of hiding in ditches, was enough to dispel their weariness. Sergeant Curtis, however, who had come over with me to greet his leader, unexpectedly showed signs of strain. As we were nearing the top of the range he called my attention to a suspicious-looking vehicle on a hilltop two thousand feet below us. I pointed my glasses:

'Looks to me like a hay cart,' I said.

'I thought it might be a German armoured car.'

I looked again. 'More like a hay cart. Even if it is an armoured car, there is nothing we can do about it. Let us push on.'

A moment later he stopped again, with a queer look in his eye.

'I think it is an armoured car. Hadn't we better get off the skyline?'

In my mind an alarm bell rang: Curtis was cracking. This strange disease overtook the strongest of us. Waterson, Locke, had gone under. I told Yunnie I would give his sergeant a period of change, looking after our supply line — he would have to replace him; Riches was the man we had had in mind for such an eventuality. A fortnight later Curtis thanked me and asked to be posted back to a patrol; I appointed him to my own 'Blitz' and found him once more cool and solid. I wondered if it would also happen to me.

I gave the German commander twenty-four hours to digest the news brought by the returned prisoner, while we kept up our fancy signalling and jammed his own messages; then the next morning I staged my show.

During the preceding days, with the help of over two hundred peasants to fell trees and cut the undergrowth, we had cleared tracks through the woods surrounding the town. Along these tracks we now drove our jeeps divided into two patrols, and, having stationed them half a mile apart in camouflaged positions from which, quite invisible, they had a view of the city walls, we opened up towards the town with every gun we had. Through our glasses we could see tracer bouncing off the walls and shattering tiles on the house tops, a senseless performance which set a few roofs on fire but otherwise could do no damage. Ten minutes later we rushed one patrol over to another position, from which it again opened up; later we moved the other, and repeated these antics throughout the day — with intervals to save ammunition — until we had fired at the town from every angle and from many different positions. I intended that the German commander, seeing fire come from woods which in his mind were inaccessible to vehicles, should assume that the weapons were fired by infantry. With this notion in his head he would naturally assume that the several positions from which we opened up were occupied by us simultaneously — as no man can run a mile in five minutes carrying a heavy gun. Finally multiplying the number of guns firing from each point by the number of these points, he would, I hoped, inevitably come to the conclusion that, being encircled by the troops of two infantry brigades or more, the best course of action for him to take was to get out before he was destroyed. On the other hand, there was the possibility that he might think that an enemy who wasted his time — and his ammunition — firing his machine guns at stone walls the whole day long was too foolish to bother about. Mortars would have been more sensible weapons for us to use in this case than guns, but we had lost all ours in the L.C.T.

Until an hour before sunset we drew no response whatever from the town. During the morning we had seen soldiers moving in a street, but from noon onwards not a soul. The place might have been evacuated, but I couldn't think how the Germans could have slipped away without being seen as we had an observation post covering their main road of retreat.

I lined up my ten jeeps on the main road and led them towards the town, determined to draw fire, and to give an extra headache to the German general by showing him that, in addition to the infantry troops crowding the woods, vehicles had now been brought against him in some inexplicable manner.

The road came out of the woods, dipped into the open fields, and wound its way amongst low hills, alternately discovering and masking the southern gate of the town, now considerably above us. I thought how embarrassing it would be for me if I drove right in to the town square and found the German general waiting to surrender. How could I bluff him to believe that, apart from the twenty-five men on my jeeps, I had a few thousands in the woods?

I had nearly reached the foot of the ramp leading up to the gate, when a black mushroom of smoke and dirt sprang up in a field to the left of the road ahead of me, then some more on the other side and behind me. Taylor, from his seat next to me, levelled his gun and fired at where he thought the enemy mortars were. I stopped by the side of the road: the other jeeps, staggered behind me, all opened up. After a while the mortars got our range and plastered us pretty freely. In a moment our position became so alarming — at any instant I expected a direct hit on one of my jeeps — that I decided to pull out. Weaving between the bursts I drove back to the tail of the column, signalling each jeep to turn back as I drove by. Then I stopped and when the jeeps came up to me in their original order, firing back as they went, I waved them on, for instead of leading the column I wanted now to take the rear position and try the smoke generators I carried at the back of my jeep — a new gadget we had not used yet in action. Yunnie, coming up last in his jeep, misunderstood my intention and waited for me to take the lead of the column. Two mortar bombs bracketed his jeep and hid him from my view; slowly the cloud dispersed: he was still alive and grinning, his face plastered with black mud. Above the din I shouted:

'Carry on, I want to lay smoke.' He made a gesture of incomprehension. Taylor shouted: 'Smoke', and put his hand to his mouth as if smoking a cigarette. Yunnie pulled his long legs out of his jeep and walked over: another burst hid him — then he was by my side, offering me a cigarette!

Off we drove, the column ahead of me, the nine jeeps still all going. I pressed down a switch on the dashboard: with a fizzling noise a cloud of white smoke rose behind me, spread and filled the narrow valley, like a curtain drawn up, hiding the town. The mortars stopped dead, the men feeding them must have thought that a happy hit had blown us all up.

Nobody was hurt, although there were a few dents in the jeeps. We stopped in the woods and waited for our observation post to come up on the wireless. Just after dark it reported a short column of trucks heading north from the town, and, later, marching troops: the German general's mind had functioned as I intended and he had fallen into my trap.

I instructed Ferri to take his men into the town as soon as the Germans were out and round up stragglers, but to avoid street fighting which would be to no purpose. Then we took two partisans each on the back of our jeeps and drove slowly along a mountain track which joined on to the main road half way between the town and the bridge over the Potenza. We had time to spare: I had no intention of taking on the whole of the German division with my twenty-five men. We dropped the partisans, who trotted off in the dark towards the bridge, under which we had laid charges with an electric detonator and a very long cable, and we waited off the road while the German troops marched by, their kit, carried in bullock carts, following behind. There was a long gap in the convoy; then, as our observation post had announced, came a last column of staff cars and troop-carrying trucks, presumably headquarters with the rearguard. We tailed on to them and when the road, with the mountainside on the right and overhanging a ravine on the left, took a long bend out of sight, we opened up. There was some confusion and for a while we had it our own way as the troops at the head of the column were quite a long time before they realized their tail had come to grief. Eventually we broke off and the remnant of the column put on speed, with us in pursuit. When we judged we were a mile from the river we fired a pre-arranged signal, two red and two green Very lights; the partisans pressed the plunger and the bridge went up with a bang. The Germans abandoned their trucks and bullock carts, and splashed across the Potenza in good order on foot. Although we fired at them from higher ground and with weapons heavier than theirs, they never broke, but organized a rearguard which kept us at a distance till the last survivors had crossed the river. We had no casualties, the partisans lost two men, the Germans about a hundred, most of their precious vehicles and nearly all their equipment, which fell as booty to the partisans. Civilians reported that the German general had been found amongst the dead, but I didn't see the body myself. We kept his staff car, bullet-ridden but still in running order, as a souvenir.

The bullocks were driven back to their former owners, the trucks which had not been burnt were driven off and hidden in the woods, the dead were buried: by noon the next day the road and the river bank were tidied up.

I drove my party back to the town, for I didn't care to sleep close to the enemy with the partisans too excited to give us protection, and also because we were nearly out of ammunition. At dawn I sent Reeve-Walker, the South African, with 'S' Patrol to recruit labour and dig approaches to the ford below the blown bridge. He got about one hundred men, but being much pestered by German snipers he could not complete the work much before dark.

I stayed the day in town to lay the basis of a civilian administration. I appointed Giuseppe Ferri, the university professor, civilian governor, with his brother, the major, under him to command the troops. Neither they nor their men were coming on with us: they had liberated their district and as far as active fighting was concerned the war was over for them. I did not press them, for I thought they had done enough, and I wanted them to keep the town tidy and enforce law and order till our military government took over. At noon the civilian governor had a problem for me: he had, he told me, about a dozen of Mussolini's Republican Fascists locked up in the town hall. What was he to do with them, shoot them or keep them to be handed over to our authorities? Knowing too well the tenderness of certain A.M.G.O.T. officers for former Fascists, I replied:

'When I leave tonight I shall have forgotten about your Fascist prisoners. Till our military government officers arrive you are the master and you do what you think best.' It would save trouble and bitterness for the future if these men got killed in the confusion of liberation. And if two or three innocents perished with them, by mistake or as a result of private feuds, well, war is wasteful of lives and many good men are killed in it every day.

Similar situations often occurred, and whenever I had at hand a sensible fighting partisan leader I made it my policy to leave matters to his discretion: if I could have guessed then what situation would develop in Italy after the liberation and in the following years, I might have been much more explicit in my suggestions.

Scores of British prisoners turned up during the day. They had escaped from the cages at the Italian Armistice, made their way south and, reaching the rich agricultural Marche region, had stayed there with the kind peasants, who fed them, clothed them and gave them pocket money. They numbered about twenty thousand in the Marche alone, but only a few hundreds had let themselves be persuaded by 'A' Force to attempt a return to our lines: the others preferred a lazy country-house life — entertained as they were now in one farm, now in another — to the risks of escape and the rigours of military life. Some of them had married farmers' daughters and talked of their estates; all had acquired an oddly exaggerated Italian appearance and many affected difficulty in expressing themselves in English (forgetting that we knew that, at most, nine months had elapsed since they had been thrown into this strange way of life). We found no New Zealanders amongst them: they had all walked back to our lines immediately after our landing in Italy; a few had remained to fight with the partisans.

I tried to organize a party of these prisoners to be guided back to our lines over the range, but they excused themselves on such pretexts that they must first settle their affairs or take leave of their friends. I believe many of them are still in Italy.

During the day a troop of three armoured cars of the Twelfth Lancers turned up. These adventurous youths had managed to slip in from the west where the German retreat was very disorderly. I liked their appearance, thought they would, with their armoured cars, be a precious addition to our strength and tried to persuade them to join forces with us. In spite of my assurance that I would, in due course, make it all right with their commanding officer, and though tempted to accept my offer, prudence and fear of authority prevailed in their minds.

That evening we had a dinner party with two hundred guests in the town hall, followed by speeches. I did my stuff and went to work again with Ferri in the mayor's office. The town was my prize and I wanted to give it a good send off: in a way it was to give these poor people a fresh start that I was fighting the Fascists and Nazis who preyed on them.

Ferri alone could not do all the work: his small band of municipal servants could not help him much in this emergency. I suggested that we set up a committee of citizens. Ferri thought they might be elected — he was a student of Political Economy and a great admirer of the British Constitution.

I said: 'You wouldn't have time to hold proper elections. This is what we shall do: we shall select the members together tonight. Then I shall nominate them according to the authority I hold from the Allied commander-in-chief, and as I shall leave tomorrow morning, nobody can undo it till A.M.G.O.T. arrives and you all go home anyway.'

We made out a list of possibles and called them for interview: we got a young doctor, the Dean of the University, three shopkeepers, three farmers, a schoolmaster, a priest, the widow of the man who had run the local bus service and who had been shot by the Germans, and five partisans, including of course Major Ferri as 'head of the police'. Representatives of the local gentry also came; they asked for improbable favours, such as to be given a car to take them to Rome, murmured names of duchesses and princesses, but refused to volunteer to do any work and then, illogically, left in a huff because they were not selected.

At five in the morning I swore in the new councillors and dismissed everyone. I was tired: these people talked so much. I embraced Ferri, had a cold bath and drove away with my men to the ford over the Potenza.

Out on the mountain road, quickened by a cool and lovely dawn, I reverted in my mind with pleasure from politics to considerations of war; turning over the things we had done since we had first crossed the range, I realized that there was an inescapable lesson to be drawn from our success: it was that operations *behind* the enemy lines, which had been for two years my main concern, had, for the present, become obsolete. No doubt, if I pursued my old plan and penetrated deeply into enemy territory, as I believed I could now do, I might enjoy an easy time in areas of relative tranquillity, and at the same time earn for myself and my men (from the uninformed) an undeserved reputation for spectacular daring. But I would be wasting my opportunities and shirking my duties, which, as I saw them, lay in remaining *in* the disrupted German front line to harass and hound the enemy: a policy both arduous and unspectacular, accompanied by many risks, but the only one likely to bring in dividends in the shape of military advantages. During the short drive to the ford I scrapped all my previous arrangements and made new plans for immediate action.

Two German snipers, who on the previous day had inflicted several casualties on Reeve-Walker's working party, were still hiding in the willows on the far bank: they fired at us with their rifles as we approached the ford, delaying us for a while. The determination of these men was a demonstration to us of what could be achieved by small means cunningly used; under a different uniform, we would have been glad to count them in our party. When, chased off by our overwhelming fire power, they took to the open, we let them escape.

Towed by bullocks, our sodden jeeps, the water rippling over the bonnets, made the far bank of the Potenza. Here we separated: I sent Yunnie with 'B' Patrol to the north-west, 'S' and 'R' Patrols to the east; with 'Blitz' Patrol I followed the second party later in the day, with the supplies we had accumulated carried in captured German transport.

My instructions were that they should operate in the high mountains, fifteen miles on each side of the watershed of the Apennines. Along this front, roughly equal to one-quarter of the width of Italy from sea to sea, and working to a depth of twenty to thirty miles into enemy territory, they were to seek out the Germans and harass them in every manner local circumstances and their own ingenuity would suggest. My intention was to compel the enemy to withdraw more

461

rapidly in the centre than on either flank. I expected that his main forces in the coastal sectors, feeling their inland flank uncovered, might open their minds to suggestions of withdrawal (to keep in step with their light troops in the mountains) and offer a less stubborn resistance to our Eighth and Fifth Armies. We were the only Allied troops in the central mountains; on either flank we were supported by armoured-car regiments with whom we made occasional contacts. For the next few months, let loose amongst the enemy in the mountains, we carried out, on the whole successfully, this plan conceived on my morning ride to the ford.

Our men were happier than at any time since we had left the desert. Engaging the enemy day after day was more on the scale of their understanding than long-range raids during which they were little more than bodyguards to their leader; constant fighting called for individual action, and their personal success could be measured unmistakably by the number of villages they liberated. They developed an enthusiasm for their work, a sense of personal achievement and an attachment to their friends in the patrol which they had never known before in their lives. Every day each one had to use his ingenuity to discover means of worrying the enemy; if they ran into danger, their companions helped them out of trouble; and, the day's work over, they rejoiced together over their narrow escapes, their stratagems and the discomfiture of the enemy: for they proved more than a match for the bewildered Germans. In seventy-eight days, although their numbers never exceeded fifty at any one time, they cleared sixteen hundred square miles of mountains, enticed several thousand Germans sixty miles back, killed over three hundred, and yet lost themselves but one man killed, and three wounded who recovered and rejoined the unit.

As there were in this area few organized partisans, our first task was to provide our own intelligence. Four or five days after crossing the Potenza 'B' Patrol had pushed on fifteen miles to the neighbourhood of Fabriano, and the remainder of the unit was in the mountains south-west of Cingoli. We found that the enemy controlled with a Jaeger Division the four main roads, had a strong garrison with artillery in Fabriano and kept detached posts in isolated villages. The forested mountainside was ours: the ranges rose to four thousand feet, with peaks over five thousand, and were not everywhere so steep that with infinite labour we could not drive our jeeps over them. The mountain villages were often linked by extremely rough and narrow tracks used by the villagers for their bullock-drawn sledges, and running at improbable angles up the slopes and through the forests. His jeeps crawling along such tracks, Bob Yunnie reached a village which he used as his headquarters for a while. From there he undertook to chase the Germans out of a town in the valley below, between him and the front line. To shake their nerve he marched his men under cover to fire Very lights from many positions, simulating preparations for a night attack. At dawn, when he expected them to have relaxed after the anxieties of the dark, he engaged them with his jeeps, rushing from one position to another to give the impression of a large force; finally in the twilight he charged up the main street with three jeeps and set the enemy on the run. The same day he appeared in another valley over a mountain range and raided a village; the following night he captured a mortar post outside yet another village. This deception work gave his men hardly a chance to rest; when they were not fighting they were hauling their vehicles over mountain ranges. The success of these schemes was based on striking at places far apart in such quick succession that to the puzzled German commander, reading the reports from his several posts, it seemed that they had all been attacked simultaneously. Three days went by, and the Germans, thinking that their positions had been penetrated by overwhelming enemy forces, called in their outposts and withdrew altogether from these valleys.

The following day Yunnie had one of his hunches, that his position was no longer secure; he suddenly took his patrol right over the ridge of the Apennines in the most difficult climb ever made by our jeeps, and descended on the other side on a small town called Gualdo Tadino, surprised and beat away a large party of foraging Germans, and, establishing himself in the neighbourhood, started operations in virgin country. Four days later, Gino, who, sick with malaria, had had to be left behind in the original village, joined them by a devious route, in civilian clothes, driving a bullock cart in which he carried some petrol jettisoned before the climb: he brought the news that after the patrol's departure the enemy had turned up a battalion strong, and made directly for a ruined monastery, Yunnie's former headquarters (informed no doubt by some Fascist). Disappointed, they had turned on to the village and captured and shot a small group of partisans who had befriended our men. Gino had escaped disguised as the village idiot. A few days later 'B' Patrol recrossed the Apennines by another route — they preferred that the same tracks should never be used twice — surprised and destroyed a battalion headquarters, then pushed a reconnaissance to within sight of Fabriano, which they found too strongly held to be attempted before the Germans' will to resist had been further softened.

Yunnie crossed the Apennines once more — three days of hard work this time, rolling boulders and cutting tracks. Travelling along the hillside, one jeep, a rock giving way under its offside wheels, turned over sideways and rolled down the mountain till fortunately stopped by a tree. The gunner, Stewart, was thrown clear; the driver, O'Neil, pinned underneath, was recovered with a broken back. The jeep, its frame warped, was still in running order but too weak to be used on patrol work. They tied O'Neil on to a plank, and, while the two jeeps remaining in the patrol pushed on, the third one drove him back along the road, through a German post and twenty miles back to where they knew of a position held by the Twelfth Lancers, who took charge of the casualty. Three months later he was back with us, weak but indomitable. I appointed him armourer for he was not fit to go into action.

I succeeded in getting through to Yunnie three new jeeps manned by members from his patrol and two recruits.

Meanwhile the two other patrols operated together further east. Sometimes driving, at times on foot, we pushed our way up towards Cingoli. 'S' Patrol, the latest-born of our patrols, was taking shape under the leadership of Reeve-Walker. The partisans here were divided into rival bands, with no strong leaders. They had a few Jugoslav

[facing: JEEPS IN ACTION IN ITALY

members who did all the work, while the others sat back and quarrelled: as a result we had to do much slow reconnaissance ourselves. We decided to capture some prisoners for information from a small village in which the local peasants reported a German post. Reeve-Walker with O'Leary and Hodgson of his patrol, Sanders, the New Zealander, and Porter of 'R' Patrol, set out on foot about ten in the morning. They worked their way into woods above the village, where Reeve-Walker, rather rashly, told them to wait while he went to reconnoitre. Later they heard some firing, and fearing their short South African leader had run into trouble, walked into the village. The time was noon on a very hot July day, the streets were empty, the inhabitants in hiding and the Germans at their meals in the coolness of the houses. They looked into several houses and finally walked into the signallers' office where three Germans were lunching. Our men held them up and made them walk away with them, carrying their wireless sets. Half way down the street, fun started: shot at from above, they fired back, and started running along the sun-scorched street. One of the Germans was hit and fell; our men, with their two remaining prisoners, darted down an alley, out of the village into a dry stream bed where they lay low till the hue and cry died down. Sending Hodgson on with the prisoners, Sanders, Porter and O'Leary walked back into the village in search of Reeve-Walker. The dead German had been removed, but they picked up his set, and having got engaged in a second street fight, gave up their search and returned.

Sitting with the jeeps half a mile away, we had fired a few bursts of intimidation in the direction of the village when we heard the rumpus. Then, quiet falling, we had waited a long time. Finally Hodgson and his two prisoners arrived; half an hour later Sanders, Porter and O'Leary, sweating under their load of wireless sets, reported their failure to find Reeve-Walker. We were getting together a relief party when he too appeared down a dry watercourse, kicking a stone and whistling to himself. He had waited to see the Germans pack up and leave the village.

The prisoners, interrogated while they were still flustered, talked willingly, and, being signallers, knew the location of the German units in and around Cingoli. With this useful information we succeeded a few days later in pushing the enemy out of another village just short of Cingoli, but the town itself we found too hard a nut to crack and gave it up for the time being.

From the reports of Yunnie, I judged that the time was ripe to make an attempt against Fabriano, and accordingly I joined him with all my men at Gualdo Tadino.

Harrying the enemy daily, Yunnie had pushed them back ten miles along the road leading north from Gualdo Tadino, and had thus cleared the way to the entrance of a railway tunnel which, passing under the ridge of the Apennines, joined our valley with that of Fabriano. The road which passed over the mountain had been blown by the Germans and could not be made practicable without considerable work. In the tunnel seven railway trucks had been crashed together and then blown up, bringing down part of the roof. The Germans in Fabriano thought themselves secure from that quarter and concentrated their defences in other directions. They had some field artillery as we found out when, to confuse them, we staged diversionary attacks from the north and the east. I recruited local labour and cleared the tunnel: we had discovered an oxy-acetylene torch and a few cylinders of gas in a workshop in a small town called Nocera Umbra, which enabled us to cut up the tangled remains of the trucks in the tunnel. While we were thus getting ready, Yunnie switched over his activities to Gubbio, fifteen miles to the north-west, and harassed the Germans there, crossing the mountains every day by a different track, his object being to deceive the enemy into believing that he had lost interest in Fabriano. Meanwhile I had observers in the town, in particular a partisan called Gigi Cardona, a former regular officer in the Italian Army, whom Yunnie had recruited earlier and who had become a brilliant member of his patrol. One night, when I judged by his reports that the time had come, I sent 'S' and 'R' Patrols through the cleared tunnel: before dawn Reeve-Walker had ten jeeps in the main square and had set fire to German Headquarters; by midday the town was ours, and by the next morning all German troops lying south of Fabriano had been withdrawn, leaving the way clear for our orthodox troops to come up and take over the town from us. Two days later the Household Cavalry, an armoured regiment, freshly arrived from home, and, I believe, in action for the first time, made its way cautiously up the road. Either our intelligence reports had not reached them from Eighth Army, or they had disbelieved them; coming within artillery range of Fabriano they sited their field guns and opened up. Reeve-Walker in the town, finding himself under fire from our own troops, drove out to Regimental Headquarters and demanded to talk with the commanding officer. An angry interview developed between our cocky little South African and a supercilious colonel of the Household Cavalry, who found it hard to accept the claim of a scrubby, unshaven ragamuffin of a lieutenant to have liberated with twenty-two men a town which he was planning to reduce according to the rules with an armoured regiment; at one stage Reeve-Walker came very near to being put under arrest, but eventually the South African made his point and led a patrol of armoured cars into Fabriano.

Our relations were much more brotherly with the Twelfth Lancers on our left flank. Knowing that greater mobility, knowledge of the enemy and the fact that our men could operate in small groups on their own initiative, without the guidance of officers, gave us advantages over the more elementary methods which, perforce, they had to use, they gave us all the support they could; they consolidated our gains for us, and set us free to pursue the enemy. I found a spirit akin to our own amongst the officers of the regular cavalry and of the Yeomanry regiments, and they generously allowed me to draw many good recruits to P.P.A. from their 'other ranks'. At one time or another during the war we co-operated happily with the King's Dragoon Guards, the Twelfth Lancers, the Twenty-Seventh Lancers and the Derbyshire Yeomanry. Their officers understood warfare, took great care of their men and invariably rose to the occasion when placed in unorthodox situations. There was an unaccountable gulf between their brilliant alertness and the infantilism of so many brave Guards officers, who, although drawn on the whole from the same class of men, knew how to die — and little else.

During these operations we were much dispersed. Scarcely a day passed without an engagement of which no more than the result was reported to me on the wireless. When we came together, like all soldiers, we talked of the fun we had had, the girls, the food and the wine, but very seldom of fighting: thus I have no knowledge, or only at second hand, of scores of actions in which our men were engaged. Corporal Owen, one of Yunnie's men, has written an account of some of his experiences (as yet unpublished), from which I shall give an extract referring to an incident which took place at the time 'B' Patrol was clearing the road leading north from Gualdo Tadino to Scheggia, while the rest of us were clearing the tunnel:

'. . . At about four o'clock in the afternoon a civilian came with the news that the Germans had evacuated Scheggia. I thought this un-likely and so did the Skipper (Bob Yunnie). "We'll go in and see, just the one jeep," he said. From the second that we sat in that jeep, the Skipper driving, myself as gunner and Gino sitting between us with a tommy gun, I knew that we were running into a trap. I was as sure as I had ever been sure of anything in my life that we were driving into an ambush. We drove round P.P.A. Corner (a bend in the road where 'B' Patrol had been heavily mortared on previous reconnaissances). . . For the first time no mortars greeted us. Then suddenly to me everything in the world, except the jeep we were driving in, stood still. The valley stretched out in front of us — the winding road along which we were travelling towards the waiting Germans — the jeep and my two companions comprised the whole of my world. Not a sound anywhere, not a movement, not even a breath of air.

'I had forgotten my pals — the unit — my people back home. My life seemed to have started the moment we came round the Corner, and how long it would last depended on how much I concentrated on my gun and that white house (a building which had been found pre-viously occupied by a German machine-gun post). Every time it was the house — the house — the house. My .50 was cocked and aimed at the enemy positions. I sat forward in my seat, my nose almost against the gun. Glancing at the Skipper, I said to him: "They are waiting for us, Skipper – they are sitting there waiting for us." He said, "I don't think so," but by his tone I could tell that he knew just as well as I. What a man! I hoped they would miss with their first burst. I could see the haystacks, the cemetery, the white house; nearer and nearer we came. Houses on the left shut out our view. We stopped. Gino said, "I think it is all right to carry on." Then he said something about having nothing to worry about as there was a cemetery ready down there. We carried on – slowly – slowly. A high bank on the right hid the haystacks – the cemetery disappeared below a rise in front of us. The Skipper said, "We'll stop here." We were hidden from the haystacks and the cemetery but the white house – now with its gable end towards us – was on our left, a little more than a hundred yards away. There was one window facing us – an upstairs window, open.

'I stepped out of the jeep, swinging the .50 towards the house. My right foot had hardly touched the ground when the awful stillness was shattered by the rattle of a spandau (the British nickname for the German equivalent of our bren gun). Something seemed to pluck at my hair and bury itself in the bank behind me. I ducked instinctively, at the same time pressing the trigger of my gun. Now I was all for it, I had come back to earth. I absolutely splattered the house with bullets, not forgetting the bushes around it, while the Skipper started reversing the jeep. I walked sideways along with it, still firing, with Gino spraying the vicinity with his tommy gun. Something began to smoke at the house as the Skipper shouted: "Jump in, Ben." I jumped into the jeep – still firing the gun with one hand. As Bob (Yunnie) backed I held on to the seat with my left hand and fired the gun at right angles to the jeep with my right.

'Bob (Yunnie) turned the jeep right hand down into a gateway, which brought the house immediately in front of me. I aimed the gun quickly and pressed the trigger – flashes of light shot off the walls. . . . Another gun opened at us from the red roofs of the cemetery as we began to move forward. I just had time to give him a burst from the .30 (the jeep carried a .50 inch gun forward and a .30 in the rear) before we were hidden by the houses on the roadside. "Get that .30

going, Ben," the Skipper shouted. I didn't say anything but waited until the house, haystacks and cemetery came into view again. They did, with a bang, as mortars fell in front of us . . . I dimly heard the crashes of the mortar shells as they exploded all around us, but was too busy to look where they were falling. We roared up the road and round P.P.A. Corner . . . We breathed again as we pulled up in Villa Colle di Canale . . . The rest of the patrol were there . . . Then we went in search of the man who had informed us that the Germans had evacuated Scheggia, but, as we expected, he could not be found. Another Fascist who had almost caused our downfall . . . It wasn't till I sat talking to Popski and Lieutenant Reeve-Walker that I realized how near a thing our latest escape had been.'

This was just a day's work. The men liked it. Owen wrote a few days later:

'. . . I was still the Skipper's gunner, enjoying myself immensely. I look on these days as Bob Yunnie's gunner as the most interesting I spent during the whole war.'

What made their life bearable was that engagements were short and they could pull out to comparative safety, and the comfort of peasant hospitality. Thus the tension was broken, and although for three months they were not one day out of danger, they showed little signs of strain. The successful soldier forgets unpleasant experiences very quickly; if he doesn't he is not a successful soldier: he finds his way to hospital as a psychiatrist's case. Brave men experience fear — only morons are never afraid — but they forget it, forget it again and again.

Breaking a long spell of administrative duties, Jean Caneri took over command of P.P.A. when I went to hospital for some weeks.

Bringing fresh ideas to the game, he led his patrol at a furious pace and extended the activities of P.P.A. over a wider territory than we had ever covered. By some accident he never even got a wound.

We pursued our games till the Germans retired behind a line of prepared positions stretching from Pesaro on the Adriatic to Pisa on the Mediterranean (which we called the Gothic Line); we then pulled

out and drove to a castle near Perugia, whence Caneri had transferred
our base. We stayed there a few days to refit.

As I thought that Eighth Army would shortly break through the
Gothic Line, I wanted to have our patrols equipped with fresh jeeps
and ready for the final chase across the Po plain up to the Alps. This
done we would, I thought, transfer ourselves to another theatre: I
wrote to friends I had on the planning staff, asking them to include
P.P.A. amongst the troops to be sent out to the Far East.

Curtis had been sergeant in my H.Q. Patrol ever since I took
him out of Yunnie's patrol, when he had given signs of battle weariness. Recovered very rapidly, he had been indefatigable with me
ever since. He had to serve the other patrols — repair and replace the
jeeps and the wireless sets, supply them with ammunition and with
petrol, and at the same time fight our own battles. He was at that
period the busiest man in the unit and the most exposed. He stepped
on a mine while clearing a ford, lost a foot and died in hospital a few
days later. He was a quiet little man with an irrepressible cheerfulness,
and the most entertaining manner of turning his narrow escapes into
funny stories. One of the pillars of P.P.A., he could not be
replaced.

Sam Taylor was not happy with me as my gunner, although I liked
him and trusted him. Perhaps, taking over from Cameron, he felt
his position difficult, as between Cameron and myself there had been
a deep friendship; more probably Taylor didn't like me and preferred
to be with his own friends in his original patrol. I made him sergeant
in 'R' Patrol when Sanders left us to go back to New Zealand, and I
chose for my companion an untried newcomer called Charles Burrows,
a butcher from Plymouth, a plain and rather shy lad of twenty-three.
Yunnie had rejected him from his patrol but I fancied there were signs
of valour in him and gave him a try. I did well for myself with this
choice, for a little more than two months later he brought me out of
a scrap in which, but for his steadfastness, I myself, along with thirty
other men, would undoubtedly have perished.

Reeve-Walker left us about this time and I appointed John Campbell to command 'S' Patrol in his stead.

Sergeant Beautyman's turn came to go home under the 'Python' scheme. At first he was disposed to let another go in his stead, then he changed his mind and asked to be released. He had not been on home leave for over five years, and yet I was surprised that he should wish to go, for I had cut my ties so completely that I had no life of my own outside the army. However, we were always ready with a substitute for any of us who might fall out: Brooks took command of the signal section, and, sorrowfully, I let Beautyman go. He went home, got married to a girl he had known all his life, served for a while in England, didn't like it and wangled his way back to P.P.A. six months later.

CHAPTER VIII

CLOAK AND DAGGER

EIGHTH ARMY forced the Gothic Line and reached Rimini, the gateway to the plain. While the town was being cleared I stayed with Nick Wilder, now in command of a tank regiment, the New Zealand Divisional Cavalry. When an infantry officer rises to command a battalion, he often shrivels up under the unwelcome strain of having to direct his men from the relative security and the awful loneliness of a command post in the rear; more fortunate, the commander of an armoured regiment actually leads his tanks on the ground and is with his men during the battle: Wilder, preparing to take his tanks into the last battle of the war in Europe (as we thought), had the same solemn boyish eagerness with which he had led a patrol of five trucks in the desert.

We waited, poised for the chase — then after three days we knew there would be no chase.

Intersected by a network of rivers and drainage canals, deeply set between banks sometimes fifty feet high, the Po plain was even less suitable for a pursuit than the mountainous country we had left behind. The map had told us this all the time, but we had hoped that the enemy would lose heart after the breach of the Gothic Line and run for the Alps. He didn't. He blew the bridges and held us up every few miles behind a canal bank. Our air force destroyed all the bridges over the Po; at night the Germans swung pontoon bridges across the river and drove bullock carts laden with supplies over to their troops further south.

It was a cruel anti-climax to the hopes of every man in Eighth Army: wondering if the war would be settled in Germany (where our troops were nearing the Rhine) before they even reached the Po, they applied themselves once more to pushing the enemy back from one river to the next.

473

I told my men that the pursuit was off, and went in search of a new role for P.P.A.

On November 1st, 1944, I crossed the Savio River on a Bailey bridge just put up by the sappers, and from the high bank looked northwards on to a desolate landscape. Rain had been falling for some days: the river in spate rushing through a breach in its bank had flooded the flat countryside as far as the next canal, its banks just visible through the mist. A few farmsteads stood out, in water up to the window sills. Bob Yunnie and five of his men walked away along the submerged road, up to their waists in the turbid flood, looking rather unheroic. When they reported back four hours later, we lifted each of our jeeps into a D.U.K.W. and drove the amphibious trucks down on to the water. By nightfall we were settled on the dry edge of a pine forest stretching from the main road three miles to a sandy sea coast.

Some partisans were camped in the wood; they told us that the next canal, one mile to the north, was held by German troops. We pushed the jeeps a hundred yards distance from a keeper's lodge which served the partisans as a headquarters, and, taking turns on guard duty, settled down to an uneasy night's rest under the rain amidst the creaking trees. The D.U.K.W.s were sent back to Savio.

The partisan leader asked me to join him at supper in the lodge. He had in two rooms some thirty men and three girls. The rest of his detachment, eighty-odd, were out on duty. Wearing the red scarves of the Garibaldi Brigade over their civilian clothes, armed with German weapons, they looked wild but their speech was low and their manners subdued, for they were weary. They had fought the Germans continuously for the last four months in the flat country around Ravenna and finally, being overrun, their detachment was separated from its brigade and left in no-man's-land, where we had now joined them. I had for some time been in wireless contact with their brigade commander, who went by the name of Bulow (a battle name derived from the word for bull in Romagnolo dialect), and I had on three occasions put out to sea in an Italian motor launch to visit him in the marshes north of Ravenna, and been forced back by the weather every time. These M.A.S. were perhaps the fastest craft afloat (the Italians claimed they reached fifty-five knots on trial), but so unseaworthy that they capsized as soon as there was any sea at all.

The leader of the detachment was a burly stone-mason of thirty-four years of age called Ateo, 'Atheist'. The name was not a battle disguise but his own by right, for he had been thus named at birth as a token of his father's anti-clericalism. His speech was rough and mixed with no little of harsh Romagnolo dialect in which, when I got to understand it, I found he expressed himself with a richness of homely imagery. There is in Romagna (the region which occupies the south-east corner of the Po Valley) an ancient tradition of independent thinking and of popular impatience with tyranny. The Romagnoli revolted early against the secular power of the Church; after the unification of Italy, contemptuous of the powers of government and asking for no one's help, the workers and peasants organized themselves in co-operatives of labour which even the Fascists could not dissolve. The Socialists found more adherents here than anywhere in Italy; when the Communist Party was formed after the first war it spread rapidly and maintained a steady underground resistance to Fascist encroachments.

After the Italian Armistice, the Romagnoli, trained to administer their own affairs in the co-operatives, and helped by the sound organization and the strong discipline of the Communist Party, soon ran the most efficient partisan formation in Italy.

Ateo was a Communist and so were the majority of his men — but by no means all. The officers were elected by their men: the appointment had to be confirmed by higher authority, who held also the power to dismiss. A political commissar in each detachment was responsible for the morale of his unit and instructed it in political doctrine, and also took his share of the normal duties of a fighting officer.

I knew nothing of the things I have just related at the time I first met the detachment: considering them with a professional eye I soon perceived that they were good soldiers and of a quality quite new to me in my experience of partisans. I decided to take them under my command and make them fight alongside my own seasoned warriors. My first favourable impression came in this way: I obtained for them British weapons, clothing and equipment and asked Ateo what in his opinion would be the best way to issue these to the men so as to avoid waste. His answer was that his quartermaster, a medical student called Camerani, would take charge and I could rest assured that there would be no wild scramble such as I had witnessed with other partisans in other places. And so it turned out: Camerani locked his new stores in a room of the lodge and entered them in his books. When he had done, he issued each man with his needs and no more: he had a nominal list of deficiencies and asking for additional items was a waste of time. Ida, our leading girl, having been fitted with a battledress, wanted also an automatic; when she couldn't get one — indeed Camerani had none to issue — I am sorry to say she swiped one off John Campbell, but returned it when she was made to understand that the young captain could be court-martialled for losing his pistol. Ida, in spite of her love of weapons, was not supposed to take a hand in the fighting; she was our chief spy and messenger. Tough but comely in her usual appearance, she dressed up for her errands as a dirty and repulsive old woman: no German soldier ever looked at her when she shuffled past them carrying a bundle of sticks. She was then indeed, to all practical purposes, invisible.

The two other girls cooked and washed for the detachment and occasionally took their turn on guard duty. They were nice, simple, hard-working peasant girls, who never thought they had done any-thing out of the way in joining the partisans; the same applied to the men, who were remarkably free from heroics. Camerani was the only intellectual in the detachment: Taschiero, Guberti and Rafuzzi, the three company commanders, and Dario Gradi, the political commissar, were stone-masons or mechanics, the rest likewise stone-masons or agricultural labourers, all born within fifteen miles of Ravenna in peasant homes. In the fertile Romagna plain every foot of land is cultivated: apart from the strips of pine forest and marsh along the coast, it provides no hide-outs, and partisan fighting had perforce been interwoven with the lives of the peasants. Their troops came out at night from the farms to raid traffic, dumps and German headquarters, and relied on their fathers, their mothers and all their elderly relations to give them refuge again until their next operation, so that there was actually no real distinction between fighters and civilians. Arms and ammunition were concealed under haystacks and in barns: when the Germans went out foraging for food the farmers' wives, who were compelled to entertain them, kept a serene face, for if they aroused the suspicions of their guests there would be no escape from the shooting party. By the time we arrived, however, the German withdrawal had filled the land with troops and pushed the partisans into the coastal strips, giving a precarious ease to the farmers.

To test my partisans I gave them the most unpalatable task of all: guarding us and our jeeps while we slept at night. They acquitted themselves of their duty so conscientiously that I decided that it would be safe to trust them further, and soon I had them attached in groups to each of our patrols. I tried to give them a defensive role, not because they lacked aggressive qualities, but I had scruples about exposing them in such actions as might cause them to be captured by the enemy: the difference in the treatment by the Germans of British and partisan prisoners-of-war was never out of my mind. The equanimity with which the Italians exposed themselves to the risk of an ignominious end by torture, which *we* would have been reluctant to accept, showed how much more passionate than ours was their determination to fight. They had emotional motives with their roots in hatred and revenge, fundamental human impulses which played but a small part in our lives; they fought in their own villages for their own homes, which had been ravished not only by a foreign enemy but by some of their own traitorous people, Mussolini's Fascist republicans, whom, as is natural, they held in extreme contempt. Lastly they were animated by a passionate desire to redress social injustice and establish a new rule in their own country, when freed at last of its hated tyrants. Although they took care not to let themselves be diverted from the task of beating the Germans, their fight was fundamentally a civil war. We, on the other hand, had been away from our country for several years, fighting in strange lands, and though our families had also suffered from the violence of the enemy, it was through the anonymity of bombing aircraft, and not the personal assault of a ruffianly soldiery. Such are human feelings that the loss of relatives crushed to death under a crumbling house is easier to bear than the knowledge that an insolent *feldwebel* has laid his dirty hands on their bodies and dragged them to a cold-blooded execution. We saw this strange discrimination in the behaviour of the Italians themselves, who accepted resignedly, as an act of fate, the terrible losses inflicted by our bombing but shook with rage at the forcing of their homes by marauding Germans.

In spite of all this it must not be thought that the partisans behaved as bloodthirsty fanatics: cheerful and good-humoured, they were soon adopted by our men as friendly companions. Each one of our patrols came to be affectionately proud of their own Italians and boasted of their high deeds and of their tricks. The partisans, on their side, ceased to feel that we were a superior kind of people and joked and fooled about with their English comrades in the perfect equality of soldiers fighting together the same battle.

Rain-drenched and half-flooded, the Pineta di Classe (a pine forest of Byronic fame) and the sand dunes on the coast were our battleground. The prospect was dismal and the scope limited after the hopes we had had of chasing the Germans to the Alps, but although we were under command to 'Porter Force', which operated on our left, we were in practice our own masters, and our men settled down happily to their task of destroying the Germans in the forest. Colonel Porter, who gave his name to a force of armoured and artillery regiments which had been put under his command for the operations against Ravenna, was one of the most brilliant of the band of cavalry officers who came into prominence during the war. He had trained his own regiment, the Twenty-Seventh Lancers, by unorthodox and imaginative methods, which had turned it into the most efficient armoured-car unit we had in Italy. He lent us his support when we required it, but otherwise gave us an entirely free hand in our sector. I learnt much from him of a type of warfare in many ways new to me.

We had a good time in our forest. With good cover and ferrying our jeeps over the floods into unexpected positions, we soon had the Germans puzzled and nervous. We pushed them out of the positions they had occupied when we first arrived, and as soon as we were comfortably established half way up the forest, we undertook to outflank them by landings on the coast. To do this we loaded our jeeps in D.U.K.W.s — one of which was fitted with a crane for this purpose — and sailed them at night from a beach in our rear. When the distance was too great to be covered by the slow-sailing D.U.K.W.s, whose speed in the water was under five knots, we loaded the amphibians (each carrying a jeep) into L.C.T.s, and, having reached a position off our chosen landing beach, drove them out of the landing craft into the sea and made the land under our own power. Thus we avoided the need to beach the L.C.T. such as had brought us to disaster at the mouth of the Tenna. The D.U.K.W.s ashore, we lifted the jeeps out of them and proceeded on our business. The empty amphibious craft sailed back and by a tricky manœuvre drove up the ramp from the water into the waiting L.C.T.s. Sergeant Porter became our chief expert on these operations, for he liked to turn fanciful projects into practical realities. He worked hard and long at his undertakings; when he was ready he demonstrated his results with a boyish smile and a tremendous confidence. We all thought how easy it all really was.

After many practice exercises we thought we had fairly mastered the elaborate technique of these operations, but one night I got into trouble when I was taking back two empty D.U.K.W.s from a landing point on the enemy coast to a beach in the rear. The distance being but ten miles the trip was to be done by the D.U.K.W.s under their own steam. We sailed at dusk: our course was to hug the coast for twelve minutes, then out to sea, due east, for twenty minutes, then seventy-five minutes on a bearing of 170° magnetic; finally a run in of a few minutes due west would take us to the beach at Cesenatico. The second D.U.K.W. ran aground on a mud bank a few minutes after we had left, just as a thick fog descended on the sea, and my own craft also got entangled. We floundered for a quarter of an hour before we both got clear, when I made directly for the open sea. To avoid losing my escort in the fog (she was manned by two R.A.S.C. drivers who were not very good at navigation) I had to slow down to a speed that I could only estimate very approximately, thus putting out my calculations. When I thought

I was two miles at sea, I turned south. There had been no wind and no sea until now, but as we turned we were struck head on by a squall, and a few minutes later the sea was covered in foam with high waves running. Even in calm water a D.U.K.W. with its tiny rudder tends to yaw as much as thirty degrees and you have to keep playing on the wheel to keep her on a course. In the gale that was now blowing we found it a problem to keep our head into the wind. Spray and rain soaked us and got into the prism of my service compass, which was all I had to steer by. I handed over the wheel to the driver while I crouched under the dashboard, trying to find a dry piece of cloth to clean the compass. I told him to keep her head into the wind: either he misunderstood me or he gave the wrong turn on the wheel, for a moment later we had broached to and were rolling in the trough of the waves, with the sea pouring over our sides. When we finally succeeded in getting her head back into the wind we were nearly waterlogged and our escort had vanished. Any precaution against being seen being now pointless, we turned on our headlights and were relieved to see our escort do the same about a quarter of a mile ahead: better sailors than we were, they had kept on their course. For two hours we remained hove to, the engine dead slow, struggling to keep in the wind. With the compass out of action I had no idea from which quarter the wind was now blowing and for all I knew we might be heading for the Dalmatian coast. In any case there was nothing we could do about it: if we had tried to steer off the wind we would inevitably have foundered. Then the gale dropped suddenly, and though the sea was still running high, the craft became more manageable and I could devote myself to the compass and wipe the prism dry. By a coincidence, for my navigation had been pure guesswork, our wheels touched the bottom less than a mile from the spot on the coast I was making for.

After this escape I got myself a proper ship's compass and had larger rudders fitted to our sea-going D.U.K.W.s.

Successive landings allowed us to outflank the Germans, who were trying to hold us on the streams which intersected the forest, and in due course we squeezed them out into the open and in view of Ravenna. They never realized how we managed to get behind them and they

[*facing:* Left: ATEO
Right: BULOW]

thought that the coastal strip of dunes was still theirs: one afternoon a patrol of theirs commanded by a lieutenant walked into the camp 'R' Patrol had made in a hollow and were all captured. The officer was sent back to my H.Q. in Savio. Judging him to be a vain man and very much of a Prussian officer, I treated him with a ceremonial courtesy that broke down his defences. I told him in French, which he spoke elegantly:

'It is the fortune of war that you should have been captured. Will you please do me the honour to dine with me?' Ivan, scowling and with rage in his heart, served us a very special meal and plenty of drinks. My guest, a fanatical little Nazi, had absorbed the ferocious teachings of his masters and had expected to be jeered at and played with. When instead he was treated as a gentleman, which he certainly didn't deserve, and entertained to dinner by a (to him) high ranking officer, his vanity went to his head and he talked more than any prisoner-of-war I have known. I couldn't stop him. When, bowing and thanking me for my 'correct attitude', he finally left for the cage, I knew as much as he did of the defences of Ravenna. I knew also that the German Army, in spite of their reverses in Russia, in France and in Italy, had no idea that they were beaten, but were sustained by an unshakable faith in Hitler's secret weapons, and I guessed that they would go on fighting till they were on their knees.

I, on the other hand, felt that the end of the war was in sight and as a consequence I relaxed somewhat from the extreme caution with which I had, for years, weighed risks and husbanded our strength. With victory assured, our lives were no longer so valuable and we could allow ourselves to attempt some of the wilder schemes with which we had toyed in imagination for a long time but which I had put aside, thinking that the risk was not justified by the results we could hope to achieve. We could now relax somewhat from our austerity of purpose.

As it happened our most precious lives were not lost in acts of daring. The day after my party with the German lieutenant, 'R' Patrol was relieved by 'S' on the coast and sailed back to Savio for two days' rest. George Lee, a young Canadian, who now commanded it, reported very sadly that laying mines across a ford so as to protect their position, his sergeant, Dave Porter, had unaccountably blown himself up, together with Trooper Croghan who was assisting him. It was a great loss to all of us. Porter had been with P.P.A. since our early days in North Africa and was part of the very framework of the unit. Tall and burly, resolute and reliable, unmovable by fear or by excitement, I had always thought him, of all our men, the most comforting to be with in a tight spot. Whatever happened he was tranquil and assured, his orderly brain working in advance on problems that might crop up he was never caught unprepared. He came the nearest to being the ideal type of soldier we tried to turn out in P.P.A., lovable and by far the most popular man in the unit. Croghan, a newcomer, was not very well known; a quiet little man, Porter had taken him under his wing and had thought much of him.

With Waterson, Locke, Sanders and Beautyman gone, Cameron, Curtis and Porter killed, the group of men who had given its character to our unit was thinning out. Their successors, Riches, O'Leary, Sizer, Taylor, Moss, Galloway, Owen, Burrows, Cokes, didn't seem to me to have the same stature, the same solidity, their personalities seemed paler; but I was under the usual delusion of the older generation when it begins to feel lonely in life—that the giants they have known in their youth can't be equalled. For, three months later, they in their turn had graduated into the old guard. In the meanwhile, with Sergeant Brooks, S.Q.M.S. Davies, Stewart, Barnes, I would chat about the old days, only two years gone at most, but time moved fast with us.

Pushed out of the forest, the Germans blew the bank of the last river which stood between us and Ravenna and flooded the land. They kept only a chain of strong-points in farmsteads and ricks which they could reach by raised paths: they mined all other approaches and sat pretty.

Before tackling these we joined with the Twenty-Seventh Lancers in an operation against a village called Fosso di Ghiaia, which, strongly held, prevented their advance along the main road to Ravenna. The Lancers put in fifteen minutes' concentrated shelling, while we opened up from the flank with twenty machine guns, then we moved in along a canal bank in our jeeps, the Lancers coming in on foot from another direction. There was a tense moment when we approached Fosso di Ghiaia, our vehicles much exposed on the high bank to fire from the sunken village; we had two men wounded but a moment later we rushed the houses on foot and the Germans gave up. As we came out with fourteen prisoners (the Lancers got the rest), mortars and 88 mm. guns opened up on us. It was a narrow squeak but we brought the prisoners into the forest into comparative safety and lined them up to be searched and interrogated. Rather dazed at first, they suddenly realized that the war was over for them, and, with hoarse jokes, they unbuckled their leather belts and threw down on the ground these symbols of military servitude. We loved these men who, ten minutes previously, we had been trying to kill — as they had been trying to do to us. They were offered cigarettes, and Burrows, my gunner, produced a *fiasco* of wine and a mug to give them a sip each. While I interrogated them one by one, I noticed that those I had done with were taken away to where tea and breakfast was cooking for them. No orders had been given, it seemed a natural thing to do to men who had just been through a heavy ordeal. We delighted to find that the enemy, whom we so seldom saw alive at close quarters, were persons like ourselves. The partisans looked on, disapprovingly. Later in the day I had a request from Sergeant Davies, who had received a slight wound, that he be allowed to keep the prisoners for a few days as they had already proved themselves so helpful with the building of a bridge over the canal: the unit was trying to acquire fourteen more pets.

John Campbell, who now commanded 'S' Patrol, had shed his inhibitions and developed a reckless personality. Stationed in a farm called La Guaiadora, he had as next-door neighbours a German post in a farm called La Favorita. Several days running he sent one of his partisans, unarmed and in civilian clothes, with a can of milk to sell to the soldiers at La Favorita. Having thus obtained knowledge of the post and of its approaches through the minefields and the floods, as well as of the habits of its inmates, he made a plan to capture them all. At first I forbade the attempt, but he pleaded so urgently that I saw it would be hard on him and his men to prevent them from carrying out an enterprise on which they had set their hearts, and I let them go.

It must be remembered that Campbell had only been in action with his patrol for a short time and had not yet proved himself. I knew he could be foolish and he had an irritating weakness – he kept losing his guns, his mortar and even his own money; but I was impressed to see that he was backed by Sergeant Sizer, O'Leary and Hodgson, sensible and experienced men. Obviously if he had won their confidence there was more in Campbell than I suspected. Anyhow I let them go. They set out on foot very early one morning, guided by the milkman: creeping along in the dark on padded feet they reached a barn outside La Favorita and concealed themselves. The Germans were nearly all on guard duty round the farm at night, for they were fearful of being surprised, yet Campbell and his men came in so discreetly that nothing was heard. At dawn the Germans, relieved that another long night was over without an alarm, walked back to the house to breakfast and rest, leaving one sleepy man on guard at the door. Campbell gave them an hour to relax and then issued from the barn with his men and rushed the farm. The sentry was overpowered before he could realize what had happened, the others, some in bed, some drowsing over their breakfast, were disarmed without a shot fired or anybody hurt. O'Leary, swift and powerful, got six men out of the loft all by himself. They tidied up the farmhouse, left everything shipshape, and returned to La Guaiadora with their prisoners. When the German ration party came to La Favorita the following night they were deeply puzzled: there were no signs of a struggle, half-eaten food was still lying on the table and yet the whole complement of the post had vanished. I don't know what report they made to their headquarters, but no attempt was made to re-occupy the farm.

Such was the first of John Campbell's cloak and dagger operations. He made several more with equal success, till nearly all the posts on our side of the Fiumi Uniti, the river covering Ravenna, had been captured. The prisoners told us that wild spooky rumours were going around the German troops: the strange fact was that none of the posts thus captured were ever replaced. The other patrols also ran cloak and dagger operations, and a competition developed between them on which I kept a watchful eye. Plain and sober as most of our men were, they had this weakness: that they tended to develop a jealous pride each in his own patrol. In our early days I had played the patrols one against the other in emulation. I had soon become very careful to do exactly the opposite, for fear that they might become over-rash, trying to over-bid their companions or even be carried away to play tricks on each other.

One farm, the Casa del Guardiano, was so well covered by floods and mines that we never managed to get near it. Rickwood, fairly recovered now from his stomach wound and, at his request, once more in command of 'R' Patrol (against my better judgment for he was still far from well), tried to find a way into it by daylight, disguised as a shepherd — the only instance I know of any one of us operating in civilian clothes. He looked pretty convincing to me and had quite a manner with sheep, but he was greeted by bursts of machine-gun fire and had to retire, having lost five sheep. We got the Lancers to shell the place, but the Germans had shelters inside ricks which were immune even against a direct hit.

I had made friends with the pilot of an artillery observation plane, and Bob and I flew several times in his tiny Auster over our area. Then we had an idea, and getting from the R.A.F. a load of small obsolete twenty-five pound bombs, we practised hand bombing on a deserted beach. When I thought I was sufficiently expert, we took off one morning with nine bombs all over us in the cockpit. We had some difficulty in taking off with the extra load, but with a very long run we managed to become airborne. We circled the Casa del Guardiano, then ran in at sixty feet: I held a bomb out of the window and let it go when I thought the distance was correct. I overshot with the first one, undershot with the second, and got a direct hit with the third. As usual the Germans had not shown themselves at first, for no one cares to give away a position to an observation plane; our strange behaviour must have shaken them — nobody had ever heard of an Auster dropping bombs — so it was not till after the fifth drop that they opened up. Being unused to these things, though I heard a distant rattle of guns over the noise of the engine, I didn't realize at all that we were the target. I asked my friend the pilot to run in once more as I had still four bombs to dispose of, which he did and I quietly took aim and dropped bomb number six, which missed, then round again and got a hit. Said the pilot: 'Do you want to go in again?' I said: 'Why not?' and in we went. As we came out he drew my attention to certain holes which had appeared in the wing above us. I said: 'Our last one, what do you think?' He was a little thoughtful but came round again and flew over the farm at twenty feet. I thought we would hit the roof and was so alarmed that I pulled in my bomb and only dropped it when we were well beyond the target. I enjoyed the party more than my friend, who was a bit worried how he would account to his commanding officer for the bullet holes in his plane. I made a clean breast of the affair to his commander, who, being a sportsman, overlooked our misuse of the aircraft and allowed us to use his planes on other occasions.

One night I received a visit from Bulow, the partisan commander of Twenty-Eighth Garibaldi Brigade. He had sailed at night in a fishing smack from his headquarters in the marshes beyond Ravenna and landed at Cierva, in our lines. He was a little man of great vivacity, born in Ravenna, who before the war had been a student at an agricultural college. He had fought in Albania (a second lieutenant in the Royal Army) until he returned to Ravenna, after the Italian Armistice, to join the partisans and the Communist Party. Discovered by Longo, the head of the Italian resistance movement, who picked him out amongst the others for no other reason, I believe, than his experience in the army, he was given command of a brigade that didn't yet exist. He raised it, trained it and led it into action, and developed an ability for partisan warfare and an outstanding gift of leadership which surprises his countrymen, 'for', they say, 'he cannot talk'; and indeed, by Italian standards, he is no speaker. He had disrupted the German communications in Romagna and speeded up their withdrawal; now, having concentrated his forces in the pine forest and the marshes on the coast north of Ravenna, he prepared for an attack on the town concerted with our own advance. After the liberation of the town his brigade became a unit of Eighth Army and took part in the final rout of the Germans.

We struck up that night a friendship that has lasted and increased to this day. Not that the little man had at that time anything pleasant to say to me: he was rightly indignant that the supplies which had been promised had not yet been delivered, and the purpose of his visit was to tell all of us what he thought of our negligence. He had been to Eighth Army Headquarters before coming to me; he had received promises, and I undertook to see that they were kept. We made plans for a concerted attack on Ravenna, arranged wireless communications and such details, then we went and visited Ateo's detachment, which was part of Bulow's brigade. I was able to give him a very good account of the work done by Ateo since he had been with us. His partisans had indeed done extremely well, fighting not only with bravery but also with skill. They had lost several men killed and made no fuss about it. Bulow, whose real name is Arrigo Boldrini, left that same night and sailed back to his watery headquarters.

The civilians made no more fuss than the partisans about their dead. A peasant woman asked to see me and, after an apology for taking up my time, told her story: during the battle which had led to the liberation of Savio she had found herself with her family between the two armies; their village being shelled, they had taken shelter in the fields under a haystack. A shell unfortunately had burst quite close killing her husband, two of her daughters, her sister and an uncle. She herself and other members of the family had escaped unhurt and had been evacuated by us behind the river Savio. 'This happened ten days ago,' she said. 'It is not fit that our dead should remain any longer unburied. I have come to ask your permission to cross the Savio and collect the bodies.' She stood, dignified and very quiet, without tears, waiting for my answer. I offered to send a truck to recover the corpses, but she would have nothing of it. 'I don't want to cause any inconvenience. I can get a horse and a cart and that is all I need. My brother will go with me.'

A high medieval tower at the mouth of the Fiumi Uniti, occupied by the enemy, gave us great inconvenience as it compelled us to put out far to sea in our navigations along the coast, and it prevented a landing we wanted to make on the far bank of the river, where a convenient road led into Ravenna. We had tried to shell it but the walls were of stone and ten feet thick so Campbell offered to capture the tower by a crowning 'cloak and dagger'. We dropped him and his party on the coast, out of sight of the tower, and off they marched in the sand dunes, to spend two days snooping and observing. When they thought they knew enough they concealed themselves at night in a shed, a hundred yards from the tower, the only cover there was — for the tower stood on a bare knoll. After dawn, as usual, the Germans retired inside the tower and closed the door, a heavy affair of oak four inches thick. Our men waited in their shed, there was nothing else they could do. At last at eight-thirty a German came out to relieve nature, leaving the door ajar. Our men sprinted, unperceived by the look-out on top of the tower, floored the piddler, dashed up the winding staircase and captured the whole garrison. At nine I got a wireless signal that all was well. We sailed from down the coast and landed five jeeps and twenty partisans at the foot of the tower. The partisans took it over, Campbell concealed his jeeps in the sand dunes to give supporting fire if needed and promptly went to sleep, while the prisoners were shipped away. At eleven o'clock the German officer's orderly came along the path carrying his master's newly-pressed coat, entered the tower and was suppressed. At one a man came to look for the orderly, and never came out again. At four a patrol of six who came to look for the orderly and for the man were let in by our partisans, and remained in. At sundown a patrol of eighteen under a captain came to look for everybody. This time there was a bit of a fight; two Germans were killed, the sixteen others joined their companions in the dungeon.

There were no more visits that night and the next morning we found the last posts south of the Fiumi Uniti all evacuated.

CHAPTER IX

WHEELS IN VENICE

RAVENNA was entered two days later by Porter Force from the south, Canadian troops from the west, Bulow from the north and P.P.A. last of all from the east, for we had lingered by the way. Bulow was wounded in the arm: I had him attended to and took him to stay with me the night. If we had formed our opinion of Italian soldiers from the behaviour of the Royal Italian Army or from that of the fancy-dress partisans further south, Bulow would have upset all our notions. Here he was on the day of his victory, a wounded hero in his liberated native town: would he stay and enjoy his triumph? Active and restless as usual, he had no peace till he left once more for his marshes, where he had led so long the life of a frog. They lived there in clumps of muddy reeds, hardly a few inches above the water: all their movements were in punts, following invisible channels. They issued to raid the Germans every night, during the day they lay in the mud.

He left me the following night: the Germans still held in strength the port of Ravenna, and their supplies, coming along the beach, were a tempting target for Bulow's forces in the marshes.

Bulow was presented with the Italian Gold Medal for Valour by General Sir Richard McCreery, G.O.C.-in-C. Eighth Army, at a parade of partisan forces in Ravenna.

I promised to join Bulow with a patrol of P.P.A. in three days' time, and in the meanwhile I pushed 'R' Patrol up a road leading north from Ravenna till they made contact with the Germans. They found them half-hearted, and after a few shots had been exchanged, they withdrew. The next day our patrol was relieved by two troops of the Twenty-Seventh Lancers and fell back two miles to the rear in support. There was another pine forest here, and I put a post of Ateo's partisans under the trees to cover a bridge over a canal half a mile to the right of the Lancers.

Back in Ravenna I made arrangements with an aged expert to take me round the churches, which for many years I had wanted to visit. A few days previously I had had the luck to save from our shelling the church of San Apollinare in Classe, outside Ravenna. I had dimly remembered that it was decorated with sixth-century Roman mosaics of great beauty, and I had prevailed with the gunners to postpone the shelling twenty-four hours while I sent a party to visit the bell tower in which the Germans were believed to have an artillery observation post. I proved the rumour to be unfounded and saved the church. This act of virtue, the first in a long career of destruction, had left me so self-satisfied that I wished to visit the other monuments of Ravenna. My appointment being at eleven, I got up early and drove out in my jeep with Charlie Burrows, before breakfast, to visit the Lancers' post on the main road and the partisans in the wood.

The road rose on a ramp to be carried by a stone bridge over a canal, which ran to the sea between banks ten feet above the sodden plain. Just beyond the bridge a Lancer sergeant with three men had sited a bren gun in the middle of the road. The two troops were on the near side of the canal with a few bren guns under the canal bank on each side of the road, and the remainder of the men on the left of the road in a hut down in the fields, against which they had driven a scout car. Unused to infantry fighting they were ill at ease without their armoured cars. They had seen no enemy when I arrived. I thought the Germans were on the run — there had been little fight in them during the last few days — and I made a plan to reconnoitre forward on the next day with 'R' Patrol. I left Burrows with my jeep on the road eighty yards from the bridge (on our side), made him turn it round facing home (the only sensible thing I did that morning), told him I would be back in an hour and strolled away along the canal bank to the right towards the next bridge on which the partisans were on guard. With me was Gigi and one of Ateo's company commanders who had come to meet me. I found the partisans happy and much better organized than the Lancers, for the job was more in their line of business. They had patrolled forward as far as the next canal in the early morning and seen no enemy.

We made our way back to my jeep, Gigi and I. As the weather was fine for the first time in a month, we walked slowly along the bank discussing the possibility of finding guinea fowl in this forest as we had done in the Pineta di Classe. The road with the jeep on it came in sight; a hullabaloo broke out on our right, in the forest on the far side of the canal. Many guns were fired, mostly German by the noise, but we discerned also the fast, dry rattle of a bren.

Gigi said: 'A counter attack?' I nodded and we both slid down the bank into the field below, which was covered in a foot of water. Gigi ran splashing towards the road, I plodded along sedately: somehow it seemed undignified to run. As I got nearer, things began to whistle and whine over my head: I saw broken twigs showering down from the trees beyond the canal bank. Three Lancers came running, head down, over the bridge carrying a bren and plumped down out of sight on the far side of the road; the fourth, the sergeant, had been killed. Burrows was crouching by the side of the jeep, his shoulders hunched up. I felt guiltily that I had left him there, eighty yards from the front line, with no other instructions but to wait for me on the road, and there he was, waiting patiently when he could have taken cover.

Hoarse cries came from the bridge: German soldiers were pouring slowly over it, six abreast, between the parapets, yelling all the time to keep up their spirits. They were in no hurry: I fancied the men behind were pushing and those in the front row were holding back hard. Burrows, seeing at last somebody to fire at, came to life, got up, stretched himself, levelled the big gun at the back of the jeep, and fired: the tracer plunged into the solid human mass on the bridge, some men fell, the others drew back beyond the bridge. At that moment something hot and very noisy whizzed past my head, very close. I put my hand to my right ear and brought it back bloody, but the ear was still there. Perhaps my duffel coat made me conspicuous, for much stuff seemed to be coming my way, but I was not going to take it off, and plodded on; worried a little that if I was hit I might fall and drown in a foot of water! Gigi now was by the jeep and firing the second gun. When I climbed up the bank on to the road he was gone; Burrows was there, still firing a burst now and then, and looking most serious. I couldn't see anything to fire at and waited with the butt of the gun in my hand. The air was thick with whistlings and whinings. An old man came riding up the road in a donkey cart; he must have been double deaf not to have heard the racket. I waved him off the road but he noticed nothing till he arrived within four yards of me, when he uttered an imprecation, jumped off his cart, pushed the donkey down the bank and toppled over, shot through the head.

The Germans came over the bridge once more in a pack, yelling as before. I could see their open mouths. When we fired they stopped on the bridge, somewhat thinned out. One of them leant against the parapet, stuck a rifle grenade into the muzzle of his rifle and took a slow aim at us. I tried to get him with careful bursts: three times he fired and missed and still I couldn't get him. I walked round the jeep to get a new belt of ammunition, when something that made no noticeable noise squashed and shattered my left wrist. The bones and the flesh of the wrist and the forearm were in a pulp, the hand was sound but hung livid and dead-like, with darkening nails, and there was no doubt that it would have to come off.

I was pleased to be wounded in this manner – more than pleased; I was filled with a joyful peace, a tranquil certainty of fulfilment. I had been chasing a phantom right through the war and now, at last, I had come on to something solid: my wound was real and nothing could take it from me.

I pushed my mangled hand into the breast of my battledress and asked Burrows to fit a new belt into my gun. He did so, still looking most serious, and went back to his own gun. The Germans came over a third time, at a run this time, filling the whole width of the bridge. A few got across and dropped promptly behind the canal bank, the others either fell or crawled back over the bridge. Though I hadn't done much good, firing with one hand, I went and sat in the jeep waiting for the next attack. After a good while the German fire eased a little; I thought they had had enough and wouldn't attempt to come over the bridge for some time: now was the moment to go and get reinforcements, or the Lancers in the hut and down the bank would all be slaughtered. I called down for any wounded men to come up to be evacuated. One man only, with a bullet through his shoulder, crawled up the bank and into the jeep. He was upset and whimpered, 'I have lost my arm, I have lost my arm.' 'So have I,' I said. 'There's nothing to make a fuss about.' He brightened up immediately.

Burrows drove us to where 'R' Patrol was, a couple of miles down the road. I told Rickwood to move up and keep the bridge covered until I could send 'B' Patrol from Ravenna to support him. At first I had expected a haemorrhage, but seeing that blood was no more than oozing from my arm, I dropped the wounded Lancer in hospital and went to find Jean Caneri in Ravenna to tell him to take over command of P.P.A. from me as I would be some time in hospital. His first job would be to extricate the survivors of the two Lancer troops and our partisans, and he jumped to it. I then told Burrows to drive me to the Canadian Casualty Clearing Station: I walked in and, feeling a bit weary, lay down on a stretcher. The duty surgeon lit a cigarette for me, injected penicillin, then looked at my hand and asked:

'Any other damage?'

'Right ear split, that's all.'

'What about the blood on your right hand?'

'Oh, that is only blood.' I looked again. No, by God it wasn't. There was a bullet hole through the palm and the fourth finger was broken. That's why I had been clumsy with my gun. He then asked a question that shattered my wonderful peace: 'How long have you been wounded?' I lifted the smashed wrist where the watch should have been: it was gone — my excellent Swiss watch which I had carried throughout the war, a watch that varied less than two minutes a month.

That afternoon 'B' Patrol, with 'R' in support, drove one of its six jeeps on to the bridge where it fired all its ammunition at the Germans on the far side, then another took its place, then another for over an hour, keeping the Germans fairly quiet while the marooned Lancers were extricated. Gigi was with them, having been wounded in the shoulder and through the chest while he was firing the second gun on my jeep that morning. Sergeant Galloway of 'B' Patrol was hit in the thigh while he was carrying a wounded Lancer out of the canal; he then went back to his jeep and went on firing till he fainted from the loss of blood. The Germans put up a heavy barrage of mortars and artillery, but our men were too close to the enemy positions to be much affected. Three Canadian Honey tanks down the road gave artillery support to our side. Ateo's partisans on their bridge had had two men wounded whom they brought back walking through the forest.

The Germans withdrew that night, leaving thirty dead behind. They were two companies of an S.S. Battalion, arrived the day before, fresh from rest, to relieve the tired troops we had been fighting so long.

This happened on December 9th, 1944. Two days later Caneri and Campbell with 'S' Patrol joined Bulow in the marshes, where they stayed till the nineteenth. Then the whole of P.P.A. was relieved and drove back to its new base near Rimini. They had been in action continuously since June 16th for six months and three days. Aggressive operations stopped for the winter along the whole of the Italian front.

I woke up from the anaesthetic that evening. My left hand had gone above the wrist, the right one was in plaster, leaving only the thumb and the tops of the second and third fingers free, I had two stitches in my right ear and I felt wonderfully hungry. There were no more than three other patients in the C.C.S. so only our ward was open, where all the sisters gathered round the stove, talking and knitting. I was fed an enormous dinner by a kind Canadian sister, after which I fell off to sleep. All was peace and kindness, I had absolutely nothing to worry about and I was completely happy. The next morning Ivan came to keep me company: he had put on a strenuously cheerful hospital face, but when he saw the stump of my left arm with its little bloody dressing, the tough Russian warrior burst into tears and I had to comfort him, which was pleasant. A sister brought him a cup of tea, patted him on the back and told him sweet things, of which he never understood a word but they made him smile through his tears.

These Canadian girls were the kindest in the world and they spoilt me thoroughly.

Most of the men in the unit came to see me during the next three days, after which I was driven to a General Hospital in Rimini. I woke up in the morning in a huge ward quite full of patients. A very busy sister brought me my breakfast on a tray; later, seeing I was not eating, she asked what was the matter. Somewhat abashed I made a helpless gesture with my stump and my plastered hand. She laughed and said:

'But you can feed yourself you know. Just try. I'll help you if you like, but I'm very busy.'

The lesson was good — I never felt sorry for myself again.

I was flown from Rimini to 104 General Hospital in Rome, where I was operated on by a woman surgeon, Barbara Stimpson, an American, but a major in the R.A.M.C. Head of a hospital in New York, she had joined the British Army long before her own country came into the war, and she now commanded an orthopaedic unit to which special cases were directed. She operated eight to ten hours every day in the theatre, and found time to visit the wards at some time of the day or the night. We all loved her; the female staff, sisters, nurses and V.A.D.s adored and worshipped her, the doctors and surgeons danced around her when they could and praised her professional skill when she was out of hearing. She looked rather severe in uniform, her hair cut straight and her manner brisk which suffered no nonsense, for she was a busy woman and very clever; but one day I called on her in her quarters, where she was confined by a bout of flu, to find her dressed in a soft flowery gown, and knitting! We talked of books, pictures, people and children — she was a very human and very remarkable person.

On previous occasions when I had been in hospital I had always had one of our wireless sections at hand and kept on fussing P.P.A. at a distance, but now, for the first time, I was without any responsibilities. It was pleasant for a few days; then when my stump had healed and the pleasure of having lost my hand had worn off, although I had dear friends in Rome, I became anxious to be back at work. On January

11th, just over a month after being wounded, I was in Viserba, worrying Jean Caneri about his plans for keeping the men happy during the winter, for we were told at Eighth Army that no operations were contemplated till the final battle in March or April. I stayed three days, during which I interviewed a number of recruits, then drove back to Rome and Naples and sailed for Liverpool in a hospital ship to be fitted in England with an artificial hand: I was told it would take six months, but I pestered the War Office so much that by the middle of April I was back in Italy. What happened to me during my extremely happy stay in England does not concern this story.

At Eighth Army Headquarters, where I arrived during the course of the Spring Battle, I fell once more into the delightful bustle of war: sleep snatched at odd hours, subdued high spirits, watchfulness, good-humoured weariness, and the unbroken, day and night, grind of work. Christopher Smuts at 'Operations', Donald Prater and John Willett at 'Intelligence', and Archie Colquhoun, in charge of Partisans, friends of mine and well-wishers, drew for me the picture of the battle and described with humour the recent antics of my own small unit. I would find them outside Chioggia, scheming for the unconditional surrender of the place. I called on General McCreery, who had befriended us more than any other army commander, and I left again to go home to my men.

During my absence Caneri had kept his men busy indeed. Apart from our routine training, he sent them to follow a course of parachute jumping, and, after that, for a month at Terminillo on a mountain warfare course, ski-ing, climbing and handling mules. In spite of these activities the men had grown restless and a little out of hand.

Bob Yunnie had left P.P.A. for good in the middle of April 1945. Perhaps he too, like others before, had borne as much strain as he could stand, but he would have fought with us the last battles of the war but for the tragic, sudden death of his only son, a boy of eight, who lived with his wife in Aberdeen: the disaster broke his determination. Although I had seen him in England with his wife and son, when he came on his first leave since the beginning of the war, I had inhumanly taken it for granted that his allegiance was only to us. When, arriving in Italy, I read in a letter he had left for me that he had accepted not leave but a permanent home posting, I remained for a long time unbelieving and heartbroken.

Caneri's patrol commanders were now Captain John Campbell, promoted to the old guard, Lieutenant Steve Wallbridge, a newcomer of great achievement, and Lieutenant McCallum, a very young officer transferred from the Twenty-Seventh Lancers. I liked him so much that I thought I had found in him at last a young man I would be able to train to perfection in my own manner and I took him in hand — but a few days after he joined us, I was wounded. He now succeeded Bob Yunnie in command of 'B' Patrol. Rickwood, disguising very gallantly the painful disorders resulting from his wound, was second-in-command of P.P.A. He exerted himself against terrible odds when, by all standards, he should have been resting in a convalescent home. The other officers we had were useful in many ways: they did not take part in the fighting. George Lee had unfortunately been recalled by the Canadian Army, and his experience was lost to us.

Thus short-handed Caneri had every excuse to follow his bent and take the field himself. He organized his own H.Q. as a complete fighting patrol, and on April 21st, when Eighth and Fifth Armies attacked after the winter pause he went into action with the whole fighting strength of P.P.A. For seven days they fought around Lake Comacchio, with the Twenty-Seventh Lancers and the Twenty-Eighth Garibaldi Brigade. On the twenty-third McCallum, leading his patrol into a village, ran into an ambush and was killed with his gunner, McDowall, by a *panzerfaust* which completely destroyed his jeep. Sergeant Galloway brought the patrol back, together with twenty-two prisoners.

On the twenty-sixth Caneri embarked his jeeps in six R.C.L.s and sailed with a mine-sweeper escort to the mouth of the Po. R.C.L.s were craft designed for inland waters, but they had been proved to be seaworthy in the course of numerous exercises during the winter. From that day P.P.A. operated in its own watery domain, on the canals, river deltas and lagoons which stretch from the mouth of the Po to Venice. The R.C.L.s commanded by Lieutenant Thomas, R.A.S.C., became part of the unit; they ferried the jeeps across the water, brought up supplies and evacuated casualties and prisoners.

The main branch of the Po was crossed the same day, and P.P.A. established beyond it with the support of local partisans. On the twenty-seventh they crossed the Adige and the Brenta, and appeared before Chioggia, a small fishing town at the south end of the lagoon of Venice, where the Germans had seven hundred men with two batteries of 88 mm. field guns, one battery of coastal defence guns, one hundred and twenty heavy machine guns, much ammunition and supplies for three months. The commander thought himself secure behind three rivers and innumerable canals on which all the bridges had been blown. Jean Caneri sent Wallbridge to him under a flag of truce, with a request to surrender within twenty-four hours, failing which he would be bombed out of the world by the air force. Concealing the fact that his whole force on the spot consisted of nine men in three jeeps, Caneri received the representative of the German commander and in five hours' talk bluffed him so successfully that he returned to his commanding officer to recommend an unconditional surrender, for Caneri would accept nothing else.

Meanwhile the other patrols had fanned out to the north-west. On the twenty-ninth John Campbell charged a battery of 88 mm. guns while they were firing on our troops outside Padova and captured them intact with three hundred prisoners, whom he handed over to the partisans; he pursued his way towards Padova and entered the town where partisans, having risen in force, were disarming the Germans. On the same day Sergeant Galloway with 'B' Patrol, making its way towards Venice, engaged the enemy in the morning, capturing ten prisoners. Later in the day they entered a small town where the Germans, barricaded in houses around the square, opened up on them from the windows. In the fierce engagement which followed Rogers was killed, Sergeant Galloway was wounded a second time and a gunner, Brown, also grievously wounded. Corporal Sonley took command of the patrol, fought in the square for forty-five minutes, killed seven Germans, captured fifteen, exhausted his ammunition and withdrew with the wounded and the dead.

On the thirtieth 'R' and 'B' Patrols sailed (in R.C.L.s) across the Gulf of Venice and landed well beyond the town, just in time to chase the Germans out of Iesolo.

When I arrived in Chioggia the poor German major, who had declared that he wouldn't surrender to anything smaller than a battalion, had realized that he had been tricked by a handful of men — but it was too late: his men were disarmed, his officers all put under guard and he consoled himself with the brandy bottle. Steve Wallbridge had spent twenty-four hours in the town before the surrender, at the German H.Q.; he had cleverly played on the dissensions amongst the German staff, some of whom, against the views of their commander, wanted to resist to the last round, and he had somehow succeeded in suggesting that he had several battalions just across the Brenta. I believe that an important element in the success of his negotiations took place on his first night in the town, when, being entertained in the German mess, he drank the whole staff under the table. Of this, however, I have no other evidence but the word of an enemy.

In the course of the last few days P.P.A. had captured thirteen hundred and thirty-five prisoners, sixteen field guns and many smaller weapons. I felt that the war in Italy would end in a few days and that the time had now come to carry out the plan I had told Cameron about when we were on our way from Taranto to Bari a year and a half earlier — a purposeless piece of swagger, indeed, but a flourish can be an end in itself. We loaded five jeeps in three R.C.L.s and, young Thomas leading recklessly amongst the German mines, we sailed from Chioggia to Venice up the lagoon, entered the Canal San Marco and moored our craft on the quay. I started my jeep and, trembling with excitement for the one and only time during the war, drove into the Piazzetta, passed between the columns, turned left into Piazza San Marco, and, followed by the others, drove seven times round the square. This was my hour of triumph.

Eight days later we were in a deep Alpine valley below Tarvisio waiting morosely for the war to end. Lazy rumours went round the leaguer. At 1800 hours I received a slip from Sergeant Brooks, Germany had surrendered.

The next day, driving in Austria, we met a group of three hundred creatures, bare-footed, in white and grey striped pyjamas, heads shaven, faces grey, eyes glazed, bones protruding, corpses that moved in fours and shuffled painfully in a ghostly semblance of soldierly order. When they reached our convoy, which I had stopped, uncomprehending, they raised croaking voices in a manner of song, a rustling Marseillaise, no louder than a whisper. They were French political prisoners, and this indignity had been done to them by their German keepers in a concentration camp up in the mountains. 'If this,' I thought, 'is what the Germans really are, we shall have a long job to cure them.'

Two days later again we were driving eastwards from Klagenfurt in Austria with a detachment of the Twenty-Seventh Lancers. At Wolfsberg the road climbs up a narrow mountain gorge: it was filled from parapet to wall with routed German troops. For eight hours we forced our way through three divisions, mostly on foot, some on bicycles, some on horseback. They had broken-down trucks, ox carts, horse carts and donkeys; no officers; the men, haggard and panicky, plodded blindly on, terrified of the Russians in their rear. At intervals, when rumours spread amongst them that the Russians were catching up, they broke and stampeded into the fields or up the hillside — then, the panic over, they took to the road again.

At dusk the last Germans thinned out. In the valley below we saw Very lights fired. It was nearly dark when, having reached the valley, I saw the mass of a tank ahead of me, covered with a red Soviet flag. It stopped and so did I. Major Lykov climbed out of the turret, we walked towards each other and clasped hands. Then the Russian stepped back, stood to attention and delivered a speech. He ended: 'There is nothing that can destroy our solidarity.'

'The war being over,' I thought, 'I might well now see to that.'

ROLL OF HONOUR

Cameron, Cpl. W.	Lovat Scouts	'Blitz'
Croghan, Tpr. T.	3rd Hussars	'R'
Curtis, Sgt. C. H.	R.E.	'Blitz'
Gaskell, Drv. W. S.	R.A.S.C.	'H.Q.'
Hunter, Pte. J.	Argyll & Sutherland	'B'
McCallum, Lieut. I. W.	27th Lancers	'B'
McDowall, Spr. R.	R.E.	'B'
McGillavray, Lieut.	Derbyshire Yeomanry	'H.Q.'
Porter, Sgt. D. J., D.C.M.	R.E.	'R'
Rogers, Tpr. A.	Recce Rgt.	'B'
Snape, Cpl. J.	R.A.C.	'Blitz'
White, Pte. A.	Oxford & Bucks.	'S'

HONOURS AND AWARDS

D.S.O.

Peniakoff, Major V.,	General List	

M.C.

Campbell, Capt. J. D. (and bar)	Argyll & Sutherland	'S'
Caneri, Major J.	General List	'H.Q.'
Peniakoff, Major V.	General List	
Yunnie, Capt. R. P.	Black Watch	'B'

D.C.M.

Porter, Sgt. D. J.	R.E.	'R'

M.M.

Beautyman, Sgt. J. E.	R. Sigs.	'Blitz'
Burrows, Pte. C.	R.A.S.C.	'Blitz'
Galloway, Sgt. D. (and bar)	R.A.S.C.	'B'
O'Leary, Sgt. W. J.	R.A.	'S'
Riches, Sgt. F. S.	K.D.G.	'B'
Sanders, Sgt. E. (with L.R.D.G.)	2 N.Z.E.F.	'R'
Waterson, S.S.M. G.	K.D.G.	'Blitz'

MENTIONED IN DESPATCHES

Hodgson, Cpl. D.	R.A.	'S'
North, Cpl. R.	R.I.F.	'R'
Owen, Cpl. B. J.	R.A.S.C.	'B'
Sonley, L/Cpl. G.	16/5 Lancers	'B'
Taylor, Sgt. S.	Bays	'R'
Thomas, Lieut. E.	R.A.S.C.	attached

INDEX

503

INDEX